SECURING PEACE IN ANGOLA
AND MOZAMBIQUE

SECURING PEACE IN ANGOLA AND MOZAMBIQUE

The Importance of Specificity in Peace Treaties

Miranda Ruwart Melcher

BLOOMSBURY ACADEMIC
LONDON • NEW YORK • OXFORD • NEW DELHI • SYDNEY

BLOOMSBURY ACADEMIC
Bloomsbury Publishing Plc, 50 Bedford Square, London, WC1B 3DP, UK
Bloomsbury Publishing Inc, 1359 Broadway, New York, NY 10018, USA
Bloomsbury Publishing Ireland, 29 Earlsfort Terrace, Dublin 2, D02 AY28, Ireland

BLOOMSBURY, BLOOMSBURY ACADEMIC and the Diana logo are trademarks of
Bloomsbury Publishing Plc

First published in Great Britain 2024
Paperback edition published 2025

Cover design: Adriana Brioso
Cover image © Olga Rai/Adobe Stock

Bloomsbury Publishing Plc does not have any control over, or responsibility for, any third-
party websites referred to or in this book. All internet addresses given in this book were
correct at the time of going to press. The author and publisher regret any inconvenience
caused if addresses have changed or sites have ceased to exist, but can accept no
responsibility for any such changes.

A catalogue record for this book is available from the British Library.

Library of Congress Cataloging-in-Publication Data

ISBN: HB: 978-1-3504-0793-0
PB: 978-1-3504-0796-1
ePDF: 978-1-3504-0792-3
eBook: 978-1-3504-0794-7

Typeset by Deanta Global Publishing Services, Chennai, India

For product safety related questions contact productsafety@bloomsbury.com.

To find out more about our authors and books visit www.bloomsbury.com and sign up for
our newsletters.

CONTENTS

ACKNOWLEDGEMENTS

This book started as a PhD dissertation, and the support of my supervisors Dr Stuart Griffin and Dr Mats Berdal was absolutely key. Stuart, thank you for leaving me to wallow in the archives and then holding me to a high standard of analytical writing to make what I found make sense to readers. Any errors or confusion remaining are entirely mine. Mats, your work has inspired mine since my Yale days – before I even knew you taught at King's. You were definitely one of the reasons I ended up at this university and I hope this research is a helpful contribution to your prodigious catalogue of work.

Crucial in turning this dissertation into a book has been the support, expertise and belief in the project from Bloomsbury's Atifa Jiwa. Thank you for buying into the project's idea from our initial pitch meeting through to the end. Your speedy, clear and encouraging support throughout the process has been wonderful. Thank you also to the editorial board at Bloomsbury for approving and believing in this book. For this piece of the process in particular, the support of Anders Reagan, Maria Kaffa and Dr Stanislava Mladenova has been invaluable.

Completing the PhD was a huge milestone for me – but also one that required taking a break from this research for a while, before thinking about publishing it. Thanks to the wonderful efforts of Dr Marshall Poe and his amazing creation of the New Books Network, I was lucky enough to interview hundreds of academics about their recently published books starting in December 2021, when the dissertation felt too close to even begin to think about adapting it for a book! I didn't expect this to help me figure out publishing my own work but I want to thank Dr Clarissa Ceglio, Dr Boyd Van Dijk, Dr Wouter Werner, Dr Nina Wilen and Dr Jonathan Fisher, in particular, for sharing their own experiences and offering guidance on putting together a book proposal and how to think about approaching publishers. Their generosity, encouragement and practical guidance have been pivotal in getting to this point.

Long before officially beginning this book, however, I have been supported by so many wonderful professors and mentors in both this specific research project and in my work in general. There are too many to name, but some, in particular, must be mentioned and thanked. To Dr Jolyon Howorth, my first-ever supervisor, who challenged me not only to think up interesting ideas but also to argue them coherently in writing – I hope I have made you proud. To Dr Stathis Kalyvas, you opened my eyes to the neverending complexities of civil wars. To Dr Steven Wilkinson, Dr Matthew Kocher, Emma Sky and Dr Clare Lockhart, you each have taught me about histories, methods and perspectives that I have built upon in my own work. Thank you to Ambassador John Negroponte, for providing the connections and communications that led to many of the interviews conducted for this research and helping me make this history a human story. Thank you also to Dr Jessica Broitman, Jane Edwards, Dr Mike O'Hanlon, Steve Blum, and Dr Betsy Bradley, who all encourage me to share my ideas on paper: you believed I could do it before I did.

For any typos or awkward sentences that remain in this book, the fault is entirely mine. The fact that there are (hopefully) so few is due to the heroic efforts of my 'PhD P(h)roofreading Posse', my friends who have volunteered their time, energy and skill to edit all of the drafts of the dissertation version of this book. Their enthusiasm and involvement at every stage have been a fabulous boost – creating not only accountability for writing deadlines but also a wonderful cheering section urging me to keep going. Thank you: Ashley Pratt, Emma Moore, Helder Toste, Justin Schuster, Esther Portyansky, Johanna Li, Peter Wyckoff, Chelsea McManus, Stephanie Saunderson, Sean Minton, Magd Lhroob, Tristan Sechrest and Meghan Iverson. Without your mental support, as well as the practical proofreading and clarifying comments, this dissertation would not exist.

Particular credit goes to Sami Melcher and Dr Anjuli R. K. Shere who, in very different ways, were key leaders of this effort. Sami, you are one of the best proofreaders I've seen and I am so grateful for your comments throughout this writing, especially the many funny editorializations that made me laugh unexpectedly even when frustrated and tired. Anjuli, you've been my writing and work partner for so long that it feels like forever, in the best possible way. I don't think I would actually have done all I planned to without your cajoling, commiserating and documentation of progress via the Wall of Anjuli.

Thank you also to my fellow PhDs who have listened to my rants, provided feedback, taught with me and just generally shared their journeys alongside mine. Dr Emily Brown, Dr Helene Olsen, Dr Saawani Raje, Dr Hillary Briffa, Meghan Iverson, Dr Becca Farnum, Natasha Boychenko, Sara Tandon, Suzie Lust, Benjamin Tan: thank you.

My parents have naturally been on this journey since the beginning – not of this research but from when I first started babbling about war (we think around age six). Thank you for not only tolerating my obsession but actively encouraging it. Thank you for the support to move away from you to London, the continued interest in my work despite the years of listening to rants about it, and the pride and support to keep pursuing this somewhat quixotic path.

Thank you in particular to my mom, Sharon, who was my first thought partner and editor back when I was just figuring out this research as an undergraduate at Yale. The conversations pacing around the living room and covering the kitchen walls in coloured sticky notes have remained key touchstones in figuring out what I actually think and why, prompted by your insightful questions and impressive memory of the various authors, arguments and historical figures in my research. I've loved sharing every step along this journey with you, from phone debriefs after editing sessions with Professor Howorth, to communal excitement about meeting Stedman and Licklider in person, to discussing hilarious details of UN archival documents even when I knew they wouldn't fit in the final book. Thank you also for ruthlessly editing my writing – without you, my proofreading posse would have had an impossible task – the readers of this book definitely have the Grammar Ninja to thank.

Finally, to Jonathan, who has gone from boyfriend, to fiancé, to husband over the course of this project. Thank you for keeping me sane and fed, for being so encouraging and excited throughout and for being patient in the amount of effort needed to cajole me away from my books for a walk. I am so excited for the rest of our adventures together, which, yes, will likely involve buying more maps!

ABBREVIATIONS

ANC	African National Congress, the party of Nelson Mandela during Apartheid in South Africa, and the ruling political party in South Africa since 1994.
CCFADM	Committee that met during the UN peacekeeping (ONUMOZ) mandate in Mozambique (1992–5) to determine the specifics of creating a post-conflict integrated military (the FADM).
DDR	Disarmament, demobilization, and reintegration, a policy package which is a series of procedures that first aims to remove weapons from combatants, then to send combatants away from their war-time organizations, and finally to more holistically enable combatants to develop peacetime likelihoods.
DRC	Democratic Republic of the Congo, one of the countries bordering Angola.
FAA	The formal name of the post-war integrated Angolan armed forces (acronym from the Portuguese name).
FADM	The formal name of the post-war integration Mozambican armed forces (acronym from Portuguese name).
FNLA	The National Liberation Front for Angola (acronym from the Portuguese name), an independence movement that fought for Angolan independence from 1961 to 1976.
FRELIMO	The Liberation Front of Mozambique (acronym from the Portuguese name), the independence movement that became the government of Mozambique in 1975, headed during the majority of the time period of the book by Joaquim Chissano.
MONUA	United Nations Observer Mission in Angola, the final UN peacekeeping mission deployed to Angola, 1997–9. This mission was preceded by UNAVEM I, UNAVEM II and UNAVEM III.
MPLA	The People's Movement for the Liberation of Angola (acronym from the Portuguese name), the independence movement that became the government of Angola from 1975, headed during the majority of the time period of the book by Jose Eduardo dos Santos.
ONUMOZ	The United Nations Operation in Mozambique (acronym from the Portuguese name), the UN peacekeeping mission deployed to implement Mozambique's peace accords, 1992–4.
RENAMO	The Mozambican National Resistance (acronym from the Portuguese name), the group contesting FRELIMO for political control of Mozambique, headed during the majority of the time period of the book by Afonso Dhlakama.

SWAPO   South-West Africa People's Organisation, the independence
                     movement for Namibia and the political party that has dominated
                     post-independence Namibian politics.

SSR   Security Sector Reform, an umbrella term that usually means changes
                     made to the institutions related to security in a country, for example,
                     the military, police and judiciary, often but not exclusively in the
                     context of post-conflict.

UNAVEM   The United Nations Angola Verification Mission, there were three
                     UN peacekeeping missions by this name, the first deploying primarily
                     to support Namibia's transition to independence (1989–91), with
                     some involvement along the Angolan border, the latter two focused
                     entirely within Angola in order to support the implementation of
                     peace treaties aiming to resolve Angola's civil war (1991–5 and 1995–7
                     respectively). UNAVEM III was succeeded by MONUA.

UNITA   National Union for the Total Independence of Angola (acronym
                     from the Portuguese name), initially one of three main independence
                     movements in Angola, and then the main group contesting for control
                     of Angola with the MPLA. UNITA was most famously led by Jonas
                     Savimbi, from 1966 to 2002.

UNSC   The United Nations Security Council, that amongst other things,
                     creates UN peacekeeping operations, including those deployed in
                     Angola and Mozambique.

Chapter 1

INTRODUCTION

Civil wars have been called 'nasty, brutish, and long', which is unfortunately an accurate assessment of what has become the most common form of mass violence since the end of the Cold War.[1] One reason these wars are increasingly long is that the number of instances where one side militarily defeats the other(s) has drastically decreased: nearly half of all civil conflicts since the end of the Cold War have ended in negotiated settlements rather than direct military victories.[2] Negotiating peace treaties is a long, complicated process with few 'best practices', 'right answers' or linear routes to 'success'. Even determining what 'success' means in the context of a civil conflict is contested, alongside what counts as 'peace'[3] or a 'civil war' in the first place.[4] This is further complicated by the fact that many civil wars recur, and this trend seems to be increasing since the 1990s.[5]

In this, civil wars are similar to other kinds of violence: pinpointing a singular root cause and designing a complete solution is rarely, if ever, possible. Civil wars, however, often have additional complexities, whether due to the size of territory, number of people involved and multiplicity of political, economic and social factors that not only interweave to create conditions for large-scale violence but are then further influenced and often intensified by the dynamics of violence themselves. Perhaps the most surprising fact, then, is not how common civil wars are, but rather how little attention this largest-scale form of mass violence routinely receives in the popular imagination and, to an extent, in academia too.

Given the millions of people impacted by civil wars – both in the present and in the future, not to mention those suffering from the legacies of past conflicts – the relative lack of attention to this form of violence demands attention. However, even when studies focus on civil wars directly, there remain subsequent issues to investigate.

While determining the causes of civil wars offers an understandable starting point for the sub-field, the unfortunate reality is that the number of civil wars is increasing, and crucially, the duration of ongoing civil wars is increasing too. To date, there is research helping shed light on the many causes of civil wars. This research supports the unfortunate likelihood that predicting the outbreak of civil conflict, as one might predict earthquakes, is likely impossible. However, this book will argue that there is an even bigger problem facing researchers; namely, that we do not yet understand how to *end* civil wars, including the increasingly common type that continue for years and decades. This problem is exacerbated by the fact that even less attention is paid to this element of civil war studies than understanding civil war causes. Intervening at this crucial juncture, this book focuses on this most common type of civil war ending: the negotiated settlement, rather than situations in which one side decisively wins on the battlefield. This book seeks to understand at least a piece of the following questions: Why are civil wars lasting longer? What are the (many) stumbling blocks in negotiating peace treaties? And, why do some peace treaties, once negotiated and signed, nevertheless fail to be implemented?

This book starts by considering possible answers to these questions, as an avenue towards investigating real-life efforts to end civil wars. More specifically, this project developed from the following ideas and logical assumptions.

First, more civil wars are currently ending via negotiation than military victory; this changes the conditions needed for a war to end – from tactical, strategic and logistical battlefield prowess to a long-term coordination of political, legal and institutional actors, which must skilfully be managed alongside military goals. This shift significantly impacts the breadth and depth of skills required for groups fighting a civil war and increases the number of variables that must align to achieve cessation of conflict. No wonder that likely takes longer!

Second, the increased complexity of this situation highlights that the signing of a peace treaty is a remarkable milestone aligning all these interests into a particular moment and document. However, it also suggests that this moment of signature (and photo opportunity) is the *beginning* of the even more arduous journey: translating the agreed-upon steps from paper into practice. As the saying goes, if 'no battle plan survives initial contact from the enemy', then surely it must also be true that no peace treaty can be implemented exactly as planned, especially when the negotiated settlement was reached through military stalemate, rather than a dictating of terms. This book, therefore, examines the entire process, from the initial effort of getting parties to the negotiating table to the end of the often years-long implementation process. This situates the book within the wider conversation of considering war as a process, which has seen scholarship begin in civil war studies as well.[6]

Third, these two previous assumptions suggest that the conditions under which a peace treaty might actually lead or even contribute to the cessation of a civil war appear functionally impossible to achieve. And yet, not all peace treaties fail. The documents themselves, the conditions under which they are created, and the manner in which they are implemented therefore seem necessary to examine in detail in order to understand what pieces can most impact this variation in outcome. Essentially, the assumption is that as with most agreements and legal documents, all sections of peace treaties (which increasingly run to tens of pages if not more) are likely not equally important in the immediate implementation stage.

This book makes a conscious choice to primarily examine the aspects of peace treaties that aim to resolve a primary issue of civil wars: who gets the military? While not all countries have militaries, the prevailing assumption is that a country, being defined by internationally recognized borders, should only have one military, not competing ones. Traditionally then, one way of defining a civil war is when armed groups end up engaging each other within a country's territory. Given this, ending such conflict necessitates resolving the issue of competing armed groups within said borders. This book makes the subjective argument that this is the most important initial task for a peace treaty: to determine who will be in the post-conflict military and what will happen to those combatants who are excluded from this institution.

This is a choice: there is, for example, substantial research conducted on the impact of elections which frames them as a critical step from war to peace. In fact, entire sections of peace treaties typically focus on elections. This book will focus attention on the former and not the latter area because there is already substantial work being conducted in the area related to the importance of elections to peace and, perhaps more importantly, real-life examples provide evidence for the assertion that elections without a pre-established resolution of who is allowed to use military force, tend to derail into significant problems, if not disintegrate peace attempts entirely.

The majority of the literature on post-conflict reconstruction focuses on rebuilding economic, political and social institutions. There is comparatively little analysis of different methods of military reintegration in security institutions, particularly in the treaty negotiations stage. This is likely because one of the most common types of treaty provisions in post-conflict security reconstruction is the disarmament, demobilization and reintegration (DDR) of former combatants, usually into civilian society, rather than into a combined military institution.

The basic premise of DDR is to turn combatants into productive civilians working in jobs unrelated to security issues.[7] This is done first through the organized Disarmament of the side(s) chosen to become civilians, usually while they are in temporary assembly or cantonment areas to facilitate the processing of turning in their weapons. The second stage is Demobilization, during which combatants disband, usually meaning leaving their military structures (i.e. battalions, squads, etc.) and returning to civilian housing and locations. The final stage is Reintegration, which is a 'longer-term social and economic process with an open time frame designed to facilitate the assimilation of ex-combatants in a way that allows them, and their families, to adapt to civilian life in communities that may not necessarily be ready to accept them.'[8] Given, however, that in many cases these young men (as they nearly always are) often lack skills suitable for the civilian workforce having spent extended periods of time as combatants. Even United Nations DDR reports acknowledge that this policy is often not successful in ensuring that ex-combatants find gainful employment and financial security.[9] Disaffected former fighters who cannot find economic or social stability in civilian life may be prone to violent provocation, leading them to take up arms again, thus threatening peace agreements.[10]

In contrast, this book argues that while ex-fighters who want to turn civilian should be given the option to go through this kind of DDR process, those who do not want to enter civilian life should be allowed to be integrated into a joint security sector. The main reason for this alternative policy to be examined is because of the inconsistent successes of disarmament in particular related to peace. This track record was highlighted, for example, in Marsh and Palik's comprehensive 2021 PRIO report on failures in disarmament.[11] A further reason for the focus on security issues is the unique kinds of knowledge and capabilities that military actors have in shaping conflict and post-conflict environments. This has been touched on in the literature, for example, by Anders Themner, who argued that military actors can help peace if they believe electoral competition and/or any power-sharing processes to be fair, as they are often the people with the most direct control over restarting or preventing conflict from breaking out again amongst rank-and-file soldiers.[12] This is a key inspiration for this book's focus on how treaty negotiations and treaty terms impact not just high-ranking military commanders, but also rank-and-file members.

Military integration can help avoid the recurrence of civil wars because it creates (1) commitment between previously warring parties, (2) security for combatants who fear that disarmament could expose them to assassination and (3) stable employment. Furthermore, it can provide a national symbol of reconciliation to the wider population. Licklider's underlying contention is that former combatants' most recent experiences, for which they received payment or non-monetary livelihood support, were in combat. Thus, many former combatants developed skills that are not particularly transferable to peacetime civilian life.[13] While in some cases ex-combatants have employment or educational experience from before the war that could assist in civilian reintegration, this is not something that can be relied upon in developing post-conflict settlements. For peace to be sustainable, all those skilled in creating violence must somehow be governed by the legal and legitimate state, which includes government security institutions. Participation in said institutions, therefore, offers the surest avenue for ex-combatants to use their skills and experiences to earn a paycheque with a minimum of transitional training or assistance. This is an important factor in reducing recurrence risk; ex-combatant financial satisfaction with post-conflict livelihood removes a potential motivation to return to violence.

However, one of the difficulties in creating an integrated military is the social element. Agreeing to join a security institution whose war-time reputation may be horrific can be a hard sell for rebels, and government soldiers may baulk at sharing space and jobs with their former enemies.[14] While at first glance this type of integration may seem risky, the potential of this idea to provide financial security for ex-combatants by utilizing their existing skills and training legally within government structures proved too compelling to ignore. Thus, this project aimed to examine how security sector institutions have been developed in recent post-conflict situations in order to determine whether more generalized practices can be ascertained through comparative case study analysis.[15]

The argument in brief

All of these premises together developed this book's starting argument: that understanding the provisions of peace treaties and their implementation processes are key to understanding how post-conflict institutions are constructed. One of the core arguments of this book is that the entire process of ending a civil war is fundamentally interconnected: how and by whom even the initial drafts of the treaty are negotiated can have significant impacts on whether or not it can be implemented successfully. This book aims to put the specific treaty terms, their implementation processes and the context in which all of this takes place into one broad understanding of how peace processes function, following the emerging focus on processes within war and security studies,[16] rather than examining only one of these aspects, as much existing scholarship tends towards.[17] Thus, the central question that this book aims to investigate is whether risks of civil war recurrence can be mitigated by peace treaties including detailed plans for security sector reform.[18] Although security sector reform is only one aspect of peace processes, it is one that has received less investigation and may have a particularly strong relationship to the outcomes of a peace process.[19] The book's argument does not go so far as to say that successful military integration is the necessary factor for a peace treaty to be sufficiently implemented to avoid conflict recurrence. Instead, the book argues that this is a helpful condition towards wider peace, but not a proxy for determining the overall success or failure of the peace process overall.

The overarching argument of this book is that for negotiations to produce treaties that can then be successfully implemented, the negotiations and treaty terms must be specific. This includes not only including details that may be contentious to negotiate, such as the number of soldiers each side will contribute to the combined military and the rules for rank designations, to name only two that arose consistently in these two case studies as difficult to agree on. This is counter to a strand of the mediation literature that advocates for leaving large issues out, strategic ambiguity, but congruent with the military integration findings regarding the need to clearly address this topic in treaties for higher likelihoods of success.

This need for specificity also includes specifying in the treaty itself, in advance of implementation, built-in flexibilities, such as conditions that must be met in the demobilization process that if not reached by a certain date, automatically extend the election timeline by a specific number of months. This book therefore does not argue that all details must be finalized in the treaty but does say that details that are not finalized should be left out purposefully and have distinct mechanisms built into the treaties specifying how and when those outstanding aspects will be determined. This includes decision-making mechanisms for how to respond to changes and other unforeseen circumstances not known at the time of treaty signing.

This book also specifies that what areas of detail can be given this 'left-out' treatment are unique to each context and can even change over time within one civil war. There is no 'one-size-fits-all' list of what terms must always, or must never, be included, this book is focused on making a more process-oriented argument about the ways in which decisions are made about what to include, or not, in negotiations, treaties and during implementation. In this sense, this book focuses both on the similarities between the peace processes in Angola and

Mozambique but also delves significantly into their differences and the importance of understanding each specific context to understand the processes that did and did not take place.

Within this overarching argument, this book makes a number of subsidiary claims. First, that treaty terms related to security issues must include realistic timelines (which can be facilitated by the inclusion of negotiators experienced in military operations as equal, not supplementary participants in negotiations) and acknowledge and account for logistical realities. One of the most consistent implementation problems that arose in both cases was that timelines and logistical preparations to carry out treaty requirements around disarmament, demobilization and military reintegration were often inadequate. This not only led to expensive extensions of timelines but also created problems around expectation management for those involved, creating distrust around the entire peace process, sometimes with violent consequences. What is clear through a detailed comparison of the Angolan and Mozambican cases is that more realistic timelines (namely two years for disarmament and demobilization rather than one) were one of the key differences between relative success versus violent dissatisfaction. There was also a distinctly more pragmatic character around both the special representative in charge of the UN's implementation efforts in Mozambique than any equivalent actor in Angola, as well as a more unified but also hands-off approach from UN headquarters that this book argues is a key reason why more realistic timelines were utilized in the Mozambican process, even if they were only included as a lesson learned from Angola's process.

Second, this book argues that a key element for successful treaty implementation is the designation of a joint committee to adjudicate issues that arise during this period that has both sides represented, but crucially has the UN or the designated international actor charged with implementation as the chair and deciding vote. Although committees along these lines existed in most of the treaties examined in this book, there is a clear difference in outcome between those in which the UN was present and more crucially between those in which the UN was present versus actually had decision-making power. This is related to, but this book argues separately from, the personality argument mentioned in the previous paragraph about the character of the UN special representatives.

Third, this book argues that a key priority of external actors during both treaty negotiations and implementation is the importance of expectation management. As shown throughout the examination of the various processes in both Angola and Mozambique, the underlying problems of both perceptions of vulnerability during negotiations and implementation as well as willingness to comply came down in most instances to failures of expectation management. Whether it was regarding Savimbi's unrealistic expectations for his electoral chances (compared perhaps to Dhlakama's more realistic ones), the decision made by the majority of Mozambican combatants from both sides in favour of the more attractive-sounding civilian demobilization package as compared to the integrated military, to the conditions and responses to conditions of those combatants processing through any of the number of assembly area demobilization camps that were attempted in both countries throughout the 1990s and early 2000s, expectation management was consistently an overlooked aspect with an array of political, logistical and security consequences.

Fourth and relatedly, this book argues that dignity and perceptions of respect are crucial throughout implementation phases (see examples earlier) but perhaps especially during negotiations. While this is relatively underexplored in the literature, this book builds on the arguments of Albin and Druckman regarding the importance of procedural equality. Importantly, aspects of dignity and respect were common themes throughout the interviews conducted for this book, with participants in negotiations consistently mentioning the impact of noticeable disparities in language, dress, bureaucratic experience, exposure to foreign travel and more on the attitude of negotiators on all sides before terms even began to be discussed. This book therefore seeks to contribute to the literature by adding nuance to the discussion around factors that impact negotiations by highlighting these less tangible, but demonstrably still impactful, elements.

Methods

Case studies are the main method of analysis because of the ability of case studies to act as deeper looks within a defined category to elucidate generalizable theories and ideas within the broader group of cases.[20] This book will use case studies as defined by Alexander George and Andrew Bennett: 'the detailed examination of an aspect of a historical episode to develop or test historical explanations that may be generalisable to other events'.[21] The benefit of using case studies for this kind of research is that it enables qualitative research into the specific processes that lead to military integration, allowing for detailed understanding of the various stages of negotiation and implementation that come together to create the outcomes this book is interested in.

A variety of methods have been used to identify the most appropriate case studies to demonstrate how integrating former fighters into post-conflict security institutions can be an effective way to increase the potential of achieving stable peace.[22] This book combines archival sources, interviews and secondary source analysis to produce a detailed analysis of the peace processes, from the beginning of negotiations to five years after the signing of the treaty.

At each stage, the cases of Mozambique and Angola are compared side-by-side, in order to understand similarities and differences between the processes in each country.[23] Although more traditional historical analysis would treat each case in its entirety and then make comparisons in the conclusion, this project aims to investigate the details of each stage for each country while also making explicit comparisons throughout; therefore, the organizational method of the book focuses on the steps of the peace processes rather than a country-by-country analysis. This organizational decision of direct comparison was further confirmed by the information gleaned from interviews and archival documents that highlighted just how closely actors in Mozambique were watching events in Angola unfold and responding to them; in fact, a number of actors from UN and NGOs were involved in the peace processes in both Angola and Mozambique in the 1990s. Putting their information and the wider literature into direct chronological conversation therefore surfaces key similarities and differences that may be less apparent if focusing solely within each country's national boundaries.

The aim of this research is to focus qualitatively on analysing the final peace treaties by looking first at the texts themselves. This is combined with interviews and written primary and secondary materials to understand the contexts around how these texts were created and implemented. The goal is to focus on comparing the two peace processes in Angola and Mozambique together, rather than conducting a case study of each country separately.

Case studies are of course limited in that innumerable aspects of both conflict and post-conflict situations are influenced by so many factors – known and unknown – that understanding cause and effect in any particular instance is always guesswork. This is further compounded when one attempts to focus on specific aspects within a country's history and even more so when theoretical understandings from literature beyond this particular country's example are brought in. Developing more general theories or understandings on the basis of one or even a few case studies is therefore fraught with difficulty. This book emphasizes the importance of understanding the specific contexts of the political situations in both Angola and Mozambique, in order to avoid over-deterministic arguments without historical nuance, while still thoroughly investigating areas in which comparisons can be made.

The cases: Angola and Mozambique

The book focuses on two examples of post-conflict military reconstruction in order to investigate the processes and outcomes in depth: the Angolan civil war (1975–2002) and the Mozambican civil war (1975–92). One of the most important factors in building a qualitative comparative analysis is case selection.[24] To choose the appropriate cases, this project engaged with a series of analytical steps to determine the cases. These two cases were chosen through a process that included combining three existing datasets to create a comprehensive list of post–Second World War civil wars, which was then culled to identify groups of conflicts most relevant to examining post-conflict military reconstruction.

Superficially, Angola and Mozambique have quite a few things in common: both were Portuguese colonies which gained independence in 1975 after years of insurgency. Both immediately fell into civil wars pitting a Soviet-backed group that was more generally recognized as the government against a rebel opposition group backed by other outside actors. Ideology was an initially important component in both wars, though in both, ideology was overtaken by economic concerns amid significant destruction as the years went on. Both conflicts were significantly affected by the ending of the Cold War, and both have gone into the post-conflict period with the formerly Soviet-backed group remaining as the main governmental actor. Both have also had similarly timed and relatively successful military integration processes, with more mixed results in terms of political power-sharing.

There are, however, significant points of difference between these two countries. Angola, by virtue of large oil resources, has a much larger GDP than Mozambique, which affected both its conflict and post-conflict dynamics and outcomes. Angola was also much more involved in the Cold War as a proxy conflict and in various regional conflicts which included Namibian independence and various wars in the Democratic Republic of the Congo. Perhaps relatedly, Angola's civil war started in 1975 along with Mozambique's, but while both countries had peace processes in the early 1990s, Mozambique's succeeded and Angola's failed, with Angola only achieving a lasting peace treaty in 2002. Thus, Mozambique and Angola provide more direct comparisons and contrasts to each other.

Sources

Because the treaties and processes this analysis is focused on all were completed over twenty years ago, the tools and framework of analysis are primarily historical. This included qualitative investigations of archival material, secondary literature, primary sources and interviews with relevant figures.

Interviews were quite informative as many of the key figures involved in these processes are now in retirement and have not all been interviewed about their involvement in these conflicts. This provided an opportunity to speak with these actors while they are no longer politically involved but still willing to participate in interviews and capable of doing so. The people interviewed were involved in the negotiation and/or implementation processes specifically related to security provisions in the peace processes in Angola and Mozambique. The especially interesting interviews were with those who were involved in the negotiations at a staff level, as their experiences have not been the focus of documentation or analysis in the available secondary literature. By interviewing them about their involvement, more information about the 'behind-the-scenes' narrative of how events unfolded, relationships developed and policies were created has now been included in the understanding of how these treaties came into being.

Information gained in interviews themselves presented challenges and ethical considerations that are of particular importance: the issues surrounding memory. While interviewees were chosen based on their direct involvement in these peace processes, the events in question happened over two decades ago. This naturally presented issues of reliability when assessing their contributions and analyses, including hindsight bias and difficulty in accurately recalling details, amongst other factors. In order to try and mitigate these concerns, interviewee information was fact-checked against contemporary archival sources and secondary material as much as possible and throughout the book is presented as memories rather than facts.

In terms of archival sourcing, investigation proved that both the Angolan and Mozambican national archives would be too biased and censored to provide useful information particularly related to treaty negotiations and implementation around security issues. Additionally, while information about the development of some of the key groups (i.e. FRELIMO) exists in other national archives (i.e. Tanzania's), they primarily are focused on the creation and development of the groups, which predates the salient part of this book's focus. However, the key archive for this research was the official UN archives. While the archives have been accessible to researchers for decades, the sensitivity rules of the UN meant that by accessing these records in early 2020, both the twenty-year and twenty-five-year restrictions had been lifted, meaning that this book was able to draw on a much wider range of UN material than has previously been accessible to researchers. This included the week-by-week minutes of the committee meeting in charge of creating the integrated Mozambican military, the after-action reports of all three UN missions in Angola, included the 'eyes-only' reports on the failures of the successive UNAVEM missions and the day-to-day memos detailing the challenges of implementing the treaties, including handwritten letters and sticky notes about conditions in assembly areas, grievances of individual peacekeepers and protests between ONUMOZ's force commander and the special representative of the secretary-general, to name just a few examples. This wealth of written primary source material gives unique insight into the processes in both Angola and Mozambique, primarily related to implementation given the UN's larger role in those stages of the processes, that this book has used to investigate these processes in much greater detail.

What existing research says

This book aims to contribute specifically to the understanding of how civil wars end and particularly the impact on post-conflict stability of how militaries are treated and organized in the transition from war to peace. This section summarizes, discusses and analyses the existing academic literature most relevant to this research question. Chapter 2 will examine the case-specific literature to provide the necessary background to understanding the peace treaty negotiations, terms and implementation in Angola and Mozambique.

Why focus on specificity and security when analysing peace treaties?

The importance of focusing on military terms is highlighted in Anne Jarstad and Desiree Nilsson's 2008 article where they introduced a new dataset that examined the implementation of power-sharing provisions in peace treaties since 1990.[25] They found that while political power-sharing processes are more common, it is military power-sharing that most strongly correlates to successful treaty implementation. They contend that this is because military power-sharing is a more costly commitment to the peace process than any other potential concession and therefore if this is successful, easier issues will likewise reach a resolution. Political power-sharing is not as significant in signalling trust between parties because it is easier to 'walk away from a joint government' than to withdraw from military or territorial power-sharing arrangements. In contrast to participating in elections or transitional unity governments, actually going ahead with military agreements involves giving up weapons and dispersing troops, or integrating chains of command and personnel intimately with the opposing side, which is much more difficult and risky to undo. This was the impetus for this research project to examine promises made around military institutions in Mozambique and Angola's peace processes to determine their salience and impact on the wider political negotiations.

This book's focus on the promise of post-conflict military integration was in part prompted by the 2008 article by Katherine Glassmyer and Nicholas Sambanis, which was one of the first articles to specifically examine military integration in post-conflict situations.[26] They argue that military integration can be successful in making peace durable, but only if it is properly structured and implemented. This idea of 'proper' structures and implementation methods became a driving query for this research project. In addition, this book very much agrees with Stedman's point that while some conflicts are likely harder to end than others, it is nearly always possible to predict *ahead of time* which those will be and prepare accordingly.[27] Charles King suggested that one type of preparation to assist in this dilemma is ensuring disarmament happens to all sides simultaneously, therefore removing times in which one side has a military dominance over the other.[28] This theme of preparation will be a consistent one throughout this book and is arguably the entire intent of the project: aiming to understand how best to plan and implement post-conflict military integration.

There are various types of structure examined in the literature and therefore investigated in this book's focus on Angola and Mozambique. One consistent theme is the importance of equality and especially perceptions of equality. For example, Cecilia Albin and Daniel Druckman argued that ensuring equality in procedures including standardized timelines for security issues (including disarmament and demobilization) can increase successful implementation of treaties.[29] This is echoed in one of the few existing analyses of Angola and Mozambique's peace processes: Dorina Bekoe's 2008 book *Implementing Peace Agreements: Lessons from Mozambique, Angola, and Liberia*.[30] In the book, she demonstrates that negotiations must maintain 'mutual vulnerability' to ensure success. This means that any concessions asked of one side must have an equivalent concession from other parties, and then any agreements about security issues in particular must aim for both sides to work along equal timelines so that one side does not feel overly vulnerable compared to its adversaries (also raised by Madhav Joshi and Michael Quinn's 2012 and Mattes and Savun, 2009).[31] Mediators therefore must aim for sides to make concessions along equal timelines and for that goal to be known to all participants. Creating joint military institutions, as opposed to some sides undergoing DDR, is an obvious extension of this argument to investigate, which has driven the research agenda of this book.

When examining how promises are made in and around treaties, this book is significantly influenced by Rothchild who argued that the more specific peace treaties are, the more likely they are to be successfully implemented.[32] He noted that although in the midst of negotiations it can be easier to use vague language to smooth over particularly contentious issues (as suggested in Zartman and Berman's 1982 practitioner-driven research),[33] this ambiguity is more likely to lead to confusion and disputes during the implementation process. The call for specificity is likewise echoed by Caroline Hartzell, Matthew Hoddie and Kees Kingma, showing consistency in the literature.[34] Hartzell, Hoddie and Rothchild in fact argue that in contexts in which political institutions have been more eroded by conflict, peace agreements must be much more specific by formally outlining the steps to ensure peace.[35] This exact circumstance helps explain the collapse of Angola's Bicesse process, as detailed in Chapter 3.

Relatedly, Michaela Mattes & Burcu Savun argue that lasting peace treaties must include both fear-reducing mechanisms to increase incentives for cooperation as well as provisions that increase the cost of returning to conflict. Their suggested fear-reducing mechanisms include third-party guarantees (following on from Walter's 1999–2002 research on commitment problems[36]) and power-sharing institutions along political, military, economic or territorial lines as appropriate to the context.[37] This is the line of inquiry prompted this book's investigation of integrated military institutions as offering a type of power-sharing.

This builds directly on Terrence Lyons' 2005 book that emphasizes how 'actions taken in the immediate aftermath of a negotiated agreement [can] play a central and previously under-acknowledged role in setting post-civil war states on a trajectory toward either continued stability or a return to war'.[38] Lyons focuses on the peace process itself and specifically incentives that can improve implementation outcomes. The first group of incentives are 'pull factors' which focus on reducing security risks and improving institutional capacities. He argues that this can be done through the setting up of electoral and oversight bodies and efforts to transform military organizations into political parties, aspects that are examined with regards to Angola and Mozambique later in this book. In examining the two case studies, the argument will be made that the involvement of military personnel with relevant expertise at the negotiations increases the chances that security provisions within the treaty will be realistic and clearly defined.

What are some of the challenges in implementing peace treaties?

The literature widely agrees that implementation is a complicated process with a range of factors that often interact idiosyncratically depending on the particular context of the conflict. Stedman, for example, contends that implementation success depends on the following factors: difficulty of implementation environment (including number and type of spoilers); willingness of outside actors to provide resources over a long-term commitment; ubiquity of valuable and easily mobile resources (both as related to financing violence and post-conflict development); and proximity of states that will or will not provide safe havens for groups to continue fighting from.[39]

Further challenges are outlined by Rothchild, who argues that implementation problems also arise where there is a lack of coordination between mediators and implementers, as well as between different implementers, an increasing issue given the multiplication in recent years of post-conflict specialists in various fields.[40] Mattes & Savun put a particular emphasis on information asymmetries amongst and between mediators and implementers and how that imbalance can lead to breakdowns during implementation.[41] With these issues in mind, verification and monitoring interventions should do the following: clearly prioritize tasks; focus on turning soldiers into civilians and leaders into politicians; making civilians feel safe, for example, through police and justice reform; and building local capacity on human rights and reconciliation issues.

Similarly, Chester A. Crocker and Fen Osler Hampson posit that agreements can fail to be implemented due to: 'inadequate enforcement mechanisms, ambiguous terms of settlement, overly rigid terms of application, unrealistic expectations, wilful defections that go unpenalized' and more.[42] International involvement is important to making sure agreements are signed, but crucially, the authors argue, this support must stay through the implementation stage as well. Additionally, a designated person or group must be in charge of mediating problems that will arise during implementation; consistent, credible and legitimate leadership throughout the process is necessary. Implementation needs to have clear goals for what 'success' means and how to get there, which could mean for example delaying elections in a situation is not ready for them rather than holding elections and violence ensuing. Having realistic time expectations that all sides agree to in advance is a good way to avoid the emergence of spoilers that could derail trust in the process. One particular risk of election models is the 'winner-takes-all' policy due to its zero-sum nature, and while elections are important, they should not be the end goal in and of themselves. Instead, demobilization and disarmament are key priorities to resolve fundamental security risks and economic reconstruction is likewise important. To ensure success, military and political timelines should be coordinated without overloading fragile situations with too-quick elections or too-quick demilitarization.

Another challenge for successful implementation particularly important in the two case studies of Angola and Mozambique is the role of UN peacekeeping in implementing peace terms. Lise Morjé Howard and Anjali Dayal argue that many UN peacekeeping missions and UN Security Council efforts towards resolving civil wars in general are actually not often specific to the particular situation and are often not crafted to be capable of keeping the peace.[43] They argue this is because of institutional inertia within the UNSC and the difficulty of reaching agreements with five veto powers. Thus, when an agreement is reached in one situation, the language is often used nearly identically in the next case regardless of suitability in order to maintain agreement between the veto powers and ensure the UNSC's place as the arbiter of international peace and security. As later chapters of this book will show, this was unfortunately very much the case in Angola in particular.

Another challenge of DDR is raised by MacArtan Humphreys and Jeremy Weinstein, who argue that successful demobilization does not in fact predict or lead directly to successful reintegration of ex-combatants into civilian society.[44] They, however, identify different factors that lead to issues with successful civilian reintegration. Those that have more success include former fighters who were part of abusive factions, fighters with lesser education and wealth backgrounds and those who were lower ranked within their military organization. On the other hand, highly educated, wealthy and higher-ranking ex-combatants seem to have a more difficult time integrating post-conflict. They conclude from these results that those who distrust the process overall, usually those with dislike or distrust of the post-conflict political situation, have less democratic involvement and thus, less successful employment integration. This finding raises questions about the likelihood of ensuring participation and buy-in across multiple ex-combatant populations.

Collier, however, casts doubt on even less economically advantaged soldiers being able to reintegrate.[45] He argues that in the short term, violence and crime are reduced if demobilized soldiers are given land, as it allows them to rebuild their lives. Collier notes that ex-combatants without land have few skills suited to civilian employment, and those who are disabled are most vulnerable in the post-conflict period and that while land can address some of those concerns, it is likely a shorter-term solution than a permanent one. Most pessimistically, Robert Muggah contends that reintegration is still the least successfully implemented piece due to shortfalls in planning, implementation and most crucially, funding.[46]

Military integration, however, as an alternative to DDR nevertheless has an important definitional parameter to set: what counts as success in a post-conflict context. This book examines these institutions' question from the perspective of enabling peace, rather than war-fighting capabilities. In this, the book agrees with Nicole Ball's critique of the usual security sector reform efforts that focus on rebuilding a functioning military institution using standards of fighting efficiency rather than emphasizing transparency or accountability to wider society. She argues this not only weakens security sector institutions but also their legitimacy within a wider peace process.[47] Further, per David Laitin, the symbol of a successfully integrated military and its ability to build a durable peace matters more than the army's actual fighting capabilities.[48] In fact, in her 2010 book, Florence Gaub shows that militaries can act as effective socializing and unifying institutions both before and after conflicts even in multiethnic societies. She highlights the importance of elite support, balanced officer corps and unified training as key factors in creating a successfully reintegrated military.[49] Laitin argues that this symbolic effect therefore eliminates the concern around the fact that many post-conflict integrated militaries are initially far larger in personnel numbers than the country needs, as was the case in Mozambique (see Chapters 4 and 5).

This literature therefore highlights a number of challenges that a peace process must negotiate, from initial meetings, to drafting treaty terms, to implementing complicated processes involving high politics and intensive logistics. The remainder of this book will examine the extent to which the peace processes in

Angola and Mozambique confirm the findings of this literature, highlight gaps and illustrate the book's main argument in favour of specificity in treaty terms.

Structure of the book

Chapter 1 has explained the context and main arguments of the book, along with details of how this argument will be developed throughout the book and how it contributes to the existing literature. Chapter 2 will examine the literature specific to the Angolan and Mozambican civil wars and peace processes and analyse the relevant historical context of both conflicts.

Chapter 3 will then build on this foundation in order to examine the process of beginning negotiations in both cases and the contents of the two treaties, the Bicesse Accords for Angola and the Rome Agreement for Mozambique and initial implementation efforts. Chapter 4 will continue this analysis chronologically, focusing specifically on the development of the integrated military in Mozambique and the return to conflict in Angola as well as the second attempted peace treaty, the Lusaka Treaty. Chapter 5 progresses through longer-term impacts of reconstruction on security and the integrated military in Mozambique, while also comparing the last stages of Angola's war and final peace treaty.

Finally, Chapter 6 assesses the peace process in thematic stages, highlighting the overall arguments and lessons from the two cases and four peace processes analysed.

Chapter 2

THE ANGOLAN AND MOZAMBICAN CIVIL WARS

Angola's civil war lasted from 1975 to 2002 and encompassed four major peace treaty processes, two of which received significant international attention and intervention, including multiple UN missions which were notorious failures. It is therefore not surprising that there is quite a lot of academic and practitioner literature examining both the country and the conflict. In organizing this extensive research, the following section will focus primarily on the four attempts made to end Angola's civil war (1975–2002): the original 1975 Alvor Agreement, the 1991 Bicesse Accords, the 1994 Lusaka Agreement and the final 2002 Luena Agreement. A large part of the existing literature that focuses exclusively on these conflicts is factual and historical. Much of the analytical literature that mentions either or both cases as examples either in edited volumes or in thematic works has been included in other sections of this literature review, for example, on disarmament, demobilization and reintegration. The remaining two sections of this literature review therefore focus on the key secondary sources directly concerned with the Angolan and Mozambican civil wars and post-conflict outcomes.

To understand the origins of this conflict, examining the colonial context is fundamental. In his 1994 article 'The Neglected Tragedy: The Return to War in Angola, 1992–3' Anthony Pereira outlines how the Portuguese colony in Angola developed, and how organized opposition arose in the final colonial period. Angola was Portugal's most important colony due to its strategic shipping location and significant oil and diamond deposits. Justin Pearce, in his 2015 book, outlines how the Portuguese government was aware of the potential problems these anti-colonial groups could pose to an independent Angola, which provides useful insight into the development of the 1975 Alvor Treaty that was meant to end the war between the People's Movement for the Liberation of Angola (MPLA) and the National Union for the Total Independence of Angola (UNITA).

The main groups that would go on to fight the Angolan civil war (MPLA and UNITA) both had their roots in the 1960s anti-colonial struggles against Portugal. Their internal histories are detailed in Fernando Andresen Guimarães' 1998 book which not only describes the development of the MPLA and UNITA but also their anti-colonial activities and the initial years of the Angolan civil war. In his 1979 book, Lawrence Henderson provides further details on these anti-colonial movements (mainly the MPLA and UNITA) and shows that by the unexpected moment of independence in 1975 boasted a combined total of fewer than 5,000 troops. One of the initial dynamics of the post-independence conflict was the rushed recruitment of fighters by both sides to bolster their positions, which is when many of the future leaders of the groups joined their respective sides. Alliances and relationships from the 1970s therefore remained salient throughout the conflict and through the various negotiations starting in 1989 and ending in 2002.

On the topic of alliances, Anthony Pazzanita's 1991 book provides a summary of the Cold War dynamics of the war, particularly the financial support of the US (to UNITA) and the USSR (to the MPLA) as well as Cuban military support for the MPLA through the 1980s. Abiodun Alao in his 1994 book outlines regional dimensions of the war, explaining the links to the Namibian independence fight, relations with South Africa and other post-independence conflicts such as in Mozambique.

As implied by the literature earlier, the 1975 Alvor Agreement that was meant to simultaneously grant Angola its independence and head off a civil war between the MPLA and UNITA achieved only the first of those two aims. The second attempt at peace did not begin until 1989, and according to Roland Paris in his 2004 book, the MPLA and UNITA were pushed to the negotiations table by their external backers, the USSR and the US respectively, rather than choosing to participate of their own accord. As Vladimir Shubin and Andrei Tokarev demonstrate in their 2001 article, Cold War dynamics heavily influenced peace attempts in Southern Africa at this time, from the deployment of the UN peacekeeping mission (UNAVEM) to the agreement between UNITA and the MPLA called the Bicesse Accords.

The Bicesse Accords fell apart within two years and became a key experience in evaluating and reforming UN peacekeeping operations going forward, both within and beyond Angola. This peace treaty has therefore received significant academic attention and has a wealth of primary source material from international actors who were involved in the process. One of the key practitioners was Margaret Anstee, who headed the UN mission during the crucial negotiations and implementation phases. In her 1996 book *Orphan of the Cold War: The Inside Story of the Collapse of the Angolan Peace Process, 1992–93*, she details the day-by-day processes that eventually unravelled. She points to a lack of mechanisms for resolving electoral and security issues as they arose, of UNAVEM II capacity in monitoring and enforcing treaty provisions and an over-emphasis on election timeline even as the DDR timeline began to disintegrate.

Anstee's observations are supported in Virginia Page Fortna's 2003 article as she agrees that UNAVEM had insufficient resources and capacity to enforce the treaty, elections were held before DDR could be completed and adds that spoiler issues were neglected. Asis Malaquias in her 2007 book builds on these findings to argue that the winner-takes-all election system raised the stakes of the election (that occurred during the initial months of implementation) too high for peace to be maintained and that the lack of UNAVEM capacity further doomed the process.

In his 2000 article, Jake Sherman lays out the immediate aftermath of the collapse of the Bicesse Accords and shows that by 1993 UNITA had control of

70 per cent of Angola. He argues that this was due to UNITA's ability to traffic in diamonds and therefore maintain access to equipment and continue to pay their members. This research is supported by Phillipe Le Billon in his 2013 book where he focuses on the economics behind the fighting in the 1990s. According to his research, even after the Cold War ended and the USSR and US stopped funding their respective proxies in Angola, both the MPLA and UNITA used natural resources to fund their fighting. The MPLA began to use oil revenues while UNITA focused on diamond mining. Billon argues that sanctions against UNITA that targeted diamond trading began to have an effect once the United States joined the effort, thus forcing UNITA back to negotiate with the MPLA. Asis Malaquias in her 2001 article further emphasizes the importance of diamond revenues in funding UNITA's activities and attributes the majority of the military successes following the collapse of the Bicesse process to diamond-backed finances.

Alex Vines, in his 1999 Human Rights Watch report argues that the targeting of UNITA diamond revenues led to territorial losses across Angola. He then states, 'The Lusaka Protocol [1994] was signed at a moment when the . . . UNITA rebels were in a weakened position and wanted to stop its territorial losses to the government.' According to David Simon's 1998 article, the US and UN thought that UNITA's leader, Jonas Savimbi, would be willing to make concessions during the 1994 peace process in order to avoid further battlefield losses and defeat. George Write, in his 2001 article, further describes how the US policy towards the Lusaka Agreement was fundamentally underlined by the goal of getting Savimbi to negotiate, and the assumption that given UNITA's weaker military position, concessions would be possible.

Initially, as Norrie MacQueen describes in a 1998 article, the Lusaka Agreement was specifically built on the Bicesse Accords. However, MacQueen notes some key ways in which the agreement was changed, specifically the increased robustness of the UN involvement through a better staffed, trained and politically motivated UN peacekeeping mission.

Despite these changes, Paul Hare, a US diplomat involved in the negotiations, and Margaret Anstee, who was still with the UN mission at the time, provide accounts from the ground that reveal the persistent problems the Lusaka Agreement was unable to address. According to both of their memoirs, Hare's 1998 account *Angola's Last Best Chance for Peace: An Insider's Account of the Peace Process* and Anstee's 1998 article 'The Fight Goes On', the primary problem of the agreement was UNITA's leader Savimbi. Both authors highlight how focused Savimbi was on obtaining the position of president, almost to the exclusion of all else, thus leading to an impasse that could not be bridged in the 1994 agreement. Hare also notes other points that were left unsolved, including the role of Portugal in the economy and the size of the unified army, but emphasized that the main issue was Savimbi's unwillingness to concede on the presidential issue.

In their 2004 book, Taisier Ali, Robert Matthews and Ian Spears lay out the failures of peacekeeping in Angola. Following the collapse of the Lusaka process, the authors describe how, 'fed up with UNITA's intransigence, the government [MPLA] launched a new major offensive in December 1998 to reclaim these territories and, as ultimately occurred, to decapitate UNITA's leadership'. As suggested in this quotation, this final military push by the MPLA was successful in forcing UNITA back to negotiations in the 2002 Luena Agreement which finally concluded the conflict. The authors also point to the MPLA's success in continuing the international momentum sanctioning UNITA's diamond trafficking and further note other attempts to isolate UNITA diplomatically, for example, by removing regional allies such as President Mobutu of the Democratic Republic of the Congo. As for the Luena Agreement itself, the authors explain the security-focused nature of the treaty by putting the main failures of the previous two agreements down to lack of trust in power-sharing provisions that inhibited disarmament processes.

In their 2009 chapter, Alex Vines and Bereni Oruitemeka propose an explanation for why the 2002 Luena Agreement was focused almost exclusively on security provisions. They posit this focus was because UNITA was divided at the time and its leaders were mostly experienced in military issues, and because there was no outside negotiator to provide a more well-rounded perspective. This builds on Vines' 2002 article when he analysed the state of UNITA's leadership and noted how the Luena Agreement was signed just weeks after the deaths of both Savimbi and his long-time second-in-command. Kelly Greenhill and Solomon Major, however, in their 2006 article argued that it was the success of the anti-diamond sanctions that forced UNITA back to the table, and that Savimbi's death was not the sole or even main motivating factor that allowed negotiations to move forward.

In terms of the treaty provisions, in their 2009 chapter, Mats Berdal and David Ucko argue that 'successful DDR (is) considered the most important precondition for post-war stability'. They note how the failures of the Bicesse Accords in particular sparked massive academic and practitioner debates within the UN around reforming UN peacekeeping, which were only compounded by the subsequent failure to successfully learn and apply the lessons during the Lusaka process. They argue that the failure of DDR was first noted following the Bicesse process and that the Luena Agreement's focus on security issues was driven by lessons learned from previous attempts at peace, not because of who was involved in the negotiations. Still, the authors found that the political aspects of Bicesse and Lusaka were kept in the Luena Agreement, and therefore found no issue with those provisions, contrary to some of the theoretical literature surveyed in the earlier sections related to power-sharing.

More authors who examine causes and effects of the collapses of both the Bicesse and Lukasa agreements include Ian Spears and James Hammill. Spears, in his 1999 book, combines both primary and secondary sources in order to analyse step-by-step how the Lusaka Accord collapsed, and analysed in particular what lessons had been learned and applied from the failures of Bicesse, and what lessons should now be taken from two failures in a row. James Hammill's 1994 article provides a useful contemporary look at what the failure of the Bicesse Accords meant for Angola. In his words: 'since September 1992, a humanitarian disaster has befallen the country [due to the failure of the Bicesse Accords] which has no parallel even during the long 30-years-war from 1961 to 1991'.

The aforementioned literature gives an overview of the scope and complexity of Angola's civil war and multiple attempts at peace. Much of the research discussed so far focuses primarily on elections and the movements' leaders rather than security issues, and this lack of focus is one of the literature gaps this book aims to address. Despite this gap, the four treaties do provide valuable insights when examining different methods of dealing with former combatants, particularly because each treaty dealt with important aspects of the peace process differently. In addition, the Bicesse Accords of 1991 and the Lusaka Agreement of 1994 have been used as the basis of multiple UN peacekeeping missions and other policy interventions in subsequent conflicts around the world, making this case study an important one to consider. The final treaty – the Luena Agreement of 2002 – led to the Angola of today, where one party (the MPLA) is both politically and militarily dominant. In comparison with the following two case studies to be considered, Angola's peace processes were much more convoluted (with four peace treaties rather than one) and show examples of both conflict recurrence and lasting peace.

Existing research on the Mozambican civil war

The variety of academic research on Mozambique's civil war (1977–92), peace process and post-conflict outcome includes extensive primary source material both from academics who were journalists or researchers involved on the ground at the time (e.g. Alex Vines), and from interviews and analyses. In addition, memoirs from practitioners involved in the process also give useful insight into the events. In the case of Mozambique, there is a lot of detail available about how exactly the peace process unfolded, with day-by-day schedules of who met with whom, how connections were made and then how security and political provisions from the treaty were implemented. However, because the civil war in Mozambique did not grow out of pre-independence contests and was successfully ended in one peace process, both quite distinct circumstances compared to Angola, the conflict and resolution were shorter, thus resulting in a smaller body of existing academic literature. In examining this case study and this material, this research project will aim to analyse the available data to explain why aspects of these negotiation and implementation steps were effective and highlight areas in which different decisions could have led to alternative outcomes.

As an overview, Alex Vines' 1996 *RENAMO: From Terrorism to Democracy in Mozambique* is one of the best sources for understanding the development and motivations of this key actor in the conflict. In particular, he focuses on the influence of external actors on RENAMO during the negotiations period, as well as outlining the internal factions that caused disharmony within its ranks. He further outlines the practical challenges that hindered implementation, particularly related to disputes over the locations of cantonment areas during demobilization and the cash incentives provided to former fighters.

In his 1999 chapter, John S. Saul describes how negotiations in Mozambique were very much organized and run by outside powers. He argues that outside backers of the Mozambican National Resistance (RENAMO) and the Mozambique Liberation Front (FRELIMO) respectively were the main ones pushing for negotiations to begin, and were primarily motivated by the humanitarian toll the continued conflict was having. These external actors included political entities on both sides of the Cold War, with the Soviet Union and China supporting FRELIMO and the Western-backed South Africa supporting RENAMO. In addition to external state actors, Saul's analysis stresses the important role that Protestant (Anglican) and Catholic institutions and leaders had in bringing both sides to the table as well as providing mediating services and discussion fora. In his analysis, the outside impetus to negotiate was resisted by both sides, though FRELIMO eventually agreed before RENAMO. Additionally, he asserts that RENAMO eventually complied not necessarily in order to negotiate in good faith but rather to continue to extract financial support and aid from the West. While this is perhaps not ideal in terms of bringing parties to the table, it highlights how coercive measures can create compliance, just as the theoretical literature discussed in earlier details.

William Minster (1994) likewise points to RENAMO as being the more recalcitrant negotiator but offers a different reason. In his analysis, 'RENAMO was afraid of peace, because its chances of winning support in peaceful political competition were so low and because its leaders had become accustomed to war as a way of life'. This argument highlights the importance of assuring RENAMO elites of post-conflict status in the negotiations and implementation process and signals that securing the elite cooperation would be key to creating a lasting peace treaty.

In his 2001 book, Chris Alden similarly argues that RENAMO's leadership was not prepared to negotiate opposite the MPLA and its lawyers and were therefore even more mistrustful of entering into negotiations than external actors expected. Alden then discusses what factors overcame RENAMO's reluctance to enter negotiations, the main one being demands from its external backers. Besides pressure from outside actors, however, Alden also points to a 'genuine weariness and concrete lack of capacity on the part of the Mozambican population and society to participate in unending war' as being another factor prompting negotiations. Specifically, he links these two drivers together by noting that due to 'the pressure of repeated drought, destruction, and famine', FRELIMO and RENAMO were both dependent on external backers for funding and that with those parties pushing for peace, neither Mozambican actor could resist entering into negotiations for long.

Cameron Hume, in his 1994 book, offers detailed descriptions of every single meeting, negotiation and discussion that occurred during the peace process. His notes reveal the importance of third-party actors and especially the commitment shown by various clergy members of different denominations. Stephen Chan and Moises Vanancio in their 1998 book also outline the entire peace process, including the various stages of negotiations and who was involved at each point. These two sources are particularly useful due to the amount of interview data that was collected and transcribed as well as the interweaving of written accounts from actors involved in the process both from Mozambique and the United Nations. These two books focus heavily on the political aspects discussed during negotiations and show that military issues were not even discussed during the negotiations until the very end. By this point, there was already a deadline put in place for the final agreement to be reached, thus putting the resolution of security issues under heavy time pressure.

In their 2014 chapter, Andrew Bartdi and Martra Mutisi also outline the stages and details of the negotiating process but go further and examine the implementation process as well. According to their analysis, Mozambique had a comprehensive interim oversight committee to run the implementation process, with both sides equally represented. Crucially, this committee had military personnel from FRELIMO and RENAMO involved, which built trust amongst military elites that allowed for problems to be more easily resolved. The first stage of implementation, disarmament, was delayed and took longer than expected to begin. A key decision was made, however, to focus on the most destructive weapons such as large artillery pieces, rather than the small arms that were ubiquitous across the country and prized for social and economic, as well as security, reasons. At first, it was difficult for both sides to concede control over these weapons, but once initial releases were made, the process moved efficiently and was considered a success by participants. In terms of integrating both sides into a unified military, despite having been successfully agreed upon, the actual implementation faced challenges. The agreed-upon training ended up being provided by multiple different external militaries, leading to confusion amongst implementers and troops. Still, some important elements were successful such as the maintenance of war-time rank amongst integrated combatants, regardless of pre-war standards for promotion. These status markers are incredibly important within security institutions, and the guarantee (especially to RENAMO troops who generally had fewer official educational qualifications) that wartime rank would be maintained was key to ensuring cooperation from mid-level and upper-level officers.

In his 1996 book, Eric Berman focused particularly on the involvement of the UN throughout the negotiations and implementation process, especially their role in monitoring and verifying the security aspects of implementation. Berman highlights the UN's credibility and preparedness as being crucial in ensuring the implementation programmes were carried out, particularly regarding the discrepancies between the agreed-upon provisions (such as the number of troops each side would commit to the unified army) and the realities on the ground.

The previous sources have discussed the development, negotiation and implementation of the peace process, and this final source examines the outcome. For the purposes of this book, the most important analysis of the outcome of Mozambique's peace process is the following quotation in Anders Themner's 2017 book: 'Mozambique remains an example of mostly successful demobilisation . . . but poor elite reintegration. RENAMO's leader . . . had failed to make the transition from guerrilla leader to democrat.' The analysis of Mozambique in the remainder of this book will attempt to show how this statement came about and how it compares to transitions in Angola and South Africa happening around the same time. Beyond this statement, Themner outlines how the agreed-upon security provisions of the treaty, both for demobilization and for military integration, had to be modified during the implementation phase. This was primarily due to inaccurate information given by RENAMO during the negotiations phase, presumably to make itself seem stronger and therefore gain more influence in the negotiation and with its external supporters. Further, Themner draws a connection between the disarmament programme of the implementation process and the provision for RENAMO leaders to keep a few hundred fighters as personal bodyguards after the treaty to the renewed violence between elements of RENAMO and the FRELIMO-dominated government in 2013. Still, he emphasizes that it is not necessarily the fault of these security provisions per se, but rather the failure of RENAMO to successfully transition into a political party.

This political failure is detailed comprehensively by Alex Vines in 2018. In this report, he outlines how RENAMO was unable to successfully transition to political power due to the lack of skills and understanding of its top leaders. Although efforts were made by international actors, including the UN, to educate and fund outreach efforts, the party has failed to make national political gains and maintains a hold only on a few municipal centres. This report is therefore the most up-to-date analysis of how the political aspects of the peace process went wrong, and, given Vines' previous work on RENAMO as an organization, offers useful insight into the pitfalls of turning a primarily military organization into a successful political institution.

While the aforementioned literature is only a sampling of the research available on the two civil wars and peace processes, these sources offer great detail in terms of what happened throughout the entire negotiations and implementation phases, including what worked and what did not. These sources also rely heavily on primary source material or include primary source material, making them invaluable in understanding what local and international contemporaries thought of the situations as they developed. This is key to understanding how decisions are made before hindsight is available, and how policies are developed, influenced and adapted in real time. The subsequent sections of this chapter will build on these literature reviews to highlight and analyse the relevant historical context to the peace processes in Angola and Mozambique, starting from their similar colonial histories.

Portuguese colonial rule in Angola and Mozambique

Although Portugal was one of the earliest European imperial forces in Africa, the formal consolidation of their colonies took place during the so-called 'Scramble for Africa' in the late 1800s.[1] The Portuguese empire's motivations and policies during this period provide essential context for understanding the emergence of the liberation movements at the heart of this book. It was under these colonial Portuguese structures that the anti-colonial movements were formed, and the organizational patterns that emerged under colonialism carried through into the civil wars after independence.

Both Mozambique and Angola were attractive colonial acquisitions for Portugal due to the development of ports as useful stopping points for the Portuguese trading route from Europe to the Indian Ocean. The colonies that eventually became Angola and Mozambique first experienced Portuguese colonial acquisitions in the early 1500s, but these were small in scale and focused mainly on natural harbours and coast-based resource extraction with minimal colonial relations towards inland communities.[2] Through the seventeenth and eighteenth centuries, the Portuguese began to expand south along the Angolan coast in order to find more arable land to support its initial coastal settlements but did not intend to move inland and negotiate difficult terrain.[3] In Angola, increased inland exploration was caused by the rise of the lucrative international slave trade in the eighteenth century, which incentivized Portugal to begin directly trading with these kingdoms in order to acquire slaves. In order to better facilitate the aforementioned trading, Portugal eventually became involved in the internal politics of the kingdoms that would become Angola and the Democratic Republic of the Congo.[4] In Mozambique, the Portuguese method of colonization was also based on the extraction of resources, including both slaves and precious metals. Portugal's territorial control focused on maximizing territory for extraction, with little settlement of Portuguese civilians in the colonies.[5]

This changed following the 1884 Conference of Berlin during which the European powers divided the continent of Africa into specific colonies based on 'facts-on-the-ground'. Fear of losing its existing ports and other territories prompted Portugal to begin more explicitly controlling territory in both Angola and Mozambique through violent conquest.[6] This not only led to various punitive military campaigns to 'pacify' the Angolan interior and bring it under Portuguese control but also to the implementation of mass settlement and infrastructure programmes. These policy changes aimed to make the colonies economically self-sufficient in order to fund the larger-scale development of extractive industries and infrastructure necessary for the export of extracted resources, without having to draw on funds from Portugal itself.[7]

These policies were largely maintained throughout the rest of the colonial period and directly set up the conditions both countries faced as they became independent and moved into civil war. The Portuguese colonial legacies around infrastructure, industrial development and labour policies are thus directly relevant to understanding what kinds of issues caused locals in both colonies to rebel against the Portuguese. They also influenced the contests that continued during the civil wars even after colonization was over.

Take, for instance, the Portuguese reaction to the dwindling Atlantic slave trade. As the slave trade was officially abolished in Europe, colonial rulers in Angola were compelled to expand agricultural production and, later, the oil trade to replace lost revenues. Even after slavery was officially banned, most native Angolans worked in indentured servitude either entirely or for the majority of their working lives for Portuguese settlers or Luso-Africans who were favoured by the colonial government due to their mixed-race status.[8] This system of forced labour was unpopular amongst most Angolans. As such, to maintain control, Portuguese colonial rule was dominated by systematic military repression.[9] This fuelled the grievances from which independent movements emerged and later influenced how these movements sought to establish political control themselves.

In both countries, colonial administration was highly centralized. Only major ports warranted urban development, and education focused on developing local talent was only implemented in areas useful to perpetuating extractive industries. There was little focus on training educated locals who might compete with Portuguese settlers for high-paying jobs.[10] Imperial funding was heavily focused on the white settler minorities: five years before independence, Angola's white population numbered 350,000 compared to the country's total population of 5.5 million, with Mozambique's numbers similarly showing 200,000 white settlers compared to an overall population of just under eight million.[11] In Mozambique, colonization also involved the imposition of Portuguese as the national language, while Angola's size and more inaccessible interior allowed for less Portuguese linguistic and cultural penetration.[12] During the civil wars, the colonial legacy of centralization became a key reason that the movements that controlled the capital cities and urban centres could remain in power, even if denied control of up to 80 per cent of the rest of the country. While these repressive policies lessened somewhat in the early twentieth century, rule by force was still the ruling policy in Angola and Mozambique even as other parts of Africa began to decolonize in the 1960s.

Aside from the structures of governance, Portuguese colonialism also had a lasting impact on the physical geography of the region. In Mozambique, one of the most physically impactful legacies of colonialism was the creation of purely latitude-based railways to move minerals from the mines to the ports.[13] Mozambique is a country that is long and narrow along a longitudinal axis, however, due to lack of colonial interest and then lack of economic ability, much of the country remained difficult to access.[14] This was an important factor in prolonging the civil war.[15] The railways and road networks were the main transportation mechanisms in colonial and independent Mozambique and were fiercely contested during the civil war both as a means of controlling access to populations and as ways to demonstrate state capacity for providing usable infrastructure or lack thereof.

Rise of anti-colonial movements

As decolonization began to rapidly occur throughout Africa, leading international support for European colonies decreased as newly independent countries joined the recently formed United Nations en masse,[16] and nationalist pro-independence movements took shape in both Angola and Mozambique. Following the end of the Second World War, most European capitals became more lax about holding onto overseas possessions due to the pressures of post-war reconstruction and the new international order that focused on economic trade over territorial acquisition. A notable exception to this was the central government in Lisbon, which was determined to maintain control of its territories and thus implemented more repressive policies. In this way, the Portuguese administration made agitation in its colonies costly for locals, thereby forcing the independence movements in Angola and Mozambique to form later than comparable efforts in other African countries.[17]

While both Angola and Mozambique had key anti-colonial movements that later became their post-independence governments, the political trajectories of both countries began to diverge in the 1960s, prior to their concurrent independence in 1975. In Angola, three competing independence movements arose from the mid-1950s onwards which led immediately to a civil war upon independence.[18] In contrast, Mozambique had only one major group prior to independence, the *Frente de Libertação de Moçambique* or Mozambique Liberation Front (FRELIMO). Therefore the transition from Portuguese colonial rule to independent government under FRELIMO was initially peaceful,[19] with the civil war only starting a few years later when competing factions evolved, separate from the independence process.[20]

In Mozambique, anti-colonial agitation started in the mid-1960s, fronted by FRELIMO, an organization founded in exile in 1962, composed mainly of well-educated expatriate Mozambicans.[21] Portugal's repressive policies and its purely export-based economy made its colonial administration in Mozambique unpopular, which enabled FRELIMO to move from popular support to successful military action against the colonial state.[22] Combined with the troop deployments to be discussed as follows in Angola, this stretched Portugal's financial and manpower resources very thin, making it difficult for the colonial regime to eradicate FRELIMO.

The first of Angola's three major independence movements was the *Movimento Popular de Libertação de Angola* or the People's Movement for the Liberation of Angola (MPLA). The group formed from the merger of smaller communist groups in 1956.[23] There is some debate amongst scholars over the extent of the MPLA's 'true' Marxist leanings, with some like Alao[24] and Legum[25] contending that the movement was merely socialist and used Marxist language to gain the support of the USSR and Cuba in the context of the Cold War. Pearce, by contrast, argues for a more genuinely Marxist ideology amongst MPLA operators, citing an internal consistency in messaging to domestic and foreign audiences.[26] The majority of the MPLA's messaging, however, focused on anti-colonialism and independence, with an emphasis on mass mobilization and better lives for the working class, without significant mention of tribal or linguistic affiliation.[27] This contrasted with the two other anti-colonial movements which formed in Angola along much more specific identity lines.[28]

Like FRELIMO in Mozambique, the MPLA's leadership was drawn from educated Angolans who had largely been educated abroad, but who were also distinct in that they generally came from mixed-race backgrounds,[29] in contrast to the majority of the Angolan population.[30] These mixed-race backgrounds were most visibly characterized by a preference for speaking Portuguese – the language of the colonizer – over indigenous languages, which was perhaps one reason that the MPLA were in general more effective in making contact and garnering support from international actors and urban communities, but had a harder time garnering support from rural Angolan populations.[31] The MPLA's support in urban centres, however, gave it the opportunity (via new recruits and safe houses) to take direct action against the Portuguese colonial administration.[32] It also made it logistically easier to communicate and recruit supporters, as well as receive material and financial support from Cuba via Angola's long coastline. Thus, by the early 1970s, the MPLA was one of the numerically largest anti-colonial movements in Angola and was best-positioned in the capital city and other key economic centres.[33]

The second important anti-colonial group in Angola leading up to independence in 1975 was the *Frente Nacional de Libertação de Angola* or the National Front for the Liberation of Angola (FNLA). It was founded in 1962 and was primarily based in the northern part of the country around the Bakongo tribe.[34] The FNLA was not only anti-colonial but also anti-communist, thus gaining nearly immediate US backing, including material support from the CIA via the newly independent Democratic Republic of the Congo.[35] The FNLA had narrow and specific goals: to amass a sufficient military force to displace the Portuguese from power,[36] and then to establish a capitalist-based economy through which they and their supporters would benefit in a similar manner to the Portuguese system of rule.[37]

The final of the three main groups relevant to the independence struggle in Angola was the *União Nacional para a Independência Total de Angola* or the National Union for the Total Independence of Angola (UNITA). This group was founded in the mid to late 1960s.[38] UNITA began in the southern area of Angola, which is primarily populated by the Ovimbundu people who possess a distinct language and culture and represent the largest linguistic identity group in the country.[39] UNITA was founded by Jonas Savimbi, an Ovimbumdu who was educated abroad and initially joined the MPLA. By most accounts, Savimbi split from the MPLA to form his own movement due to his desire to be in charge of his own organization. From the outset, UNITA was very much structured around the person of Savimbi and was portrayed as such to both domestic and international audiences.[40]

Given the MPLA's dominance in urban centres and the FNLA's dominance in the north, UNITA focused primarily on the south where it had Ovimbundu support. Savimbi explicitly linked this strategy not only to Maoist insurgency tactics (but not Maoist ideology more broadly),[41] but also to the aims of preserving indigenous rulership structures and practices, in opposition to the imposition of colonial and colonial-style organizational structures (therefore making an implicit criticism of the MPLA's mixed-race leaders).[42] These gains notwithstanding, UNITA remained insufficiently powerful in terms of economic or human potential to be able to substantially move against either Portuguese or MPLA forces in strategic urban areas, either before or after independence.[43]

The regional or ethnic dimensions of these three Angolan liberation movements described earlier should not, however, be overemphasized. While each movement was initially founded in specific geographic areas and to some extent with specific identity focuses, scholars largely agree that all three groups broadened their appeals to become more generally nationalistic. Therefore, while their differing bases of support are important for understanding tensions at the time, the civil war that ensued between them is not a straightforward or even primarily identity-based conflict.[44]

Independence and immediate aftermaths

The single biggest catalyst for independence in both countries did not occur in Africa, but rather in the army barracks in Lisbon.[45] By 1974, the colonial wars in Angola and Mozambique and in Portugal's other African territories had been ongoing for at least a decade, with increasingly large numbers of Portuguese soldiers being conscripted and deployed from Europe only to face frustrating and seemingly pointless stalemates in Africa.[46] This was economically challenging for Portugal, and war in the colonies also reduced the economic output that was gained from holding these territories in the first place.[47] Under these circumstances, the dictatorship that had long ruled Portugal was losing support, and in 1974 the army rebelled and overthrew the government.[48] The new military-dominated government decided in 1975 to grant independence for all of Portugal's colonies.

In Mozambique, independence was accomplished quite smoothly, as FRELIMO by this point was popularly supported, militarily proven and overwhelmingly the only major anti-colonial force in the country.[49] The new Portuguese government was more concerned with getting out of its African entanglements than strictly adhering to Cold War ideology due to the economic burdens of maintaining colonial rule, and so plans moved quickly to transfer power directly from the colonial administrators to FRELIMO without elections.[50] This transfer of power was conducted via treaty, but was primarily negotiated and implemented by the Portuguese army (instead of the foreign ministry or executive).[51] Given the speed of this change, Portuguese who had settled in Mozambique received little compensation from either the retreating Portuguese army or the incoming FRELIMO government. The majority of the Portuguese settler population fled in fear of retaliation by local populations who had been indentured workers and in many cases also actively destroyed Mozambique's infrastructure in anger at the reversal of colonial policy.[52] Mozambique at independence was therefore left with an entirely export-based economy, mostly destroyed infrastructure and a dearth of skilled workers.[53]

In Angola, on the other hand, the three liberation movements each used the relaxation of Portuguese rule to campaign openly for support both amongst the Angolan people and in the international press in order to gain a seat at the negotiating table to determine the terms of Angolan independence. Given the speed at which the Portuguese wished to depart, an agreement, the Alvor Accords, was soon signed, determining that independent Angola would have a transition government equally composed of the three liberation movements that would then hold elections after ten months. While some monitoring and verification procedures were mentioned in the treaty, it had barely been signed, much less gone into effect, before it fell apart, starting the official civil war.[54]

Angolan civil war

This book firmly agrees with the scholars who note Angola's civil war as being primarily a contest between the MPLA and UNITA over legitimate right to exclusive rule over Angola. Given this assumption, it was these motivations that led to the recruitment of international actors for support, and not, as some propagandists on either side of the conflict have claimed, a war that was exclusively either a Cold War proxy fight or a South African ploy for regional dominance.[55] Discussing the role of international actors is, however, key to understanding the development of peace negotiations as well as their progression. Therefore, motives and involvement of the main international actors in the Angolan civil war will be the focus of this section.

In the initial years of the Angolan civil war, the main international actors involved directly were the Soviet Union and Cuba. Although it is still difficult to determine an exact chain of events,[56] what is clear is that within a few weeks of war breaking out in mid-1975, there were Cuban troops on the ground in support of the MPLA and South African troops on the ground with UNITA,[57] a situation that would remain unchanged until 1989 when peace talks began.[58] Cuba had been supporting the MPLA since the 1960s, as there were ideological and linguistic similarities between the two groups that Castro and Guevara in particular noted.[59] Much of Cuba's involvement in Angola was funded by the USSR, which preferred to have Cuba involved on the ground rather than deploying Soviet troops directly.[60] While Cuban policy in Angola cannot be simply reduced to acting as a Soviet proxy, the importance of Soviet funding cannot be ignored.[61]

UNITA, on the other hand, was backed primarily by South Africa. This is what sparked the true beginnings of the main part of the civil war as the MPLA was unable to eradicate UNITA as they had with the FNLA due to South African support for UNITA, countering the MPLA's Cuban advantage.[62] Thus the conflict transitioned from being a spillover of anti-colonialism to a true civil war in an independent country, with famous and long-running internationalization.[63]

During this period of the conflict, UNITA increased its efforts to find international supporters,[64] aiming mainly to gain US support.[65] The involvement of the United States in the Angolan civil war was from the beginning more complicated and less overt than South African, Cuban or Soviet intervention. Given that the group the United States initially backed, the FNLA, became a non-entity by the end of 1976, their first plan for uprooting the communist MPLA was derailed, leading the United States to switch to supporting UNITA.[66] Savimbi very much focused on cultivating US support, including through an embassy-like outpost in Washington, DC, hiring lobbying firms to secure Congressional support, and personal visits which received extensive media coverage.[67]

South Africa's apartheid policies made it a more awkward source of support for UNITA as those policies were increasingly unpopular amongst UNITA's American allies and therefore were a high-value propaganda target for MPLA messaging.[68] South Africa was committed to UNITA, however, due to South Africa's interests in maintaining a colonial hold on what became Namibia, which the MPLA was actively fighting against.[69] Still, South Africa's military support was key for UNITA to be able to fight against the Cuban-backed MPLA forces and UNITA assiduously maintained South African support through the 1980s.[70] Interestingly, there was some amount of controversy on the South African side as up to this point, South Africa had only supported white African forces in the region, and this was the first time South Africa directly allied and fought with an indigenous African group.[71]

Mozambican civil war

Compared to Angola, the transition to independence in Mozambique was relatively straightforward and was accomplished with minimal violence amongst Mozambicans. FRELIMO was deemed to be the legitimate government of Mozambique by nearly all international actors. In its initial years, FRELIMO's use of highly centralized, extreme political and economic measures (such as Soviet-style collectivization) to secure and maintain power yielded few economic benefits and did not alleviate the political repression of the colonial regime.[72] The harsh domestic economic measures as well as undercutting traditional structures of leadership within provinces and villages in Mozambique created the environment in which the *Resistência Nacional Moçambicana or* – the Mozambican National Resistance (RENAMO) was born.

The group was formed around 1977 as an explicitly anti-FRELIMO movement, but exactly how these factors combined to create the group is still contested. Likewise, there is debate over to what extent RENAMO had an initial political agenda in addition to executing military attacks, and at what point and with what amount of autonomy a political agenda was created.[73] The important points are that RENAMO was initially founded in Rhodesia within the first two years of Mozambican independence in 1975;[74] was explicitly anti-FRELIMO and anti-Marxist;[75] and claimed to speak for the disgruntled population of Mozambique.[76] Rhodesia's support for RENAMO lasted until 1979, when it was made to cut ties with RENAMO as a condition of its transformation into an independent Zimbabwe.[77] South Africa took up support for the resistance movement around that time as a way to combat FRELIMO's efforts to overthrow South Africa's apartheid government.[78]

With South African backing,[79] RENAMO's membership soon increased to at least 10,000 members (gained through abduction or convinced to join due to anti-FRELIMO sentiment)[80] and attacks into Mozambique against both government infrastructure and civilians in government areas began to increase significantly by the mid-1980s.[81] Like the MPLA in Angola, FRELIMO was predominantly influential in towns and cities,[82] but RENAMO operated throughout much of the countryside, particularly in geographically inaccessible areas. By 1984, the FRELIMO government began taking RENAMO seriously as a threat rather than purely a South African proxy that could be eliminated through the removal of South African support,[83] especially as successful RENAMO attacks on Mozambique's relatively few and therefore especially-key infrastructure links were spectacularly costly to the government's ability to govern and be seen as legitimately capable by domestic audiences.[84] FRELIMO meanwhile was also battling with periodic cycles of floods and droughts, leading to serious food shortages and famine as well as increasing already-rampant poverty;[85] neither side was in a position to win.[86]

Towards peace talks

By the late 1980s, the military situation in Angola had been stalemated for ten years. Despite massive battles over the decade, the main state of relations remained the same: the Cubans and Soviets were providing military and financial assistance to the MPLA who controlled mainly towns and cities.[87] UNITA operated throughout the countryside with South African and American support.[88] On the other hand, in Mozambique, FRELIMO had finally admitted to its lack of economic success and opened itself up to Western financial help, thereby deconstructing much of its explicitly Marxist rhetoric and structures and defanging one of RENAMO's main anti-FRELIMO claims.[89] FRELIMO was desperate to come to an accommodation with South Africa to stop RENAMO's economically devastating attacks, but while South Africa was happy to negotiate to improve the trading relationship between the two countries, the agreement reached in 1984 was entirely to South Africa's benefit (FRELIMO stopped harbouring the ANC) and did nothing to halt RENAMO's influence in Mozambique.[90] FRELIMO thus continued to need significant Soviet financial support and still had great difficulty working with Western financial institutions and companies who were eager to invest in and develop Mozambique's economic potential, but hesitant to commit given the violence on the ground.[91]

At this point, the various international actors involved in both conflicts were weary of wars that they saw as not intrinsically important to their interests and increasingly long, exhausting and expensive commitments. Additionally, with the changing Cold War context causing former adversaries to be more interested in cooperation than continued conflict, there was a wider global context in which commitments to funding and supporting ongoing war in Angola and Mozambique were being recalculated.[92] From the mid-1980s onwards, the US and USSR were increasingly reaching detente on various issues, including resolving proxy conflicts throughout the Third World. This meant that both superpowers were becoming more interested in getting reasonable peace agreements in Angola and Mozambique quickly in order to reduce both potential hotspots and foreign entanglements, causing both sides to begin to pressure Cuba and South Africa as well as the MPLA and UNITA respectively to think about going to the negotiating table.[93]

For exactly the same reasons, the US and USSR also began pushing for peace talks in Mozambique, as well as for resolution on the related South African regional wars in what became Namibia and internally with the ANC.[94] In fact, it was the situation in Namibia that was the first conflict in Southern Africa deemed sufficiently 'ripe' by the external actors to try to bring to the negotiating table. This situation will be discussed in the next chapter, along with its implications for moving parties towards negotiations in Angola and Mozambique.

In both cases, while the international actors were ready to begin discussions, the groups on the ground – the MPLA and UNITA in Angola and FRELIMO and RENAMO in Mozambique – were generally much more reluctant to make the necessary concessions to even acknowledge the legitimacy of the other to talk directly with, as it would require conceding that military victory was not possible.[95] Still, international financial pressure as well as diplomatic incentives from regional actors (to resolve the Namibian issue in the case of Angola and to provide diplomatic access and backing to RENAMO from Zimbabwe, Kenya, and an alliance of Protestant and Catholic churches in the case of Mozambique[96]) slowly brought the parties to the point of being ready to begin negotiations.

Conclusion

There are a number of interesting points about the similarities and differences of these two civil wars and how they began to be brought to an end. In terms of the origins of the groups and their organizational principles, the question over to what extent either conflict fits into the academically rich category of 'ethnic conflict' is worth considering. The origins of the four major groups in these two wars have mainly ideological origins but with some identity-based organizational markers. This examination, however, has found that while there may be some identity-based groupings within UNITA especially and to some degree in both the MPLA and FRELIMO's more mixed-Portuguese backgrounds, the identity-specific cleavages were at most used for some specific recruitment, internal communication and patronage methods, rather than providing an all-around blueprint around which to structure any group's identity or main goals. Thus, while these conflicts definitely had ideological elements, calling them 'ethnic' wars would be a misnomer.

In terms of the dynamics of the conflicts, both wars were lengthened by three key geographical factors: sparse colonial infrastructure, inaccessible territory and foreign safe-havens. Both UNITA and RENAMO benefitted from the fact that Portugal had in both countries focused its infrastructural building efforts on developing port cities, roads between ports and resource-specific transport links from the interior to said ports. This meant that the majority of both countries was rural and much of it was inaccessible either due to poorly maintained infrastructure or a simple utter lack thereof, showing the long-lasting impact of colonial decision-making on the conflicts and development prospects of both countries. This inaccessibility gave both groups wide swatches of territory in which to safely operate that were difficult for their respective governments to access militarily or administratively, much less actively contest. Furthermore, both UNITA and RENAMO benefitted initially from having sympathetic regimes across borders to allow for safe havens from which to receive supplies, training and plan attacks. However, both the MPLA and FRELIMO quickly targeted these safe havens and changes in regimes most notably in the DRC and Zimbabwe in turn increased pressure on UNITA and RENAMO to operate within their own countries and rely mainly on South Africa as their regional backer. This increased the pressure on both groups to contest territory, populations and eventually politics within their own countries as there was nowhere else to retreat, and also meant that once pressure grew on South Africa to withdraw its foreign military involvements, both groups lost an important ally quite quickly.

Finally, the extent to which superpower pressure was the main driver of bringing parties towards negotiations is a key point that will be further expanded on in the next chapter. While the motivations for the various international actors to become and stay involved in the conflicts has been discussed in this chapter, divergences have become clear between international and local incentives to keep the conflicts going. This is a significant factor in both how negotiations began, developed and resolved and how they had implications for implementation as well.

Chapter 3

TOWARDS PEACE?

Towards peace talks in Angola: The Namibian dimension

Unexpected as it was, Namibian independence created a new impetus towards negotiating peace in Angola.[1] As the 1980s continued, the country that became Namibia was still a South African colony called South-West Africa, which was a holdover from South Africa's days as a colony of the UK. For decades, South Africa had been fighting a pro-independence insurgency movement in Namibia known as SWAPO, which had received support from myriad independent African states including Angola's MPLA and their allied Cuban forces.[2] The MPLA's involvement was particularly significant due to the lengthy border shared between the two countries which enabled SWAPO to have safe havens outside the conventional reach of South African forces.[3] This was a primary reason for sustained South African involvement directly in the Angolan civil war, as the removal of the MPLA in favour of UNITA would eliminate one of the most significant backers of what South Africa saw as an internal insurgency.[4]

As the tensions of the Cold War began to subside, the problems of Namibia and Angola were seen as linked by diplomats in Washington, DC, and Moscow, as many of the actors overlapped,[5] including South Africa, Cuba, the MPLA and, to a lesser extent, UNITA, according to interviews with US diplomats who were involved.[6] The United States continued to worry about the implications of a significant number of Cuban troops fighting successfully abroad and what it could mean for Cuban policy closer to home.[7] Cuba itself was beginning to feel the strain of having so many troops and non-military personnel (most significantly doctors)[8] abroad and was therefore looking for ways to end their involvement successfully.[9] At the same time, the Soviet economy was rapidly deteriorating and the state faced an increased impetus to quickly reduce financial aid to both Cuba and African allies.[10] South Africa wanted to reduce military expenditures, particularly as global sanctions in reaction to the country's policy of apartheid were becoming economically significant and wanted to move to the majority side of decolonization.[11] South Africa, however, also wanted to end its involvement in both wars without losing further prestige or suffering military defeat that could make maintaining domestic control in a climate of rising internal dissent and violence more difficult.[12] Thus, all the main foreign actors involved in Namibia, most of whom were also partisans in the Angolan civil war, began to turn towards negotiation as a way to resolve the Namibian conflict, bringing to the same table many long-standing enemies in both wars.[13]

In 1988, discussions began between the US, USSR and South Africa about Namibian independence, alongside an agreement for Cuban withdrawal from both Namibia and Angola.[14] The US-led Tripartite Talks, which were followed closely by the United Nations and regional countries,[15] including the Democratic Republic of the Congo, another player in the Angolan conflict, ultimately resulted in the signing of a UN-backed peace deal.[16] This treaty also provided for the simultaneous withdrawal from both Namibia and Angola of South African and Cuban troops, allowing both sides to save face,[17] reducing the financial commitments of both superpowers, and removing one significant proxy layer in this part of Southern Africa.[18]

This, however, left the MPLA and UNITA without two foreign actors who had been present since 1975, no proxy issue of their own (Namibian independence) to focus on, and two opposing superpowers who had now successfully worked together on the public international stage to end a conflict just over the border. The military situation in Angola continued to be one of stalemate, particularly following the withdrawal of foreign support, and the pressure from the US and USSR to negotiate along the successful lines of the Tripartite Talks grew.[19] For both sides, there was also the pressure to ensure the success of the UN peacekeeping mission, UNAVEM I across the border in facilitating elections. The outcome of these elections after Namibian independence was eagerly watched by both sides of the Angolan conflict, especially as comparatively, SWAPO was much less organized and developed than either Angolan group and yet managed to easily win a popular vote. This begged the question: if SWAPO could succeed, why not either of the Angolan groups?[20] The MPLA saw the convergence of the two superpowers as a way to gain US recognition and support, which would significantly boost Angola's trading prospects and political standing,[21] and in fact successfully negotiated direct US-Angolan diplomatic contact as a reward for cooperation with Namibia.[22] UNITA, on the other hand, saw this as a threat to their own US backing and was confident that in a US- and UN-backed election, UNITA's ethnic majority support would win out definitively, as long as the MPLA was not given too long to adjust from their communist policies and win over the population.[23]

There was one significant problem with the Namibia comparison and enthusiasm spilling over into Angola: it was simply assumed that the losing party would accept the result and that the winning side would not punish them. In fact, both Angolan parties saw electoral victory in more existential terms.[24] Namibia's independence had been guaranteed by treaty and SWAPO was the only political party in the country – Angola was in a far different situation, a fact that in the enthusiasm over superpower cooperation and UNAVEM I's success in achieving its mandate for a successful post-conflict election, was mostly overlooked,[25] with dire consequences.[26] The first two UN peacekeeping missions in Angola shared the same name, UNAVEM II and UNAVEM III, respectively, suggesting a link with UNAVEM I, and indeed, the missions were initially thought of as being related. However, as subsequent discussions in Chapters 3, 4 and 5 will show, both Angolan missions were given a much wider mandate than primarily setting up an election with only one major party with much simpler logistical and geographic challenges.[27] The continuity in naming, therefore, is perhaps less contiguous than was hoped.

Angola: Beginning negotiations

The combination of these factors enabled the beginning of peace talks. The first summit was conducted by a coalition of eighteen regional leaders, including Mali, the DRC, Zambia, Nigeria, Mozambique and more. These regional leaders were aiming to achieve peace locally and saw negotiating the end of one of the largest and longest-running conflicts in the region as a way of boosting Southern African diplomatic prestige on the regional and international stages. Initially, the negotiations began well, and for the first time, the leaders of the MPLA and UNITA publicly met and shook hands.[28] Talks even progressed to the point of draft terms being discussed, but while the parties left the talks feeling like discussions had been concrete, problems soon arose that derailed the entire scenario.

The issue was specifically regarding the role Jonas Savimbi would play in any upcoming negotiations and elections, and a particular problem was one of language.[29] This particular negotiation had taken place mainly in English and French, the shared languages of those involved. However, upon returning home and reporting publicly on the progress of these high-level talks, it soon became clear that there was either a conceptual disagreement or a linguistic one over what both sides had agreed Savimbi would do to calm the situation such that negotiations could continue without escalated violence. According to a US diplomat who was involved, the problem was that according to the French-language media reports coming from this discussion, Savimbi's role was described as 'stepping away' from direct involvement in day-to-day military operations of UNITA in order for peace negotiations to begin. According to English-language reports, however, Savimbi had in fact agreed to 'exile,' with differing accounts as to whether this would be a permanent state or merely temporary.[30] The idea of voluntarily agreeing to what Savimbi saw as a permanent removal from political and military power was too much for him to agree to,[31] and so all progress made via this forum was quickly scuppered by UNITA and further attempts at beginning negotiations were rebuffed.

This next round of negotiations culminated in the signing of the Bicesse Accords in 1991, named for the town in Portugal in which the negotiations were based. This agreement was seen as a huge step forward, as it was the first time the two sides had signed anything together since the abortive Alvor Accords prior to Angolan independence in 1975.[32] However, the Bicesse Accords failed to be implemented and within two years of being signed, the country had not only returned to war but in fact the years following the failure of the Bicesse Accords were amongst the most violent of the entire conflict. Unlike the initial negotiations in Gbadolite, the Bicesse process was initiated and maintained through coordinated international pressure and involvement, rather than primarily through regional actors. Thus, while the MPLA and UNITA had fewer personal prestige reasons for participating, the fact that both sides' financial backers were pushing so heavily towards negotiation was the main factor in the resumption of talks towards peace.[33]

The two main outside actors in these negotiations were the Americans and the Portuguese. As previously discussed, the US State Department under Presidents Ronald Reagan and George H. W. Bush had a strong Bureau of African Affairs that saw the end of the Cold War and the withdrawal of Soviet support to its erstwhile client states as a prime opportunity to resolve long-running conflicts peacefully so that the United States could stop spending military and economic aid to bolster insurgencies or prop up dictators.[34] Given how successful the process of Namibian independence had been from the United States' point of view – peaceful withdrawal of thousands of Cuban troops and personnel from Southern Africa, effective joint negotiating with Soviet diplomats, a free and fair election that saw a popular insurgency become a legitimate government – it seemed appropriate to move on to try and resolve issues in Angola.[35]

In addition, the personnel available from the State Department had already gotten to know some of the Angolan actors, especially those from long-time US foes MPLA, which helped begin to establish the idea that the United States could be a helpful broker for peace, rather than an antagonistic partisan solely seeking unilateral UNITA victory as had been previous US policy. Furthermore, the US diplomats had a decent working knowledge of the issues at stake, the personalities involved and some even had Portuguese language skills.[36] This established a key basis of trust in US expertise and commitment that enabled both sides to engage with the United States as one of the key mediators.[37] Finally, the Soviet Union was willing to cooperate to end the conflict, allowing diplomats from both superpowers to unite and pressure both Angolan parties to the table. All of these factors meant that there was real impetus and effective international pressure to move towards US-mediated and joint-sponsored talks.

The other important international actor was Portugal, who hosted and funded the discussions. At first glance, Portugal's involvement perhaps is less obvious, given that its last significant involvement in the Angolan conflict had been primarily as an instigator.[38] However, decades had passed and Portugal was eager to show that they could not only improve their record on Angolan affairs, but they could also contribute productively to international peace and security in the new post–Cold War era.[39] Portuguese sponsorship had the additional benefit of providing a level of linguistic and cultural comfort, especially as leaders and senior figures in both movements had spent significant time there either in their youths or during the conflict.[40] Portugal's method of sponsorship was primarily the provision of a negotiating space: a newly completed hotel training complex outside of Lisbon near the suburb of Bicesse. Furthermore, the relative isolation of the environment allowed for concentrated discussion. Given that the majority of the negotiations that became the Accords took place in a three-week stint in the environs of this hotel in Bicesse, it proved itself to be an effective location in which to negotiate.[41]

Negotiations were conducted primarily in Portuguese, with the help of US State Department translators for some of the US diplomats and advisors who did not speak Portuguese.[42]

The final outside actor was the previously mentioned Soviets who were present in Bicesse but were not significant actors at the negotiating table. This was because the three-week intensive stretch of negotiating took place in the winter of 1990–1, which was when the Soviet Union was in the throes of disintegrating. According to the senior US diplomat at the Bicesse negotiations:

> during these 21 days of being sequestered, the Soviets spent almost all their time watching CNN. They were concerned that the Soviet Union was going to completely collapse, there were going to be riots, civil disorder in Moscow . . . they were also concerned that their families would not get enough to eat because there was no food in the shops . . . the Soviets basically checked out [of the Angolan peace process].[43]

Therefore, while Soviet involvement was significant in signalling united superpower pressure to achieve progress towards peace regarding the situation in Angola both during the weeks in Bicesse and beyond, they were not important actors in discussing and finalizing the details of the agreement.[44]This had important implications for the MPLA, as their main financial backer was therefore both not hugely involved in negotiations but also patently interested in financing further MPLA war efforts if negotiations failed. This increased the need for the MPLA to either sign and implement peace properly or at least gain time to secure alternative financing.

Unlike the Mozambique negotiators, who will be discussed later, there was relatively little educational discrepancy between UNITA and MPLA figures negotiating in Bicesse. The MPLA had been acting as a legitimate government for the past few decades and therefore had representatives with official government ministerial experience. UNITA had also generally received foreign education and legal training, as well as coaching from American private consultants and support from US congressional members throughout the 1980s.[45] In fact, UNITA's experience dealing with US politicians was perhaps greater than the MPLA's given the lack of relations between the MPLA and the United States due to Cold War tensions.

The MPLA's main goal for these negotiations was to maintain as much power and legitimacy as possible while working to ensure an MPLA victory[46] but if forced, allow elections in which UNITA could freely compete. The MPLA also very much wanted to show democratic progress in order to gain international, and especially American support, to bolster its international standing, domestic legitimacy and economic strength.[47] UNITA's focus was very specifically on winning elections.[48] Similarly, the United States, bolstered by the successful transition in Namibia which hinged on the combination of free and fair elections coupled with a light observer UN mission, was also hyper-focused on elections as the solution to the Angolan conflict. Other issues were important to the negotiations, and there were two separate fora set-up, one for political issues and one for military ones, but the political room is where the bulk of the discussion was focused and where the stakes were perceived by both sides to be nearly existential. This was both because political power in Angola had always been dictatorial and therefore there was no tradition or model of shared power available that both sides could agree on.[49] Also, the history of violence until this point meant that many in leadership positions feared for their safety if their side lost.

Mozambique: Beginning negotiations

The success of a multi-party diplomatic effort to end a long-standing Southern African civil war, the conflict in Namibia, was watched with interest from Mozambique.[50] This was particularly true given the direct involvement of South Africa in Namibia and Angola, as South Africa was also the main foreign backer of Mozambique's RENAMO and as such had a stake in the conflict in that country as well.[51] Likewise, the USSR was both the main backer of the Mozambican FRELIMO government and Angola's MPLA and the same economic pressures that pushed the USSR to favour peace in Angola were apparent in Mozambique.[52] This was particularly true as FRELIMO was not nearly as prolific a weapons-purchasing government as the MPLA (due to lack of oil revenues), and so the USSR's financial ties to the regime were weaker from the start.

In Mozambique's case, the diplomatic and economic pressures of regional countries were also significant, though for different reasons than with Angola.[53] Mozambique's civil war had long had cross-border implications, most notably with the now-former Rhodesia being the initial base for RENAMO. As the war developed, however, RENAMO's focus on attacking infrastructure led to further attacks on now-independent Zimbabwe and neighbouring Malawi, with both countries also suffering from refugee flows and economic trade disruptions.[54] There was therefore regional pressure to relieve the conflict in Mozambique because of the deleterious effect it was having not only on Mozambique's economy and ability to trade with its neighbours but also on the regional economy more broadly.[55]

In addition, there were distinct domestic pressures facing Mozambique that changed FRELIMO's calculus about its willingness to negotiate with RENAMO, which it saw exclusively as a terrorist insurgency. Mozambique habitually suffered cycles of drought and flooding, and towards the latter half of the 1980s, the country was yet again in the throes of severe natural disasters.[56] Coupled with FRELIMO's earlier disastrous economic policies, the country's already struggling economy was suffering even beyond the depredations of RENAMO's attacks on infrastructure.[57] FRELIMO had recognized this problem earlier in the decade; it was the impetus behind trying to negotiate with South Africa to stop backing RENAMO in order to hamstring the insurgency and allow FRELIMO to focus on the economy.[58] This 1984 accord failed to stop RENAMO and therefore the combined problems continued. As a result, FRELIMO was more willing to take the pragmatic approach of trying to resolve the conflict with RENAMO, in order to be able to focus on opening up the economy and government coffers to international (mainly Western) aid and development, which foreign investors had strongly signalled would only be possible if there was no further insurgency.

On RENAMO's side, there continues to be a debate about the extent to which the group had organized political goals at any point during the civil war[59] (see earlier sections on the development of RENAMO). By this point, the political demands that were clearly known focused on the reversal of FRELIMO's destructive economic policy as well as seeking political representation for RENAMO in national politics.[60] Given the economic demands FRELIMO was facing, and – increasingly as the 1980s progressed – the global decline of communism that lessened ideological stances, both sides of the Mozambican conflict began to consider the benefits of negotiating.[61]

Notably, what brought negotiations in Mozambique, to a starting point, was distinctly different from the process undertaken towards negotiations in Angola. In Mozambique, talks about negotiations and then the formal negotiations themselves were consistently and explicitly under the auspices of Sant Egidio, a Catholic charity headquartered in Rome with close ties to the papacy.[62] Mozambique had both Protestant and Catholic populations, though even combined these counted for fewer than half of the population. Nevertheless, bishops on both sides of the Christian divide had been active in trying to protect civilians in their dioceses throughout the civil war and had thus developed ties with both sides, particularly RENAMO who was not ideologically hostile to the idea of organized religion in the way that Marxist FRELIMO was.[63] By 1985, both Protestant and Catholic bishops in Mozambique began working together to try and bring both sides towards negotiations, and the NGO of Sant Egidio became key for a number of reasons.[64]

First, Sant Egidio was a known entity in Mozambique, as the charity had worked to alleviate poverty throughout much of the country since independence, thus giving it some contacts if not deeper relationships with both RENAMO and FRELIMO.[65] Second, its status as an NGO meant that it was distinctly a facilitator and mediator, and not an outside government or political actor with its own agenda, allowing both sides to feel Sant Egidio represented a truly neutral party with conflict resolution as its sole focus.[66] Third, the organization's links to the papacy and the attention paid to these efforts by the Vatican was also encouraging, as it lent international weight and recognition to the peace process, even in nascent stages.[67] It allowed FRELIMO to still feel secure by being treated as a legitimate government by a fellow government-like organization with the weight of substantial history behind it.[68] While FRELIMO's traditionally communist ideology would on paper present a barrier to accepting the explicitly religious organization of Sant Egidio as a mediator, the weakness of the organization to exert political control, as well as the personal relationships many organization members had within Mozambique from decades of humanitarian work made this concern mostly irrelevant.[69] On the other hand, the Vatican's neutrality in the Cold War meant RENAMO was not put off by assuming the Vatican would side with the recognized government automatically. Thus, both sides quickly approved of the idea of Sant Egidio as the mediator and loci of discussions, which remained constant throughout the peace process to come.[70]

Mozambique: Getting to agreement

Once Sant Egidio was established as the forum for peace negotiations in Mozambique in 1990, other governments began to take the idea of talks seriously and became involved. The United States had little direct involvement in Mozambique but was distinctly involved in trying to resolve issues in Southern Africa (see Angola, also US involvement in the end of Apartheid in South Africa). Thus, in a US climate of trying to bring peace to this region, high-level US diplomats focusing on the entirety of sub-Saharan Africa began to take an interest in the negotiations ongoing in Mozambique.[71] This mainly took the form of working with other Western ambassadors in the country and in neighbouring capital cities, particularly Harare, to form a working group of observers to maintain a united Western presence.[72] The objective was to assure both sides that the West was watching and hoping that the talks would continue.[73]

In Rome, the US embassies to the Italian government and the Holy See played a more direct role in participating in negotiations in advisory capacities, similar to the role played by American legal and military experts in the Bicesse negotiations in Angola.[74] This was made possible to some degree by the small size of the US embassy to the Holy See and also by the fact that the diplomats stationed there happened to have a strong command of Italian and Portuguese, the two key languages of these negotiations.[75] This close attention at the Holy See enabled both Mozambican parties to feel that the United States considered them a priority and gave both sides confidence that what they were negotiating was being watched and could be backed up by what quickly became the sole remaining superpower.[76]

Another key foreign actor for the Rome-based talks was the Italian government. The most significant way in which the Italian government was involved in these discussions, however, was not diplomatically but rather financially. Not only did the Italian foreign ministry underwrite the entire cost of the negotiations at Sant Egidio (specifics of which will be discussed later),[77] they also provided the bulk of the funds to support RENAMO's transition into a political party during and following the last stages of the Rome-based negotiations.[78] There is some debate over the motivations for the Italian government's willingness to raise millions of dollars on this effort, with the majority of interviewees for this book either professing no concrete knowledge of motivations or theorizing that it was a combination of historically close ties to the papacy and thus a willingness to support their efforts as well as a broader foreign ministry goal of signalling Italy's commitment to peace and progress as a global player.[79]

One tangible way in which the Italian government supported the negotiations based in Rome was through the provision of suits, shoes, hotels and restaurants for the RENAMO delegation.[80] According to a foreign advisor to RENAMO, whose covert involvement supporting RENAMO has become increasingly known in the decades since these events, he suggested to Sant Egidio that 'if you want them [RENAMO] to behave like civilised humans you must treat them like civilised humans and the big carrot is to give them respectability. Give them things that they never had, like driving in a nice car, walking through a shopping mall, things like that. And it worked'.[81] According to former US ambassador to Mozambique Dennis Jett, who was ambassador from 1993 to 1996, when the RENAMO delegation initially arrived in Italy, they felt visibly disadvantaged compared to the FRELIMO delegation.[82] In his summary, RENAMO fighters felt that '[they] had come straight from the bush, and all we have are our combat fatigues or military uniforms. Yet all of these people from the government, they're going to show up in their nice shoes and we're going to start off feeling inferior'. In his interview, the ambassador continued his recollection of the situation 'So the Italian government bought them new suits. So they [RENAMO] put on their new shoes and that's the kind of indication of their level of sophistication and exposure internationally.' This account was seconded by a colleague at the State Department who was based in Rome as well as the head of the Bureau for African Affairs at the time. The latter also mentioned that some of RENAMO's delegation also required eyeglasses, which was addressed by Sant Egidio in Rome.

Other foreign governments were tangentially involved in these negotiations, mainly as members of the ambassadorial advice group in Maputo.[83] In addition, the Portuguese government offered mediation services on the back of the at-the-time successful Bicesse negotiations completed for the Angolan civil war. Given that Portugal had just successfully facilitated negotiations for that conflict and had the requisite linguistic and logistical skills, this offer was seen by the Portuguese as somewhat obviously the necessary next step for Mozambique, given the lack of government weight, logistical support and cultural ties that Sant Egidio could provide. By this stage, however, negotiations in Rome were well underway, and the relative weakness of Sant Egidio as a political entity was seen by both Mozambican parties as a benefit towards allowing them to negotiate on their own terms without external political pressure.[84] Therefore, Portugal's offer was refused, though the country did remain peripherally involved, similarly to the efforts underway from the United States and Italy.[85]

RENAMO's delegation throughout the Sant Egidio negotiations underwent some personnel changes but was relatively stable. This was due less to the perception that negotiations would be more successful with consistent participants and more due to the fact that RENAMO had very few high-level leaders who were willing and able to participate in negotiations and thus there were few options for rotations or replacements. Additionally, given RENAMO's foundation and structure as a primarily military movement with few coherent political goals, the majority of negotiators for the group were generals who had relatively little formal education, minimal exposure to the international stage and often little formal military training.[86]

On the other hand, they had substantial understanding of the conditions within Mozambique[87] and were heavily invested in the discussions around what demobilization and disarmament might look like and how RENAMO members would be treated in peacetime. This meant that discussions around these issues were high on RENAMO's agenda and they were deeply invested in agreeing on details regarding payments, training and the integrated military.[88] However, there was often limited understanding of the practicalities behind the processes needed to put these policies in place, requiring a large amount of technical information support from advisors (mainly from the United States) to explain military procedures such as ceasefires and humanitarian corridors. In order to explain these procedures and give RENAMO negotiators ideas to consider, US diplomats and advisors spent a large portion of time educating RENAMO about different options, using models from various countries and other peace processes as examples.[89]

RENAMO's leader Dhlakama did not attend the negotiations and instead remained based in RENAMO's bush headquarters. This meant that any potential agreements had to be wired back to him for final approval and that when he did come to Rome towards the end of negotiations, drafts had to be explained and sometimes re-negotiated in order to give him psychological control over the process.[90] In interviews with a US diplomat in the Office of Southern African Affairs, circa 1990s, described multiple direct experiences interacting with Afonso Dhlakama and other senior RENAMO leaders, and mentioned time and again the lack of knowledge the senior figures had, for example: '[Dhlakama] knows nothing about the world. He's only heard of . . . he's heard of the Soviet Union, surely the United States. He's heard of Italy. And he's heard of Portugal. But he has no idea where these countries are in relationship anything. He's never heard of World War Two.' The idea of RENAMO leadership lacking understanding of basic geography and political structures was echoed by a long-time foreign advisor of RENAMO, a native-Portuguese speaker who, while lecturing at a university in South Africa, clandestinely travelled to Mozambique to educate and liaise with RENAMO fighters throughout the 1980s and early 1990s.[91]

FRELIMO's negotiators on the other hand were generally quite well trained as government ministers and often had a lot of experience dealing with outside actors.[92] This meant that their agenda was much more heavily focused on the political, namely ensuring FRELIMO's recognition as the legitimate government of Mozambique, even if that meant accepting free elections. Their second priority was to develop FRELIMO's institutional ties to other international actors in order to bolster legitimacy but also open up Mozambique's trading potential with the outside world in order to alleviate the economic issues that were eroding domestic support for FRELIMO. FRELIMO therefore needed much less educational support to participate in the negotiations and was also more able and willing to switch up negotiators in Rome based on the needs of the negotiations and the governmental processes back in Maputo.[93]

On the military side, however, FRELIMO was much less invested in the specifics of disarmament and demobilization and considered these issues subservient to ensuring legitimacy, sovereignty and governmental control over the country. Additionally, the negotiations gave FRELIMO more direct insight into the lack of political experience of RENAMO which perhaps also increased their willingness to allow elections, given both the financial incentives being provided by the post–Cold War international community,[94] but potentially also the knowledge that in future elections, FRELIMO's governmental and institutional capacity would likely allow for an electoral victory over the politically juvenile RENAMO.

In this context, the process of negotiations was largely for each side to remain in separate rooms within the Sant Egidio compound, with diplomats and Sant Egidio members shuttling between the rooms.[95] Negotiations with RENAMO were generally more discussion based, with models mentioned earlier, before Sant Egidio would begin to draft RENAMO's ideas onto paper.[96] These would then be ferried back to FRELIMO for comments, reactions and changes, then back to RENAMO. Once a draft on an issue was somewhat negotiated, it would be wired back to Dhlakama and the FRELIMO government in Maputo for further input.

There were very few direct meetings between the two sides, for a variety of reasons. First, the FRELIMO government still saw RENAMO as illegitimate politically and of little organizational consequence institutionally, and did not want to grant RENAMO the legitimacy of sitting across the table as equals.[97] Relatedly, RENAMO's negotiators felt at a psychological disadvantage to the knowledge of bureaucratic procedures and government policies compared to FRELIMO and preferred to have intermediaries who were able to additionally provide information.[98] In addition, both sides had a long history of antagonism and very little history of direct contact throughout the conflict, making direct meetings a prime opportunity for grandstanding and political manoeuvring that was nonetheless not conducive to actual negotiations and compromise, thus the mediators had an interest in keeping the two parties more often separated.[99]

Angola: The Bicesse Accords

Once negotiations got underway at Bicesse, the majority of the terms were agreed upon within three weeks of intensive rounds of discussions.[100] The main priority for all sides was to agree on election procedures. The specific details of election procedures were strongly contested, but some basic premises were assumed by all parties, to the ultimate detriment of the successful implementation of the agreement. For the purposes of this analysis and its focus on the military integration aspects of the peace processes, these election-related issues will be only briefly discussed here.

Likely due to Namibia really only having a single party aiming to take over government, that situation did not require a particularly long period of preparation, and in fact given the South African government's interest in withdrawing in order to deal with political changes within its own country, a long transition period was in no one's interest in Namibia. In fact, the eleven-month[101] timeline was considered by some international observers to be too long, and with too much potential for retaliatory clashes between the South African defence forces and SWAPO. In Angola, the election timeline was a cause for some argument between the two sides but was resolved via American mediation.[102] UNITA wanted to have elections within twelve months in order to use their existing political capital, capitalize on the public good of UNITA's US-backed international profile and quickly win the election.[103] The MPLA, on the other hand, wanted a 3–4 year lead up to the elections in order to build up support in areas previously denied to it and to continue their administration as long as possible.[104] Faced with these competing demands, a senior US diplomat working on African affairs devised an eighteen-month framework that was accepted. He stated in an interview for this book, 'at the time it just seemed like a good compromise between the two demands'. In follow-up questions, it was clear that the number eighteen months was chosen almost at random; it was not based on any particular metric or example but merely as a compromise between the numbers proposed by each side.

A further way in which Namibia's example was relevant to the Bicesse negotiations around Angolan elections was in the supremacy of elections relative to other components of the peace plan. Again, given that in Namibia one of the two main combatants was not contesting the elections and was withdrawing from the country entirely, the main issue for the country was to set up an independent government; there was no need to create an integrated military nor was there particular pressure to demobilize and disarm fighters immediately. Despite the fact that Namibia's conflict was specifically an independence conflict whereas Angola's was a civil war, the discussions at Bicesse failed to take into account this key difference and likewise focused all efforts on getting to a successful election. While security issues like disarmament, demobilization and the creation of an integrated military were discussed and included in the treaty (which will be discussed in more detail in subsequent paragraphs), the key feature was that all of those processes were rigidly set to be completed before the elections, for which there were no provisions for delays to either the security processes or the elections. This was to have dire consequences for the implementation of the process.

In terms of the security provisions of the treaty, both sides agreed quite quickly to the premise that Angola should have a united military that answered to an elected civilian government. Given that the MPLA had already agreed to an elected government and both sides already exercised (at least nominally) civilian control over their own forces, this was a straightforward aspect to agree on.[105] The idea of integrating the two sides was also a simple principle, as neither side was at all comfortable with being unilaterally disarmed. The difficulty lay in the specifics of this integrated army, particularly the proportion that each side would contribute in absolute numbers, relative ranks of officers and the stages through which these steps would take place. These specifics were discussed at the table, but because agreement could not be reached on the issues, these details were not mentioned in the final agreement.[106]

When determining the size of an integrated army in any post-conflict situation, there are a variety of factors that influence the numbers put forth by either side. On the one hand, both sides want to make sure that they will have as much representation as possible, ideally fifty per cent, but if not, as high a percentage comparatively as possible. Additionally, the higher the percentage claimed during negotiations, the more the side can posture about its current strength of arms in order to maintain leverage in negotiations, particularly as a sticking point if negotiations look like they are breaking down. However, a balance must be struck between the level of strength one side wishes to project and the actual number of fighters they can contribute. While both sides know the other is inflating their numbers, neither wants to be more grandiose than the other, relatively speaking, and then be shown up to be relatively less powerful than agreed upon during implementation. Therefore, the final number agreed by each side is usually higher than they could actually contribute, but the proportional numbers for each side are usually relatively accurate.[107]

This was the case in Angola, with the MPLA initially proposing a contribution of 20,000 fighters each,[108] whereas in reality neither could field so many, but the ratio of 50/50 remained relatively realistic.[109] What was not specified, however, were key numbers of officer ratios, nor guarantees of equal UNITA involvement in the police at either enlisted or officer levels.[110] Additionally, no mention whatsoever was made in the treaty about the intelligence services.

What is significant about these calculations, however, is that they are distinctly political and not at all about the capabilities of the military as a fighting force.[111] This is both because in the case of Angola, especially with the situation in Namibia resolved, the main threat to Angolan security was internal, rather than external. Therefore the size of the integrated army did not need to reflect fears of invasion. Due to the calculations discussed earlier, however, there was also little incentive to downsize the army for practical reasons – that is the relative lack of need for a massive army given the lack of fear of invasion nor need for expeditionary capability – and so no discussion was held about the military capabilities of the integrated army. Therefore, from the start, the idea of an integrated army was for political and symbolic purposes, not for war-fighting ones. Therefore, when assessing later on the success or failure of military integration, it is these intentions that are important to measure against, not more traditional metrics of military war-fighting capabilities.

The specific process, then, of integrating the security forces on both sides set out the following steps. First, cantonment camps (assembly areas) were to be formed across the country for both sides, determined by each side's leadership over the course of four weeks.[112] These camps would then welcome, register, house, disarm and prepare combatants from both sides for integration. These camps and their internal registration and disarmament processes were to be overseen by UN peacekeepers with a verification committee composed equally of MPLA and UNITA members to resolve any issues, with the US, Portugal and the UN as observers on the committee.

Once combatants were registered in camps with their arms requisitioned for the integrated army, they would either be allowed to choose to be discharged to civilian life or sent to new locations to form new units in the integrated army. The new army would be officially constituted before the September 1992 elections with the senior military leadership joining first and then new units building out from the top down as combatants processed through the camps.[113] Importantly, all of this was to have taken place before the election. In no stages of this ceasefire, cantonment, disarmament and integration process were provisions made for delays.[114] The plan for cantonment, for example, was for the combatants to be registered in one of the fifty camps within sixty days.[115]

The role of the UN was a consistent sticking point during the negotiations, though primarily not between UNITA and the MPLA and instead due to broader geopolitical factors. In fact, both Angolan parties agreed with the idea that the United Nations should not become particularly involved. Likewise, they preferred to have a peacekeeping mission based on the Namibian one: that functioned primarily as election observers and more general monitors, with a distinctly observational character.[116] The UN itself, however, wanted to be more involved in the peace process at the top levels of decision-making to be able to effectively act as a curb on violent posturing during the campaigning process and beyond. However, there were myriad demands on the international community, resulting in this plea being mostly unacknowledged even once the implementation process began.[117] One of the main barriers to further UN involvement was the changing dynamics and demands of the superpowers. While the ending of the Cold War released some of the habitual blockages in the UN Security Council around peacekeeping, what kind of interventions would be accepted in the new world order had yet to be determined via discussion or precedent. In addition, other factors included the increasing number of hotspots around the world at this point in the early 1990s that required UN attention as well as the UN's relative lack of robust peacekeeping missions in its past, thus making funders and troop contributors unsure of what kinds of mandates were necessary to solve the issues arising.[118]

When the peace treaty was finally signed, there was a clear timeline for demobilization, disarmament and integration in advance of the elections. However, there were tensions from the start, about whether and to what extent both sides would live up to the demobilization and disarmament provisions, especially as some on both sides, though particularly UNITA's leader Savimbi, began to see the usefulness in keeping soldiers deployed during campaign events in order to intimidate voters.[119]

Mozambique: The Rome Agreement

As previously noted in the Rome-based Mozambican discussions the two sides rarely sat directly across the table from one another, whereas in Bicesse, both UNITA and the MPLA negotiated directly with mediators present, and were instead divided into a 'security issues' room and a 'political issues' room, with the latter generally taking precedence and the majority of the attention.

In the Mozambican negotiations, on the other hand, military issues were from the start considered by both parties, RENAMO especially, to be central negotiating points.[120] This was for a variety of reasons and still not fully agreed upon today by those involved, but the most commonly put forward reason for this focus is clear. RENAMO's background, as discussed in the earlier part of this chapter, was fundamentally as a military group, with political aspirations developed at least a few years after its insurgent campaign began. Therefore, the senior leadership of RENAMO was promoted far more for military abilities than political ones, thus giving them more knowledge and interest in security issues than political ones.[121] Furthermore, while RENAMO did have political demands by the time of the negotiations in Rome, there was by this point the precedent of Angola and Namibia (and others from sub-Saharan Africa) to draw on in terms of frameworks for elections and winner-takes-all political structures that neither side saw reasons to deviate from in the case of Mozambique. The security situation, on the other hand, was quite pressing and it was RENAMO's persistent insurgency that brought FRELIMO to the table, rather than RENAMO's political legitimacy or breadth of political support. Thus, FRELIMO hoped that by focusing on and resolving security issues, it could simultaneously stop the insurgency that had plagued it for so long and successfully contest the internationally backed elections, thus both winning the military conflict as well as the one for international prestige in the aftermath of the Cold War.

By 1992 when these negotiations were firmly underway, the Bicesse Accords from Angola had been signed and were in the process of being implemented. This treaty provided a direct framework and basis for comparison for the Rome talks for four key reasons.[122] First, given the similar colonial and independence trajectories of the two countries, both local and international actors hoped that both countries may be able to achieve similar peace outcomes, and like the similarity in actors that drove both sides to the table, there was some utility seen in treating the two conflicts almost as siblings. Second, the MPLA and FRELIMO in particular had very similar backgrounds and goals coming into the negotiations, and thus FRELIMO especially watched the MPLA's negotiating stance and outcomes closely to model themselves after any perceived successes.[123] Third, many of the American diplomatic and military officials who consulted in person or ad hoc in the Rome negotiations as experts and mediators had previously worked on the negotiations in Bicesse and were thus able to directly draw on their experiences from those negotiations in discussing terms for Mozambique.[124] Finally, RENAMO's long-time foreign advisor was responsible for the physical drafting of RENAMO's demands which often formed the drafts for discussion in the Rome negotiations 'essentially copied the political parties legislation [provisions] from Angola['s treaty] and made a few adjustments'.[125]

In 1992, the Bicesse Accords were in their initial implementation stages, the election was not set to be held until September of that year. Thus, the full effects of the Bicesse Accords were not yet known, and yet important lessons began to emerge from the implementation stages that began to trickle over to the Mozambique negotiations through the shared US personnel who were involved in both processes. These lessons will be explored in the following paragraphs discussing the terms agreed on in the Rome treaty and the similarities and differences with the Bicesse agreement.

In general, the two treaties were very similar: both called for multi-party elections to be contested by both sides, with the winner assuming the majority of political power and further elections to be held at regular intervals. Likewise, both called for an integrated army, with the exact same rationale applying in Mozambique as in Angola, with the only difference being a known power imbalance in Mozambique: regardless of posturing, both sides knew RENAMO would never be able to achieve parity with FRELIMO forces in terms of numbers or official training at the beginning of integration, and so the calculations about numbers to offer were about relative proportions, not aiming for an equal split.[126] In addition, the procedure for demobilization, disarmament and integration into both civilian life and the unified military was in broad strokes the same as was the UN's role as an observer and verifier of the peace process. Like the Bicesse Accords, the Rome treaty did not discuss the intelligence services or police officer ranks,[127] though it did go into more detail about the number of police each side would have in the unified forces, which was a level of detail absent in the Bicesse Accords.

What is significant is how the Mozambique agreement deviated from the Angolan one: not in principle, but in the details, either by changing certain procedures or by specifying them to a degree absent from the Bicesse Accords. First, while both sides were to have split cantonment areas like Angola, the locations were chosen in consultation with the UN peacekeeping forces and a group of seven observer countries led by the US, in order to ensure the camp sites chosen were in protected but accessible areas, rather than in purely strategic locations that could be used as fighting bases with little hope of outside moderation, as had become the case with primarily UNITA camps in Angola.[128]

Second, the disarmament process focused on identifying and removing large-scale military equipment (i.e. artillery) from both sides as the first priority, with personal weapons coming as a distant second priority. This was both a lesson learned from the Angolan process of disarmament during which a significant number of the weapons turned in were historical artefacts and the lack of focus on large weaponry did little to alleviate the security dilemma or significantly curtail either side's capacity to renew conflict.[129] It was also a concession to RENAMO's fears of persecution and FRELIMO's goal of restoring functioning transport links. RENAMO combatants' ability to keep their personal arms during subsequent stages of the process engendered more trust in their ability to protect themselves.[130] This was because personal weapons were considered status symbols and signifiers of personal wealth in Mozambican society, due to their importance for personal safety during the years of war, and so maintaining possession of personal weapons was seen by demobilized combatants as important both in protecting their physical safety but also their status within their new communities.[131] For FRELIMO, the main threat to its ability to restore economic progress to the country which would subsequently bolster its political popularity and thus electability was RENAMO's heavy artillery which habitually blew up the few railways and roads that Mozambique relied on for the bulk of its economic trade both internally and with neighbouring countries. Thus, a focus on heavy weaponry in the disarmament process was favoured by all.

Third, the integration process offered the chance to return to civilian society as well as join the unified army, like in Angola. Specifically, however, those who chose the civilian path had to choose a specific town or village in which to receive their integration payments over the course of two years. This was in order to ensure that ex-combatants actually and at least semi-permanently dispersed and demobilized, to avoid militias without uniforms forming surreptitiously as had happened with UNITA combatants staying in cantonment areas past their official end date in order to remain intact should they be needed to restart conflict.[132]

The two key differences, however, between the two treaties, were the election timeline and the role of the UN peacekeeping mission, both of which were directly based on the implementation failures of the Bicesse Accords. As previously discussed, the Bicesse Accords called for a strict timeline of eighteen months during which the entire security processes would be completed and then elections would be held. Even within the first few months of this process, it was clear that the deadlines would not be able to be met, from delays from posturing or logistical challenges.[133] Still, as there were no provisions for delaying the elections and the international community was eager to 'finish' the Angolan process, the election schedule went ahead even though the demobilization and disarmament processes were barely half complete, much less the integration process which had barely taken even symbolic steps. Even before the election was actually held, multiple internal and external actors were warning of the dangers of this decision, and these warnings, while not heeded in Angola, were written into the Mozambican Treaty. Therefore, while a strict timeline for demobilization, disarmament, integration and then elections was written into the Mozambican Treaty with little extra time added on to the Angolan numbers,[134] explicit mention was made throughout the treaty that the security processes must be completed before elections could be held, even if that meant elections were delayed. Likewise, specific procedures were written into the treaty about how and when to delay elections in order to complete the security provisions of the treaty. Interviews with US diplomats and military experts who were involved in both negotiations as well as a South African lawyer who was RENAMO's main legal aid and drafter of much of the treaty all independently agreed that this delay mechanism was a direct result of watching the unfolding chaos in Angola.[135]

The other significant difference from the situation in Angola was the role of the UN peacekeeping mission in Mozambique, ONUMOZ. It started with the same mandate as the Angolan UNAVEM II missions, to primarily observe and verify the steps and stages of the Rome agreement. However, the international community and the UN itself very successfully lobbied the two parties in Mozambique to agree to a more substantial role.[136] The updated mandate included a voting role on the verification committees in charge of dealing with unexpected issues or disputes during the implementation process, a position that the UN in Angola was only allowed to observe.[137] It also essentially put the UN peacekeeping mission in the directing role of the entire implementation process: while the mission was not responsible for carrying out all aspects of the treaty, it was charged with oversight of nearly all of its provisions either on equal footing with the two sides or in a supervisory role above both parties.[138]

This was acceptable to both Mozambican parties for the following reasons. For RENAMO, a more robust peacekeeping mission was considered a protection mechanism from potential FRELIMO aggression given its governmental legitimacy and superior experience as a political and national movement.[139] In addition, given RENAMO's already discussed relative lack of implementation and certainly negotiations knowledge, having more UN officials available to support developing the group into a viable political party was seen as a valuable resource. For FRELIMO, a stronger UN presence signified the increased attention of the international community and commitment to assist Mozambique recover from war, which FRELIMO believed would improve FRELIMO's international standing as the legitimate government of Mozambique at least during the implementation phase, if not also following a successfully contested election. Thus, both sides had an interest in there being a more directly involved UN peacekeeping mission and in cooperating with its suggestions, mandates and actions.[140]

Like with the Angolan process, there were of course outstanding disagreements even as the treaty was signed and began to be implemented. They mainly focused on financial issues – specifically, the amount which RENAMO would be given to transform itself into a political party, and the specific amounts given to senior RENAMO leadership in order to maintain their support for the treaty.[141] However, once the government of Italy agreed to a fund of around $17 million, RENAMO accepted the final provisions and began to cooperate with the implementation process.[142]

The General Peace Agreement was signed between RENAMO and FRELIMO in Rome in October 1992 and the UN mission ONUMOZ was authorized in December 1992 and first deployed in early 1993.[143] In many respects it followed the same format and principles as the 1991 Bicesse Accords, but in key areas related to security provisions, the role of UN peacekeepers, and in the relationship between security provisions and election timeline, had taken specific lessons from the implementation problems of the Bicesse Accords and made a treaty that was both more detailed and more flexible.

Angola: Implementing the Bicesse Accords

Signing the Bicesse Accords was merely the first step in achieving peace in Angola; the larger challenge lay in trying to implement them. The timeframe given for the security provisions to be put in place was twelve months, with elections to follow.[144] The immediate priority was securing the ceasefire, for which the UN mission UNAVEM II was meant to observe and monitor compliance.

The first problem in implementing the Accords was the sheer size of Angola. The fifty cantonment areas for the combatants were scattered across a massive country.[145] Furthermore, it quickly became apparent that the locations that each side had chosen for their camps was not necessarily neutral or chosen with the best interests of the peace agreement in mind. MPLA camps, for example, tended to be near urban centres; while this made transport of troops to these camps and the delivery of supplies and monitoring relatively easy, the enticements of urban life also proved tempting to the assembled fighters and increased issues with discipline and desertion within MPLA camps. UNITA camps, on the other hand, were not only in deeply inaccessible areas,[146] making the provision of supplies and transport of UN monitors supremely complicated.[147] The locations also tended to be chosen primarily for military strategy instead of as a first step towards a unified army or demobilization into the civilian population. Camps were located on high ground, at key intersections or near secret weapons caches, all of which seemed to indicate UNITA's ambivalence about complying with the accords from the start.[148]

In New York, there were also challenges, namely regarding the funding and therefore the size and capabilities of the UN mission UNAVEM II.[149] Although it had been authorized relatively easily given the agreement between the USSR and US regarding the need to resolve conflict in Angola, actually determining the particulars of the mission was more difficult. Not only was the USSR going through its own crises and thus unable to fund efforts further afield,[150] the other large funding powers were likewise focused on the collapse of the Soviet Union, the Iron Curtain, and a variety of civil wars popping up all over the developing world.[151]

Fundamentally, UNAVEM II was authorized to be an observance and monitoring mission, but the debate raged over exactly how many monitors and observers were needed and what kinds of equipment were required in order to carry out this mission. Also, the distance between Angola and most of the troop-contributing countries meant that even once numbers were agreed upon, deploying to Angola was a time-consuming process. Furthermore, skills – logistical, military, legal and linguistic also varied widely amongst the deployed troops.[152] Finally, even once peacekeepers had arrived in Angola, deploying them to the cantonment areas was highly difficult, particularly to the UNITA camps given their inaccessible locations.[153] All of these factors combined to make UNAVEM II an unpopular mission, both with the funders on the Security Council and with the countries contributing troops; no one was eager to pour more into Angola than deemed necessary.[154] Therefore, at peak strength, UNAVEM II had 350 military observers and 126 civilian police.[155] There was also a civilian air unit and a medical unit, as well as some eighty-seven international civilians and 155 local staff. In addition, during the polling, UNAVEM II fielded a total of 400 electoral observers.[156]

In addition, UNAVEM II also had constant logistical and communication challenges. The mission barely had any of its own equipment beyond personal kits and weapons for its peacekeepers.[157] Given that many of the cantonment locations could only be reached by helicopter (or a pathless trek through the jungle lasting over a week), in combination with the fact that the UNAVEM II mission only had three aircraft, transport to and from camps was a constant issue.[158] Additionally, the same terrain that made air travel the only reasonable way to move from place to place made the communications equipment available in the early 1990s work at less than optimal conditions. This meant that updates on problems with compliance or adherence to the timelines and stipulations of the agreement were delayed in being reported and therefore received slow follow-up and enforcement as well. Furthermore, this isolation made the UN mission and the individual peacekeepers both appear and actually be quite vulnerable, as evidenced by fatal attacks on peacekeepers.[159]

Even once the camps were set up, however, maintaining discipline and compliance was a further challenge. In MPLA camps, there was little ideological unity to the MPLA army, and the draws of peacetime and non-soldiering opportunities began to seem more attractive than staying for an unexpectedly long time in camps with nothing to do far from home for many soldiers.[160] In the UNITA camps, on the other hand, internal discipline was generally quite effective, as the fighters were drawn together on ideological and often linguistic lines anyway, and had fierce inter-unit loyalties.[161] On the other hand, this cohesion in and of itself, as well as the relatively unsubtle strategic placement of the camps meant that while UNITA soldiers were not deserting and causing problems interacting chaotically with civilian populations, they were also not making any efforts towards actually demobilizing or, in some camps, complying with UN disarmament procedures.[162]

Even beyond the problem of individual behaviour within the camps, ensuring compliance with the terms and especially the deadlines of the overall agreement of the Accords was a fundamental problem. Although the treaty specified that all demobilization into and then from cantonment areas was to be completed prior to the September 1992 elections, by that date, even optimistic UN estimates acknowledge that merely 59 per cent of combatants had reported to cantonment areas, with fewer having properly disarmed or demobilized further.[163]

Running parallel to the security processes in the camps, of course, was the election campaign for a winner-take-all presidential contest.[164] With the election date fixed, all efforts on both sides were turned towards gaining victory in the polls. Both parties were explicitly allowed to campaign throughout the country, both in current strongholds but also in areas previously denied to them.

As has been discussed earlier in this chapter in the section detailing each group's origins, the MPLA tended to draw more support in urban areas, whereas UNITA's main base of support continued to be the southern-based Ovimbundu group which was the largest single identity group in the country, but still accounted for less than half of the population. The MPLA's campaign strategy tended to focus on the party and mainly led with a message of economic growth. Given the decrease in Soviet funds and the collapse of global communism, ideology was largely absent from the MPLA's strategy, and while incumbent President dos Santos was the face of the campaign, the messaging tended to focus on the party rather than revolve around him as a central figure.

UNITA's campaign, on the other hand, was deeply focused on Savimbi, who was styled as a saviour and father to the nation. UNITA's messaging focused on Savimbi as creating and leading an Angolan identity with some references to democratic ideology,[165] but primarily focusing on 'big-man' politics of the style that has become increasingly familiar to audiences around the world since the end of the Cold War.[166] One way in which this focus on Savimbi and the grand terms in which he saw his role in Angola became clear was through his increased use of military language, military dress and soldiers in his campaign events as the election drew nearer.[167] This not only served to make UNITA seem more militaristic to both local and international observers[168] but also began to raise tensions significantly as the election neared, as the MPLA began publicly calling into question Savimbi's willingness to allow the elections to be free and fair.[169] Given the delays that were mounting in the security processes, with fewer than 62 per cent of soldiers in the cantonment areas,[170] much less completely processed through the various stages by the election, tensions were high.[171]

Nevertheless, elections were held on schedule and were generally considered to be sufficiently free and fair by the variety of international organizations who sent observers, despite Savimbi's militaristic posturing.[172] Results were to be announced three days after the polling, which created a very tense few days. As results began to come in, it became clear that though initial polls at the start of the campaign had pointed towards a UNITA victory, results were now showing the success of the MPLA. Savimbi immediately started questioning the results and demanding recounts and special examinations of specific polling places he alleged were fraudulently interfered with. Despite pleas from various diplomats as well as the head of the UN peacekeeping mission, Savimbi began to go public with his doubts as to the election's validity and refused to publicly state his acceptance of his loss.[173] In the midst of all this doubt, all steps towards completing the now-seriously-behind-schedule security provisions completely stalled, with the MPLA focused on stemming desertions and preparing for a potential attack, and UNITA troops likewise gearing up.[174] Within three weeks of the election, the results had been officially declared in the MPLA's favour, Savimbi had officially withdrawn his approval and participation from the plan and the war was fully back on.[175]

From the day of signing to the day of UNITA's first attack, the Bicesse Accords had managed to get over 50 per cent of fighters into cantonment areas, managed a symbolic ceremony with the top generals of each side pledging to be part of a unified army in the week before the election,[176] and the holding of an internationally recognized free and fair presidential election. Within less than three months, however, of signing the piece of paper, there was no more peace for the UN mission to keep; the war renewed and was more deadly than before, and UNAVEM II's mandate ended in tatters.[177]

Mozambique: Implementing the Rome Agreement

As with the peace treaty, Mozambique's implementation process benefitted from a variety of lessons learned from Angola as well as unique differences between the situations in the two countries; this combination contributed to a more successful implementation process in Mozambique. While the peace was by no means complete following the initial years of implementation, Mozambique's civil war has not restarted, even if issues remain between the two sides over two decades later.

The initial stages of putting the treaty into practice were the same as in Angola: the setting up of cantonment assembly areas, the authorization and deployment of the UN peacekeeping mission and beginning to process combatants from both sides. The cantonment areas had been discussed during the Rome negotiations, and once the contentious provisions for the ceasefire were determined and agreed to, deciding where to put the camps within each group's area of influence was relatively straightforward. While logistical considerations of transporting food and equipment to the camps were a concern, this was less to do with purposefully difficult-to-access locations being chosen and more about the condition of transport infrastructure in the country overall after so many years of war.[178]

The UN peacekeeping mission, ONUMOZ, was eagerly anticipated by both sides, who saw a UN mission as a sign of the international community's commitment towards the peace process. Thus, there was minimal internal opposition to the UN taking on a larger role within the peace process than any previous UN mission had been authorized. Likewise, with the abject failure of UNAVEM II fresh in the minds of politicians and administrators in New York, there was little debate about the need to ensure more troops and more funds for the mission in Mozambique.[179] There was proportionally still a dearth of peacekeepers compared to Angola, but given Mozambique's much smaller geographic size, this did not end up having a significant impact on the mission's ability to succeed.[180] Nevertheless, the role of the UN was more symbolic than enforcement, as even with the higher troop numbers, had substantial violence recurred, the 6,576 maximum deployed peacekeepers[181] would not have been able to significantly stop determined efforts by either side to escalate back into full-scale war.

Once the camps and the UN peacekeepers were set up, the processing began. Initially, the number of combatants from both sides turning up to the assembly areas was within the expectations of the treaty, but delays, especially on the RENAMO side, quickly began to crop up. By January 1994, barely 4,000 RENAMO fighters had been registered at the camps.[182] This was for a variety of reasons, both those publicly claimed by RENAMO leaders as well as those inferred by outside observers. The official statements from RENAMO leadership complained about the conditions of the camps as a direct cause. Behind these statements, however, RENAMO was struggling to transition into a fully political entity and decided to pursue a strategy of delay.[183] Additionally, RENAMO was constantly pushing for more outside funding and support and used assembly delays to keep the spectre of a RENAMO army for gamesmanship purposes in ongoing funding negotiations.[184]

Still, the complaints about camp conditions were not entirely fabricated, especially for RENAMO combatants who had been fighting with guerrilla tactics for years, based in the jungle, many of whom had actually been captured into the group in the first place.[185] This dissatisfaction led to significant demobilization delays that looked to potentially derail the entire peace process as RENAMO fighters seemed to no longer be willing to move to and stay within cantonment areas.[186] Within a few months, however, UN records show participation increasing, and while elections were eventually delayed, the process stayed on track. Through the course of qualitative interviews, the following explanation was given by RENAMO's long-time foreign advisor:

The possible carrot [came from] what I experienced to be one of the biggest hardships in the normal camps, which is the absence of toothbrushes and toothpaste, and tooth and dental ailments. People go crazy with a . . . tooth abscess and the cure was that somebody would actually take a screwdriver and a hammer, and hammer the tooth. Some people will die as a result of this from infections in their bones. So I said okay, we have to have welcoming packs. And in the welcoming packs, we put the things that everybody in RENAMO dreams of, which is a . . . large tube of toothpaste, a good toothbrush, a pair of decent . . . shoes, and some underwear . . . [also] people in the bush don't have soap. And if you cannot wash with soap for several years . . . you develop skin problems, it's not nice. So, that became very, very attractive to people. So this [the camps] are a place where we have luxuries and it was a big fight with the UN.

He then went on to describe the following solution, which was corroborated in a separate interview with one of the senior UN officials in ONUMOZ.[187] According to his recollection,

he [the senior ONUMOZ official] managed somehow through a contact in France to convince Colgate and Colgate sponsored, I think 50,000 packs of toothpaste and brushes. And so we got a couple of these things sponsored and had so many people started trickling in and then there was a big big [improvement, with RENAMO soldiers arriving in camps] 20 hours a day.

This is an example of the kind of practical and logistical challenge that came up often in the cantonment and demobilization processes in both Angola and Mozambique, requiring pragmatic and flexible responses.[188]

Relatedly, the senior ONUMOZ official via interview mentioned a further example in the same vein:

The cultural difference within the United Nation system itself was a problem [in setting up assembly areas]. The cult of peace-keeping operations vis-a-vis the culture of development and of humanitarian operations proved in practice to be quite different and sometimes conflictual . . . [the development side was in charge of organising camps and] they decided that the traditional African farm hut was more suitable than military tents. Unfortunately the soldiers, when they reached the Assembly Areas – often after a long and extenuating march – did not appreciate the highly pedagogical approach of the UN volunteers. . . . Exhausted, they were furious when no accommodations were ready. Those who were confronted with this situation concluded that the United Nations was unreliable and disorganised. They were also offended as soldiers for being treated like peasant farmers. In the end, they had no choice but to build their own huts. Furthermore, on the incorrect assumption they would remain only for [a] few days in the Assembly Areas, they built very basic shelters which quickly proved unsuitable. This became a source of resentment and even occasional mutinies. . . . The organisation of the Assembly Areas was one of the more serious mistakes we made.

Once fighters were in cantonment areas, disarmament began. This was an explicitly UN-led stage of the process and specifically targeted large-scale arms rather than personal ones. While this did lead to quite a few symbolic turnovers of arms and likely did eliminate some significant weaponry from both sides, local and international observers acknowledged during, immediately after, and in the long term after the peace process that disarmament had largely failed to significantly change the number of weapons available for conflict in Mozambique.[189] In fact, UN peacekeepers running the assembly areas quickly noted that while the number of arms turned in was consistent with the number of fighters registering, the quality was much lower or older than expected for functioning weapons.[190] Nevertheless, this was not considered an adequate reason to delay the demobilization process, nor worth the efforts of the thinly spread ONUMOZ mission to use exhaustive expeditionary measures to verify disarmament more broadly.[191] Both secondary diplomatic sources as well as internal UN documents suggest that this was a policy interpretation from the ONUMOZ commander Ajello himself: 'it seems to have been agreed between ONUMOZ and the government, with the recent example of the collapse of the Angolan peace process after the 1992 elections, that to insist that RENAMO submit to a rigorous and comprehensive disarmament process was to risk pushing them too hard'.[192] While this was noted as the biggest regret or biggest area of improvement by some involved in the implementation process, most others conceded that this was a necessary concession to ensure general compliance with the accords.[193]

Following disarmament, the treaty planned for the majority of combatants to then integrate into a unified Mozambique army, with only those physically unable to serve demobilizing instead into civilian life. The treaty, however, specified that demobilization would be on a self-selected basis, on the assumption that most former combatants would choose to stay within the known military institution, especially with the benefit of a government salary, rather than start from scratch in a new profession. To the surprise of leaders on both sides as well as the UN mission and international observers, in both groups, the vast majority of non-officers chose to demobilize into civilian life.[194] The specifics of how this impacted the creation of the new integrated military will be discussed in depth in Chapter 4.

This choice was likely due to the attractiveness of the civilian demobilization package offered.[195] This consisted of cash payments over two years, to be collected from a specified location, to ensure combatants began to develop roots in a particular place and to monitor locations of former combatants.[196] It was hoped that this physical scattering across a country with relatively few modes of long-distance travel would weaken RENAMO's ability to reform as a coherent military group.[197] This two-year period was seen by former fighters as sufficient time to get 'a farm, a wife, and a baby', according to an English-language journalist who has been reporting on events in Mozambique since 1979. According to him, this demobilization package compared favourably with a stagnant government salary and continued discipline and rigour of military life seem less than enticing by comparison, an idea confirmed by a senior UN official in the ONUMOZ mission.[198]

All of these stages, especially the early cantonment processing and then the expanded demobilization programme, took longer than had been specified in the treaty. This, however, is where the two provisions came into effect: first, the UN had the power in the verification and monitoring committee to recommend and vote through a delay to the elections, and both sides had already agreed to said delays in order to ensure the security provisions were successfully implemented. Thus, elections were delayed with very little chaos, confusion or threats from either side.[199] Although there were tensions throughout the campaigning process and RENAMO's leadership threatened not to participate in the early days of elections – it was clear they would not win a majority – the process was overall much smoother than in Angola. The official demobilization numbers stated that over 57,000 FRELIMO fighters and over 20,500 RENAMO fighters had gone through the UN process.[200] Ultimately, the unified army was successfully created before the election and the elections took place with both turnout and results – a FRELIMO presidential victory – verified by the international community and accepted by both sides.

Discussion and conclusion

Though both were Portuguese colonies for nearly 300 years, Angola and Mozambique embarked on parallel but separate paths towards peace in a tumultuous era of global, regional and internal conflict. This chapter has shown the initial negotiation and implementation stages for both countries in the order in which they developed, this section will now directly discuss major findings and themes.

One key theme of the negotiations processes for both conflicts was the impact of superpower pressure towards bringing parties, both the local actors themselves as well as other smaller powers involved in the conflict or in the mediation, to the table. Motivations for the US and USSR to resolve these proxy conflicts have been clear throughout the latter half of this chapter, but what the investigation of the terms, negotiating process and implementation of the treaties showed is that superpower pressure may have been enough to bring all parties to the table, but it was not always sufficient to get parties to reach an agreement, nor to enforce one. These two cases clearly showcase the contrast between negotiations solely motivated by outside actors, versus those that local participants have internal incentives to actively participate in. This confirms Beardsley's argument that third-power mediation can be hugely impactful on peace efforts in the short term, but can therefore get in the way of more endurable peace in the long term by over-emphasizing external preferences for peace over local ones.[201]

Resolving the issue of Namibia was a key to 'unlocking' peace in Southern Africa for a variety of reasons. First, it brought opposing sides to the same table for the first time, enabling relationships to be developed, knowledge to grow and a platform for informal discussions that could reduce the risk for actors like the MPLA to consider entering negotiations on the Angolan issue.[202] Namibia was also key for removing the added complications of Cuban and South African troops, thus reducing the Angolan civil war to a much simpler, if not at all less lethal, battlefield calculus. The Namibia negotiations also developed a blueprint of joint superpower negotiations and pressure, brought in the UN as an approved observer and implementer and set up elections as the key success criteria recognized by the outside powers. While this blueprint had very different outcomes for Angola and Mozambique, Namibia is noteworthy for the example and lessons it provided for both cases.[203]

Within the multi-party negotiations for both peace processes, it is interesting to note the important role that secondary powers played, mainly: Portugal and Sant Egidio, with some involvement from the Vatican and Italian government as well. Significantly, both had deep cultural and linguistic knowledge of Angola and Mozambique, something not shared by any of the other powers involved in these negotiations, notably the United States. While US diplomats were generally reluctant to ascribe significance to linguistic knowledge in discussing the impact of Portugal and Sant Egidio as the host of their respective negotiations, it seems unlikely that the ease with which negotiations were facilitated by having drafting legal and linguistic help from these two actors would have been so seamlessly achieved otherwise.[204] Particularly given the example of the aborted Gbadolite talks and the linguistic challenges that arose when moving from general principles to specific details, the importance of cultural and linguistic familiarity with the main parties surely contributed to the ability for these negotiations to move beyond general principles, especially during the weeks of intensive negotiations on site. Still, the fact that most of the US diplomats who were involved in both negotiations were either the same individuals or had worked closely together in the past likely provided a significant basis of pooled knowledge that benefitted particularly the Mozambique negotiations, even without specific knowledge of Mozambique.

While Sant Egidio's role as an NGO makes it relatively unique as a mediator of a modern civil war, understanding the extent to which its perceived weakness, as a non-state actor without significant military or financial leverage,[205] must first determine to what extent it was seen by participants as weak as well as comparing against other mediators and perceptions of them. Sant Egidio was selected by both sides for reasons described earlier, a key one being that it was seen by both sides as being popular and perceived as legitimate by a significant portion of the citizenry of Mozambique[206] – perceptions of domestic support can in fact be hugely powerful levers to influence organizations that seek to achieve similar status. Additionally, on the Angolan side, Ethiopia was not a country with particular ties to either side nor a country with relevant military or economic levers regarding the conflict, and yet this did not help the Ethiopian government become a relevant mediator in that conflict. In fact, in Angola, talks initially happened far away in Portugal with a colonial power that had long since left and literally removed itself from the Angolan context nearly wholesale (see Chapter 2). Talks then occurred in the

DRC which was heavily involved on both sides, then in nearby Zambia which was heavily involved in the conflict primarily on UNITA's side, and then finally the last treaty was negotiated in Angola itself, hardly neutral territory. Therefore, the idea that Sant Egidio succeeded because it was a neutral and weak mediator seems not to take into account the various nuances of who and where mediators are and how they are seen by the key conflict actors themselves at the time.

During the negotiations, gaps in negotiating capabilities between the government and rebel sides became clear, especially between FRELIMO and RENAMO. Although the MPLA and FRELIMO both suffered from having been ostracized from the US-led international community due to their Marxist policies and alliance with the Soviet Union during the Cold War, both nevertheless had been acting as governments for decades and therefore not only had access and experience of international politics but also a developed government infrastructure with a full political and economic programme and ministers capable of representing their portfolios.[207] While UNITA had senior leadership that was highly educated and internationally experienced, it was a relatively small group that had no government experience to draw on and had a much less politically experienced constituency to report back to.[208] RENAMO, in contrast, had a barely literate leadership with almost no educational experience, much less acumen for international politicking.[209] Therefore there were significant gaps in legalistic and political strategy between the government and non-government actors in both negotiations.

UNITA and RENAMO focused heavily on elections and security provisions as ways to secure their own power, without developing a broader political portfolio or platform that would enable them to appeal to a sufficient constituency to win the elections they were demanding so strongly in negotiations.[210] Thus, the structural imbalance between the two different kinds of actors became clear as negotiations concluded and then implementation began, beyond the particular charismatic or educational qualities of UNITA and RENAMO's leadership. This was a structural gap that was recognized more clearly in Mozambique than in Angola due to RENAMO's leaders being both deeply uneducated and mostly coerced into joining, but was a problem for both groups in terms of being able to successfully transition from armed insurgency to political party.[211] This is a transition process that received mainly ad hoc attention from outside actors, which mainly took the form of financial support to mount a campaign and private sector advisors on campaign strategy that was often ignored, irrelevant to the situation of the particular country, or inadequate.[212]

Another problem that UNITA and RENAMO suffered more than the government actors was communication within their groups, most notably through the negotiators sent abroad and their superior leadership back on the ground. In both cases, negotiations were often slowed by the length of time needed for communication in the early 1990s, exacerbated by the fact that both groups' main bases were in relatively inaccessible areas that required further technological and logistical coordination to maintain communication to Bicesse and Rome respectively.[213] In addition to the practical challenges, there was also the psychological fact that both groups relied heavily on a single charismatic leader who structured his decision-making and leadership around his personal goals and idiosyncrasies, and therefore was highly paranoid about being 'left out' of decision-making and having his authority 'usurped'. Therefore, despite the logistical efforts needed to keep both Savimbi and Dhlakama appraised of negotiation efforts in Europe, it was politically necessary for negotiators to constantly seek approval from their leaders in order to maintain their own positions within the groups.[214] This meant that while there was no splintering within the groups that would have resulted in the proliferation of combatants or negotiators in the conflict as a whole, talks were definitely slowed by the need to keep both dictatorial leaders psychologically satisfied.[215]

In terms of the main goals of combatant negotiators, both negotiations tended to split issues into either political or security-related topics, with the former receiving more attention in written memoirs whereas the latter were deemed more significant in the majority of interviews conducted for this book.[216] When asked to explain this discrepancy, one senior US diplomat who both wrote a memoir within five years of his experience working on the Mozambique negotiations and was interviewed for this book in September 2019 recounted that 'at the time, elections were seen to be the big thing, but [in hindsight] I think the security issues mattered more for making [the Mozambique peace process] work'.[217] In both cases, the security issues were often more closely insisted upon by the two rebel groups, potentially due to their need to maintain personal security for leaders, both from government opponents and potential internal challengers once the strict controls of the battlefield were relaxed.[218] In contrast, from the start of negotiations, the headline issue for the MPLA and FRELIMO was security, international recognition and legitimacy as the sitting government of their respective country. This was likely caused by the knowledge of the Cold War ending, thus removing their main international backer and ideological raison d'etre. Interestingly, one feature that was part of neither negotiation was the admission of moving both countries to multi-party elections-based systems, a concession both formerly Marxist governments had made prior to negotiations beginning due to Cold War atmospherics.[219] This missing feature removed what could have been a significant barrier to agreement, but also a key part of RENAMO and UNITA's Cold War-era political platform – for which neither had an effective replacement.[220]

The main security provision that this book is concerned with is military integration, which was the operating assumption in both cases with seemingly little debate about alternatives. None of the interviewees mentioned that other alternatives were considered, and so it seems that because neither side was confident of a military victory, an integrated military was seen as a necessity to ensure neither side was able to command military dominance, even in peacetime.[221] In Mozambique, both sides from the outset of negotiations seemed to not only assume an integrated military as the basis for a post-conflict security institution but also acted both during negotiations and implementation in relatively good faith in complying with this assumption. Delays, some of which were real, were raised by both sides throughout, but relatively few 'all-or-nothing' type withdrawal threats were made regarding the integrated security structure as a concept. On the other hand, in Angola, while no other methods of post-conflict security institutions were discussed, both sides not only delayed implementation but seemed to make very few even symbolic gestures towards actually forming an integrated army, thus suggesting that while both sides had agreed to the institution, both also thought that once they won the election, they would be able to rewrite the provisions in their favour, something neither side seemed to act towards, if not consider, in Mozambique. It remains unclear whether this is a full picture of the motivations around the idea of an integrated military in either country nor why both sides in Mozambique seemed more willing from the outset to comply than in Angola. Suppositions regarding the amount to which UNITA and the MPLA wanted to comply in general with the Bicesse Accords rather than were forced to by outside pressure can be made, but as yet gaps in understanding the incentives and thought processes remain.

In terms of implementing the security provisions, both processes faced significant delays in the initial stages of cantonment and assembly, with the majority of complaints relating to logistical delays, especially for RENAMO and UNITA fighters moving through generally inaccessible territory, as well as poor conditions in the initial set-up of the camps.[222] This is one of the key ways in which Mozambique benefitted from following Angola, in that the international community learned three key lessons from the failure of compliance in Angola. First, more time needed to be given for combatants to arrive at and process through cantonment and assembly areas, which themselves needed to be in conveniently located and psychologically safe areas, but not purely strategic ones.[223] Second, the living conditions of the camps needed to be appropriate to the climate conditions of the countries (e.g. no tents during the rainy season) and perceived to be dignified to combatants living there, which included basic hygiene kits and orderly processing.[224] Finally, the role of the UN was significantly stronger in the Mozambican process overall, which directly translated to more coherently administered camps with improved communications between UN headquarters, cantonment areas and the leadership of both sides, to ensure the process moved along with as few delays as possible and that problems were solved relatively quickly.[225] Nevertheless, cantonment and assembly was delayed in both cases, due to logistical issues but also as a way for the two rebel sides – seen as institutionally weaker compared to their government counterparts – to extend their campaigning time and thus try to win over more support for the election.

These delays jeopardized and eventually doomed the entire process in Angola due to the single most significant difference between the two treaties and implementation processes: a fixed election date.[226] As has been described and analysed in this chapter, the specified deadline in Angola meant that delays in cantonment and assembly reduced the possibility for any realistic disarmament and demobilization, much less the building of an integrated army and the prospect for an election result that would not be contested in the event of a UNITA loss. In Mozambique, on the other hand, this was one of the most important lessons learnt from Angola and was used to great effect by the head of the UN mission who made a number of relevant executive decisions. The focus on elections has been explored in the context of each case previously, but one point is worth highlighting further. Extensive interviews with every US diplomat involved in both the Angolan and Mozambican negotiations, the majority of whom were also directly or tangentially involved in the Namibian process, made one thing clear. The US State Department and political administrations really did think that holding a free and fair election would resolve the conflicts in all three countries permanently, and only after the disaster of the Bicesse Accords did they begin to somewhat reevaluate that stance.[227] This signals a deeper problem in US foreign policy and conflict resolution capabilities but is beyond the scope of this book to explore further here.

In fact, the UN missions were systematically different on a number of levels. First, UNAVEM II in all of its iterations was drastically undermanned and underfunded compared to the sheer size of Angola as well as the scale of its conflict.[228] Second, UNAVEM II's role in implementing the Bicesse Accords was strictly one of observation and verification, with little ability to direct, mitigate or enforce processes and provisions.[229] Third, UNAVEM II received insufficient political backing from the superpowers and regional actors to exert political pressure on either side to comply.[230] Finally, the head of UNAVEM II, Margaret Anstee, was accused by both local and international actors for being habitually unaware of details on the ground, incapable of managing the UN resources available and unwilling to take the necessary political risks to pursue the full extent of the mission's mandate.[231]

ONUMOZ, on the other hand, was more appropriately sized in both personnel and funding for the geography and scale of Mozambique, due to its improved superpower and regional backing.[232] Additionally, ONUMOZ's institutional role in the accords was firmly one of enforcer and implementer, which was not only accepted but welcomed by both FRELIMO and RENAMO, following the lead of the disaster in Angola but also due to the relative institutional weakness of both actors compared to their Angolan counterparts. Finally, multiple secondary sources and interviewees noted the importance of the personality, background and actions of the head of the UN peacekeeping mission, Aldo Ajello, an Italian diplomat chosen to head this mission due to UN bureaucratic policies, not aptitude.[233] Nevertheless, by all accounts, he was key to the mission's success, mainly because of his focus on the big picture of achieving the main goals of the peace settlement, even if that meant sacrificing some of the details, such as ignoring personal disarmament in favour of removing heavy weaponry and hidden caches or appeasing RENAMO hardliners by allowing personal patronage networks funded by UN cash rather than demanding exact financial transparency.[234] One interviewee noted, 'Ajello was Italian, he was used to dealing with the mafia. He would even say in public that he "bought off" RENAMO leaders, and you know what, it worked.'[235] While this approach left some corners cut, for example, the lack of personal disarmament was regretted by one US diplomat in 2019 as being 'my biggest regret of the peace process', most agree that Ajello's leadership was key to ONUMOZ's success,[236] though the mission's stronger institutional basis compared to UNAVEM II surely was also important.[237]

One aspect of implementation that was surprising in the case of Mozambique in both the secondary literature and throughout the interviews was how few combatants of FRELIMO and RENAMO actually wanted to join the integrated military once the accords were signed. The assumption and compliance with the idea of the integrated military had already been discussed and was not contested, but when it came time for combatants to choose whether or not to join the institution, numbers on both sides were drastically lower than anyone had predicted. Through the interviews, the main theory for this unexpected outcome became clear: the two-year demobilization package offered to those who chose civilian life over a military career. As has been previously discussed, this long timeline for demobilization was seen as attractive to combatants, but while this is a view that became clear with hindsight, it was a surprise to everyone involved in the process.[238] As will be analysed in detail in the next chapter, although some learning was taken from this experience by international actors in Mozambique and within the UN more broadly, gaps remained particularly around funding for these efforts and coordination with wider economic reconstruction.[239]

This chapter focused on outlining the negotiation process, the provisions of the two major treaties and how they were both implemented in Angola and Mozambique. While there are three further peace treaties that will be analysed in further chapters, they are all explicitly based on and in addition to the Bicesse Accords. Parallel to ongoing cycles of conflict, negotiation and attempted implementation in Angola, implementation continued in Mozambique which will likewise be explored in subsequent chapters. While the conflicts and conflict resolution processes in both countries moved, as has been shown, in relative parallel from colonization through independence and into civil war, it is at this point in the early 1990s that the trajectories of the two countries begin to significantly diverge in some ways, but remain surprisingly similar in others. The remainder of this book will continue to trace these progressions to determine what lessons can be learnt for post-conflict military integration processes in Angola and Mozambique, as well as be broadly applied to other processes.

Chapter 4

DIVERGING PATHS

This chapter investigates the parallel trajectories of the peace processes in Angola and Mozambique and how by 1998, they were on distinctly separate paths. It covers the events from the collapse of Angola's Bicesse process in 1993 to the successful negotiations of an adapted treaty, called the Lusaka Protocol (1994), and its partial implementation and eventual collapse. The chapter will then consider Mozambique's contemporaneous process of implementing its 1992 Rome Accords and how that peace process was kept on track through the successful negotiation of elections, before analysing in detail the creation of the integrated military. Finally, the chapter will conclude by comparing both processes and investigating lessons that can be learned by comparing the divergent processes.

By the end of 1993, Angola's Bicesse process had completely fallen apart after the 1992 election results were rejected by UNITA. As the demobilization process in Angola had been hampered by implementation and cooperation issues from the start, the failed elections that UNITA took as the last affront to return to armed violence. Conflict resumed within days of Savimbi's declaration. In fact, UNITA's conspicuous failure to demobilize once its soldiers were in assembly areas[1] allowed it to go back to fighting almost immediately, with stunning results.[2] Despite the MPLA holding the majority of Angola's cities and main roads since independence in 1975, the mass desertions and disillusionment that afflicted many of its soldiers during their Bicesse demobilization process meant that as soon as conflict resumed, UNITA was very much in the ascendant. In fact, within seven months, UNITA controlled roughly two-thirds of Angolan territory, far more than it ever had in the past. Angola's second-most important city, Huambo, was firmly UNITA headquarters and control of Luanda was once again contested.[3]

While both sides had lost their foreign military allies and equipment backers, UNITA had historically been less reliant on outside funding and support than the MPLA. UNITA was also able to leverage the large rural population, through its knowledge of terrain, its arms caches and the discipline it maintained during the peace process to its clear advantage. The MPLA was scrambling with a lack of strong foreign alliances and support, especially in the wake of the end of the Cold War and the collapse of the Soviet Union. The international reaction in response to the renewed violence was universally condemnatory, particularly against UNITA. This was a notable shift in US policy towards UNITA, which would escalate further.

However, the relative lack of direct international involvement, aside from the underfunded and understaffed UNAVEM II, meant that there was little leverage the international community could exert in the initial months of the renewed conflict. This chapter will trace how those negotiations to achieve peace in Angola unfolded and resulted in the 1994 Lusaka peace agreement, focusing on how the negotiations built on and tried to learn from the mistakes of the Bicesse process.

Simultaneously, Mozambique's peace process was underway, with elections postponed but demobilization on track, and a coordinated UN-led effort focused on ensuring that the problems that beset Angola in 1992 would not be mirrored across the continent. Demobilization had suffered some key setbacks in terms of getting soldiers into assembly areas, satisfying their demands while there and sending combatants to their various post-demobilization lives afterwards. The UN mission ONUMOZ was holding together an international coalition of NGOs, UNOs and foreign donors, but still faced a difficult coordination task – made trickier by continued logistics and supply scarcity. The spectre of Angola, however, loomed large, especially as internal conflict in that country went from bad to worse. All actors in Mozambique were determined to keep the peace process intact. The civilian support schemes were a key feature of Mozambique's demobilization and integration programme, which will be briefly discussed in this chapter. However, as the focus of this book is on military integration, this chapter's sections that address Mozambique will look primarily at the processes and formation of the new integrated Mozambican military, as well as the wider context of civilian reintegration of former combatants, the impact of the election results and broader reconstruction issues for the country as a whole.

Moving towards negotiations in Angola

From almost the moment that the Bicesse process broke down following Savimbi's failure to accept the election results, the international community put as much diplomatic pressure as it could to compel both sides to go back to the negotiating table and complete the peace processes laid down in the Bicesse Treaty. For the first few months, both UNITA and the MPLA were more focused on prosecuting the renewed conflict and calls for peace negotiations did not result in any concrete actions. Additionally, the international community was deeply concerned for the UNAVEM II peacekeeping mission that was still on the ground in Angola. There were hopes that this pre-existing tool could be leveraged to bring parties back into treaty compliance, but as violence escalated, fears about the ability to maintain this deployment began to divert much of the UN's attention as well. Essentially, the UN became more concerned about the viability and safety of their mission and personnel, which is common to peacekeeping deployments facing unexpected instances of violence.[4] This focus on safety, however, while clearly the first priority of mission command and the UNSC funders, nevertheless meant that UNAVEM II became a much less active player in trying to bring both sides of the Angolan conflict back into treaty compliance.

Structural changes that enabled conflict

The increasingly brutal and widespread violence after the peace process broke down was not expected to last for as long as it did, especially because both superpowers (the US and USSR) had withdrawn their diplomatic and, more importantly, their financial and military support, which was assumed by all observers to be necessary factors in enabling both sides to continue prosecuting violence.[5] In the years immediately prior to the Bicesse negotiations (excluding the mass manoeuvres of primarily South African versus Cuban troops along the southern border of the country that was quite directly a function of Cold War rivalries and in many ways separate from the Angolan domestic contest), these expectations began to be revealed as deeply inaccurate. The first change that was overlooked was that both UNITA and the MPLA had found effective financial resources outside of superpower contacts, namely, Angola's massive rentier resources: diamonds for UNITA and oil for the MPLA. While oil had been a financial lifeline for the MPLA previously,[6] UNITA mining and selling significant quantities of diamonds was not only relatively new for this stage in the conflict but also made a significant difference in their ability to operate without substantial foreign support and continue the conflict despite international pressures.[7]

The second change that quickly became apparent from this post-Bicesse conflict was that ideology had in many ways mostly disappeared from both the propaganda, statements and publicized goals of both sides.[8] Instead, both the MPLA and UNITA were now explicitly fighting for control of the political centre of power. The structure of this central power was no longer contested; both sides accepted that Angola would be a multi-party democracy with elections. UNITA no longer was calling for democracy or freedom from communist oppression. The MPLA was no longer calling itself communist since the withdrawal and collapse of the USSR removed both the ideological appeal and financial incentive to conform to Soviet standards. The conflict from 1993 onward suddenly no longer looked like the Cold War proxy war many outsiders had assumed it was. This revealed that Angola's conflict was, and had likely always been, an internal contest for political power: UNITA and the MPLA had taken advantage of outside support through the externally imposed Cold War lens to further their own goals.[9] At this point, international actors began to understand that getting parties to the negotiating table again was likely to be much more difficult than previously thought, as the financial levers of superpower support were gone, and neither UNITA nor the MPLA needed outside legitimacy or support to continue the fight. Essentially, outsiders were no longer as relevant, and therefore their ability to coerce, persuade or incentivize either side to negotiate dropped significantly.

Attempted talks in Addis Ababa

Despite this decreased level of involvement, UNAVEM II's continued presence in Angola gave the international community an influence on the ground, if only a slight one, and the head of the mission Margaret Anstee was determined to save her now failing peacekeeping mission (as of November 1993) from total collapse.[10]

She began by convincing both sides to agree to renewed negotiations through a planned summit in Addis Ababa, Ethiopia, a previously unused location for Angola-related talks. At this stage, it was easier to convince the MPLA to attend for two key reasons. First, since they were on the back foot militarily, negotiations would create a break in the conflict and therefore some breathing space. Second, as the internationally recognized electoral victors, they now held what they saw as the international moral high ground – a resource they were unwilling to squander given both their recent history of being seen as anti-West and also potentially because Western countries remained the largest and best oil customers. UNITA, on the other hand, with its control over Angolan territory increasing and an increasingly unambiguous claim that the Bicesse process was fundamentally unfair and had been implemented in a biased way, felt little desire to engage with either the MPLA or international community. While this effort to get the summit to happen was mainly the work of Anstee, UNITA agreed to participate less from her persuasion than from the efforts of a long-time Savimbi ally, the outgoing president of Cote d'Ivoire, Felix Houphouet-Boigny.[11]

The talks began in January 1993, with a stated focus on 'four main issues: a) the establishment of a ceasefire; b) the implementation of the Bicesse peace accords; c) the definition of the UN's role regarding the ceasefire accords and the second round of presidential elections; and d) the release of prisoners'.[12] Although both sides had agreed to participate in the Addis talks, neither agreed to send their top leaders. The meetings were attended mainly by high-level military officers and politicians from each side instead of people who were actually able to make significant decisions or move discussions forward.[13] The talks quickly broke down and a break was called, and the talks never resumed. It was at this point that the international community began to fully understand that neither side was planning to pay more than lip service to continued international efforts towards peace and that something more drastic than calling for the peace process to resume was likely in order.

Changing people and places

This breakdown in talks sponsored by UNAVEM III resulted in the mission becoming defunct in theory as well as in practice (despite a three-month extension from the UNSC)[14] and changes were quickly made in the UN to change which senior representatives were on the ground in order to move towards a more robust peace negotiations process. Most notably, this meant the replacement of Margaret Anstee with Alioune Blondin-Beye; replacing an English-speaking woman with a French-speaking man was seen by some as making it more likely for Savimbi to take the UN seriously.[15] While this was discussed in some of the literature and hinted at in UN documents, it is hard to tell whether this made any appreciable difference beyond UN documents pertaining to Angola now switching primarily from using English to French.[16] The main similarity between the two lead UN negotiators was that they were both used to and prepared to work within the UN bureaucracy, rather than practically oriented like ONUMOZ's Ajello.[17] This meant that they were both concerned with ensuring UN headquarters in New York were kept constantly apprised of developments in Angola and adhered quite strictly to the mandates, with all the restrictions, that they were given. This perhaps meant that aside from using personal appeals, both Anstee and Blondin-Beye operated as relatively interchangeable UN bureaucrats, even though this had already been shown to be less effective in Angola. While the new diplomatic effort still focused on building on the treaty and implementation that had been started with the Bicesse process, diplomats from the UN and other relevant countries (South Africa's foreign ministry got quite involved in negotiations about negotiations at this stage) began to look at drafting an addendum to the Bicesse Treaty, which eventually became the Lusaka Treaty.

Lusaka, Zambia was chosen as the city for another round of negotiations. Its key selling point was its proximity to Angola, which in the minds of the international diplomats was seen as a way of encouraging participation from MPLA and UNITA leaders who did not want to travel long distances from the frontlines.[18] This proximity seems to have encouraged both sides to agree to participate in talks, though location was likely the least relevant reason for negotiations to have resumed at this stage. According to one UN report from the time, however, the location was deemed still too far from the conflict. This may have delayed the talks simply due to diplomats and negotiators wanting to spend more time in peaceful surroundings.[19] Additionally, Zambia had not played much of a role in the conflict so far on either side and so was seen as more neutral than other neighbours: the DRC, Namibia or even South Africa. Zambia's government was not particularly involved in the discussions but served as an effective host. The location itself was not hugely significant though, indeed, there were more important political and military factors for why both sides were willing to participate in negotiations at this point.

Political and military incentives to negotiate

There were both political and military incentives to participate in the Lusaka talks for the MPLA and UNITA. First, there was a significant change in international attitudes towards UNITA. In a previously unprecedented move, the international community imposed sanctions on UNITA, after the group refused to accept the election results.[20] While this did not necessarily affect UNITA's ability to use diamonds to fuel their conflict (though that would change later on, see Chapter 5), these sanctions were an important symbolic blow as for the first time UNITA's key superpower ally, the United States, was publicly against them.[21] This damaged UNITA's international political legitimacy quite significantly,[22] though it does not seem to have made a substantive impact on UNITA's internal messaging within either the group or amongst its Angolan constituents. Still, the pressure from the loss of international political prestige from the imposition of UNSC sanctions was enough to bring UNITA to the negotiating table in Lusaka and at least pretend to act in good faith and calm its military actions while talks continued.[23]

These UN sanctions placed the MPLA on the same side of the conflict as the United States for the first time. This had been an MPLA goal since the late 1980s, both in order to be part of US-led international institutions without the stigma of US disapproval, and for the potential foreign aid that could come with no longer being a political pariah.[24] After ideological messaging had been removed from party slogans and propaganda, the MPLA's key internal messaging began to exclusively focus on their ability to best provide for the people of Angola, which was given credence by their new access to trade internationally and to acquire foreign aid.[25]

On the military side, UNITA's initial momentum and success meant that the group now had to maintain significantly more territory than they had previously, which was a test for their resources and capabilities. While the group was certainly better disciplined and generally more loyal than the MPLA,[26] it was still difficult to operate and control areas that for the past few decades had been firmly in MPLA hands.[27] UNITA at this point in early 1994 saw participation in the Lusaka talks as a practical way to gain time to consolidate their holdings on the ground, especially because they felt that gaining further territorial control gave them more leverage at the negotiating table. They wanted to make political use of this land while they still controlled it.

The MPLA, while immediately on the back foot militarily in late 1993,[28] were in the process of regrouping, mainly by hiring foreign mercenaries using their substantial oil revenues that were no longer prohibited from being traded in standard international markets, unlike UNITA's diamonds which had a more convoluted economic transfer process.[29] MPLA troops had demobilized more than the government wanted during the Bicesse DDR process,[30] and so reforming the MPLA army took time, and their loyalty was sometimes weaker. Participating in the Lusaka process gave the MPLA time to reform and strengthen its army through massive arms deals,[31] raise money for improved weapons and foreign mercenaries and essentially prepare for a 'take-it-all-back' offensive.[32] The MPLA in particular had reason to delay in negotiations as long as possible, as it gave them more time to arrange a military counterstrike,[33] whereas UNITA had some pressure on it negotiating quickly, it still had quite a strong feeling of military success (as evidenced by the territory so quickly acquired) and so also did not see the talks as needing to progress with much urgency.

Politically and militarily, both sides had incentives to cooperate in the Lusaka process, but not because either side had exhausted their military options. In fact, both sides likely saw participation in negotiations as a way of furthering their military conquest for total power. This is exactly what mediation theorists and expert mediation practitioners do not recommend when pursuing negotiations. According to Dudouet (2010) and Jett (1999), both of whom have written extensively on the topic of what makes for good mediation and negotiating, in Jett's case with direct Angolan involvement as a senior US diplomat, the conditions for the Lusaka process were not promising from the start. Dudouet and Jett argue that for a negotiation to succeed, the combatant actors must fulfil three criteria: desire to achieve a political rather than military settlement, the ability to enforce the treaty provisions amongst their own constituents and political legitimacy to maintain support during the transition period. While both the MPLA and UNITA fill the latter two categories, the even more basic stipulation of wanting to find a political, as opposed to a military, settlement rings false in the circumstances illustrated earlier.[34] While the diplomats involved in Lusaka tried hard to learn lessons from the Bicesse negotiations and implementation, their cooperation amongst themselves and improvement at setting more realistic timelines and expectations[35] was fundamentally hindered by the parties' refusal to seriously cooperate.

Thus, it becomes clear from the combined analysis of these sources that the motives of both groups essentially doomed the talks from the start as both sides saw the diplomatic moves merely as facades and boosts to military ones.[36] To give a sense of the delicate military balance that existed in early 1994 during the Lusaka negotiations, a private meeting between Blondin-Beye and newly elected South African President Nelson Mandela suggested that the UN estimated that 'UNITA controls about 60% of the terrain and the government controls about 80% of the population'.[37] These, then, were the convoluted and pre-emptively fatal conditions of the Lusaka talks.

The Lusaka negotiations

Learning from Bicesse

When the negotiations in Lusaka began in November 1993, the international actors were generally focused on building on and learning from the Bicesse Treaty.[38] It was agreed amongst all parties that the Bicesse Treaty was not useless; it merely needed to be amended and added to in order to fully achieve lasting peace treaties. This required understanding what lessons needed to be learnt from the failure of the Bicesse process, both in terms of specific provisions and implementation requirements. The three main lessons that set the stage for the negotiations themselves were the importance of finishing security issues before elections, the need for a capable UN peacekeeping mission, and the impact of conditions in assembly camps on combatant compliance.

The first lesson learned by those in Lusaka about the problems of implementing the Bicesse agreement is the same lesson that had so clearly been learned by Mozambican negotiators: disarmament, demobilization and reintegration into either a joint military or into civilian life must be completed before elections can be held. This was clearly an issue with the Bicesse process and one that no one wanted repeated.[39]

Another outcome of the Bicesse agreement analysis was a new appreciation for the role of the UN and a deeper appreciation for the need for peacekeeping missions to be larger, better funded and have a stronger mandate in order to be able to not only carry out their assigned functions but also to more broadly keep the peace on track both on the ground and at the leadership level.[40] This was a lesson that was being learned from other UN peacekeeping missions at the time and from the last 1990s onwards was a consistent part of the UN peacekeeping agenda. The problems of UNAVEM II were widely recognized within the UN and, combined with similar problems in other missions, led to significant developments in the thinking and planning around UN peacekeeping going forward, for Angola and beyond.[41]

The third lesson was the importance of the conditions for combatants in assembly areas.[42] This has been discussed in previous chapters, the conditions in assembly areas were often deemed deeply inadequate by combatants due to lack of sufficient housing and food. This had been a problem on the UNITA side as it had been the main reason given by UNITA leadership for not encouraging their soldiers to participate in the DDR process. On the MPLA side, it was easier to get soldiers to register. It was quite hard to convince them to stay in these inhospitable camps leading to a massive outflow of desertions which made it difficult for the MPLA to maintain its fighting ability and therefore the sense of security going forward, and created potential problems for peacekeepers who now had to potentially face rogue fighters around the country.

The intangible elements

The importance of intangible and interpersonal elements of negotiations remains a key element of this book, because they help explain the dynamics behind the treaty terms, how they were understood by participants and thus help reconstruct the full environment in which these issues were negotiated and implemented. Despite anecdotes being mostly ignored in wider literature, they provide useful insight into the progress and tenor of the negotiations. First, as with the previous negotiations in Portugal, translators were a key part of the negotiations due to the different languages spoken by the participants. While the primary language of the Angolans was still Portuguese, the main UN mediator spoke in French and others involved spoke English, once again introducing opportunities for misunderstanding based on linguistic differences.[43]

Another personal element perhaps of note is that General Ben-Ben, now one of the senior-most political and military leaders in UNITA, who was the head of the Lusaka negotiations delegation, was in fact the nephew of Savimbi.[44] This highlights that Savimbi thought of the negotiations as important enough to send a relative, but not important enough for him to become personally involved, which became an issue during the negotiations themselves. UNITA was increasingly an organization centred around Savimbi as a person, rather than an ideology or broader political platform, making it both more robust in terms of it being centralized around him and requiring his personal approval for any peace to go forward, but perhaps also weakening the institutional resilience of the organization.

At the initial meeting in Lusaka, American diplomat Paul Hare noted that there were visible differences in skin tone between the two delegations, pointing to the continued salience of perceived ethnic differences between the two groups.[45] It is interesting to note that identity differences along specifically Angolan lines: the debate between assimilation with former Portuguese colonists versus drawing on indigenous Angolan languages and cultures remained a relevant dividing idea between the two groups.[46] Despite the ongoing fighting and the collapse of the Bicesse process, however, when the two Angolan delegations met in Lusaka, they greeted each other warmly, without apparent animosity, thus suggesting identity differences were not the entire root of the conflict nor necessarily insurmountable to cooperation.[47]

One final issue that is worth raising and bearing in mind throughout the subsequent discussion of the specifics of the treaty is that the negotiation at every stage, on every issue, individually and collectively, suffered from significant and impactful delays.[48] There were delays in both sides determining which representatives to send to the talks, delays in one or both sides appearing at negotiations, delays in coming up with terms and counterarguments, last-minute delays about confirming agreed-on provisions before moving to the next section, delays about who within each side was allowed to make final decisions and more.[49] The negotiations began on 15 November 1993 but the final treaty was not signed until November 1994.[50] Given that this treaty was meant to be an addendum to the Bicesse Accords in order to continue an already begun peace process and therefore should have been a relatively quick process, many outsider actors felt that both UNITA and the MPLA were purposely delaying talks unnecessarily in order to further their military goals.[51] A noteworthy example of this was the capture by the MPLA of UNITA's second-most important city, Huambo, just a few months before the treaty was initially signed in 1994. This was the MPLA's first major success and increased the perception amongst some MPLA generals that a military victory was the only way forward in defeating Savimbi and UNITA.[52] This action was condemned by the international community as inflaming tensions that would inhibit the confirmation of the new treaty, and yet the city remained under MPLA control.[53] This contributed to a tense and distrustful atmosphere throughout the entire negotiations process and beyond, an intangible factor that is worth remembering when analysing how the treaty itself developed and how implementation subsequently unfolded.

The Lusaka Treaty

From the beginning of the negotiations there were more immediate priorities that needed to be resolved through the Lusaka process even as the lessons learned from Bicesse were becoming clear to mediators. At this stage, the goal was to add on to the Bicesse Treaty by clarifying some of the vague areas, not rewrite the treaty entirely.[54] Therefore, while some ideas about what could be changed if the negotiations were to start from scratch were beginning to be floated, the central focus was on getting parties back into a peace process as quickly as possible.[55] Therefore, the priority issues were, in order: determining an acceptable status and settlement for Savimbi, a timetable and new composition arrangement for the integrated military, a mandate for a new UN peacekeeping mission and how to divide ministerial power in a government of national unity (to be called the GURN). These issues were considered by all sides to be the main gaps that the Bicesse Treaty had failed to address.

The status of Savimbi

Of all the issues to be resolved, clearly the question of how to satisfy Savimbi was the largest.[56] According to the senior American diplomat involved at the time, 'I believe emphatically that if UNITA had accepted the result of the election in good faith as they had promised, the Bicesse agreement would have survived',[57] clearly showing the shift in US thinking from backing UNITA to believing it was the main barrier to peace. Such a shift was also signalled by the UNSC resolution imposing sanctions on UNITA that the US allowed to pass.[58]

Prior to the Lusaka negotiations both sides accepted that the Bicesse process calling for a presidential run-off election was the next step, at least in principle.[59] However, it quickly became clear that Savimbi was not pushing for a speedy conclusion of that election. UN documents from October 1993 reporting on a classified meeting between Blondin-Beye and the UN Secretary-General state that Savimbi was willing to allow the MPLA to retain the presidency for a few years before the next elections,[60] presumably in order to give Savimbi and UNITA time to either take over the country militarily or, more likely, increase its control enough to guarantee victory in the following elections.

According to that same report, Savimbi's goals at this time were to gain 'special privileges and a special status', seemingly instead of winning the presidency which he had failed to achieve in the elections he disputed.[61] The difficulty lay in determining what this special status could be that would be acceptable to the MPLA and, perhaps more challengingly, to Savimbi.[62] Despite months of negotiations including face-to-face meetings between Savimbi and MPLA President dos Santos, the issue of a special status was not resolved in the eventual Lusaka Treaty.[63] The closest the treaty came to including a privileged status was a stipulation that 'taking into account his position as the President of the largest opposition party, the President of UNITA shall be guaranteed a special status',[64] but that the nature of this status would be clarified after the signing of the treaty through bilateral discussion between the two leaders.[65] Given the amount of influence Savimbi maintained, unspecified sticking points such as this special status increased risks that conflict would resume. The agential aspects of treaty success demand more research and better-qualified metrics to truly unravel the causal links but are broadly evident in this instance.

Integrating UNITA into security institutions

Another central issue was developing a plan for successfully integrating UNITA into the army and police forces. Resolving this successfully would avoid the cantonment area disaster of the previous process and create a unified security institution making it more difficult for either side to have sufficiently staffed armies to continue the conflict. These negotiations were generally handled by the chiefs of staff of both militaries. As they were already familiar with each other and the general steps from the Bicesse process, negotiations tended to progress quickly through more technical issues.[66]

Unlike in the previous negotiations, there were immediate areas of agreement, beyond the need to prioritize military issues over electoral ones.[67] First, both sides agreed that generals should make formal integration overtures to join the army before the new cantonment and processing stages were complete. This would send a signal through the chains of command that the top military leadership was in full compliance with this renewed peace. There was a determination to avoid a repeat of the mistakes of the Bicesse process – the first attempt to create an integrated military involved the top generals on each side making a symbolic integration move only the day before elections in a clearly rushed attempt at fulfilling treaty obligations.[68]

According to UN reports, the two sides easily reached agreements on how to proceed with troop disengagements, demining and communications. Commanders agreed to visit garrisons personally in order to ensure these procedures were properly communicated and implemented.[69] Also, while verification and monitoring protocols were not developed in detail at this stage and instead were left for the creation of a more robust UN peacekeeping mission, the principle of technical agreement was clear in these discussions.[70]

The issue of determining how many generals there would be in the new army was important for reasons of status, balance of power and salary. This was more contentious because it was clear the international community was no longer equally backing both sides of the Angolan process. When UNITA requested forty-nine generals, the MPLA countered with three; the compromise backed by mediators was a mere nine positions for UNITA, providing clear evidence that the international community was no longer egalitarian in their support. Notably, UNITA was allocated the high-ranking chief of staff position,[71] which may have incentivized acceptance of the nine-general stipulation.

UNITA was also forced to accept the provision that its troops be required to enter cantonment areas to undergo disarmament. Once there, troops would either be slated for full demobilization and civilian reintegration or integrated into the new national army.[72] In contrast, MPLA troops would not have to go through this process; they could either retain their positions in the military and transition over to the integrated forces without a period of cantonment and disarmament or choose to utilize existing discharge procedures to leave military life.[73] This was one of the most significant changes between the Bicesse and Lusaka treaties, as it marked the first instance of a clear preference by mediators for confirming the MPLA as the government and military of Angola, where international observers treated UNITA not as a legitimate alternative government and military but as rebel forces.

The MPLA's forces were explicitly considered the national army, into which UNITA would integrate, rather than requiring both sides to disarm and demobilize and then create a new institution equally together, as had been the stipulation under the Bicesse Treaty. This likely changed as a result of the international perception of UNITA as the bad actor due to their refusal to accept the Bicesse election results and the decision to back out of the nascent combined military. The Lusaka Treaty was directly built on continuing the Bicesse process; the implicit assumption was that the new treaty provisions were aimed at bringing UNITA back into compliance, rather than treating both sides as equally likely to renew conflict and disregard the treaty.

The final significant change in the Lusaka Treaty was a change in timelines for these agreed-upon security procedures to take place. This applied both to the disarmament and demobilization processes as well as the integration and training into the new joint military. Unlike the Bicesse Accords which stipulated all of this was to be completed in two months,[74] the Lusaka Treaty called for a 455-day process, to be verified by the UN.[75] This was quite a substantial improvement and showed how clearly the lesson had been learnt about the need for devoting sufficient time to security provisions before elections could take place.[76] Still, unlike the Mozambican agreement, the Lusaka Treaty still did not include specific provisions for delaying elections if there were delays in the military processes, nor did it include the stipulation that the military processes must be complete before elections. While that seems to have been the intent from memoirs of negotiators involved,[77] that particular provision was not explicitly included in the text of the treaty. So, while more time was allotted to the process, there still was not a mechanism to adjust the chronology once the process began.

A new UN peacekeeping mandate

The key to making sure all these pieces were implemented was the creation of a mandate for a new UN peacekeeping mission that was acceptable to the parties in Angola as well as the international community.[78] There was general agreement on the need for a more robust mission, sorting out specifics was of course less straightforward, particularly around how much authority the mission would have over carrying out the peace process.

One priority for the MPLA was retaining their sovereign status as the Government of Angola, regardless of the contested election results.[79] As discussed, the MPLA was quite conscious of their status as an internationally recognized government, especially with their fledgling ties to the United States and within international institutions like the United Nations, and wanted to make sure that a new peacekeeping mission would neither jeopardize MPLA actions within Angola nor their international standing. The clearest manifestation of these concerns is in the myriad letters from the Angolan office at the UN headquarters requesting information and influence over which countries would contribute troops to the new peacekeeping mission,[80] likely in order to ensure that none were obviously pro-UNITA. Specifically, these letters consistently requested that MPLA allies like Brazil were included in large numbers in peacekeeping missions, as opposed to other countries that the MPLA either expressed scepticism about by virtue of unfamiliarity, or hinted at UNITA partisanship. Whether UNITA was less concerned with the composition of UN troops or did not have an easy way of relaying their concerns, given their lack of institutional access to the UN's peacekeeping headquarters, is unclear.

One issue both Angolan parties were equally interested in was to what extent the new UN peacekeeping mission would in fact not only oversee and monitor the new peace process but implement and enforce it. While the mediators in Lusaka were clear about the need for the UN to have a stronger hand in keeping the peace process on track the second time around,[81] both UNITA and the MPLA were more ambivalent about allowing the UN so much sway, which is likely one reason why delays over this particular aspect of negotiations began. Additionally, the UNSC, further away from on-the-ground developments, was hesitant about sending in and funding so many additional peacekeepers given how badly the first attempt in Angola had gone.[82] Again, this was a consistent challenge for peacekeeping missions around the world, particularly as the number of missions increased as the 1990s progressed. Nearly every mission deployed by the UN has been considered insufficient in size, most commonly due to lack of funding and concerns over personnel safety.[83]

Still, despite all of these misgivings, the newly created UNAVEM III was eventually authorized with 7,000 troops (as opposed to UNAVEM II's 1,200) and a mandate to not just observe and monitor steps like disarmament[84] but to chair the joint military committee charged with implementing the security processes within the broader peace agreement.[85] While some of the mediators were still not sure whether this would be a sufficiently large mission, this was a clear improvement over UNAVEM II that the international community hoped would suffice.[86]

The other change to the Lusaka Treaty as compared to the Bicesse Accords was the composition of the national government beyond the presidential and executive levels. Given how much territory had changed hands since the failed Bicesse elections and the relative absence of provincial-level provisions in the Bicesse Treaty, this was seen as a good opportunity to address unity politics at the provincial level as well.[87] The final treaty contained over four pages of lists of various provincial, municipal and administrative posts designated for UNITA members, a clear change from the Bicesse Treaty.[88] Some of these provisions were implemented, but as with much else with this treaty, the process was not completed.

Notable changes and omissions

The fundamental challenge for the Lusaka Treaty was its foundation on the Bicesse Accords, perhaps most pointedly revealed in a quote from Herman Cohen, a senior American diplomat who was instrumental in both the Bicesse and Lusaka processes. He wrote in his memoirs about the Lusaka process and his analysis in hindsight is damning: 'If we could do it all over again, a more plausible scenario would have been a coalition government of national unity, cohabitation and governance for three to five years, military transition to one national army over to three years, liberalisation of political life and elections after five years.'[89] Not a single one of these ideas was included in any of the Angolan treaties.

Once the Lusaka treaty had been drafted, there were clear ways in which it had built on the Bicesse Accords and made progress in delineating areas whose previous ambiguity had caused significant problems for implementation. It is worth noting, however, which key issue that has not yet been discussed was omitted; namely, diamonds. This shows the extent to which the Lusaka Treaty was narrowly focused on resolving the perceived gaps in the Bicesse Treaty, rather than making changes to grapple with the shifting dimensions of the conflict. Savimbi publicly claimed to control two-thirds of the diamond production in Angola, amounting to $400 million per year[90] even given the illegal channels and methods that often had to be used given UNITA's non-governmental status. Despite this diamond trade being public knowledge, as was the evidence of how effectively UNITA could mine, sell and then use these resources to prosecute violence, no mention of diamonds was included in the treaty, nor is this issue mentioned in contemporary accounts of negotiations. This omission is a key component of the treaty that has been relatively overlooked in both diplomatic memoirs and academic articles.

In terms of the big picture, aside from additional specifications and details added into the Lusaka Treaty as compared to the Bicesse Accords, there is one quite significant change that begins to emerge as all these pieces are analysed together: a radical shift in the international perception of UNITA and by extension, the entire Angolan civil war. In the Bicesse Accords, although the MPLA was at the time the Government of Angola, Cold War ideologies and allegiances meant that both sides were considered relatively equal in terms of international legitimacy. The treaty reflected that perception in that both sides were essentially treated equally in terms of their required participation in disarmament, cantonment, demobilization and military integration processes, their equal status in contesting the elections, their equal requirement to give up external support and so on. As much as the Lusaka Treaty was officially a mere continuation of the Bicesse process, the provisions, language and attitude indicated through memoirs and UN reports at the time reveal quite a different atmosphere. UNITA was no longer treated as an equally legitimate potential government actor: they were required to disarm and go into cantonment areas whereas the MPLA is not; UNITA alone was required to unilaterally withdraw from its newly acquired territory; UNITA politicians were not given any extra-governmental positions and were instead enjoined to merely take up their Bicesse-accorded seats; the integrated military was not recreated but rather it was assumed that what was the officially established joint forces, the FAA, which by default became purely MPLA when UNITA pulled out, will become again the joint forces once UNITA rejoins the institution.

The entire tenor of the Lusaka Treaty is therefore focused on UNITA coming back into compliance with the Bicesse Accords, with the main changes to the treaty focused on increasing enforcement measures to ensure that result, including longer timelines and a more robust UN mission. Still, in this context, those two improvements begin to seem less like incentives and more like enforcement mechanisms targeted particularly at UNITA rather than at both sides equally. The UN resolutions passed around this issue, including the sanctions passed against UNITA, confirm this impression that UNITA was treated specifically as a bad actor; that 'bad actor' status also thereby confirmed the international legitimacy of the MPLA as the Angolan government, regardless of UNITA's stance on the election results. The Clinton administration's shift regarding UNITA has been clearly analysed by Wright, who demonstrates how the United States therefore went from being a UNITA ally to considering UNITA as a destabilizing actor.[91] This book goes further to argue that the shift in US attitude was the main driver for the distinctly different tone that UN documents (including the imposition of sanctions and the wording of peacekeeping mandates) took regarding UNITA from 1994 onwards.

While this book is not interested in determining whether this shift in perception and treatment of UNITA was factually accurate or morally correct, it is worth noting that this change was likely visible to all involved in negotiations. This likely had an impact on UNITA's willingness to participate in the Lusaka negotiations, how the treaty was implemented and why UNITA again failed to live up to its commitments. This confirms a theme of this book that perceptions of equality in treatment, compliance and timelines are an important reassurance mechanism in successfully implementing treaties, a principle which was very much ignored in the Lusaka Treaty. Blaming UNITA for the breakdown of the Bicesse process focused narrowly on the events around the election, which UNITA felt ignored its wider claims about MPLA interference in the campaigning and voting procedures themselves. The international negotiators' emphasis therefore on needing to bring UNITA specifically, rather than both sides equally, back into treaty compliance, was seen by UNITA as being fundamentally one-sided and therefore both unfair and untrustworthy. Given the existential nature of disarmament and demobilization, including of Savimbi's personal guard, it is unsurprising in this context that UNITA was such an uncooperative actor in the Lusaka negotiations.

Implementing the Lusaka Treaty

Given the problematic experience of the Bicesse process, the mediators were keenly aware that negotiating a new treaty was one thing, but implementing it was a much larger and more important challenge. Unfortunately, as has been described in earlier sections, there were pre-existing reasons that meant neither the MPLA nor UNITA were entirely invested in seeking peace at this point in the conflict. This section will investigate the security-specific implementation of the relevant provisions of the Lusaka Treaty. Many of these steps are the same as were undertaken in the Bicesse implementation process and so were either repeated entirely (assembly areas, disarmament, civilian demobilization), or proceeded from the point at which they had failed in the prior process (integration into the military and the new UN mandate).

The most significant issue was the significant continuing ambiguity about the linchpin of the whole situation – the future status of Savimbi. This problem in particular became publicly clear when Savimbi refused to attend the Lusaka Treaty signing ceremony on 20 November 1994. He cited security concerns, but this was a symbolic problem that already signalled wider concerns and uncertainties about the ability of this treaty to stop the conflict. While his refusal to participate in person did not derail the signing ceremony, it did show the importance of the international community in compelling both parties to commit to the deal, thus once again creating a situation in which the international community seemed more invested in this peace process than either Angolan party.[92]

On the positive side, the Lusaka Treaty did create a peace process that calmed conditions in the country from the brutality of 1993–4, but only relatively. As with the Bicesse Accords and the Mozambican Rome Agreement, the first step in the renewed peace process was a bilateral ceasefire with the same process as had worked in Bicesse but with a more robust UN mandate to verify the ceasefire; more focus in the treaty and from the international community on ensuring compliance, especially from UNITA; and a slightly longer timetable for all the steps of the ceasefire to be implemented.

According to UN primary documents, the ceasefire generally held throughout 1994 and early 1995, with only minor incidents.[93] This is more likely due to the fact that a temporary halt in fighting was in both sides' strategic interests than any good-faith interest in upholding the treaty terms. For UNITA, it enabled the consolidation of their territorial gains, estimated in June 1994 to consist of 60 per cent of Angola's land.[94] For the MPLA, this pause allowed for the consolidation of their troops and military capabilities, especially as they were not required to go to cantonment areas, disarm and demobilize. Thus, a simple ceasefire was not in fact a signal of either side fully committing to the peace process, and it is understandable why both sides complied relatively easily in the absence of good-faith desire to achieve peace. This immediate compliance also showed clearly that despite questions about UNITA's internal coherence and loyalty to Savimbi and the MPLA's now well-known problems with desertion, the leadership of both groups remained sufficiently in control to enact nation wide ceasefires once they agreed to do so. Although an issue with many civil wars, splintering was not a particular problem for either of Angola's main combatant actors at this stage.[95]

Assembly areas

Although the ceasefire held until war officially resumed in 1998 (after much of 1997 saw small-scale 'banditry'), there were immediate problems with the implementation of the new security provisions of the Lusaka Treaty. Although the conditions at the assembly areas had been a noticeable problem throughout the Bicesse process and were one of the main complaints both sides had about UNAVEM II's efficacy, the conditions in the cantonment areas under the Lusaka process were not a significant improvement, according to the UNITA troops registered there.[96] The Lusaka Treaty specified that the assembly areas would be in conveniently accessible areas (to forestall the problems of UNITA choosing strategic and inaccessible areas) that would be monitored and verified by the UN mission (again to avoid the problems of the Bicesse Process).[97] However, despite conditions in the camps being a recognized failure, there was no mention of conditions, or how to improve them, in the Lusaka Treaty itself. Therefore, just like in the Bicesse process and in the cantonment process in Mozambique, the living conditions in the camps were notably poor. This raised the ire of UNITA combatants who were already reluctant to take part in this one-sided disarmament and demobilization-through-military-integration process and now felt further alienated by what they saw as unfairly poor camp conditions. There were complaints about quartered combatants being required to participate in the construction of the camps[98] which was seen as demeaning by the combatants. There was insufficient food, and what there was was of poor quality. A lack of sufficient housing repeated the problems from the Bicesse assembly areas that had not taken into account Angola's rainy season when requisitioning tents to be sent along with UNAVEM II.[99] Camps also struggled with inadequate access to fresh water.[100] These logistical problems have plagued other peacekeeping missions as well.[101]

Throughout the quartering process, from its start following UNAVEM III's delayed deployment (see later section) in mid-1995 until the formal resumption of hostilities in 1998, UNITA was constantly behind the timetable for fighters reporting to assembly areas to undergo the Lusaka disarmament process, even after a longer (revised) timetable was enacted.[102] This consistent delay was the primary reason that the MPLA and international community continued to doubt UNITA's commitment to the peace process. For example, in February 1996, an internal UN report stated that 'only about 16,000 troops had been quartered out of 62,000 troops declared by UNITA'.[103] According to American diplomat Paul Hare, who was involved in this process, by June 1996, the UNITA numbers were still only at 52,000, which did not include any police officers or the highest level of 'presidential guards'.[104] In addition, beyond the numbers, UNAVEM III observers began to notice that many UNITA fighters were quite young or not particularly able,[105] or would register in camps but then disappear, sometimes reappearing with stories of being summoned to leave the camps and then sent back by UNITA while completing military missions in between. These allegations and reports increased perceptions that UNITA was complying with only the minimum of the Lusaka provisions in terms of registering combatants and nothing more substantial.

Disarmament and demobilization

The same held true for the disarmament portion of the Lusaka process, though in this case there were issues on both the UNITA and MPLA sides. In terms of demobilization, in a change from the Bicesse process, the Lusaka Treaty called for all UNITA combatants to register in cantonments, disarm, be integrated into the FAA and then at an unspecified future point, some would be selected for demobilization into civilian society. For UNITA, the issues with registration continued as the combatants who did register in camps often brought weapons that were of markedly low quality, thus raising suspicions of secret/unauthorized weapons caches, another problem the UN began to face with increasing regularity in other conflict areas.[106] This was heightened by the fact that UNITA turned over no heavy weapons or mines.[107] There was no doubt that UNITA retained significant stocks of weapons it was not planning to turn in.

In addition, UNITA was still using diamond revenues (not mentioned in the Lusaka Treaty) to buy weapons from the Republic of Congo and the Democratic Republic of the Congo (the latter in particular a long-term ally) despite the Lusaka Treaty's provisions against the acquisition of weapons and UNAVEM II's mandate calling for neither side to rearm.[108] The MPLA also broke this provision with a purchase of tanks and artillery likely acquired in May 1995 after the treaty was put into effect. Additionally, the government made little effort to disarm the civilian population, many hundreds of thousands of whom (some estimates suggested one million) had acquired small arms during the initial outbreak of post-Bicesse violence.[109] Clearly, disarmament was not a serious commitment by either side.[110]

There were two key problems with civilian demobilization under the Lusaka process: coordination and long-term execution. Once soldiers decided to opt for civilian demobilization,[111] there were no fewer than six international and governmental agencies who provided mandatory identity information and/ or benefits to each demobilized combatant and their dependents, thus creating obvious pathways for confusion on the part of aid providers as well as combatants, along with the inevitable delays and mix-ups. This quote from a think tank report written on Angola's various DDR process from 1991 onwards gives a useful listing of the complexity of the civilian demobilization coordination problem: 'Upon leaving the camps[,] soldiers were issued with travel cards (by the International Organisation for Migration), demobilisation cards ([by the] FAA), benefit cards ([by the] Unit for the Coordination of Humanitarian Affairs), subsidies ([by] IRSEM), reintegration kits ([by] IOM), a "Portuguese kit" supplied by the Government of Portugal, [and] a World Food Program food ration.'[112] Unsurprisingly, this was not a smooth operation; while fewer than the declared 62,000 troops reported to assembly areas, only about 40,000 received any of this assistance in 1996 and 1997, and by 1998 when the war resumed, only 60 per cent of those soldiers had received the second payment and only 25 per cent the final payment.[113] Civilian demobilization, to most UNITA members who went through the process, seemed quite clearly to be more along the lines of 'much ado about nothing' than actual resettlement assistance or good-faith efforts from either the international community or the MPLA government. This increased perceptions amongst soldiers that peace via this process was not likely to lead to an immediate improvement in their lot, therefore increasing pressure up their chains of command to negotiate for, or if necessary fight for, a better deal.

FAA integration

While the integration of UNITA fighters into the FAA as agreed in the Bicesse Accords was one of the top priorities of the Lusaka negotiations and the main focus of the eventual treaty,[114] this renewed attention did not make much difference in the implementation's success. Continuing the trend from negotiations and cantonment, there were massive delays in the designation of UNITA soldiers for the FAA and the attendance of UNITA combatants in training camps throughout the years of official Lusaka Treaty peace.[115] After all, perhaps even more than cantonment, symbolic disarmament and demobilization, actually joining forces with the MPLA in a unified structure controlled by the MPLA-led government was a true step towards UNITA giving up its ability to unilaterally re-engage in hostilities. As delays began, progressed and further mounted throughout 1995–7 it became increasingly clear that UNITA was not particularly willing to make more than token attempts to integrate into the FAA.

The one contrast point to this trend was the attendance of UNITA generals alongside MPLA generals in an official symbolic rejoining of the FAA in December 1996;[116] both sides abided by the agreed-upon meeting points and arrived at the appointed time with respect to the joint verification and military issues committee chaired by the UN to deal with implementing the security aspects of the treaty.[117] In addition, dos Santos and Savimbi met personally under UN auspices multiple times after the signing of the treaty,[118] ostensibly to ensure that any implementation issues were given appropriate attention and enforcement from the top, and of course also in order for both sides (and the international donors) to see them working together for peace. However, relatively little came from these meetings beyond public statements and the implementation of the security provisions of the treaty continued to drag on.

These delays were particularly clear when looking at the assembly areas, demobilization and integration of lower levels of UNITA into the FAA. Despite an extension to the timetable in late 1996, UNITA did not live up to the majority of its commitments for FAA integration as laid out in the Lusaka Treaty. More UNITA fighters than expected opted for civilian demobilization over FAA integration. While on the surface this looks similar to the issue encountered with Mozambique's integrated military (discussed later in this chapter), it was perceived by many in Angola at the time as a way for UNITA to keep its soldiers out of the integrated military structures and available as 'civilians' to be called upon in a future armed conflict. Compounding this distrust was the fact that many UNITA fighters appearing for registration in assembly areas were young with little training, too old for FAA service or otherwise impaired. Questions began to arise about where UNITA's best fighters were, and why they were not participating in the cantonment process.[119] Therefore, the peace generation mechanisms of demobilization looked to be in serious jeopardy, especially when combined with the increasingly obvious retention of UNITA's key military equipment and weaponry.[120] According to a UN report from September 1996, UNITA was at that time claiming that fewer than 3,000 of its troops wanted to join the FAA when UNITA's contribution had been initially envisioned as 26,300.[121]

Even once these troops had been designated for the FAA, however, there remained the problem of housing, training and fully integrating both sides, which likewise ran into problems. The existing FAA fighters were meant to stay in barracks throughout this process, but soldiers soon complained that the promised housing was actually poorly suited tents rather than the barracks that had been expected.[122] Given that the MPLA had previously had issues with desertions, this was an issue that could potentially escalate for the government and likewise increased pressure for the existing FAA to do more than 'wait-and-see' whether UNITA would cooperate. Therefore, due mainly but not exclusively to UNITA delays and refusal to commit, the integration into the FAA barely occurred beyond the symbolic level at the top of the hierarchy before the tenuous peace entirely broke down.

UNAVEM III

As has been previously discussed, international mediators considered a mandate for a new UN mission to be essential in preventing the same mistakes that dogged the Bicesse process implementation; they successfully convinced the rest of the international community of that fact. However, as with every peacekeeping mission discussed in this book, the newly created UNAVEM III was immediately beset with logistical issues that delayed its deployment by nearly six months, only finally deploying in Angola in mid-1995, despite the treaty having been in force since November 1994. Thus, there was a delay in actually beginning the assembling, disarmament and demobilization process, as with the UN mission firmly in control of these operations as opposed to merely observing them, there was no alternative to waiting for the peacekeepers to deploy.[123]

Furthermore, even once deployment began, there were still political problems preventing UNAVEM III from fully carrying out its mandate. In order to ensure successful implementation, various committees had been created with UNAVEM as the chair in order to oversee and discuss both political and military implementation issues that might arise during the process. The political committee, however, was hampered by the fact that while dos Santos participated as requested, Savimbi generally declined to attend the joint meetings or even sometimes to meet with UNAVEM III personnel.[124] This exacerbated the problems with lack of UNITA participation seen across the assembly areas; Savimbi's behaviour made it clear that any claims of internal UNITA issues that prevented clear communication, leading to issues on the ground, were unfounded. Perhaps it was the case that UNITA fighters themselves did not want to cooperate, but Savimbi's lack of participation in the process suggested this was a problem with UNITA not just from Savimbi, but further down the ranks of leadership too, not an issue of his inability to enforce compliance internally.

Aside from the military and political issues already mentioned, there were also severe logistical issues. Although the assembly areas had been mandated in the treaty to be in accessible areas, Angola was still one of the most heavily mined countries in the world, particularly on key roads, and the peacekeepers had issues getting sufficient helicopters to enable access to the assembly areas.[125] In addition, once in place, few peacekeepers spoke Portuguese and certainly none spoke the relevant indigenous languages, so communication with the demobilized soldiers remained a consistent problem.[126] Furthermore, although with 7,000 peacekeepers UNAVEM III[127] was significantly larger than UNAVEM II's maximum of 250 'military observers',[128] it was still insufficient for a country of Angola's size.

All of these factors combined meant that UNAVEM III's mandate to conclude the implementation of the Lusaka Treaty by February 1997, two and a half years after the signing of the treaty, was unrealistic from the start.[129] Unsurprisingly, the mandate had to be extended, but the international community was wary of allowing UNITA more time because of suspicions (discussed earlier) that UNITA was drawing implementation out on purpose.[130] Therefore, the mandate was only extended three months in order to put pressure – officially – on both parties, but likely mainly on UNITA.[131]

Still, there were some benefits to UNAVEM III's deployment. The ability of the mission to enforce the creation and running of assembly camps, registration, disarmament and demobilization was likely the main reason any of those processes happened at all. It is also likely the main factor that enabled peace to last as long as it did. Second, the UN's direct control of those processes meant that they had the ability to patrol, monitor and report on compliance, thus compiling information useful both at the time and in hindsight for understanding exactly how the opposing sides were or were not complying. As the peace broke down, it was useful to have the UN peacekeeping mission more involved on the ground in order for the UN and other observers to collect accurate information to aid in analysis of what had gone wrong in order to apply those lessons within Angola and beyond. Third, the presence of more active peacekeepers who engaged in patrols and investigated claims of violations gave both sides the feeling that their complaints were being listened to, which increased their trust in the UN and acceptance of UN presence.[132] This suggests that there was a signalling effect in the presence of a more robust UN mission, indicating to the civilians that the peace process was real and trustworthy. On the other hand, the blatant inability of the mission to curtail the escalation of violence in late 1997 and into 1998 likely eroded this trust faster for it having existed in the first place.[133]

The Lusaka negotiations process, the treaty itself and the implementation were an improvement over the Bicesse process mainly in that the UN was given a larger role, more time was allowed for security measures to be executed and the process involved a heightened emphasis on ensuring demobilization and military integration before attempting another round of elections. However, the international community in general and the outside mediators, in particular, failed to understand both the political and economic dimensions of the conflict. They, therefore, left out of the treaty entirely the main leadership challenge (the status of Savimbi) and the main economic drivers (oil and diamonds). While some of the Lusaka Treaty's provisions were successfully implemented, even sustained international attention from 1994 to 1998 was insufficient to keep the peace process on track once the two Angolan parties had regrouped sufficiently from demobilization to resume conflict. The Lusaka Treaty therefore shows not only the failures of the Bicesse and Lusaka processes but also the limits of international influence. Additionally, it shows the pitfalls of trying to fix previous peace processes or relying on previously agreed-on issues as a blueprint for peace going forward: Angola's war in 1994 was not the same as it had been in 1990 and would continue to change.

Implementing peace in Mozambique

In the last chapter, Mozambique's FRELIMO government and RENAMO opposition group successfully reached a peace agreement in Rome in 1992. As they began to implement the treaty, leaders on both sides, as well as the leaders of the UN mission ONUMOZ, kept a close eye on Angola in order to avoid the problems rapidly appearing in the Bicesse process. The last chapter explored how many of these initial steps, especially with regard to security provisions, were more successful in Mozambique than in Angola, though whether elections would be able to be peacefully and successfully held and accepted was still a challenge.[134] Guided by the observations of Angola and the changes already discussed as part of the Rome Agreement regarding demobilization prioritization,[135] elections were successfully held in Mozambique in 1994. Although there were some concerns about RENAMO participating in the process,[136] the election saw widespread participation and no serious problems.[137] Both sides accepted the results and FRELIMO won the presidency and a majority in the new parliament.[138] This section, however, focuses on the creation of the new Mozambican integrated military, the FADM.

Creating the integrated Mozambican military (FADM)

The analysis of Mozambique's DDR programme addressed thus far has focused on disarmament and demobilization, whereas this section will concern itself with the last frontier of reestablishing security: the creation of a new military. The development of the integrated military, the *Forças Armadas de Defesa de Moçambique* (FADM), was seen as a key benchmark by all the parties involved in the Mozambican political process for a number of reasons.[139] First, it had been difficult to negotiate in the treaty, and so success would be seen as validating those efforts and the treaty itself. Second, the creation of the FADM, even if only with a symbolic inauguration, was one of the treaty's requirements for elections to be held and was seen as the official ending point of the demobilization process.[140] This demobilization was considered the riskiest part of the treaty, as evidenced by fears of an Angolan situation and the stipulation so rigorously adhered to – even at the cost of renewing ONUMOZ for a full year beyond the original mandate – that demobilization and the creation of the new FADM be completed before elections could be held.[141] Thus this section will go into significant detail as to how the new FADM was conceived and developed in practice, examining the goals for the new institution, the size of the force, the organizing committee in charge of sorting out technical issues, how the new force was trained and then what the FADM became in practice in its first few years. Each section will lay out the initial aims of the peace plan, before describing the actual implementation and analysing the outcomes. In general, while there were significant deviations from the peace plan during the implementation phase, the new FADM generally succeeded in becoming a combined and non-political military institution. Its ability, however, to act more effectively as a unifying symbol and stable employer was undercut by wider economic problems that hindered Mozambique's overall reconstruction.

Goals for the FADM

When building the new FADM, there were a variety of stakeholders and priorities between international donors, FRELIMO and RENAMO that ONUMOZ, in particular, was in charge of managing. First, the international community had particular goals their vision of the new FADM had to encompass, specifically that it would function as part of the wider security sector reform process in limiting the ability of either side to revert to armed conflict.[142] Relatedly, the new FADM was hoped to be sufficiently strong and integrated to ensure that the government was once again the only organization in the country capable of organized violence. This priority references Weberian sovereignty theory and the basis of international law, which is also built into more recent scholarship on evaluating the effectiveness of DDR and SSR programmes.[143]

Additionally, the international community wanted the new FADM to be distinctly non-political, in the standard of Western militaries that hold themselves apart from civilian politics and in contrast with a perceived 'African problem' of coups. Aside from wanting the military to be civilian-run, little detail or thought went into the other principles, design or functions of the military, leaving problematic ambiguities the organization would struggle with going forward.[144]

FRELIMO wanted the new FADM to be in many ways the continuation of their previous military and saw the integration process as a method of incorporating the smaller RENAMO force into their large military, thus neutering it. This was one of the main reasons that FRELIMO pushed hard during negotiations for a large FADM, an issue which will be discussed further in the next section. Additionally, FRELIMO wanted the new FADM to have access to further professionalization training through new ties with Western militaries (including the British, Americans and Portuguese). Any of the existing officer corps saw the new FADM as a continuation of their decades-long military careers.[145] For lower ranking FRELIMO members, the new FADM was mainly thought of as a source of stable employment with high-status salaries, something that FRELIMO had run into difficulties providing in the past – lower-ranked soldiers saw the international community's participation and sponsorship of the FADM as hope for a better-funded institution going forward.[146]

RENAMO's priorities for the new FADM, on the other hand, were very much focused on symbolic changes between the FAM and the FADM and ensuring high ranks, status and salaries for their top officers. RENAMO also saw the FADM as being a much more suspect institution that they were wary of joining because of its seeming similarities to FRELIMO's FAM. In addition, due to the size difference between the two groups, RENAMO worried about being swept up in a FRELIMO-dominated institution and therefore lobbied hard for a much smaller force. Additionally, RENAMO officers generally saw the new FADM less in terms of a space for a long-term military career as these officers generally had less exposure to formal military institutions to begin with and often had not volunteered to join RENAMO in the first place.[147] The officers, therefore, considered participation in the FADM as a method of guaranteeing salaries and pensions that would not only allow for a much higher standard of living than they had managed during the war but would also allow them to disperse patronage to war-time followers, even amongst now officially demobilized soldiers.[148] While these were not all contradictory goals to what either FRELIMO or the international community wanted, there were enough differences between these three main stakeholders that negotiating and implementing plans related to the creation of the FADM was a tricky process.

In addition to these priorities, it is worth considering potential goals that were not discussed or included in plans regarding the FADM. The lack of discussion around these topics is useful in understanding how some of the gaps in the eventual FADM came into being – showing an ambiguity and gap from the outset. There was little focus in the negotiating stage on the desired capabilities or standards of the new FADM, with issues like corruption, professionalization and training left to the implementation committee, discussed in more detail later in the chapter. Even in those discussions, however, it will be shown that types and amount of training were considered relatively low priority and that the measure of success of the FADM focused much more strongly on its ability to satisfy the demands of soldiers on both sides in order to prevent immediate recurrent violence than the ability of the FADM as a functional fighting force.[149]

External influences explain some of the design challenges facing the FADM. Its symbolic role as a mechanism of treaty implementation took priority over functionality. Furthermore, improved capabilities were a double-edged sword: offering both the potential to ensure security, but also exacerbate violence should the peace plan go awry. When examining the FADM as a purely military structure, these gaps seem like large issues to be left out. However, analysing the international community's priorities for the FADM as a barometer of the peace process rather than primarily as a military institution explains this seeming discrepancy. Examining these motivations is key to understanding why the FADM developed the way that it did, particularly in terms of short-term versus long-term developments. The international community's focus was on securing the creation of the force before the October 1994 elections and maintaining salary payments in the immediate aftermath of the elections to maintain stability. The priority was not to embark on a multi-year total rehabilitation of the standards, training and capabilities of the new forces that was necessary to make the FADM a fully fledged military institution.

One reason for this was that funding the FADM's capabilities specifically around elections was a shorter-term and more targeted commitment, making it easier to solicit and maintain international financial support. This was especially true as the initial agreement between the parties and then with international donors had been for a much larger military, but with demobilization completed and donors having spent more than planned on demobilization and reintegration, it was a relatively straightforward proposition to convince donors to simply finish a 'last piece' (the elections). This was particularly persuasive given the importance given to the elections going smoothly, as the creation of the FADM at least symbolically was one of the key markers of whether elections could be held according to the terms of the treaty, which the international community was deeply invested in happening both to avoid the breakdown as had occurred in Angola and to allow the withdrawal of the expensive ONUMOZ operation on time.[150] Therefore, these gaps were probably unintentional to some degree, as this issue was not mentioned in the meeting minutes of the CCFADM at all. However, it may have been discussed by ONUMOZ and UN headquarters. Regardless of whether these gaps were purposeful or not, the experience of the FADM suggests that these omissions were not relevant to the institution's post-war trajectory.

While these topics were perhaps purposefully excluded, it is also worth noting the academic and policy context in which both negotiations and implementation in Mozambique were operating in terms of developing these plans for the FADM. In the early 1990s when the plan for the new FADM was being negotiated, and then in the following years towards the middle of the decade when it was being implemented, there was a relative dearth of scholarship and policy materials on best practices for what is now commonly understood as DDR and military integration. This meant that the plans made for the FADM in Mozambique were for the most part drawing off of wishes to avoid the fate of Angola and received wisdom about demobilized combatants being the likeliest safe option for removing capacity for renewed violence. Although by 2000 the UN had developed wide-ranging expertise on UN peacekeeping, DDR and other related issues, when the Rome Agreement was negotiated and signed in 1992 and then began to be implemented over the next two years, these wider peacekeeping experiences were not yet being comparatively analysed.[151]

Size of the FADM

The size of the FADM was the main discussion point during the negotiations.[152] From the start, there is little evidence that anyone was concerned about the size of the FADM in relation to either Mozambique's ability to defend itself or having too few or too many soldiers in uniform – creating either too small or bloated security institution.[153] The debates around size were much more narrowly focused on the relative strength – measured in number of soldiers – and proportions of the two sides being integrated. All of those debates, however, had to be revisited during the implementation phase when it became clear that for both sides, many fewer soldiers than expected were willing to join the new FADM. Thus, the talks began again about what shape and distributions the new FADM would consist of while ONUMOZ and international donors scrambled to expand the demobilization benefits and logistics for the vast majority of combatants who chose civilian over military life.

From the onset of negotiations, FRELIMO's stance was in favour of a large army. Some of those reasons have been discussed in previous chapters. Essentially, a large army was seen as a guarantee of continued FRELIMO dominance;

while RENAMO's total numbers were still not clear during the negotiations, it was undoubtedly the case that FRELIMO's military significantly outnumbered RENAMO's. FRELIMO thought having a large army guaranteed continued dominance of the security forces even once merged with RENAMO fighters.[154] Additionally, as an already existing and hierarchical state institution, FRELIMO felt that a large military would be able to provide stable and therefore attractive jobs for many FRELIMO members even after the war ended, enabling them to maintain their base without having to create entire new large-scale employment schemes from scratch.[155] In this vein, FRELIMO successfully proposed that the new FADM would offer salaries to rank-and-file soldiers nearly three times what they had been paid during the conflict, backed by the international community.[156]

RENAMO, on the other hand, facing the same numerical calculations as FRELIMO, was in favour of a much smaller army, to maintain a favourable ratio and to not be overwhelmed.[157] In addition, a smaller FADM would mean that RENAMO could contribute its required troops while also perhaps keeping some fighters back in either bodyguard or reserve capacities, giving it a hedge against a possible reversion to conflict. With a larger army, RENAMO would face the humiliation of not being able to contribute sufficient soldiers for its agreed-upon quota while also not being able to keep back fighters for protective purposes.[158]

Additionally, RENAMO likely felt that the government should not have such a large military at its command. While RENAMO was planning to contest the post-treaty elections, it was clear both to RENAMO leaders and outsiders that the group was ill-prepared to turn into a political party and there was much fear on the part of top RENAMO leaders about their ability to win such a contest. Thus, limiting the size of the government's military regardless of who was in government was seen by RENAMO as having a greater curtailing effect on FRELIMO than itself.[159]

The treaty therefore compromised between these two positions and agreed that the new army would have 50 per cent from each side totalling 30,000 soldiers total, meaning that each group would contribute 15,000 fighters.[160] This was larger than RENAMO's demand but much smaller than FRELIMO's and international mediators eventually persuaded both sides that this was a workable compromise.[161] This new FADM would focus primarily on the army, as RENAMO did not have air or naval units to bring to the new FADM. Importantly, the decision about which fighters would demobilize entirely versus which would join the new FADM was left entirely up to the leaders of each group,[162] with decisions about whether to factor in individual soldier preferences left ambiguous in the treaty. This was the plan as cantonment in the assembly areas began, with the assumption that soldiers would mainly choose to join the FADM rather than opt for civilian reintegration once at the assembly areas and presented with the two options.

In a surprise to all involved, the vast majority of combatants on both sides of the conflict chose civilian reintegration, as has been discussed in Chapter 3.[163] Therefore, the principle of parity that had been agreed on in the peace treaty was undermined by soldiers' own preferences about joining the FADM. At ONUMOZ's recommendation, the quotas were therefore reduced for both sides, meaning that the agreed-upon total of 30,000 instead became just 12,353, and the principle of 50 per cent from each side had to be abandoned. When the FADM was inaugurated, it comprised 8,691 FRELIMO soldiers (or 70.36 per cent) and about 3,662 RENAMO fighters (or 29.64 per cent).[164] While on the one hand the inauguration of the FADM was considered a success in and of itself, the uneven balance from the beginning did not decrease tensions and likely contributed to RENAMO's continued feelings of being at a dangerous disadvantage. However, no alternatives were seriously discussed either within ONUMOZ or CCFADM documentation, likely because starting negotiations on the size of the FADM from scratch was seen as both far beyond the mandate of either the CCFADM or ONUMOZ and also deeply detrimental to keeping the disarmament and demobilization plans on track.

The role of the CCFADM

Determining the size of the FADM was really the main technical issue of the new military that was discussed and debated during the Rome negotiations; all other aspects about how the new military would function were left to the CCFADM. The treaty designed this committee to include representatives from both RENAMO and FRELIMO to be chaired by ONUMOZ and with other interested international actors allowed to be present, mainly the British, French, Americans and Portuguese. In a distinct change from the Bicesse Accords, this committee had the UN as an active participant in order to act as a chair, tiebreaker and assist with implementation of decisions and was specifically designated as a military technical committee, separate from a different committee focused on big-picture political issues.[165] This allowed the CCFADM to be somewhat divorced from politics and ensured that the main participants would be military leaders with the necessary technical expertise rather than politicians. It is unclear where this particular aspect of the CCFADM's structure came from; no evidence suggests it was a lesson learned from observing Angola, but it is consistent with Ajello's pragmatic problem-solving approach to treaty implementation. The CCFADM, therefore, became an important forum for building the actual structures of the FADM, including key issues like rank standardization (which had direct implications for status and salaries) and training. As these are generally considered more technical issues, there is a relative dearth of academic literature on this topic. However, the UN archives, which include detailed minutes from every single one of these meetings over the course of the two years of ONUMOZ's deployment, have recently become available and will be analysed extensively in this section to recreate exactly what was debated and decided on.

One of the first issues that the CCFADM and ONUMOZ more broadly dealt with was the topic of standardizing ranks across FRELIMO and RENAMO.[166] This had immediate implications both for the creation of the FADM and the disbursement of demobilization packages, as both were tied to conflict-era ranks in determining the amount of either wage or reintegration assistance packages given out.[167] As this became publicly known, especially to soldiers awaiting processing in assembly areas, this became a particularly high-stakes topic, albeit for different reasons. For FRELIMO, their military had been organized along standard European models, with ranks, training, promotions and uniforms all drawn from decades of Soviet support.[168] Given this existing international standard, FRELIMO officers held strongly to these principles and wanted to ensure that the system of rank and status would be continued in order to maintain their power and prestige and also the professional reputation of the institution as a whole.[169]

RENAMO, on the other hand, had very little Western-style organization or tradition of ranks and training, as they had developed primarily as a guerrilla group with little international backing.[170] The priority of these officers therefore was much more focused on attaining the financial benefits that came with high ranks with little understanding of the traditions of education and training that on the FRELIMO side were standard prerequisites to attaining high ranks.[171] The problem that existed in both groups was that officers on both sides were the soldiers most likely to opt to join the FADM rather than be demobilized, as they felt their skills were best suited towards continued military careers rather than starting from scratch in the civilian world and wanted to maintain the status and patronage systems they had run during the conflict.[172] This, however, meant that there was a surplus of officers from both sides leading to a bloated command structure,[173] with a lack of enthusiasm from rank-and-file soldiers on both sides.

There were therefore fierce debates over how many senior officers each side was allowed to have within the FADM and what the qualifications were to be included in that group.[174] This not only was a topic during CCFADM meetings but also throughout the demobilization and FADM training processes more broadly.[175] It often came up in seemingly insignificant ways, such as over hotel accommodations during training courses, uniform allotments in training camps, vehicle allocations or ensuring that equal numbers of equally ranked officers were included in various programmes and meetings.[176] These comparative status issues may seem small, but were in fact considered symbolic of wider issues of parity, recognition and respect that were treated as highly contentious and possibly volatile issues if not resolved.[177] The solution that was eventually settled on was spearheaded by the deeply pragmatic head of ONUMOZ, Aldo Ajello,[178] who stated that titles held at the end of the war would continue,[179] but that future promotions would be tied to a standard education and knowledge-based testing system.[180] As the FADM continued, however, the formal pre-FADM rules for promotion came to the fore and RENAMO officers quickly became quietly retired or prevented from rising in the ranks.[181]

Training the new FADM

In order to form and then maintain the FADM, negotiators had to decide what kind of training would be available and useful. This started in parallel to the Rome negotiations, with the 1993 Lisbon Declaration focused specifically on gaining international support for training the FADM. In this document, the UK, France and Portugal agreed to train the new military, with Portugal focusing mainly on senior leadership, naval and special forces training, while the French would undertake training in demining and the British would focus on infantry training.[182] While this showed commendable international support for the FADM, ensuring coordination, cooperation and general applicability of a military receiving training from three different institutions was a challenge that seemed under-recognized.[183] One important aspect that changed from the planning stages was the designation of ONUMOZ as being the sole organization in charge of organizing and maintaining the training facilities used by the international trainers. While this was not originally part of ONUMOZ's mandate, Ajello undertook to add this to the responsibilities given that ONUMOZ was already overseeing the assembly areas which were being turned into training camps and saw their continued involvement in facilitating the logistics and supplies for these areas as a way to ensure training could commence with as few delays as possible.[184] This is another example of how Ajello's personal focus on pragmatism – a continuation of this book highlighting the importance of less tangible aspects to successful peace implementation – had a significant impact on the outcome of ONUMOZ's activities and the reconstruction efforts more broadly.

The Portuguese courses began soon after the creation of the FADM and generally proceeded without much incident, which is likely due to the fact that the senior officers selected for leadership training were predominantly FRELIMO officers who were used to such sources, had sufficient educational backgrounds to participate well and had decades of experience working with formal Portuguese. Similarly, as the FADM navy was entirely the FAM navy,[185] there were structural, educational and historical linkages that made training quite straightforward. Perhaps unsurprisingly, there is little information available on the progress or outcome of the special forces training administered by Portugal.

The French demining training programme started with 100 students to form a special FADM brigade to focus on this issue.[186] This was a French-led effort that received significant support from ONUMOZ in terms of staffing and logistics. This was also a well-funded effort from the international community who saw demining in Mozambique as an important priority to allow for economic reconstruction. This was also a popular option for trained non-commissioned officers from both sides in the new FADM as it was quite well-paid compared to other technical jobs.[187]

The British infantry training programme was meant to start with 1,500 students who would then go on to set up their own training centres to further train thousands of more soldiers into new brigades.[188] These plans had to be revised due to the lower-than-expected number of soldiers who opted to join the FADM and then again due to the lack of assembly camps that could be immediately turned into training camps.[189] Still, despite these much smaller numbers, getting the programmes running ran into immediate logistical problems.[190] As with the assembly areas, three of which became the primary base for the infantry training, the conditions in the camps were woefully and immediately inadequate for human habitation.[191] Trainers and programme participants complained incessantly to ONUMOZ about lack of electricity and running water, inadequate food supplies and even lack of secure fencing around more than one facility.[192] Another persistent problem was a lack of translators for British trainers in order to communicate with Mozambican participants, an ongoing issue that resulted in significant delays in training programmes.[193] Fixing these problems was made difficult by the continued lack of air and land access to these camps due to the poor condition of roads and the lack of ONUMOZ aircraft available (they were simultaneously trying to finish demobilization and transport, the election campaign and organizing of polling places and the training of the FADM).[194]

In terms of the content of the British-run infantry training programmes, the curricula seem to have been clearly adapted from standard Western understandings of the capabilities an infantry should have – a decision that does not seem to have been debated in either the treaty negotiations or CCFADM meetings. This meant that infantry training for officers and trainers planned to focus heavily on military actions such as drills, weapons handling, fieldwork, tactics and physical fitness, with only 4 out of 278 class hours (1.4%) dedicated to teaching the laws of armed conflict and military law, with the same amount given to teaching administrative skills.[195] This original training plan was meant to last sixteen weeks, but due to delays in starting training and the pressure to complete training before the elections, the plan was reduced to ten.[196] While it is not exactly clear which lessons were omitted from the training, it is clear that the focus of infantry training was very much on traditional military skills, not on reconciliation, military conduct, ethics or non-tactical professionalization. This is significant because it shows the bias in perceptions of what military training needs to be, which is heavily based on Western histories where pre-military education can be assumed to include societal norms around civilian protection and rule of law, therefore meaning that military training needs to focus on equipment and physical aspects of soldiering.[197] In post-conflict contexts, however, what soldiers already know before training is often exactly the opposite, as they have joined the FADM by virtue of surviving a civil war. Therefore, the aspects more needing to be learnt at this stage are more likely to be around use of force, rule of law and civilian protection,[198] as these, not how to use rifles, are more likely to be novel to those emerging from nearly two decades of civil war.

In addition, the section of training designated specifically for the lowest ranks of the military lasted only four weeks[199] and maintained the section of classes on administration, but eliminated the classes on law in favour of first aid skills instead.[200] So the lowest ranks, and thus the largest ranks, of the FADM were given no legal, ethical or behavioural training at all through the British-led programme. This was likely not considered an issue at the time for two main reasons. First, the content of the training programmes was, as far as can be ascertained, left to the discretion of the three international actors providing the training, in accordance with general goals agreed on in discussion with both sides. Second, this was likely adapted from British infantry training which deals primarily with soldiers with no combat experience and perhaps lower physical skills, but who, having grown up or at least been exposed to peacetime democracy, likely need less instruction on the basics of military conduct and ethics. Both of those expectations, however, did not fit the Mozambican experience: having just come out of a conflict, basic infantry skills were likely relatively straightforward for most soldiers willing to join the FADM to grasp, whereas education had been disrupted throughout most of the country for at least a decade, in addition to the lack of any democratic experience. Thus, while the numbers suggest success in training 500 military instructors, five infantry brigades and 1,000 officers, altogether totalling 5,000 trained FADM members prior to elections,[201] the content and quality of that education is perhaps less than salutary.

The reality of the FADM

As stated at the beginning of this section, the international community saw the creation of the FADM almost exclusively through the lens of providing stable institutional employment for former combatants that could act as a symbol of national reconciliation and a source of reassurance for both sides that the war was truly over. It was not seen as necessarily needing to be successful as a fighting force. For FRELIMO, the FADM was about providing employment and maintaining reputational strength, whereas for RENAMO the FADM was potentially suspect and to be engaged with warily. This concluding section of the formation of the FADM will assess to what extent these various goals were met, and how the initial years of the FADM lived up to the treaty obligations and hopes of the parties involved.

By 1996, the FADM was clearly in existence and had successfully seen the formal and actual disbandment of both FRELIMO and RENAMO's individual military organizations. In this respect alone, this fulfilled one of the most important criteria of the Rome Agreement and succeeded in achieving what had so blatantly failed in Angola. The 1996 FADM had rank-and-file as well as middle and senior officers from both FRELIMO and RENAMO who were being paid equivalently and equally for their rank and were suffering roughly the same amount from Mozambique's wider economic reconstruction challenges. Symbolically, a new uniform had been agreed upon and manufacturing rushed such that soldiers were able to return even from pre-election training camps in their new uniforms.[202] In many ways, therefore, the FADM looked to be a great success, by the standards of the international community, FRELIMO and RENAMO.

Looking more closely at the FADM as a military structure rather than a political one, however, problems become apparent. The training conducted by the Portuguese, French and British had been both piecemeal and short-lived; by 1996 the programmes had been long completed with nothing further scheduled.[203] While the demining team had been trained and continued to operate alongside ONUMOZ for the rest of the peacekeeping mission, the extent of mining in Mozambique was such that a 100-strong brigade was not sufficient. Additionally, Mozambique's Navy and Air Force were not significant parts of the country's security forces, nor did they have any RENAMO representation and thus did not factor usefully into conversations about political reconciliation. Perhaps because of the focus on the FADM as a political rather than a military force, in addition to the lack of threat from any neighbour, by 1996 the FADM 'consisted of a navy with no functioning ships, an Air Force with no planes that flew, and an army with almost no operable heavy weapons' according to a senior American diplomat involved in Mozambique throughout the late 1990s.[204] There were some international concerns that Mozambique, given its smaller-than-expected army, may not be able to maintain security following the departure of ONUMOZ. However, these fears quickly proved unfounded thus eliminating any political will for increasing the capabilities of the FADM as a robust fighting force.[205]

Additionally, within the military structure, problems were beginning to emerge. The senior political figures in charge of the Defence Ministry took seven months to be appointed after the October 1994 elections, leaving the organization in limbo for much of its formative initial year.[206] Furthermore, many of the top military officials were considered hard to work with by international donors,[207] perhaps making it difficult to negotiate continued support from the international community.

From the rank-and-file's point of view, the corruption and salary delay problems that had plagued the FAM prior to the creation of the FADM looked set to continue, with the government struggling to keep up with payment schedules for soldiers as well as the latter of the twenty-four-month payments promised as part of the demobilization packages. Thus, payments started to be given out late to all participants, but particularly RENAMO combatants as ex-FRELIMO fighters received their allotments first, causing tensions between the groups both within and outside the FADM.[208] This showed that not only was the FADM meant to exist more for political than military reasons, but that FRELIMO's economic goal of the military providing a source of satisfying employment was also failing.[209] These economic challenges only continued, and by 2000, the functionality of the FADM militarily and economically had further deteriorated as the country failed to recover economically, thus further hampering the government's ability to pay its soldiers and improve its military.[210]

The structural effects of this economic challenge and exclusive focus on high politics began to have deleterious impacts on the reconciliatory aspects of the FADM. Overall troop strength decreased to just over 11,500 in 2000, with the majority of the decrease coming from former RENAMO fighters. This was particularly acute for RENAMO officers who in the later 1990s and into 2000 began to feel that they were passed over for promotion due to insufficient educational backgrounds that they had not previously been penalized for during the creation of the FADM. These officers began to retire in large numbers, with ongoing debates about the extent to which these retirements were coerced, engineered or encouraged by FRELIMO.[211]

By 2000, therefore, the FADM was a strong enough institution that its existence was no longer in question and as a signal of Mozambique's continued progress towards sustainable peace, particularly to the international community, it was quite successful. Within the country, its lower size and capacity, as well as lessened morale and status had decreased its ability to influence political events, which was likely also welcomed by outsiders. As a source of stable employment and as a strong symbol of reconciliation, however, it was being eroded as the larger economic situation threatened Mozambique's reconstruction more broadly. This section has described in detail the processes through which the new FADM was formed, highlighting contrasts with the attempts in Angola. The next chapter will investigate how this new FADM fared as Mozambique's post-conflict reconstruction process continued, and new comparisons will be drawn with Angola's further versions of military integration.

Conclusion

By 1998, the situations in both Angola and Mozambique were clear, if not necessarily optimistic: Angola's Lusaka Treaty was completely defunct. Even its peacekeeping mission was pulled out in favour of mere observers as renewed conflict raged. In contrast, Mozambique seemed firmly on the path to peace, although the structural flaws of the reconstruction process and misaligned focus of the treaty organizers made it a deeply impoverished peace that held few hopes for the country gaining any amount of economic stability, increased political freedom or sovereign agency. As these two countries' attempts at peace have been considered in parallel throughout this book, it is worth comparing the two cases more directly.

As evidenced throughout both primary and secondary source material on Mozambique, the spectre of Angola was looming over the entire Mozambican peace process, in ways that seem to have moved negotiating parties to mostly avoid the problems of the Bicesse process. Measures included authority resting in the hands of a pragmatic and coordinated UN peacekeeping mission[212] for the following functions: running assembly areas and demobilization, chairing political and military committees to determine outstanding issues for institutional structures going forward, managing the coordination between different international actors and NGOs to create one demobilization process and successfully ensuring the completion of Mozambique's first contested elections. Much of this, however, would not have been possible without RENAMO's willingness to participate in elections and then accept defeat,[213] a decision which arose from a combination of factors explored earlier.

In Angola, on the other hand, the lessons of Bicesse were unfortunately only somewhat learned – there was a significant gap between understanding what the problems were and being able to make significant enough changes to the subsequent Lusaka Treaty. While a more robust UN peacekeeping mission, amongst other changes, was implemented, its inability to enact much long-term change points to the importance of local actors cooperating with international efforts: something evident in Mozambique but not in Angola. In fact, a lesson that emerges from the Lusaka negotiations, treaty and process is the importance of ensuring that peace treaties do not go ahead before both sides actually want peace, which very much conforms to the theoretical idea of 'ripeness' discussed in the opening chapter's literature review.

One of the most interesting comparisons between the Mozambican Treaty and the Lusaka process is the similar manner in which they discuss the 'government' versus the 'rebel' sides, that is, RENAMO and UNITA. While RENAMO had consistently been treated as a non-sovereign rebel actor, UNITA had received much more prestigious billing in the Bicesse process, the treaty, UN resolutions around the treaty and international discourse in general. In the Lusaka process and treaty, however, this status was markedly decreased and UNITA was very much the focus of frustration, suspicion and strict security provisions, whereas the MPLA's position as the legitimate government of Angola seemed much stronger.

Even as the implementation process was delayed, the suspicion generally fell more on UNITA than on the MPLA. There are a few possible reasons for this. First, determining the extent to which the MPLA planned to comply with the treaty was somewhat difficult, as the most stringent security provisions in the treaty applied primarily to UNITA. So, whether or not the MPLA would have agreed to and undergone cantonment, disarmament and demobilization remains an open question. It is, however, much easier to determine the ways in which UNITA did and more importantly did not comply with the Lusaka Treaty, thus making their breaches much clearer and more condemnable.

Second, there is an element of source bias that is interesting to investigate. The majority of primary sources used in this section of the research have been from the UN archives and from interviews with key, mainly non-native, figures involved in the Bicesse and Lusaka processes. Given that the MPLA was the recognized government of Angola throughout this entire period, they had inside access to the UN apparatus. It could therefore easily reach out to UN officials at various levels and times and do so in a way that was easily documented by the UN system and thus preserved in its archives. Additionally, even though prior to the Bicesse elections the United States and West in general were more in favour of UNITA as the 'legitimate' voice of Angola, especially once the Bicesse Treaty was signed and Western diplomats were based in Luanda, there were easy methods and means of communication with MPLA officials. Their UNITA counterparts, on the other hand, were much less physically accessible. Finally, the majority of the MPLA's officials at both senior and middle levels were educated in Western styles of diplomatic processes and spoke at least one European language, Portuguese, if not more. While Savimbi as an individual was highly and flamboyantly educated,[214] many other UNITA leaders were not, thus further inhibiting communication with the outside both formally and informally. These intangible factors influenced the historical record with regards to the amount of negative focus on UNITA and the lack of sources that explain their internal thinking and operations. However, the shift in international perceptions of UNITA came quite distinctly following the failure of Savimbi to accept the results of the Bicesse elections, when the MPLA had been the Angolan representative at the UN since independence in 1975 and had been hosting foreign diplomats since the Namibian negotiations in 1989. Therefore, this particularly noteworthy suspicion of UNITA as opposed to both sides of the conflict could entirely be a result of these institutional, linguistic, access and educational factors and not just a result of source and archival bias.[215]

Another issue that seems specific to Angola is the omission of restrictions on the use of resource revenues – oil for the MPLA and diamonds for UNITA – to perpetuate armament and the prosecution of conflict. As will be seen in subsequent chapters, this exclusion was to have deadly consequences. On a more comparative level, however, there is a contrast that can be gleaned from the two countries' experiences, namely the importance of treaty specificity. The Lusaka Treaty was in many ways an attempt to edit the Bicesse Treaty and to make it more specific in order to avoid what had been tried and had failed, before. The Mozambican agreement had a similar intent but went much further in the changes it implemented. While some of the reasons that the treaty was able to make more adaptations from the Bicesse process than was possible in Angola was due to FRELIMO and RENAMO being more willing to hand authority to the UN, the content of the treaty itself cannot be fully understood as a product of UN peacekeeping mandates that were, in all three cases, written after the treaty was signed.

What both the Lusaka and Mozambican negotiators learnt from the failures with the Bicesse Accords was the importance of specificity and timetable flexibility, along with a robust UN mission. But the flexibility, as shown by the success in Mozambique, must include restrictions specified ahead of time, to avoid processes being dragged out for the purpose of military preparation as happened in 1997 in Angola.[216] In Mozambique Treaty, there was a simple fail-safe built in to protect elections: if disarmament, demobilization and military integration were not complete within the year specified, then the elections could be pushed back. Importantly, however, they could only be pushed back once, and only by one year. Thus flexibility was coupled with specificity in order to maintain pressure and expectations on both sides, as well as clear benchmarks for success or failure. Relatedly, and perhaps more importantly for the prospect of creating integrated militaries, it was understood in all three negotiation processes that there were specifics about the integrated military institutions being proposed – such as exact numbers of soldiers each side would contribute, ranks, salaries and so on – that were best left to a later time to be determined. The Mozambique Treaty allowed for such contingencies/flexibility by mandating the creation of two UN-chaired committees, one to deal with political issues and the other (the CCFADM) to be more concerned with technical military issues. The CCFADM committee was able to successfully debate, negotiate and resolve these contentious issues within the pre-existing and politically settled framework of the peace treaty. In the Angolan processes, however, these issues were neglected and when addressed were hampered by confusion over whether they were political or military topics, and thus military conversations were overtaken by political scuffles. The specificity of laying out a framework for how to deal with outstanding political and, separately, military issues was a key structural difference between the Mozambican Treaty and either of its Angolan counterparts.

Finally, the creation of integrated militaries – the issue that remains most central to this book – had by this point only been achieved by Mozambique. This chapter has detailed how the CCFADM discussed structural issues such as the size of the new military, its ranks structure and balance and related issues such as salaries and benefits. The emphasis on size in terms of balance between the groups has been investigated, as well as the pragmatic approaches both groups took in adjusting their expectations when demobilization versus integration numbers became clear. Also, the importance of the issue of rank has been discussed, with the argument on the impact on status and respect being strongly made, as opposed to an argument about balance on a purely numerical or monetary basis. What has emerged from this analysis of the creation of the FADM has framed it in both a positive and negative light. The work of the CCFADM appears crucial in turning the provisions of the peace treaty into a functioning military that still operates today. There were initially encouraging efforts to bring in foreign training to boost the capacity of the new FADM. However, the coordination efforts that were so carefully monitored in other aspects of the peace process were less considered here. Similarly, the training that was completed does not seem to have had much follow-up. This leaves the FADM institutionally sound, but militarily of low capacity and with an incredibly minimal focus on military ethics, professionalization or rule of law-related norm-building.[217] Furthermore, there was a similar lack of long-term consistency in the inclusion of RENAMO officers at senior levels in the new FADM, leading the integrated military to increasingly look dominated by FRELIMO, especially at the top. Combined with FRELIMO's consistent victories in the ballot box, this two-sided peace treaty begins to look more uneven. When examined in isolation, the FADM looks coherent and beneficial to peace. However, as will be explored further in the next chapter, political and economic aspects of Mozambique's post-conflict reconstruction process begin to negatively and permanently impact the FADM's ability to function as an integrated institution.

Additionally, the next chapter will continue investigating the final peace process in Angola and draw comparisons between the situations in both countries.

Chapter 5

PEACE AT LAST...?

This chapter covers the last historical sections of the Angolan and Mozambican civil wars. The sections on Angola include the final stages of the breakdown of the Lusaka Treaty, including the failures of UNAVEM III and its successor mission MONUA to keep the peace process on track. The chapter then goes into depth on the final years of the Angolan war, especially on the role of diamonds and oil in changing the dynamics of both the war and the subsequent peace. The chapter contests a dominant strand in the literature regarding the importance of the death of Savimbi in bringing the war to a conclusion, agreeing with more nuanced claims that Savimbi's death was just one of a number of factors leading to the final peace treaty in Angola's war. The chapter then goes on to analyse the Luena Treaty's terms and implementation, with direct comparisons both to Angola's previous peace processes as well as Mozambique's.

In the second part of the chapter, Mozambique's longer-term post-conflict reconstruction processes are examined. This will focus specifically on how the international community handles and mishandles civilian reintegration of former combatants, the key role of international financial institutions in curbing Mozambique's post-war growth and finally the implications for the integrated military and Mozambique's peace prospects more broadly. Overall, this chapter traces the historical processes in both countries in parallel. It will find areas of similarity and contrast as a natural extension of case study analyses and explore various ways that international actors can have positive and negative impacts, the centrality of understanding demographic and economic factors on the ground, as well as the importance of specificity, coordination and flexibility in creating and implementing peace treaties.

The breakdown of Angola's Lusaka Treaty

The breakdown of the Lusaka Treaty, as documented in the last chapter, was at first a relatively slow process. For much of 1995 and 1996, the ceasefire was held across the country, UNAVEM III successfully set up demobilization camps for UNITA members, and thousands of combatants began to register and begin processing for either demobilization or FAA integration. However, by 1997, it was clear that UNITA was not sending either its top fighters or best equipment into UN hands[1]and was stalling in returning territory to state (aka MPLA) control. Savimbi was avoiding meetings with both President dos Santos and international mediators,[2] and both sides were rearming.[3] In the face of this descent back to war, the international community had increasingly less leverage, especially as by this point, neither side relied on international governments like the US and USSR for funding, instead relying on diamond and oil revenues.[4] As has been explored in Chapter 4, the contest between the two sides from this point forward was not about ideology or superpower politics, but rather a straightforward fight for control of the state.[5]

As demonstrated in the previous chapter, the Lusaka Treaty had built-in weaknesses, most notably the lack of restrictions on the use of resources to fuel conflict by either side (primarily diamond revenues for UNITA and oil revenues for the MPLA) as well as the lack of a satisfying position for Savimbi.[6] More importantly to many outside observers at the time, the Lusaka Treaty was seen as being built on shaky foundations regardless of the content of the treaty. One reason for this was the perception that little trust remained between the two sides, following the post-Bicesse violence, especially as senior UNITA leaders had in fact been targeted during this time period.[7] In this explosive atmosphere, no treaty terms could have persuaded UNITA to legitimately lay down its arms, especially without believable international guarantees to protect them.[8] Given the one-sided nature of the Lusaka Treaty's demands for UNITA to disarm and demobilize (MPLA troops were required only to stay in their barracks during this process), the prospect of UNITA trusting the MPLA or international community to either protect its continued existence at all or uphold its safe and equitable involvement in national politics was unsurprisingly lacking.[9] This is not to say that the international community's focus on UNITA as the instigator of post-election violence was incorrect or unfair. It was, however, one-sided in seeming to assume that the MPLA was blameless and acting entirely legitimately, whereas in fact both sides were routinely accused of human rights abuses and dictatorial policies.[10]

Therefore, while there were clear military incentives for both sides to negotiate and sign the Lusaka Treaty (see Chapter 4), conditions from the beginning were such that it was more likely that both sides saw the negotiations and initial implementation of the treaty as a facade for rearmament and planning for future military campaigns, rather than an actual move to peace.[11] In fact, this is exactly what happened, as UNITA continued its lucrative diamond trading and stalled regarding the disarmament and demobilization of its top fighters.[12] Indeed, although the unity government was sworn in on time, the demobilization and integration of UNITA soldiers into the FAA that was meant to run in parallel had only seen just over 10,000 soldiers and ten generals (none considered closest to Savimbi) inducted into the FAA, well under the 36,300 initially proposed.[13] In addition, UNITA's de facto control of key diamond-producing territories and symbolic strongholds continued.[14] Interestingly, while diamonds remained a key income source for UNITA, the group did in fact officially give up some of its key diamond areas during the Lusaka Treaty implementation process, but outright refused to hand over any symbolic strongholds.[15] However, while some diamond areas were turned over, local hostility, although officially not organized by UNITA commanders, inhibited the government from actually establishing administrative control over these areas.[16] Meanwhile, the MPLA used its oil revenues to hire mercenaries, train soldiers and buy weapons. Additionally, the MPLA began to work to isolate UNITA diplomatically, with efforts likely influenced by the one-sided nature of the Lusaka Treaty and shift especially in US presidential policy from being pro-UNITA to pro-African governments. By early 1998, the MPLA was publicly stating that its goal was to defeat UNITA militarily, on the battlefield.[17] From this point onwards, if not before, the Lusaka Treaty was functionally dead.[18]

One immediate impact of the MPLA's declaration of renewed war came from the international community and was twofold. First, the UNSC no longer wanted to continue funding the increasingly risky UNAVEM III mission. It was therefore drawn down and replaced with a much smaller, Luanda-based, observer mission, MONUA. This was received well by both the MPLA and UNITA who did not want a UN mission trying to stop any military progress. Second, the UNSC and international community more broadly began to understand that stronger measures would have to be taken against UNITA if the war was to conclude quickly, with the implicit backing of the international community firmly on the side of the MPLA by this point. Therefore, much tougher sanctions against UNITA began to be enacted by the UNSC from 1997 onwards, as well as wider campaigns on the issue of conflict diamonds more generally, resulting eventually in the establishment of the Kimberley Process in 2003. This cemented the MPLA's status as the legitimate government of Angola in the eyes of the international community, a position that was significantly strengthened by the MPLA's continued control over the capital city of Luanda.[19]

On the subject of international involvement, an important ambivalence requires mention here and throughout this chapter. As funding for both sides of the Angolan war moved from predominantly being sourced from foreign governments to foreign companies, it is important to understand the competing interests the foreign governments began to more clearly face as the conflict continued. While the United States, for example, no longer funded UNITA and in fact was an increasingly vocal proponent in the united UNSC for enforcing sanctions against the group, the United States still did not directly fund the MPLA war effort and essentially advocated for an end to the conflict, but without wanting to remain directly involved on either side.[20] In fact, the Clinton administration had a large effort focusing on developing economic trade ties with African countries, including Angola, a policy that would be greatly enhanced by peaceful conditions in which to facilitate economic growth.[21] Outside of government corridors, however, US oil companies were the key source of foreign income and indeed overall revenues for the MPLA throughout the entire Angolan war, but especially from the early 1990s onwards, as Angola's off-shore oil reserves were revealed to be some of the largest in the world. Therefore, although the US government was not funding either side of the conflict, US companies, which were likely to have some domestic influence with their own government, were key financial backers of the Angolan war effort. Thus, the US government had incentives, perhaps, for this conflict to continue or at the very least, to see the maintenance of a strong MPLA. This blurry separation between US actors is worth keeping in mind in assessing US motives and incentives as the war continued.

End of UNAVEM III

UNAVEM III had been the most robust peacekeeping mission approved by the UNSC in Angola, explicitly drawing on the lessons of UNAVEM II and trying to improve from the mistakes of the Bicesse process. Still, as has been demonstrated in Chapter 4, UNAVEM III was insufficiently manned and funded for carrying out the scale of the tasks assigned to it, even if both the MPLA and UNITA had been fully cooperative.[22] UNAVEM III was impeded at every turn by UNITA and did not have the funding, political coordination or capacity to succeed in the face of this opposition.

In addition, throughout the Lusaka Treaty's implementation process, there had been significant delays on the part of the international community, further eroding the legitimacy of the UN as a conflict-resolving actor to parties on the ground.[23] Beyond the delay in deploying UNAVEM III, much of the promised humanitarian and civilian reintegration that had been seen as a key and perhaps the only way in which UNITA fighters would truly be able to leave conflict behind was delayed. In the four years that the Lusaka Treaty was under implementation (1995–8), less than half the international funding was actually made annually available. This created massive delays and implementation problems in trying to make demobilization and civilian reintegration a reality on the ground, entirely separately from UNITA's unwillingness to fully participate.[24] The failure to manage this process is an important aspect of how the UN was perceived across the country, as this was seen as a further failure on top of the various problems seen to be externally imposed since the Bicesse process itself.[25] Additionally, it perhaps goes some way towards explaining why international organizations associated with the UN during this time who failed to live up to their promises (CARE, World Food Programme, etc.) continued to try and provide humanitarian aid even as the conflict fully escalated, creating the ethical dilemmas mentioned earlier in this chapter.

Furthermore, as political negotiations and progress began to break down, the UN felt increasingly unable to influence the progress of events in Angola,[26] especially as both sides began to more obviously rearm and plan military campaigns. Despite repeated warnings from the UN Security Council in the form of resolutions more strongly sanctioning UNITA from 1997 onwards, public statements from the UN secretary-general, and the efforts of the UN Special Representative Blondin-Beye, it became clear to the UN that neither side in Angola was going to remain committed to political reconciliation and conflict resolution as 1997 ended. Given these circumstances, UNITA's refusal to cooperate with UNAVEM III in the field became pronounced and UN headquarters began to worry increasingly not just about UNAVEM III's ability to carry out its mandate but also for the safety of those in the mission. UNITA's intransigence on the ground was particularly important when understanding the extent of UNITA's control of Angola: 'In March 1997, some 50% of Angola's territory was still under UNITA control, although 80% of the population was in government-held areas.'[27] This situation, similar to the discrepancy between population and territorial control noted in the initial post-Bicesse fighting discussed previously, suggested a high likelihood of continued conflict between the two sides. Additionally, the Special Representative Alouin Blondin-Beye, who had shepherded the Lusaka Treaty into being and was seen by both sides as being a legitimate and helpful mediator, died in a plane crash in June 1998. This was the final nail in the coffin of a robust UN presence in Angola.[28] Thus, when the UNSC was faced with the choice of either pulling out or substantially increasing the scale of the mission in order to make peace, the UNSC unanimously chose to pull out.[29]

Establishment of MONUA

MONUA was established with just 3,026 peacekeepers assigned to complete tasks the 7,000 UNAVEM III peacekeepers had left unfinished. Importantly, although there was direct continuity in the assignments, the name change signalled a different attitude by the UNSC towards Angola: UNSC switched from the third iteration of the 'Angola Verification Mission' to 'United Nations Observer Mission in Angola'.[30] This could be a means of acknowledging the progress both sides were seen making politically, with the successful swearing in of the GURN and the hopes of the international community that the conflict in Angola was inexorably moving towards political rather than military means of resolving disputes.[31] Or, the replacement of a verification mission with an observer mission could have been an attempt of the UNSC to signal the decreasing importance of Angola on its agenda and a way of stepping back from active conflict resolution while still having some way of staying on top of changing events.[32] Furthermore, it could have also been a means of trying to distance itself from the increasingly unpopular UNAVEM interventions both within and outside of Angola. Given the decreased role that the UN was to play in Angola going forward, whether the intention of the name switch was to step back or not, that became the de facto consequence.

Essentially, the 'gamble for the UN was that the pace of the process, although still extremely slow, was fundamentally irreversible and that UNITA's continued obstructiveness had become mere habit rather than a purposeful political strategy'.[33] As will be demonstrated through this chapter, this is a bet that the UN fundamentally lost and was likely doomed for all the reasons previously outlined in this chapter and Chapter 4 by the time MONUA was put into place in June 1997. This quotation is interesting for its mention of the slowness of the pace of negotiations, which is not a factor mentioned significantly either in the literature, or therefore, in this book. Pace of negotiations remains an interesting area of analysis for its impact on peace negotiations (see Chapter 6, areas for further research). However, this is not a focus on this book due to the complexity of untangling the impact of pace, if any, from other impacts on the peace processes, such as the political economy of conflict (see sections on diamonds, oil and local geopolitics), as well as its lack of mention in the secondary literature, UN archival material and interviews conducted for this research.

MONUA on the ground

MONUA deployed in July 1997, a mere month after the mandate was officially passed in June 1997.[34] Initially, MONUA took over the assembly areas and demobilization processes established by UNAVEM III, reporting that by August 1997, nearly 80,000 UNITA soldiers had been demobilized with fewer than 20,000 remaining to be processed and over 10,000 joining the FAA.[35] This was a significant increase in the number of UNITA soldiers registered in assembly areas, suggesting an initial improvement in MONUA's abilities over the progress made via UNAVEM III.[36] However, these numbers were not representative as truly denoting a cessation of armed fighters in UNITA areas, especially as the trend established under UNAVEM III of 90 per cent of UNITA soldiers in assembly areas requested demobilization back into UNITA-held areas. According to UN reports, sending UNITA soldiers back to UNITA areas, even if technically demobilized, amounted 'to recycling UNITA soldiers [and] . . . defeats the spirit of Lusaka'.[37] Significantly, this 'recycling' of UNITA fighters which continued under MONUA,[38] was given as a key reason for increased UNSC sanctions against UNITA in 1997.[39]

Beyond the problems of demobilization locations, the assembly areas themselves were a constant headache for MONUA. As had been the case throughout the missions of both UNAVEM II and UNAVEM III, conditions in the camps were constantly insufficient. This was caused by a variety of reasons, including difficulty accessing camps due to mined roads and insufficient UN helicopters, creating delays in provisions of supplies and necessary housing infrastructure.[40] This was exacerbated by the fact that neither the assembly camps nor the demobilization processes had been planned or built to accommodate the thousands of dependents that came along with UNITA fighters,[41] rapidly escalating conditions of overcrowding and therefore low morale and disciplinary issues. Furthermore, issues within the camps included UNITA officers not wanting to live next to subordinates and openly be given the same provisions as them and divisions arising between UNITA groups based on their post-assembly areas destinations. Additionally, local populations in UNITA-controlled areas were often directly adversarial to MONUA work, including threatening the personal safety of MONUA personnel.[42] As tensions mounted and war became increasingly likely, direct obstructions from armed and uniformed UNITA personnel in areas surrounding MONUA camps became prevalent as well.[43] Both of these last two threats to the ability of MONUA to function were likewise cited in UNSC resolutions sanctioning UNITA.[44]

In terms of the integration of UNITA fighters into the FAA, problems remained with fewer than 12,000 UNITA soldiers integrated by the end of 1998:[45] an increase of fewer than 2,000 above the numbers managed by UNAVEM III despite eighteen months of MONUA deployment. There are a variety of likely reasons for this, both within the FAA and UNITA. An initial MONUA report suggested that the FAA was less organized than expected and that the chain of command seemed less than fully functional. This included divisions between junior and senior officers over the extent to which they were prepared to accommodate integrating UNITA forces, with junior officers distinctly less willing to comply.[46] There were other reports about how the FAA command was more hardline than the MPLA's political sides during the Lusaka negotiations (see Chapter 4).[47] This observation helps explain the internal constituencies the FAA leadership was trying to manage while also trying to stay unified with the MPLA senior political leadership. The key grievance identified in the MONUA report was the feeling that the FAA could not become so large that it would lose its preferred economic and job status and that if the agreed-upon number of UNITA fighters joined, junior MPLA officers would be unhappy.[48] In order to combat this while still publicly complying with the terms of the Lusaka Treaty, the FAA published its criteria for which soldiers it would allow from UNITA, which was deemed by both UNITA and MONUA to be unnecessarily restrictive.[49] This showed another gap in the treaty itself, which did not put limits on the FAA's ability to unilaterally create the selection criteria.[50] This gap is likely due to the fact that the FAA was so dominant in these negotiations due to its battlefield position. However, this is also consistent with Angola's earlier treaties that also did not often include sufficient specifics about how provisions would be implemented.

All of these delays – demobilization, FAA integration and the turning over of UNITA territory to the government (the latter of which made no progress under MONUA) – meant that MONUA was unable to complete its mandate within the initially allotted timeframe and had to be extended by the UNSC through 1998.[51] The UNSC signalled its unwillingness to continue to accept delays especially from UNITA by imposing further sanctions resolutions in late 1997 and early 1998 as well as extending MONUA's mandate for only six months, in the hopes that these deadlines would require faster progress in implementing the terms of the Lusaka Treaty.[52] As has already been noted in Angola in previous peace processes, deadlines had previously not been effective in this context and likewise MONUA's extended mandate saw not only no further progress towards peace but increasing signs towards war.[53]

End of MONUA

MONUA's previously unexamined 'Lessons Learnt' report from the end of its mission, only released to researchers in 2019 after being given in confidence to the UNSC and UN secretary-general, highlights a number of factors that at the time were well understood to have been problematic aspects of MONUA. While seeing an explicit guide written to inform and better prepare future UN peacekeeping missions is encouraging, it is disappointing to note how many of the practically focused 'lessons learnt' had already been apparent following both UNAVEM II and UNAVEM III and yet had not been resolved prior to MONUA's deployment. These lessons included:

> In missions where quartering sites are to be established suitably qualified and experienced staff should be identified early and earmarked for this important task . . . the composition of the planning team determines the quality of the final product. The experience of Angola shows the importance of including a senior mission official in the planning team who will then be involved in the implementation of the plan.[54]

This is clearly the case when assessing the performance of ONUMOZ and the key role played by the mission commander, Aldo Ajello, as has been discussed in Chapters 3 and 4.

A UNAVEM III report from 1997 had cited the importance of UNAVEM III staff members who had worked previously on ONUMOZ to take lessons about assembly area construction,[55] but this unofficial knowledge transfer was insufficient to create sustainable infrastructure solutions for Angola's assembly areas. Deciphering the reasons for the lack of organized UN learning is beyond the scope of this book but nonetheless remains a consistent theme, particularly with regard to the Angolan case study.

Once the MPLA officially declared its aim of trying to oust UNITA unilaterally via military defeat, the UNSC knew that MONUA's capacity to carry out its mission was over. The mission officially ended in February 1999 after withdrawing to Luanda in October 1997.[56] MONUA was replaced by ONUA,[57] a traditional small-scale observer mission based almost exclusively in Luanda with a mere thirty personnel.[58] The new mission head was mainly based in New York and tried to maintain that the UN was still optimistic about political reconciliation in Angola.[59] For the remainder of the Angolan conflict, UN peacekeeping was to play no major role for the first time since 1988.[60]

Angola's last treaty: The Luena Memorandum of Understanding

This section will establish the overall dynamics and context important for understanding the specifics of the treaty that will then be discussed subsequently. The chapters covering the trajectories of the Angolan and Mozambican peace processes so far have illustrated the importance of understanding the dynamics of opposing sides at the start and during the course of treaty negotiations as a key factor in understanding the terms of the signed treaty as well as how and with what degree of success those terms are then implemented.[61] Angola had three peace treaties, in 1975, 1991 and 1994, all of which were successful in gaining the requisite signatories and all of which were implemented to varying degrees. All three treaties, but especially the last two – which have been investigated in detail in this book – fell apart fundamentally due to the same underlying cause: problems in implementing the security provisions, especially those related to military integration, created insurmountable roadblocks to the continued progress towards peace. While continued violence was also an issue in Angola from the breakdown of the Bicesse elections onwards, even moments of ripeness were routinely underutilized for during negotiations and implementation. In the case of Mozambique, on the other hand, the security provisions in the treaty were more detailed from the outset, which this paper has argued influenced the more straightforward success in implementation, and also helps explain why – despite the many initial ideological positions and levels of brutality comparable to Angola's conflict – Mozambique's conflict only required one peace treaty to end the war. This book consistently argues that specificity about treaty terms is important, particularly around security issues, including creating an integrated military.

This book argues that the Angolan conflict definitively ended in 2002 for structural economic, political, international, regional, leadership and process-building reasons. It considers Savimbi's death to be a key factor in hastening and cementing the peace – the process benefitted from his absence, mainly because there was no longer the spectre of Savimbi agreeing but then reneging at some point in future.[62] However, his death was not the causal mechanism for UNITA's ultimate defeat.

The next few subsections will examine the state of the conflict from 1999, outlining each side's tactical strategies and progress in order to understand the impact of the conflict on the subsequent peace process, as this had significant impacts on the different conditions that UNITA went into negotiations with, as compared to the Lusaka process. The first subsection demonstrates that control over physical territory was an increasingly important aspect of the conflict in its final years. The second section explains how the end of the Cold War significantly changed the international diplomatic element of the conflict, with the MPLA's political and economic future secured and UNITA losing its international standing. These two changes are combined in the third section which examines how UNITA's once-lucrative diamond profits were inhibited by the loss of international standing and protection in organizations like the UN and by an economically bolstered MPLA's advances into formerly UNITA territory. The fourth section will then examine how UNITA was forced to stay in this weakened position by the MPLA's regional diplomacy which eliminated UNITA's remaining regional allies and cross-border havens and smuggling routes, irrevocably weakening the economic, social and military structures of the group.

Territorial contestation

As of 1999, civil war (ongoing since 1975) was fully renewed throughout Angola, without any pretence of progress on finishing the implementation of the 1994 Lusaka Treaty. This abandonment of the peace process was solidified by the 1999 withdrawal of the UN peacekeeping mission MONUA, signalling the cessation of the international community's direct involvement to try and end the conflict. This withdrawal was welcomed by both parties of the Angolan civil war: the MPLA (recognized by this time as the Angolan government) and UNITA (rebel group led by Jonas Savimbi).[63] Although UNITA maintained that the war was restarted solely by the MPLA, the attitude of the MPLA as well as the UN was that UNITA had so purposefully been delaying the implementation of the Lusaka

Treaty that UNITA had clearly been the initial bad actor.[64] Thus, UNITA's claims of innocence fell very much on deaf ears, and the MPLA's goal to defeat UNITA conclusively on the battlefield received no significant international resistance after the withdrawal of MONUA.[65]

Another key reason that the international community of states was, for the first time in Angola's long war (1975–2002), no longer particularly involved was the removal of outside government funding supporting either side. The end of the Cold War had eliminated the incentive for countries like the United States and the Soviet Union to financially support opposing sides in civil wars, so neither the MPLA nor UNITA had international funding from state actors for the fighting that commenced in 1998 and continued until 2002. Instead, both sides were primarily funded by exploiting their regions' natural resources: off-shore oil for the MPLA and alluvial diamonds for UNITA. The buyers of these exploited resources were mainly international commercial actors. This meant that unless foreign governments, especially the United States, were willing to rein in powerful companies, governments no longer had financial leverage to intervene in the conflict in Angola, either for or against peace.[66]

The early stages of the 1998–2002 conflict were characterized by an initially successful UNITA push towards MPLA territory followed by a concentrated FAA (the military arm of the MPLA) counterattack that by 2000 meant the MPLA was pushing UNITA out of territories it previously controlled. Initially, both sides very much fought using conventional means, organizational frameworks and weapons, heavily featuring tanks, large formations and military aircraft. This was a surprise to many who had previously seen UNITA as primarily a guerilla group without either the interest or the means to launch conventional campaigns against the MPLA. However, UNITA initially made a large push towards MPLA centres of power, at one point in 1999, gaining ground close enough to Luanda to threaten the capital itself.[67] This was accomplished mainly via conventional means and equipment, bought from Eastern European countries offloading post–Cold War Soviet weaponry and paid for through diamond revenues.[68]

The MPLA, however, had been planning their rearmament since 1992, and unlike UNITA, had not been forced to either hide their continued rearmament or slow it significantly during the one-sided Lusaka Treaty process.[69] Any internal debate within the MPLA about whether to negotiate with UNITA or try and defeat them had also been resolved, with FAA generals very much at the forefront of driving the military effort.[70] Furthermore, the international community continued to recognize the MPLA as the legitimate actor in the conflict, including by allowing the MPLA to receive loans reserved for legitimate state actors from international financial institutions like the International Monetary Fund (IMF) and to sell its oil on the international market.[71] Meanwhile, the international community continued to impose UNSC sanctions on UNITA's diamond resources. While this was not particularly successful for reasons that will be more fully developed in the later section devoted to diamonds, it nevertheless signalled an important shift in the international community's position on the MPLA as the legitimate government of Angola.[72]

The MPLA was initially worried about UNITA's ability to challenge its control of key cities including Luanda. Therefore, the organization concentrated on defeating UNITA, focusing the majority of government spending on the war and ignoring most other state functions. This had disastrous consequences for the people of Angola, millions of whom fled either to Luanda or abroad. By 1999, Luanda had an estimated population of three million, despite only having the infrastructure capacity to accommodate one million people.[73] Munslow suggests that in early 1999, 'Over 10% of the male population aged between 15 and 39 are soldiers in the rival armies; in addition there are literally hundreds of thousands of armed "civilians", members of irregular or paramilitary forces, or people holding arms for their own protection.'[74] This illustrates the scale of the conflict across the country and how entrenched fighting and warfare was three decades since both independence and the start of the war between the MPLA and UNITA. Furthermore, with the MPLA solely focused on military contest, shoring up infrastructure and basic services for either Luanda or Angola more widely was ignored.[75]

Although UNITA's military push towards Luanda was initially successful, it quickly became clear that the group had overextended itself, both in its ability to maintain control of this vast stretch of territory – especially in areas with hostile civilian populations – and in its ability to continue facing the conventionally competent FAA in direct combat.[76] UNITA returned to its previous methods of organizing and fighting,[77] which changed the character of the conflict from one of mostly conventional military tactics back to one of guerrilla tactics, shifting territorial control and deeply blurred demarcations of influence.[78] Most of the population resided in MPLA territory but UNITA still maintained significant influence in more rural and inaccessible areas,[79] denying full sovereignty to the MPLA even if UNITA was unable to contest the control of the MPLA at a national level.[80]

Importantly, UNITA was still claiming national goals and nationwide grievances even as their territorial control was shrinking, claiming to have been shut out of national politics and nationwide economic decision-making following the Bicesse process which Savimbi maintained had been rigged against UNITA.[81] Although millions had fled UNITA territory, implying little sympathy for the cause or belief in the group's ability to provide, UNITA still organized itself with state-like principles, claiming to administer its territory as a state. During these initial years of renewed conflict, UNITA successfully maintained good ties with local communities in remote areas that had been under UNITA control for decades.[82]

However, even these long-standing ties began to crumble as by 2000, the FAA continued to advance into UNITA strongholds, losses which were both symbolic and economically vital.[83] Being forced out of symbolic towns was detrimental to UNITA's authority with local populations, although UNITA still claimed the loyalty and support of locals, the increasing number of children fighting for UNITA suggested a lack of adults willing or available to fight for the group, therefore necessitating kidnapping or coercing children to fight instead.[84] Additionally, as international sanctions increasingly tightened the noose on UNITA support and the FAA intervened in other regional areas,[85] UNITA's external sources of support began to dry up.[86] Although UNITA continued to release public statements claiming impressive purchases of military equipment, there was little evidence of Soviet warplanes or tanks on the battlefield.[87] The FAA, on the other hand, was able to continue funding itself using oil revenue which had not been affected by the conflict, given the oil rigs' physical location off the coast of the country and far from UNITA's reach.[88] Therefore, the FAA was able to not only continue equipping its forces but also expand its technical military capabilities as it advanced further into the hinterlands long controlled by UNITA but increasingly coming under FAA influence.[89]

Following the death of Savimbi and UNITA's ensuing inability to find a clear successor for the mantle of UNITA leadership, the remaining senior members of the group quickly realized that the prospect of the FAA's campaign of 'surrender-or-die' was even nearer to reality than had been previously understood. In addition, there was little economic and military capacity to continue the fight to defeat the FAA and gain political power through military conquest, and the prospect of further decades in the bush launching small-scale guerrilla attacks was clearly no longer compelling. It was a combination of these leadership, economic and military realities that hampered UNITA's leverage during the Luena negotiations and allowed the MPLA to dominate both on the battlefield and at the negotiating table.[90]

In order to come up with some sort of leadership structure, the various branches of UNITA began to discuss potential leadership candidates, mainly between one of the remaining senior generals (Paulo Lukamba or General Gato), the current head of UNITA-Renovato (Eugenio Manuvakola) one of UNITA's remaining international diplomatic figures (Isaias Samakuva). Leaders within the various components of UNITA held an internal vote in mid-2002 and General Gato emerged as the nominated leader at least for the immediate negotiations process.[91] This again emphasized the nature of the military-centric talks and expertise allowed by the MPLA.

Prior to the actual signing of the Luena Treaty, the FAA announced a ceasefire in early March 2002, which also included a blanket amnesty for UNITA fighters (as well as FAA soldiers accused of crimes) as well as a reaffirmation of the continuation of the Lusaka Treaty.[92] This blanket amnesty faced international disapproval. This was because it was deemed to inhibit investigations into human rights abuses as well as any attempts at broader reconciliation. However, given the lack of international leverage and involvement in the Luena discussions and the dominance of the MPLA's political position, these protests were ignored by the MPLA.[93] Furthermore, plans were announced for the immediate demobilization and sheltering of fighters and displaced peoples.[94] As the treaty itself remained narrowly focused on strictly military matters, resolving the issue of thousands of displaced Angolans remained a persistently unresolved issue.

Diamonds

By 1998, UNITA had very little international support due to changes in the MPLA's international standing (discussed earlier), with sources of international funding likewise drying up.[95] This meant that diamond revenues, which had previously comprised a large part of UNITA's funding, now became the sole means by which the group continued to survive financially.[96] This increased the incentive to accelerate production, requiring more low-skilled and physically intensive labour. This was not an appealing prospect for locals in UNITA-controlled areas, as lower levels of funding meant that UNITA was unable to continue providing the quasi-state services that it had managed for populations under its control in previous years – efforts it had abandoned in favour of a focus on maintaining arms supplies.[97] This had the direct result of tying UNITA to its diamond revenues, and elevating the continued control and access to diamond-mining areas as existential to the group's survival, replacing the support of the largest demographic group in the country, which had previously been UNITA's basis for both support and legitimacy.[98] Furthermore, this economic distancing between rural populations and UNITA worked in tandem with the forced conscription of people in UNITA-controlled areas into mining or fighting to increase fear, mistrust and hatred of the group, significantly eroding popular support for UNITA.[99] This is evidenced by the tens of thousands who fled UNITA areas for either coastal cities controlled by the MPLA or for other countries. This exodus was particularly acute in the 1998–2002 phase of the civil war, directly impacting the group's ability to fund continued military operations.[100]

UNITA became famous for mining and selling diamonds to fuel their war-fighting capacity from 1997 onwards, as it became clear to the UNSC that UNITA was rearming surreptitiously mainly via diamond funding.[101] However, UNITA had been in control of the diamond-rich areas of Angola since the 1970s and had, in fact, been mining diamonds and using the revenue to fund its war efforts throughout the 1990s, not just as the Lusaka Treaty began to fail.[102] This experience meant that by 1997, UNITA had established internal structures and organizational knowledge of international diamond-selling procedures which enabled them to quickly ramp up mining during the peace instigated by the Lusaka Treaty and maintain it once the conflict began again.[103] What is significant about UNITA's post-Lusaka use of diamond revenues is therefore not the initiation of this practice, but the expansion of it and the sole reliance on these profits to continue their military campaign.

The scale of UNITA's use of diamond revenues is important for three reasons. First, the sheer amount of money was significant, with various sources quoting UNITA diamond revenues in excess of $400 million in 1999,[104] $3.7 billion from 1992[105] or, most conservatively, the UN-estimated $500 million per year.[106] While this was not necessarily sufficient capital to maintain arms and supplies for a full conventional army (as the MPLA was consistently capable of doing),[107] it was certainly sufficient in Angola's war-torn economy to maintain UNITA's control over its territory and allow them to launch attacks throughout much of the country.

Second, the geographic distribution of Angola's diamond deposits explains which territories UNITA prioritized maintaining physical control over. Diamonds were not directly mentioned in the Lusaka Treaty, although at the time of signing, UNITA controlled two-thirds of the country's diamond-rich areas.[108] However, many of these areas were designated as some of the initial territories the group was meant to give back to government administration during the implementation of the Lusaka Treaty and, perhaps unsurprisingly, were some of the territories UNITA most delayed relinquishing control over. The impending loss of control over diamond-rich areas was a key reason for UNITA to delay in complying with the Lusaka Treaty, leading to the eventual unravelling of the treaty.[109] This also explains why some of these territories with otherwise little strategic or symbolic significance were some of the first areas that the FAA targeted once the war officially resumed in 1998.[110] Even though the FAA did have some initial success in driving UNITA out of some diamond-rich areas, UNITA maintained control of sufficient resources even after 2000 to continue to fund guerilla efforts.[111]

UNITA was able to mine diamonds effectively even while fighting the MPLA for both geographic and economic reasons. Geographically, Angola's diamonds are primarily alluvial (mainly found in rivers), meaning that the mining process is low-cost and does not require specific expertise.[112] These were ideal economic conditions for UNITA, as they had access to easily exploited labourers with little education or alternative economic prospects, and could keep costs of extraction low in order to make the most profit from selling the diamonds. The fact that the physical process of mining diamonds did not require education meant that it was also easy to keep the process heavily centralized within the UNITA leadership, as few needed to have specific knowledge to carry out and manage the process. This appealed to Savimbi's drive for personal centralization throughout the group but made UNITA overly centralized in terms of decision-making, developing a dangerous brittleness.[113]

Another geographic benefit was the situation of these riverbed diamonds primarily in Angola's interior, making them harder for the coastally based MPLA to take over.[114] The deposits' proximity to Angola's borders with other countries also enabled expedited smuggling to international buyers, primarily through the Democratic Republic of the Congo (DRC) and Zambia.[115] The proximity to these borders inhibited the MPLA's ability to physically isolate UNITA from cross-border smuggling networks, perhaps incentivizing the MPLA to take more drastic action in the DRC in order to limit UNITA's cross-border supply capacities.

UNITA's diamond profiteering is also significant for a third reason: the massive international commercial and criminal networks that the group became a part of, which were sufficiently complex to inhibit the effective implementation of either UN Security Council-imposed sanctions or crackdowns by individual national governments.[116] Thousands of dollars worth of diamonds mined in eastern Angola might, for example, be sewn into the lining of a suit (diamonds do not show up in metal detectors),[117] worn by a mid-level UNITA member who flew on a small plane to Lusaka, Zambia, to negotiate medical supplies and sold to both legitimate and criminal commercial buyers in Lusaka. From there, these Angolan diamonds might be mixed into a bag with South Africa and Congolese diamonds (tracing the specific geographic origins of diamonds is scientifically difficult),[118] then bought by another middleman, perhaps an Israeli, then sold in the diamond capital of the world, Antwerp, Belgium, to be made into jewellery and sold to consumers around the world.[119] If governments like the United States, for example, tried to stop Belgian diamond purveyors from working with Angolan diamonds, by the time the diamonds reached Belgium, their origins would be nearly impossible to untangle.[120] To add complexity, in the late 1990s, South African diamond-mining giant De Beers was responsible for over 80 per cent of the world's diamond supplies and was accused of mixing in Angolan diamonds amongst South African ones in order to maintain its domination of the market while avoiding the perception of profiting from a bloody conflict.[121] Companies with substantial monopolies like De Beers are naturally resistant to external audits, and, as a private company, relatively impervious to sanctions regimes imposed and intended to be implemented by governments against other governments, not corporations.[122]

The UNSC attempted to impose sanctions on UNITA's diamond industry in 1997 and multiple times in 1998. These efforts were significantly hampered by the fact that although most of Angola's diamond deposits were in UNITA-controlled areas, not all of them were.[123] That meant that although UNITA was the primary actor using diamonds to fund its military campaigns, there were also diamond mines operated by the MPLA, specifically the FAA.[124] Therefore, even if a diamond could be definitively confirmed to have originated in Angola, that fact alone was not a guarantee that it had been mined by UNITA rather than the internationally recognized MPLA government. There was no international appetite for UNSC action against the MPLA because it was the internationally recognized government of Angola. The UNSC sanctions were specifically against UNITA's sale of diamonds. Naturally, the inability to accurately assess which diamonds came from UNITA versus the FAA also made the MPLA less willing to assist in the implementation of these sanctions, for fear of decreasing their own diamond revenues.[125] The MPLA therefore focused on cutting off UNITA's cross-border access more broadly, rather than assiduously working with the international community to stop the mining of diamonds in their country.[126]Furthermore, there had been a negative shift in the international perception of UNITA and Savimbi which perceived them as the instigators of the failure of the Bicesse and Lusaka processes. Additionally, there were much higher legal barriers to sanctioning the MPLA's use of diamond revenues due to state sovereignty protections fundamental to the UN Charter.[127]

In fact, this was one of the key reasons that the Kimberley Process, an international regime meant to track and eradicate blood diamonds, was not in fact ratified until 2003, after the conclusion of Angola's civil war. Without the cooperation of the Angolan government, a country with some of the largest diamond deposits in the world,[128] the process could not go forward.[129] It is likely not a coincidence that the 2003 post-war Angolan government was willing to join this programme to regulate diamond mining and international sales,[130] but was not even willing to participate in discussions around this possibility when the conversation began around 1998.[131]

In addition to the geographic, economic and international implications of UNITA's reliance on income from its diamond sales, that reliance also had consequences for UNITA's leadership and relationship with the people who lived in territories it controlled. Throughout its history, UNITA had portrayed itself as the champion for the Angolan people, particularly for the Ovimbundu identity group which represented the largest demographic in the country.[132] Although UNITA's international ideology shifted in a myriad of ways from the 1960s onwards, UNITA's domestic messaging was consistently about representation for this group and for Angolans more broadly, contrasting with the MPLA that was described as being mainly by and for those with Portuguese descent and focused on the capital of Luanda. Despite all of UNITA's other ups and downs throughout the conflict, this messaging was consistent and relatively well received by the rural populations in its strongholds.[133] During the 1998–2002 fighting, however, this messaging began to break down as a direct result of UNITA's increased reliance on diamond revenues.[134]

The loss of popular support was not actually a decisively weakening factor for UNITA's ability to continue fighting, as it could operate diamond mines by using the revenues to buy or coerce the necessary labour to keep the mines going. Instead, as long as UNITA could still mine and sell diamonds, it was able to fight, regardless of the support or needs of the population it still spoke of defending.[135] Diamonds, therefore, were crucial to funding UNITA's war effort but also fundamentally tied to a loss of popular support, a narrowing of reasons to fight, reduced claim to legitimacy, a brittleness in leadership and a reliance on a single source of funding that is dangerous to any movement.

Oil

The previous section discussed how diamond revenues were used to fuel the last stage of the Angolan conflict from 1998 to 2002; in the previous section the discussion focused primarily on UNITA, but as the MPLA began to take over diamond-rich territories from UNITA in 2000, a similar dynamic continued to play out as the MPLA also had issues securing sufficient labour to operate diamond mines in order to gain revenue for further fighting. This section will discuss the other natural resource that played a massive role in funding Angola's continued conflict during this period: oil. The use of oil to fund the MPLA's war effort was a function of geography as well as international political networks and regimes of international law. It had similar consequences for the MPLA's ties to Angolan populations and the progress of the conflict. However, there are key differences in how oil fuelled the MPLA's war effort that arguably contributed significantly to how this resource was able to sufficiently fund the MPLA to the point of a military victory, whereas UNITA's diamond revenues were sufficient to keep UNITA in the conflict, but insufficient for the group to win. These differences are partially a function of international law and politics, but have their roots primarily in geographic facts that the MPLA was able to take advantage of, rather than circumstances they intentionally created.

Angola has the second largest set of oil deposits in Africa (after Nigeria), making Angola one of the richest oil countries in the world. Since independence in 1975, this has been one of the main sources of revenue for the Angolan government, but for much of the early stages of the Angolan war, oil exportation was hampered by

Cold War dynamics that inhibited Western oil companies from fully investing in developing and extracting Angola's oil wealth. Although some Western companies like Chevron had operated in Angola for decades by the end of the Cold War,[136] it was only during the Clinton administration's push for expanded free trade in Southern Africa that the US government and more oil companies began to fully engage with the MPLA through trade.[137] Angola was considered to be in the Soviet sphere of influence and the then-Marxist MPLA had laws prohibiting trading with the West. Following the end of the Cold War, these restrictions were lifted; by the late 1990s, oil revenues were one of the largest contributions to Angola's GDP. The MPLA government was able to extract the maximum possible revenue from this resource in order to fund the conflict.[138]

At no point during the entire 1975–2002 conflict was UNITA ever in a position to challenge the MPLA for control of Angola's oil resources. This is not a function of military, political or economic factors, but geography: Angola's oil resources are located either off the coast of Angola or in Cabinda, a northern territory exclusively controlled by the MPLA since independence in order to maintain control over its oil reserves.[139] Since its founding, the MPLA has been based along the Angolan coast and from independence has kept exclusive control of the coastally located capital city of Luanda. Subsequently, UNITA never contested control over off-shore oil resources – the same geographic isolation that protected many of UNITA's diamond mines and cross-border smuggling routes for much of the conflict also entirely protected the MPLA's oil resources from any attacks from UNITA.

This basic geographic fact had important political, military and economic consequences. First, the MPLA was able to build its entire patronage network around reliance on oil revenues as there was no chance of losing those wells to military contest.[140] Likewise, the certainty of continued MPLA control calmed Western investors and oil companies who otherwise were reluctant to invest in any shore-based industries that could be physically disrupted by war.[141] The off-shore nature of oil production gave the FAA a secure funding stream for its military endeavours and also meant that few military resources were needed to guard these all-important resources from potential attack. This was especially true given that the MPLA had a naval force, which UNITA never did;[142] naval units, which had no other part to play in defeating UNITA could easily focus on guarding the oil wells without compromising the combat strength of the rest of the FAA. Economically, the fact that the MPLA's main GDP contributor was oil meant that the government was fundamentally tied into international oil markets and economies in a very direct and relatively powerful way, and, given the strategic importance of oil and therefore the weight given to countries with large oil reserves in international politics and economics.[143] It also enabled the MPLA government to continue its political and military efforts within the country without requiring much economic buy-in from the populace, thus further distancing the MPLA from the Angolan people, similar to the way that diamond revenues distanced UNITA from its former core constituents.

Beyond geography, however, international law was another significant factor in the MPLA's open reliance on oil revenues to directly fund the 1998–2002 conflict, contrasting with UNITA's use of diamond revenues reliant on smuggling and secretive methods. This is quite simply due to the fact that as has already been outlined, by 1998, the MPLA was internationally recognized as the legitimate Angolan government, with all the rights to operate on the international economic market entailed by that designation and without any remaining Cold War-era political barriers.[144] As the sole recognized government, the MPLA was able to negotiate contracts with oil companies to extract and develop oil or take out loans from international financial institutions paid by oil revenues without questions as to the legitimacy of the MPLA's authority over these resources.[145] Likewise, companies could trade directly with the MPLA government without worrying about international sanctions or domestic repercussions.[146] This freed the MPLA from relying on secretive middlemen and smugglers, all of whom would require their own cut of the profits, thereby diminishing the overall returns. UNITA did not have this luxury and its profit margins suffered.[147] Similarly, the UNSC never once sanctioned the MPLA or its sources of revenue, nor tried to minimize or halt oil production in Angola, even as it became increasingly clear that these revenues were primarily and directly funding a brutal war effort and not at all into infrastructure improvements, service provision or transparent governance.[148] Although the norm of non-interference was undergoing substantive changes elsewhere in the world by this time, for the reasons explored so far, classical national sovereignty still protected the MPLA from external constraints on its internal governance.

A shift in international politics mainly due to changes in US policies under the Clinton administration also benefitted the MPLA and further empowered it to use oil revenue. As has already been demonstrated, the Clinton administration broke with decades of precedent by sanctioning Savimbi and refusing to continue monetary or political support for UNITA. In addition, beyond merely recognizing the MPLA as Angola's government,[149] Clinton had a broader agenda to develop US economic ties in Africa, including in Angola, with a parallel agenda of economic liberalization.[150] In Angola's case, economic liberalization encouraged the MPLA to strengthen economic ties with US companies and develop private markets, moving away from its Marxist past but did not improve transparency, entrench democracy or combat corruption, especially as Angola's trade activities expanded, making individual transactions harder to track.[151] Regardless of the failure of Clinton's democratizing efforts in Angola, economic ties continued and oil was central to this trading relationship.[152] This massive oil industry also gave the MPLA other diplomatic channels through which to engage with international actors, including key trading partners like the United States.[153] This likely contributed to ensuring a consistent external angle of approach that was distinctly anti-UNITA from the late 1990s onwards.

All of these factors combined meant that the MPLA was able to fund its war effort primarily through protected and lucrative oil revenues with international cooperation, rather than interference – to great effect.[154] Even with the international oil market slump in the late 1990s,[155] the MPLA was still able to extract so much money from selling oil that the FAA continued improving its military capabilities. The FAA purchased additional conventional land weaponry but also increased its aerial power and technological surveillance capacities, key for searching out guerilla-style UNITA hideouts in dense remote areas. Although the FAA's use of conventional tactics against a guerilla force was not especially efficient,[156] their clear capital dominance and therefore equipment advantage was sufficient to begin to push UNITA back from 2000 onwards.

In contrast, the reliance on oil revenues had a direct negative effect on the millions of Angolans living in MPLA territory. The fact that the government did not need to rely on the population to fund its war meant that there was essentially no pressure the population could leverage against the government in order to obtain improved infrastructure or service provisions for a populace devastated by decades of violence.[157] The humanitarian situation, even in theoretically prosperous coastal cities, was dismal.[158] This was further exacerbated by the environment of extreme corruption facilitated by the overwhelming focus on defeating UNITA militarily in pursuit of that goal, oil revenues were funnelled directly to the FAA, rather than distributed more equally via normal government channels or mechanisms.[159] Official government wages became useless, and corrupt patronage networks were the only substantial sources of wages that existed throughout much of the country during the last years of the war.[160] Funnelling oil funds directly to the FAA also incentivized some generals to continue the fight against UNITA, with the understanding that their access to huge amounts of money was predicated on continued warfare. This feedback loop created incentives to draw out the conflict for their own economic gain,[161] thus creating even worse humanitarian conditions and increasing corruption in the country.[162] This strengthened the influence of the FAA within the MPLA, which weakened moderate politicians who had less of a role in the war effort and therefore less money and consequently less leverage in deciding the trajectory and agenda of the party. Similar to UNITA, this centralized the MPLA's leadership structure to the point of brittleness, lending a significant advantage to those most closely aligned with the military who had a vested interest in continuing the conflict.[163]

Oil, therefore, was crucial to funding the MPLA's war effort but also fundamentally tied to a loss of popular support,[164] a narrowing of reasons to fight and a brittleness in leadership and funding.[165] In the MPLA's case, however, the combination of protected geographic location and active international support meant that this oil revenue was necessary and sufficient to fuel the war effort; without it, the MPLA lacked the ability to unilaterally defeat UNITA in battle without international military support.

Local geopolitical changes

Aside from the difference in funding streams and tactics discussed in previous sections, there is one other important aspect of this last stage of the Angolan conflict that helps provide context for the negotiations around the Luena Treaty – regional dynamics. This section will explore the international dimensions of the last stages of Angola's civil war, specifically the MPLA's efforts to cut UNITA off from its last few allies, mainly the Mobutu regime of the country that is now, and throughout this book, is called the DRC. The MPLA also enacted a nearly identical campaign against another UNITA ally, the Lissouba regime in the Republic of Congo.[166]

The regimes in both Congos had initially supported the FNLA in the Angolan civil war (see Chapter 2). Following the MPLA's defeat of the FNLA within the first few years of the conflict, both regimes switched to supporting UNITA,[167] with President Mobutu developing both a personal and business relationship with Savimbi,[168] as evidenced, for example, by Savimbi being willing to participate when Mobutu hosted the failed Gbadolite summit in 1989 (see Chapter 3).[169] In the late 1990s, UNITA controlled most of the shared Angolan-Congolese border, providing the perfect route for UNITA to smuggle diamonds out and military and medical supplies into the country. Smuggling operations mainly used small aircraft[170] that could easily travel from the DRC into UNITA-controlled territories of Angola without crossing any hostile territory.[171] Although the FAA did have a far-superior air force to either the DRC or UNITA, the breadth of Angola as well as the dense and inaccessible nature of the UNITA-controlled areas meant that these smuggling planes were generally quite safe from FAA threat.[172]

The FAA began to push to reclaim strategic symbolic and diamond-rich areas from UNITA and successfully worked with the international community to isolate UNITA from former allies. This is evidenced by the closing of UNITA offices abroad[173] and the repeated attention from the UNSC on sanctioning UNITA's diamond revenues. However, these sanctions were difficult to enforce, as discussed in the previous section on diamonds. Therefore, the MPLA decided to disrupt UNITA's funding streams in parallel by cutting UNITA off from its regional allies.[174] To the MPLA, the continuation of a pro-UNITA regime in the DRC had to be eradicated if UNITA's supply routes were to be fully cut off and the group definitively defeated.[175] Additionally, the MPLA wanted to take advantage of the fact that in 1997, two regional organizations were both headed by MPLA allies and thus would help ensure that there was no coordinated regional response to counter the MPLA's overthrow campaigns in either Congo.[176]

Thus by 1997, the MPLA allied with a faction within the DRC led by Laurent Kabila to overthrow the Mobutu regime.[177] The comprehensive analysis of the First Congo War is beyond the scope of this book, but the fact that the MPLA was a direct ally of this overthrow is directly relevant, as this alliance was made explicitly for the purpose of denying UNITA supply and retreat routes that could potentially ensure its survival just across the Angolan border.[178] The MPLA wanted UNITA to be completely defeated, not harried into a safe haven across an international border.[179] Under such a scenario, the MPLA would receive strong international condemnation for crossing international borders, thus forcing the MPLA to live with a still-existing UNITA threat. Thus, the intervention into the DRC to help install an anti-UNITA government was seen as a worthwhile investment, even though it split FAA military efforts and financing.[180]

This concentrated effort against the Mobutu regime was successful with Laurent Kabila installed as the president of the DRC in 1997, thus cutting off UNITA's official relationship and access to the DRC.[181] Fully policing the entire

2,421-kilometre-long border between UNITA-controlled parts of Angola and the DRC was still beyond the scope of either the MPLA or the Kabila regime.[182] Still, UNITA did have to spend more effort and money hiding their cross-border efforts, which further cut into their organizational, labour and economic capacities.[183] This was especially true as the MPLA left 7,000 soldiers in the DRC to police the border from the Congolese side.[184] From the MPLA's point of view, therefore, this was a successful operation to weaken UNITA.

In addition to acting against pro-UNITA regimes in the Republic of the Congo and the DRC, the MPLA was also increasingly hostile towards Zambia; another country through which UNITA laundered diamonds and imported arms.[185] The MPLA started with a pressure campaign for Zambia to comply with international sanctions against engaging in UNITA's diamond trade.[186] However, this generally went unheeded as a large portion of border-dwelling Zambians (as well as senior Zambian officials)[187] had developed economic incentives to continue engaging in cross-border smuggling with UNITA.[188] The MPLA then resorted to threats of violence,[189] which, given the FAA's involvement in the overthrow of two other neighbouring regimes, was potentially more convincing.[190] While there were plots to bomb parts of Lusaka, these plans went awry when the bombs exploded prematurely in the Angolan embassy, making the would-be perpetrators clear.[191] Following this incident, the MPLA stopped threats of violence, helped by mediation from Swaziland, but accusations of contravening UN sanctions to help UNITA continued until the end of the conflict.[192] Still, an important oil refinery in the north of Zambia was blown up, leaving the country short in fuel in late 1999, at the same time that UNITA ran out of fuel in trying to defend two of its most important strongholds.[193] While it remains unclear whether this was an MPLA-orchestrated attack or merely a coincidence, this incident illustrates how targeting Angola's neighbours for their support of Savimbi and UNITA changed dramatically from 1997 onwards.

This had significant consequences for UNITA's ability to combat and survive FAA assault, as well as setting a very different regional stage for the next peace treaty. Essentially, the MPLA's successful regional diplomacy, backed by economic and military coercion, removed the majority of UNITA's regional supporters. By 2000, UNITA had lost not only local support within Angola, international support in the UN and from the US, but also nearby regional support which had previously provided diplomatic weight, safe havens for UNITA leaders and access to international economic and diplomatic circles. Thus, the group was fundamentally weakened on a number of structural levels and cut off from nearly all previous support networks, showing how the pace and impact of the conflict directly influenced UNITA's negotiating position during the Luena process.

Content of the treaty

The Luena Treaty, technically a Memorandum of Understanding, was explicitly based on the Lusaka Treaty. It therefore billed itself quite narrowly as aiming to fix the military issues that had impeded the full implementation of the Lusaka

Treaty and made no further changes to the previously established mechanisms of Angola's peace processes. In fact, the document opened with the statement that: 'The subject of the Memorandum of Understanding is the commitment of the parties, through fraternal and active collaboration, to guarantee the achievement and activation of the cease-fire and resolution of all pending military issues.'[194] These outstanding security aspects were considered to be the 'definitive resolution of the armed conflict, and the renewed undertaking of the complete execution of the task of finishing the formation of the Angolan Armed Forces.'[195] Therefore, the Luena Treaty focused specifically on the military issues that had been left incomplete during the Lusaka process rather than create an entirely new peace treaty.[196]

This MPLA-centric conception of the Luena Treaty undoubtedly made it easier to negotiate quickly for multiple reasons. First, as there was less content to cover, there were no outside actors to pressure for a more inclusive treaty model.[197] Also, all the provisions were all within the areas of military and security issues, requiring only one set of expertise from either side – something both sides had in ready supply given the twenty-seven years of conflict.[198] While the Bicesse and Lusaka treaties were fundamentally flawed, as previous chapters have argued, this was primarily related to the security provisions and the plans for their implementation. By redrafting these sections, the Luena Treaty therefore resolved some of the flaws of the previous treaties.

Like the Lusaka Treaty, the Luena Treaty was fundamentally centred on the understanding that UNITA was to blame for the conflict[199] and that there would be no prospects for further conflict once the group's military capabilities had been eradicated through demobilization. This demobilization would mainly be into civilian life, though some soldiers were to join the now officially MPLA-dominated FAA. As the MPLA still considered the Lusaka Treaty to be in effect, they still planned to implement the provisions for UNITA involvement in national and provincial politics. One major reason these provisions were not changed is likely due to the fact that although the Lusaka Treaty guaranteed UNITA political involvement, the treaty generally made sure that any such involvement was in a politically subordinate position. Ensuring the continued political dominance of the MPLA had been a significant sticking point in the last treaty, as Chapter 4 discusses with regard to the challenges of finding an appropriate position for Savimbi. Therefore, with his death in 2002, these political plans could go forward, and the MPLA could both maintain claims to international legitimacy by appearing to uphold the terms of the Lusaka treaty while also resting assured that UNITA would not become a political threat.[200] As such, there was no need for the Luena Treaty to address any political issues, as the MPLA considered them already taken care of.

The agenda of the Luena Treaty was entirely concerned with military issues, the list of which is worth including in full here:

a) 'Ceasefire;
b) Disengagement, quartering and completion of the demilitarisation of UNITA Military Forces;

c) Integration into the Angolan Armed Forces of general officers, senior officers, junior officers, non-commissioned officers and junior enlisted personnel of UNITA Military Forces, in accordance with existing vacancies;

d) Integration into the National Police of general officers and senior officers of the Military Forces of UNITA, in accordance with existing vacancies;

e) Demobilisation of excess personnel from UNITA Military Forces and the extinction of the Armed Forces of UNITA;

f) Social and professional reintegration into national life of personnel demobilised from the ex-UNITA Military Forces.'[201]

This list is interesting for a number of reasons. First, it is a much shorter agenda than in previous treaties, showing the importance of learning from the experiences of previous treaty negotiations. It was by now a familiar process and one that could rely on previous treaties to cover wider aspects of the conflict. This allowed the Luena Treaty to narrowly focus on addressing only the areas deemed still problematic. This list highlights quite clearly how the Angolan peace process created both its own norms and momentum. Throughout all the negotiations from 1989 onwards, certain expectations and provisions were fixed and carried through to subsequent treaties. These were mainly around the primacy of elections over completed demobilization and an insistence on comprehensive disarmament without sufficient time allotted for verifying this. Both of these prompts stemmed from a single underlying assumption that democratic elections would be solely necessary and sufficient to permanently resolve political tensions that had previously only been negotiated through violence.[202] Even as circumstances changed and implementation continually failed, these assumptions were not adjusted sufficiently.[203] This shows a lack of mental flexibility, bureaucratic inertia and other organizational psychological barriers.

Second, this list is, for the first time, directly explicit about the goal of fundamentally disarming and demobilizing UNITA entirely, without any remaining military capability. Given the security dilemmas present in the breakdown of the previous two treaties, this declaration (and the fact that UNITA signed the treaty despite its inclusion) shows just how militarily depleted UNITA was in 2002.[204] Third, UNITA lacked agency in negotiating their influence within these institutions. The fact that an explicit limitation on integrating UNITA personnel into the FAA and police forces only 'in accordance with existing vacancies' appeared in the treaty's agenda – as opposed to appearing merely in the provisions and modalities included in the treaty's appendices, as had been the case in the Lusaka Treaty – shows the dominance of the MPLA and FAA.[205]

Finally, the inclusion of 'social and professional integration' as a key agenda item shows an increased understanding of the importance of comprehensive integration to remove the temptation to return to conflict. This is one of the most significant changes from the security provisions of the previous two treaties, which had considered disarmament and demobilization the immediate challenges requiring the most focus and assumed in relatively broad terms that reintegration would necessarily follow. This is one area in which the Luena negotiators seemed to be learning from the failures of the previous two implementation processes.

Another significant change between this treaty and the previous two was the international community's comparative lack of a role in either the negotiations process or in the implementation terms. The negotiations were undertaken entirely by the FAA and UNITA-in-the-bush military command; no outside actors had any official involvement in the negotiations. After Savimbi's death, President dos Santos did immediately fly to Portugal and the United States to consult with the heads of both countries, but this was considered a behind-the-scenes discussion, not official involvement in negotiations.[206] The reasons for this lack of international involvement are still unknown, though evidence suggests that the MPLA did not want international interference in favour of UNITA. In fact, the discussions took place in former UNITA territory and not in Luanda, a more diplomatically accessible location. This is likely a further explanation for the speed with which the negotiations were finalized: without the need to adhere to diplomatic conventions of bureaucracy and posturing, there were fewer barriers to simply sitting down and writing plans. In the implementation plans as well, no concession was made to directly include any international actors in either verification, monitoring or implementation roles. The FAA explicitly took on the role of setting up and administering assembly areas, as well as overseeing disarmament and demobilization.[207]

The one area in which international actors were involved was the creation of a joint military commission between UNITA and the FAA to monitor any unforeseen issues that arose during implementation.[208] The troika of the US, Russia and Portugal, as well as UN military officials, were invited as observers to this commission.[209] However, the impact was limited, since outsiders were invited primarily as observers or had a minimal role as technical advisors. In fact, the creation of a commission to adjudicate issues mirrors quite closely in principle the committee used in Mozambique to significant success, as discussed in Chapter 4. This was also the first time a committee like this had been explicitly outlined in any of the Angolan peace treaties. This signalled an important lesson learnt from previous implementation failures, namely, the need to ensure that there was a practical solution to delays or unforeseen circumstances on the ground that could be resolved rather than devolving into larger political problems.

Furthermore, designating this committee in charge of the implementation schedule was another modification that allowed for adaptability in a way that had not been possible in previous treaties. While the improved flexibility was more in line with what had been agreed on in Mozambique, the mechanism of adjustment was different, as instead of having a firm schedule laid out in the treaty, with a built-in extension method, the Luena Treaty outlined some of the schedule but then gave this committee authority to make an unrestricted number of adjustments to the schedule once implementation began.[210] While this could have resulted in compounded delays as had been seen after the Lusaka Treaty, the lack of a coordinated or strong UNITA likely reassured the FAA that this flexibility would continue to be under their control. It does suggest, however, that in a more equal military situation than that in Angola in 2002, this kind of mechanism for scheduling adjustments may have run into significant problems.

In terms of the actual numbers of UNITA combatants and dependents that would need to be processed, the Luena Treaty definitely learnt from the UN numbers that came out of previous DDR processes in Angola and planned from the outset to provide room for 50,000 UNITA combatants.[211] Considering estimates of UNITA's fighting strength in 2001 numbered at most 30,000 (UNITA's estimates) and perhaps closer to 8,000 (FAA estimates),[212] this was a much more comprehensive plan than any that had been undertaken under UNAVEM II or UNAVEM III, which habitually underestimated the number of UNITA soldiers they would need to provide capacity for (see Chapter 4). Interestingly, the Luena Treaty also designated the number of positions within UNITA that these assembly areas would hold: 'Approximately 12 generals and 47 brigadier generals, around 1,700 senior officers, about 17,350 junior officers, around 3,150 sergeants/non-commissioned officers and about 27,740 other enlisted personnel.'[213]

This specificity might suggest that the FAA had a very good idea of UNITA's composition at this point, suggesting further military and intelligence weaknesses on UNITA's part as well as a lack of negotiating room in concealing this information.[214] Alternatively, it could suggest that the FAA was prepared to impose these categorizations and felt sufficiently comfortable in their abilities to make reality fit these numbers that they were willing to include them in the treaty itself. Given that an addendum to the treaty was quickly added to expand the numbers to 70,000 UNITA members and up to 400,000 dependents once implementation began and the assembly areas began to fill up,[215] these initial numerical estimates perhaps give more weight to the theory of UNITA's poor negotiating position. The FAA's willingness to accept UNITA's estimations and not later accuse UNITA of purposefully obfuscating information shows that the MPLA and FAA felt strong enough compared to UNITA that numerical discrepancies with regard to UNITA's fighting forces were no longer a source of military concern.

In terms of what would happen to these UNITA combatants after processing in the assembly areas, the treaty noted that six lieutenant generals and fourteen brigadier generals would be included into the FAA general staff,[216] which is actually more generous than the Lusaka Treaty's terms of a total of nine UNITA generals, without the promise of their inclusion onto the general staff (see Chapter 4). This perhaps signals that the FAA, as they were themselves military leaders and were directly negotiating with UNITA's military leaders, knew the importance of status that this concession would give and hoped that including this term in the treaty would enable the MPLA to avoid having to make any other political or leadership changes. This likelihood is strengthened by the fact that after the Luena Treaty was signed, both of the main military signatories on each side received important diplomatic and administrative posts.[217] In addition, this could also signal an attempt by the FAA to split UNITA's military leaders from their subordinates, who, after all, were only promised inclusion into the FAA 'according to existing vacancies', which is much less promising than guarantees of general ranks. Especially since the treaty expects 50,000 UNITA members, and then later says that up to 45,000 of these may be 'subject to social-professional reintegration',[218] this implies that a mere 5,000 UNITA members would be allowed to join the FAA and police.[219] Although UNITA's forces may have been sufficiently depleted for this number to be accurate, it still represents a significant downsizing in the promise of inclusion from the Lusaka Treaty's 30,000 UNITA members and the 26,300 who had been officially integrated prior to the resumption of war.[220]

Implementing Angola's Luena Treaty

The following sections will explore the four main stages of the Luena Treaty's implementation. First, the section will analyse the quartering, disarmament and initial demobilization phases, which generally were more successful than previous attempts due to fewer structural barriers and a secure military situation. Second, the section will address the integration of UNITA combatants into the FAA, which was fundamentally straightforward because it simply saw the absorption of 5,000 fighters into an institution without any structural changes. Third, the section will discuss the wider programme of civilian integration, showcasing how these programmes face logistical challenges and delays regardless of the institution responsible for carrying them out. Finally, the longer-term political, military and economic integration elements of Angola's post-conflict reconstruction situation will be briefly described and assessed.

Assembly areas, disarmament and demobilization

Almost immediately following the signing of the Luena Treaty, the creation of assembly areas for UNITA troops began. This speed, notable compared to the previous two treaties, was likely for two reasons: first, without international involvement, there were no travel and logistical delays in initiating processing or coordination issues with local actors; and second, with the FAA firmly in charge on the ground, a unilateral ceasefire reduced security risks.[221] For these reasons, the eighty days given for the quartering, disarmament and demobilization of UNITA troops outlined in the Luena Treaty[222] was a somewhat more reasonable prediction than the timeframes in the previous treaties. Still, it did not take into account the massive scale of the UNITA members who arrived, particularly as it vastly underestimated, as had previous processes, the number of dependents who would arrive for registration along with combatants.[223] Due to higher-than-expected numbers, the eighty days required extension, though registration was still announced as completed in August 2002,[224] even as official plans noted that some assembly areas would remain open until early 2003.[225] The number of assembly areas expanded from twenty-seven planned to thirty-five total,[226] and by the end of July 2002, these assembly areas held a total of over 85,000 UNITA combatants and over 280,000 dependents.[227] By February 2003, these numbers had increased to 435,000 total combatants and dependents across the assembly areas.[228]

As occurred in previous quartering processes, the condition of housing and food supplies in the camps were insufficient, especially as the number of people arriving for registration far outstripped the expanded camp number capacity. The general economic conditions in Angola at the time included rampant corruption and a near-total lack of public services. Combined with the even greater deprivations common in formerly UNITA areas due to the stresses of twenty-seven years of war, malnutrition, lack of sufficient food and other resources were common across all of the assembly areas.[229] Furthermore, as the number of registrants was larger than expected, this then delayed the next steps of the demobilization and reintegration processes, meaning that thousands of people were in camps for several months to a full year.[230] This was insufficient time to grow crops to sustain themselves or engage in sustainable economic activities.[231] This worsened the food security and overall economic situation for these hundreds of thousands of formerly UNITA-related Angolans.[232] Although the MPLA was soliciting humanitarian aid and reconstruction funding from a variety of international actors, in the initial months little came of this, likely due as much from overstretched resources of international charities as from the inaccessible geographic nature of most of these camps, given the geography already discussed in this book common to formerly UNITA areas.[233]

In terms of who these UNITA combatants were, a World Bank report from 2002 suggested that 99.8 per cent of registered combatants were male, with an average age of thirty-three and an average of fourteen years claimed as fighting for UNITA, suggesting a general trend of young people and legal children being involved in the conflict. Furthermore, 70 per cent of those surveyed by the World Bank claimed no formal education beyond fourth grade, and many additionally noted that so many years fighting in the bush had eroded many educational skills, including literacy.[234] All of these demographic indicators suggest that this would be a population generally considered at risk for recidivism into violence, especially given worsening attitudes towards hopes for the future as delays in assembly areas lengthened. Interestingly, this combination of data did not lead to worries either from MPLA or international actors regarding renewed violence, yet again confirming how militarily dominant the FAA was seen by all actors at this point. Another contributing factor was a general finding by the World Bank that few combatants wished to join the FAA,[235] though this was both because of war weariness and also distrust of the security institution that had been responsible for UNITA's military defeat. Therefore it is not possible to conclusively determine how many UNITA combatants were interested in joining the security services in general as a livelihood provider, given the psychological barriers around the FAA in particular.

By late 2002, demobilization was beginning to occur in some assembly areas. The Luena Treaty had called for all UNITA combatants to be formally integrated into the FAA as a first step. Second, most were meant to be discharged immediately and then receive integration payments in the guise of military discharge stipends for five further months. The FAA preferred this option because it enabled them to directly process and therefore compile information on former UNITA fighters,[236] and by the World Bank who preferred to funnel money through existing government institutions rather than setting up new agencies or commissions. It quickly became apparent that due to the larger-than-expected registrants, it would be more logistically feasible to process most UNITA combatants through a parallel system of going into civilian life immediately from the assembly areas.[237] Throughout late 2002 and 2003, these processes proceeded, organized by Angolan administrators and funded mainly by international donors including the World Bank. The last assembly areas were closed in October 2003 with the World Bank reporting that over 100,000 UNITA combatants had been officially demobilized and disarmed.[238]

This quartering, disarmament and demobilization process was undoubtedly more efficient, effective and faster than previous processes that had been undertaken in Angola in the past. This was in large part because the entire process was run by the MPLA, which reduced the coordination, linguistic, personnel and equipment shortages experienced by every UN mission in Angola. The other key factor was the military dominance of the FAA which meant that security risks or delays over security dilemma concerns were largely eliminated. Still, conditions in the assembly areas were still problematic, signalling the larger impact of Angola's lack of infrastructure and greatly underdeveloped economy.[239] Outside observers commented that the disarmament processes were not comprehensive either in terms of UNITA's entire caches of weapons or the potentially up to 2.5 million small arms freely circulating in the civilian population.[240] Importantly, civilian defence groups, regardless of political allegiance, were left out of this process.[241] As the groups had primarily been created by the MPLA,[242] leaving them outside the peace process and therefore tacitly enabling their continued possession of weapons was likely a deliberate ploy of the MPLA's to hedge against any future UNITA resurgence.

In many ways, these stages of the reconstruction process were similar to comparable stages of the Mozambican reconstruction effort. Both processes had some but relatively few extensive delays due to gaps in expected versus realistic numbers of combatants and dependents. Both processes had problematic conditions in the assembly areas that had short-term consequences but did not lead to long-term insurrection. Both processes included disarmament but focused much more on registration and demobilization, and both processes had fewer than expected combatant requests to join the state security forces. What is of course a significant difference between the processes is the role of the international community, as the Mozambican process was overseen rigorously by UN peacekeepers. This therefore suggests that the problem with UN peacekeeping missions in Angola previously had not been their presence per se, but their capacity to carry out their role. Comparatively, ONUMOZ was more similar to the FAA in terms of its ability to guarantee security, access the entire country, work as the coordination hub and centre of all reconstruction efforts and dictate timelines and priorities. In contrast, neither UNAVEM II, UNAVEM III nor MONUA had many, if any, of those attributes. This, therefore, suggests that in these initial stages of quartering, disarmament and demobilization, the uniform of the administrators matters less than their resources, agency and capacities.

Integration into the FAA

In terms of FAA integration, this part of the demobilization process began early, with 5,000 UNITA members joining the FAA in April 2002 just after the treaty signing.[243] This was of course merely symbolic, and the more practical integration began in August 2002, when eighteen UNITA generals were formally included into the FAA.[244]

As mentioned in the earlier section, initially all UNITA soldiers were meant to join the FAA and then be discharged into civilian life, and this did occur for just under 80,000 UNITA members in July and August 2002.[245] The rationale for this idea was twofold: a combination of goals from the FAA and international donors. The MPLA and FAA wanted UNITA combatants to transition through the FAA in order to ensure a regular accounting method for UNITA's potential fighting force, though statements were also made about the potential for reconciliation.[246] The World Bank also had an interest in demobilization being organized in this way as due to its institutional structure; it was easier to give aid to permanent government institutions, such as the military, than to either temporary structures or to non-government agencies overseeing reconstruction.[247] However, as the number of combatants requiring demobilization became clear, the World Bank assisted the MPLA in creating a new government programme to centralize efforts.[248]

This meant that in terms of civilian reintegration, there were nearly 80,000 UNITA members who were treated as discharged FAA soldiers, whereas the other over 20,000 UNITA combatants were processed straight from assembly areas and given supply-based 'reintegration kits', rather than FAA discharge salaries. While this did not lead to significantly different outcomes between the two groups due to consolidation efforts made to centralize reintegration efforts in 2003,[249] it shows the extent to which the integration process was being reconfigured in real time. Once again this suggests a gap in the planning that went into the Luena Treaty, and a lack of sufficient learning from the previous two integration processes that had been attempted in Angola, not to mention lessons available from other countries by this point in 2002. It remains an untested counterfactual whether more international involvement in the drafting of the treaty could have alleviated these problems. Still, the international community had leverage at this time as the main donor of the process and could have used that to step in. However, given the lack of sufficient learning evident between the two internationally led processes previously in Angola, citing lack of domestic knowledge as responsible for this mildly unwieldy dual programme seems insufficiently supported.

The FAA did integrate 5,000 UNITA members, including eighteen generals into its forces, as outlined in the Luena Treaty, on time. However, there were no provisions in the treaty for guaranteed input of UNITA members into FAA structures or decision-making, and no provisions made to guarantee promotions, educational access or any other special support for former UNITA combatants to succeed in the FAA. Essentially, instead of being an equal or fully integrated institution on a structural level, the FAA simply absorbed 5,000 new soldiers into its ranks and thereafter treated them according to pre-existing FAA procedures.[250]

Given that the FAA was a typical state-centric conventional force, and with the demographic data represented in the World Bank numbers discussed in the previous section, it is unlikely that UNITA combatants who joined the FAA were in such position to succeed in this new environment. UNITA combatants had not previously received standardized military training that would have been recognized or valued by a state-centred conventional force like the FAA, thus meaning that UNITA fighters had to adapt to an entirely new system that was not built nor planning to adjust in order to maximize their existing knowledge or productively build upon it.

Civilian integration

In parallel to the FAA integration, demobilization into civilian life was progressing. By January 2003, it was estimated that 80 per cent of former UNITA combatants had been given their necessary documents and paid their reintegration payments either via lump sum or FAA discharge, both the equivalent of five months' pay in the FAA.[251] The influx of this money into assembly areas and other formerly UNITA territories was an apparent increase in immediate consumer purchases, especially alcohol, in celebration of demobilization.[252] Despite this initial success, the scale of the reintegration challenge was massive. According to a World Bank report from 2003: 'Almost 80,000 former UNITA soldiers and around 360,000 of their family members must be reintegrated socially and economically, as must the 33,000 troops due to be demobilised from the Angolan Armed Forces (FAA).'[253] A key priority noted by the World Bank and other international donors was making sure that assistance to ex-combatants worked within a wider programme of reintegration of Angola's displaced peoples, refugees and the country as a whole, to ensure that these funds helped communities regenerate more widely, especially in rural areas that had seen both the largest depopulations and the heaviest violence of the war.[254]

Under World Bank pressure to ensure more comprehensive reintegration as well as faster processing, the MPLA set up a government body to organize reintegration, starting in June 2003.[255] The plan was that all ex-combatants from UNITA as registered in assembly areas from April 2002 onwards would be eligible to receive five months of FAA salary, $100 for reintegration assistance and a toolkit for agricultural work with the programme planned to progress over three years.[256] Initially, these plans did not include the former combatants who had either been registered and begun demobilization or merely registered during either the Bicesse or Lusaka processes but were not included in post-Luena assembly areas.[257] As this population numbered over 100,000 this was potentially a massive oversight. The international donor community, however, successfully negotiated for these 'old caseloads' to be included in the ADRP programme,[258] even though this raised the size of the funds needed and the disbursement of international funding to the ADRP was already facing chronic delays. In addition, continued difficulty related to mined roads, rainy seasons and keeping track of the hundreds of thousands enrolled in the programme as well as the parallel humanitarian aid for Angolan civilians who were internally displaced or became refugees and were now returning to the country created further logistical delays.[259]

By March 2004, these delays meant that fewer than 8,000 UNITA combatants had received their full benefits from this programme.[260] This led to discontent amongst many who had not yet been processed as expectations had been raised and not yet met, including statements by UNITA's political leadership condemning the delays.[261] By June 2005, this number had expanded to 45,000 combatants who had received financial assistance, but not the equipment or tools for agricultural work that had been promised.[262] However, over 10,000 UNITA members had been given either government jobs or training (primarily by the Ministries of Health and Education) and a separate 8,000 UNITA members had found their own jobs independent of ADRP efforts.[263] Nevertheless, by 2008 when the ADRP officially closed, over 97,000 UNITA combatants had been officially demobilized, with over 50,000 receiving reintegration packages of supplies and nearly the full 97,000 receiving some form of financial support.[264]

Longer-term reconstruction in Angola

The MPLA and World Bank generally considered the reintegration schemes a success, pointing to the nearly 100,000 former UNITA combatants who had been processed and received financial reintegration support. Recent scholarship has acknowledged that despite the FAA's many failings, it remains the most integrated and representative public body in the country, because of the Luena and Lusaka goals and processes of integration.[265] However, surveys undertaken in 2008 of samples of up to 40,000 former UNITA members suggest that employment has been more of a struggle,[266] with 4 per cent reporting formal employment, 61 per cent reporting self-employment of some kind and 35 per cent still unemployed.[267] But more positively, over 90 per cent of these respondents nevertheless reported significant feelings of reintegration into their communities, citing support such as from church groups and local NGOs.[268] This exists within a larger picture of Angola's oil-focused and infrastructure-dominated aims of economic development and physical reconstruction, largely centred around urban areas and subject to rampant corruption, including by leading FAA generals.[269] Yet there has been little progress made in developing Angola's smaller urban areas, connecting rural areas into the national economy and improving government provisions that could inhibit corruption, such as rule of law, justice systems, educational access, human rights protections and so on.[270]

In terms of the political sphere, the MPLA remains dominant and has won every election in the post-conflict period.[271] Although over 100 political parties technically exist and UNITA remains the largest opposition party, the MPLA's control over state resources, especially media, makes it difficult for other parties to contest the MPLA's control.[272] UNITA has now regularized its leadership and developed a new generation of politicians and has rebuilt some of its local community ties in rural areas, building on decades of messaging around UNITA as the voice of the marginalized.[273] This is particularly pertinent to many rural communities as MPLA control over government services including education also means that the pro-MPLA war narrative has dominated the country's discourse. A blanket amnesty policy for both UNITA and FAA atrocities that is officially upheld by the state creates strong discouragement from investigating war experiences or memories in public. MPLA membership for government jobs, even in rural areas, remains a requirement, thus alienating many former UNITA members from one of the few sources of stable jobs in this still highly corrupt and patronage-based economy.[274] Thus, discrimination against those formerly of or from former UNITA areas remains a salient political cleavage in Angola,[275] though one without security implications given the dominance of the MPLA and FAA.

The FAA stayed quite large, with over 100,000 soldiers under arms through the 2000s,[276] though it also discharged 33,000 as well to reduce the numbers slightly. Interestingly, a secondary demobilization programme was announced when the ADRP closed in 2008 to deal with excess fighters who had for apparently technical reasons been unable to be processed in the main programme. In an apparent coincidence, this new programme was designed to have capacity for 33,000 fighters and was run and financed entirely by the Angolan government.[277]

Overall, this reintegration process saw the same funding concerns and logistical delays as previous efforts in Angola. Reconstruction was a multi-year effort that cost billions of dollars and ran into coordination and logistical delays both within and outside Angola. This suggests that any expectations of completing this kind of process in fewer than four years with a much lower price tag and without administrative access to the entire country were doomed to fail, regardless of who was in charge of the implementation. The MPLA and FAA were not significantly better at managing this process than the UN peacekeepers had been, nor were either the steps of the process nor the reintegration support provided significantly different than during either of the two previous implementation processes. The difference of course is that the FAA had won on the ground and UNITA's leadership was still very much lacking. This separates the cases for which this piece of the Angolan peace process can be used as a more generalizable study, as the treaty was negotiated and implemented under conditions of near-victory. This does not negate its usefulness as a case, however, it merely separates out the situations for which it can serve a salutary purpose as being different from the cases for which Mozambique's process may be a more relevant lesson.

The relative success of peace in Mozambique

By the late 1990s, peace seemed firmly in place in Mozambique, as the first set of free and fair elections had been successfully completed in 1994 and then replicated in 1999.[278] For this reason, this chapter's discussion of the continued peace process in Mozambique will be much shorter than the previous section on Angola. The wider picture of Mozambique's entire post-conflict reconstruction is beyond the scope of this book, but the impact of the economic reconstruction has important implications for the formation of the FADM and will be discussed in brief here.

Economic inequalities and implications

Mozambique's post-war economic problems were caused primarily by the IMF, whose focus since the 1980s had been the provision of loans and technical assistance in order to help Mozambique participate in the international economic market.[279] There were deleterious side effects of these policies. They either directly or indirectly exacerbated poverty and income inequality within the country,[280] and had direct political and security consequences, despite important macroeconomic reforms Mozambique implemented from the late 1980s to the early 2000s.[281]

When the failure of FRELIMO's Soviet-style economic policies became clear to the population and government of Mozambique in the late 1980s, FRELIMO began taking loans from the IMF in order to save the economy.[282] This continued during the peace negotiations and immediate implementation years. The combination of IMF loans and international post-conflict aid meant that by the mid-1990s, the majority of Mozambique's GDP was generated from foreign aid and mostly controlled by non-Mozambican actors.[283] This decreased the government's ability to provide for purely Mozambican services such as healthcare and education and made the government more dependent on the goodwill of the international community funding the country than on providing for the increasingly poor Mozambican people.[284] A 2004 report found that poverty in Mozambique was likely around 70 per cent across the country, with notable income inequalities present, especially in Maputo.[285] This was a similar dynamic to how the MPLA in Angola was more beholden to international oil deals and companies than their own population, and in both cases had the effect of eroding funds and attention from infrastructure, poverty reduction and the provision of services for local populations.[286] This was exacerbated when areas in northern Mozambique were discovered to have natural gas and coal deposits, which were developed almost exclusively for export, funnelled through Maputo rather than to local communities.[287]This was especially detrimental in light of the civil war and the challenges inherent in transitioning away from a wartime economy. Military leaders remained plutocrats while citizens remained economically disenfranchised.

Most foreign actors left the country in 1997 when the reintegration programmes were declared complete. As the 1990s continued, however, the IMF was still very much in charge of the government's macroeconomic policies. As such, the focus was exclusively on implementing reforms to ensure Mozambique's ability to participate in regional and global trade and thus pay off its immense loans.[288] This left very few resources available for improving domestic economic conditions within Mozambique,[289] which had three important consequences for the post-war settlement: increasing discontent within RENAMO, raising RENAMO grievances against FRELIMO and stagnation within the FADM.

As has been mentioned in previous sections, many former RENAMO combatants had reintegrated into civilian life near comrades and commanders, meaning that RENAMO social networks from the war largely stayed intact into the post-war period.[290] While most former combatants genuinely preferred non-violent careers at this point, this preference was also predicated on the often faulty assumption that veteran status would lead to better post-war economic outcomes.[291] While this was the case in the initial reintegration years, given the narrow focus of internationally funded reintegration packages being tied directly to veteran status, once these payments ran out, most former combatants were not left well off economically. Without a growing national economy, they turned to their RENAMO social networks with the expectation of patronage and support.[292] However, the retired commanders found themselves in the same position, especially as they had not been treated differently in the reintegration programmes, nor were their wider social circles of dependents taken into account. The need to provide for these networks and the lack of planned methods of doing so likely explains the preponderance of former officers appearing in new criminal networks throughout Mozambique in the late 1990s and early 2000s.[293] Another consequence of this patronage expectation was that it maintained RENAMO social networks, which is also a factor that enabled the continuation of RENAMO's political coherency as a party, as RENAMO politicians began to shift blame for lack of economic prosperity from their own shoulders to the FRELIMO government.[294]

The rising frustration regarding lack of post-war economic opportunity within RENAMO began to have larger effects, as the FRELIMO government was increasingly seen as at fault for the lack of economic development.[295] In addition, the continued FRELIMO majority both in parliament and in the executive meant that RENAMO politicians began to feel permanently designated as the opposition party, without a true say in government.[296] This gave rise to suspicions of election rigging, leading RENAMO to boycott the 1998 parliamentary elections (though this was short-lived as RENAMO participated in the 1999 presidential elections).[297] These economic trends and accompanying frustrations continued into the 2000s,[298] especially as FRELIMO continued to win all national-level elections and governance was still centralized,[299] ensuring that even regions of primarily pro-RENAMO populations (mainly in the north of the country) were given little autonomy and economic development was seen primarily in the south.[300] This is one of the largest reasons that in 2013, a few hundred former RENAMO fighters followed Dhlakama when he declared the Rome agreement to have been abrogated by FRELIMO and claimed the continued marginalization of RENAMO politically and economically.[301] While this did lead to some low-level violence, it has not yet risen to the level of renewed civil war, especially with Dhlakama's death in 2017.[302] Furthermore, these same economic conditions are likely the cause for the current Islamist violence plaguing the north of the country.[303]

Another impact of these stagnated economic conditions was that the government was unable not only to provide services such as healthcare and education, thus entrenching rampant poverty across the country[304] but also was often unable to pay wages for those who worked for the government.[305] This included wage delays within the FADM, which began to create cracks in integration efforts within the military. Given the ties that the government had with those who had fought for it during the decades of the civil war, as well as concerns about those same soldiers overthrowing the government should they become dissatisfied,[306] it is perhaps not surprising that of all government employees, former FRELIMO soldiers in the FADM were paid their salaries with fewer delays than other government workers including former RENAMO fighters in the FADM.[307] However, this was often done relatively surreptitiously to avoid claims of corruption. Nevertheless, by 2000 it was apparent that the FADM as an institution did not have sufficient funds to provide for training, development and professional opportunities as a professional employer attractive to eligible Mozambicans and former combatants who had joined in the initial post-war period.

In addition, it was clear that FRELIMO was supporting the FADM by paying the salaries of former FRELIMO fighters.[308] This immediately ignited tensions between former FRELIMO and RENAMO fighters within and beyond the FADM, especially as it highlighted the numerical imbalances between the two sides that the treaty provisions had initially planned would not exist, but which had become the de facto reality when faced with a lack of volunteers on both sides and the overwhelming numerical majority of FRELIMO at the end of the war (see Chapter 4 for more details on the size of the FADM). Furthermore, the lack of professional development opportunities meant that promotions were essentially stalled, leaving former RENAMO soldiers at a seemingly permanent educational and skills disadvantage compared to their FRELIMO peers, solidifying what had been hoped would be a temporary disparity in abilities.[309] It is not surprising that by the early 2000s, many senior RENAMO soldiers in the FADM felt entirely unable to continue working in an institution that preferred their FRELIMO colleagues in terms of education, wages and rank and was seen, along with the rest of the government, as being fundamentally corrupt and inept.[310] Although numerically the FADM barely shrank from its 1996 numbers, by the mid-2000s, only a handful of senior RENAMO officers remained.[311]

Mozambique: Short-term success but long-term challenges

It is not an insignificant measure of success that despite these economic problems, political tensions and stagnation of the FADM, Mozambique's level of crime and two insurgencies in the north have not risen to the level of renewed civil war and certainly not on the scale of the one million dead that the 1975–92 conflict created.[312] The attitudes and actions of international actors in the treaty negotiations and implementation phases were noteworthy in prioritizing Mozambican needs and knowledge (exemplified best through the coordination of the international community around Sant Egidio and the pragmatic attitudes of Aldo Ajello and his ONUMOZ mission).[313] As post-conflict reconstruction processes continued, however, most international actors left to deal with other crisis areas, leaving Mozambique to fall prey to more standard policies of 'development', with very particular internationalist agendas, rather than having a focus on local conditions.[314] The later years of Mozambique's reconstruction are thus in stark contrast to the successes of the early years and show in sharp relief the importance of attention to detail, flexibility and coordination in not only devising a sufficiently specific plan to work in the relevant conditions[315] but also commitment in implementing those plans for short and long-term success.

Conclusion

This chapter has covered the final peace treaty in Angola and the continuation of the peace process in Mozambique and highlights some clear parallels in both outcomes. Both RENAMO and UNITA gained and then stagnated as the permanent parties of opposition. This occurred despite Mozambique having a seemingly more politically equal attitude towards RENAMO, as opposed to the Lusaka and Luena treaties explicitly prioritizing the MPLA in Angola. This suggests that additional factors beyond inclusion and enfranchisement are necessary to offset factionalization such as measures to ensure opposition parties can contest national elections even when long-standing parties in power control access to most media; achieving equal status within the military in fact as well as on paper and perhaps more and longer-term training in electoral politics, party-building and campaigning.

In both cases, the focus of treaty implementation was on disarmament and demobilization, with additional attention paid to reintegration efforts, but those initiatives did not see long-term success in either country. Similarly, the influence of the international community is clear in both cases, with some beneficial consequences in Mozambique, especially around political and practical coordination around ONUMOZ.[316] What seems to be the more dominant trend with international actors in both cases, however, is a focus on continuing their respective missions without alteration, even when local conditions and needs change drastically.[317] This included the IMF's focus on macroeconomics and global trade at the expense of improving living conditions and microeconomics in Mozambique, and humanitarian actors continuing to aid displaced and war-affected populations in Angola even as this loosened accountability ties between both the MPLA and UNITA and their respective local constituents. While working towards the priorities of one's specific organization is of course the mission, it seems problematic for these particular organizations to pursue such out-of-touch agendas in both Angola and Mozambique since they define themselves as being service-based. In fact, both peace processes were most effective in implementing their treaties when the security provisions were undertaken by those with the attention to detail and knowledge of local conditions, which, as ONUMOZ proved, did not preclude these attributes from being held by international actors.[318]

This chapter also highlighted the important role that non-state elements played in both conflicts[319] and particularly in Angola. The role of diamonds and oil was key to funding the 1998–2002 section of the conflict, but without international markets and trading networks, these political economies would not have been possible. These aspects of the Angolan conflict show the limits of international institutions and politics to intervene in civil wars and further underline just how central national politics were to Angola's conflict. Additionally, they demonstrate how much the Cold War dimensions of the civil war had been created specifically in response to financial incentives of the US and USSR and not due to fundamental ideological divides within Angola. In Mozambique, the role of non-state actors has been discussed in previous chapters, with Sant Egidio as the key mediator placing Mozambique's Treaty negotiations making it one of the few civil wars with an NGO so central to its peace process. Nevertheless, the role of the IMF as a non-state actor is crucial to understanding the stagnated trajectory of Mozambique's longer-term post-war reconstruction.[320]

In terms of specific security provisions, both the Rome and Luena processes focused on demobilization and reintegration fuelled by monthly payments over the course of months and years as the key method of reducing combatant populations. This is an interesting departure from policies tried earlier in Angola that focused more on the disarmament aspect, suggesting informal learning or perhaps merely coincidence between the two cases, which saw disarmament as technically part of the process, but not one to be emphasized exhaustively. On the other hand, physical scattering was considered central to Mozambique's demobilization, and while similar efforts in Angola were less successful, the idea of instalments of reintegration funding and support was similar in both processes as a way to create sufficiently long-term incentives (though only five months in the case of Angola) for combatants to build civilian lives for themselves. In the longer term, however, both processes ran into issues regarding political dissatisfaction stemming from failed expectations around economic development and opportunity. This suggests that while demobilization and reintegration are necessary for peace processes to stay on track in the three- to five-year period following the signing of a peace treaty (as evidenced by the failures of these processes following the Bicesse and Lusaka treaties), economic opportunity eventually becomes more important for opposition parties, demobilized combatants and the progress of the integrated militaries.[321] While these two points have been separately made in the literature,[322] the combination of these elements, as demonstrated particularly in the case of Mozambique, is of particular note.

Angola and Mozambique both ended up with integrated militaries, albeit ones in which opposition members (UNITA and RENAMO respectively) were brought into an organization either officially or unofficially dominated by the government party, with relatively few structural changes taking place. Nevertheless, these integrations were successful in two important aspects. First, there was no in-fighting within either institution, despite the fast combining of forces from previously opposing sides. Second, both institutions remained subordinate to civilian politics, without coup threats or attempts. What these integrated militaries have failed to do, however, is guarantee equal opportunity for advancement and professional development within their ranks, primarily due to educational disparities that predate integration as well as lack of funding in Mozambique's case. It remains an open question what the trajectory of the FADM in Mozambique could have been if the government had sufficient funds to be able to develop the institution as had been planned by ONUMOZ and military trainers from Portugal, France and the UK.

This chapter does not suggest that elections are a particularly important marker of either longer-term reconstruction failure or success. There were concerns about violence around both the 1998 and 1999 elections, but although RENAMO boycotted one and participated in the other, in neither case did violence occur or conflict resume. In fact, it was not until RENAMO's position as a permanent opposition party became clear in 2013 (over twenty years after the signing of the Rome Treaty), and importantly, compounded by economic disenfranchisement of RENAMO areas, did violence break out again. This suggests that early assumptions that elections were key to creating and cementing peace were not nearly as important as the Bicesse negotiators assumed and that ONUMOZ's push to focus on security issues before elections and treating elections as a potentially destabilizing moment were more accurate.

All of these factors combined, as well as the analysis of the treaties themselves from earlier chapters of this book, suggest that treaties in both countries succeeded when they were: specific, focused in detail on the implementation of security provisions, had coordinated implementation actors and prioritized demobilization and reintegration over comprehensive disarmament.

Chapter 6

LESSONS LEARNED AND IMPLICATIONS

This chapter brings together the four peace treaties and academic literature review to analyse in depth the main lessons learned from this book and identify contributions to the literature, gaps and areas for further research.

Moving towards negotiations

Throughout this book, the period prior to the negotiations beginning has been examined in order to understand the motivations, incentives and conditions of the conflict and the parties involved. This is necessary because, as this research argues, negotiations do not happen in a vacuum and thus cannot be divorced from the domestic and international politics, domestic, international, economic and other pressures immediately prior to negotiations officially beginning. Broadly this book finds that external political pressure is a necessary, but insufficient condition for negotiation commencement. Adding external financial incentives (positive and negative) can also guarantee the signing of a treaty. However, external influence (both political and economic) cannot guarantee successful implementation of a treaty and is especially limited in enacting provisions that require a reduction in fighting capabilities. This suggests that external political pressure, financial incentives and signatory status cannot create peace. This is a conclusion demonstrated in existing literature on UN peacekeeping missions and security sector reform; this book strengthens these findings through an in-depth case study analysis of Angola, long considered a UN failure, and Mozambique, considered one of the UN's earliest successful multi-dimensional missions. Additionally, this book combines the examination of treaty negotiations, treaty terms themselves, along with implementation, a combination rarely seen in this literature. Furthermore, the analysis of factors including language, dignity and decision-making bodies are understudied in peacekeeping and security sector reform literatures and broaden the findings of this study.

This book shows that a better mechanism for reducing conflict includes effectively implementing treaty provisions that require parties to reduce their fighting capabilities. Force reductions, more than anything, signal a sincere commitment to conflict cessation. It is an imperative condition that trumps successful negotiations, signatory status or economic development. This research shows that alternative employment options for former fighters are needed to break the conflict cycle. Furthermore, those employment options must meet certain criteria to outweigh a return to war. As such, gainfully employing former fighters in roles that offer status and economic opportunity are critical measures needed to enforce successful force reductions that lead to sustained peace. This is a consistent finding across much of the post-conflict reconstruction literature, however, this book examines this conclusion specifically through the lens of security institutions, especially an integrated military, as providing these job opportunities, rather than focusing on civilian methods, as is most common amongst DDR literature.

Beyond external pressures, this book finds that there are a few other potentially significant aspects that may assist in the beginning of negotiations. In particular, there is evidence that the impact of battlefield stalemate leads to a certain 'ripeness' for negotiations, as theorized by authors including Zartman.[1] In examining the peace treaties discussed in this book, battlefield stalemate does seem to have some impact on when and how treaties were signed. However, the relationship is not a particularly clear one, especially as the line between short-term battlefield stalemate, long-term battlefield stalemate and war weariness is blurry. Battlefield stalemates were in fact the norm going into both failed and signed peace treaties in these two cases. Therefore, both cases demonstrate that battlefield stalemates are not sufficient to keep negotiations going, much less ensure signature and implementation.

This section will compare the four treaties that were signed, as well as the two other attempted negotiations in Angola (in Gbadolite and in Addis Ababa) to argue that collectively these negotiations show that external pressure is consistently enough to force domestic parties to the negotiating table. In some cases (Rome and Bicesse), it was consistently applied with sufficient financial incentives (positive and negative), to guarantee the signing of a treaty. However, external pressure alone could not guarantee the successful implementation of the Bicesse and Lusaka treaties. This is especially apparent for provisions that require parties to reduce their fighting capabilities. Thus, when looking at the civil wars in Angola and Mozambique, external pressure is necessary but not sufficient for negotiation commencement and treaty signing.

External pressure

Examining and comparing these four treaties consistently shows that outside backers wanting peace may be sufficient to get a treaty signed, but are not enough to ensure the treaty will be successfully implemented.

The fact that external pressure was enough to start negotiations and sometimes even guarantee the creation of a treaty, but fell apart during the implementation stage is consistent with issues highlighted in the existing academic literature.[2] This book adds weight and depth to the literature by conducting in-depth analyses of the negotiating processes and the treaty terms themselves. For example, the examples of Angola and Mozambique concur with Walter's identification of a commitment problem being a barrier to implementing security provisions,[3] along with Stedman, Rothschild and Cousen's discussion of the need for long-term involvement from international actors to ensure successful peace rather than merely pressure to negotiate and sign a treaty,[4] confirmed by DeRouen et al and Doyle & Sambanis' analyses.[5] This is even more clearly outlined by King's analysis of the importance of security provisions being implemented for peace to stick,[6] beyond the mere signing of official pieces of paper.

This book's analysis finds that negotiations for three of the four treaties began as a result of external pressure, specifically from reductions in foreign aid that enabled continued fighting. Timing and the international context are also important. The negotiations that ultimately resulted in the Angolan Bicesse Treaty and the Mozambican Rome accords both took place within the context of the ending of the Cold War. This therefore meant that the MPLA and FRELIMO in Angola and Mozambique respectively lost much of the financial and military support that had previously been supplied by the USSR to MPLA in Angola and FRELIMO in Mozambique. Ipso facto, the United States was less interested in supporting UNITA when the MPLA was no longer considered to be a Soviet proxy. Economic liberalization was linked to political progress towards democratization. Another outside change in circumstances was similarly important: the end of Apartheid in South Africa had carryover effects in contiguous Mozambique and removed foreign backing from RENAMO (see Chapter 2).[7]

Beyond the political fallout of the end of the Cold War, there were also shifts in the global financial system from the 1990s that especially influenced Angola. From 1992 onwards, the MPLA was influenced by the financial incentives of economic trading partnerships with international financial institutions and Western oil companies. In contrast, UNITA now faced UNSC pressures – without US aegis incentivized by a need to counter the USSR – that developed into multiple resolutions imposing UN sanctions. From this we see that external financial incentives to entice the MPLA and external financial pressure against UNITA factors in Angola's second treaty, as well as the first.

In the discussion of how negotiations for treaties began, it is important to consider not only successful negotiations but also failed instances that started but did not mature into signed resolutions. For these purposes, this book examined the three treaties (two for Angola's conflict and one for Mozambique's) that did not reach the point of treaty signing, which share interesting similarities. The Nkomati agreement in 1984, the Gbadolite discussions of 1989 and the Addis Ababa talks in 1993 all were attempts at regional negotiations to resolve Mozambique's and Angola's wars respectively. While being primarily civil wars, each nonetheless had clear military, economic and humanitarian impacts on their neighbours. In all three cases, regional pressure was the key organizing mechanism for these talks to be conceived of and begin, but all three had notably little great power or international institutional involvement. This regional focus was clear to participants at the time, who uniformly approached these negotiations with much smaller and more junior delegations and presented demands in a much more declarative, rather than discussive, manner. Unsurprisingly, while the Nkomati talks did lead to an agreement between the Apartheid South African government and FRELIMO, neither the talks nor the agreement actually addressed the entirety of the conflict, and in the two Angolan-focused discussions, barely a press statement was successfully made. This illustrates that external pressure could facilitate the initiation of negotiations, but more levers were needed to reach signatory outcomes.

Framing Mozambique's process as internally driven, rather than externally imposed, was foundational to success in Mozambique. While external financial changes and allegiances were definitely part of the backdrop of the move to negotiations for Mozambique's Treaty, changes to internal group dynamics and influences from countervailing organizations had a direct impact on the beginning of negotiations. Specifically, internal changes within FRELIMO (moving away from a Soviet-style economy and informally recognizing RENAMO as a legitimate group) combined with pressure from domestic civil society, primarily the Church, had a much more immediate and effective impact on the beginning of negotiations than external regional pressure. The idea that Mozambique's negotiations were fundamentally founded on 'Mozambicans talking to Mozambicans'[8] has been confirmed through secondary sources, memoirs and interviews and is widely considered to be a key basis for the success of negotiations and eventual treaty implementation. A key piece of this was the fact that the mediator for this treaty was Sant Egidio, a Catholic NGO without the financial or political power to force either side into either negotiations or treaty compliance, therefore ensuring that what was agreed upon was done so without coercion, making actual implementation of the terms more likely. In this sense, Mozambique benefitted from a comparative lack of international interest in its war, as there were few outside actors' opinions to consider or pressures to endure, as in Angola. This example highlights how perceptions of neutrality were helpful, and potentially linked to the absence of Cold War politics and former colonial interlocutors, which confirms conclusions in existing literature about the importance of committed external actors.[9] The UN was unable to fulfil this role in Angola because the UN was not seen as a neutral actor, given the dominance of the US and USSR in backing the initial UN peacekeeping missions into the conflict, and then the continued pressure of the United States' position vis-a-vis UNITA as opposed to the MPLA via the UN continuing the impression of partiality. Additionally, the UN's direct involvement via the deployment of troops meant it was yet another external actor in a conflict that had seen multiple interventions. Unlike Sant Egidio, therefore, the UN was neither invited by the domestic parties nor seen as safe from military meddling once involved.

To contrast, this is particularly salient when examining the one treaty of the four that had barely any outside involvement: Angola's Luena Treaty, which ended the conflict in 2002. Not only was this treaty far enough removed from the Cold War to not have to consider the same political and financial pressures as previous efforts, but by this point the MPLA had been firmly established as the legitimate government. As such, it no longer worried about losing access to international economic markets. Furthermore, UNITA had already had three rounds of sanctions imposed against it from 1997 onwards, signalling the maximum penalty and involvement the UN was willing to implement at this stage in the conflict. This divergence between the Angolan and Mozambican cases, with one conflict ending through one of the UN's first multidimensional missions versus the other concluding in essentially a battlefield defeat and an entirely internal process, demonstrates how each case study can be used as examples for different kinds of conflict conclusions. Mozambique offers a clear lesson in how external mediation and then UN peacekeeping can create positive short-term change, while Angola demonstrates the many pitfalls of external interventions of various kinds but also demonstrates how treaties are nonetheless relevant to conflict cessation even in instances of battlefield victory.

It is not unrelated that the Luena Treaty was explicitly negotiated away from international observers, who perhaps were seen by both Angolan sides as no longer being relevant players, and in fact perhaps inhibitory ones. There is no direct interview evidence to confirm that the choice of negotiating location and lack of participation invitations to international actors was deliberate. However, comparisons to Angola's previous treaties and implementation failures strongly suggest that Angolans had generally lost faith and interest in involving international actors in treaty negotiations and saw outside participation as inhibiting, rather than assisting, peace. Given the demonstrated and repeated biases of international actors who had been involved in Angola to date, (especially US insistence on using democratic procedures such as elections without supporting evidence that they are essential peace components), this is a reasonable suspicion.

In light of the aforementioned examples, this book finds that the impact of foreign pressure to begin negotiations was clear: they started but did not necessarily progress. Each instance finds that negotiations were initiated and treaties were signed, but foreign pressure was insufficient to ensure implementation actually proceeded once parties were required to take significant steps to give up military power in favour of peace. In light of these conditions, the two treaties created mainly through foreign pressure (Bicesse, Lusaka), could not be fully implemented. War resumed well within five years of the signing of each treaty as outsiders became the actors most invested in peace, rather than the indigenous groups.[10] As has been discussed in previous chapters, even going into both negotiations, both the MPLA and UNITA saw these negotiations as merely a step towards outright victory in the contest for political control. While both sides were willing, to a degree, to participate in political competition via the Bicesse elections, the reduction of military strength was not successfully implemented with either treaty, signalling that foreign pressure was not enough to resolve the commitment problem.

What role of war weariness? Same as battlefield stalemate or defeat?

As we consider the role of timing, the issue of battle fatigue is important to consider. The four treaties did not have a uniform driver in terms of amount of or type of battlefield fighting prior to negotiations. In some cases, there were high levels of fighting immediately prior to negotiations (Lusaka, Luena). In others there was a recent history of high-intensity combat, but a more immediate stalemate that preceded negotiations (Bicesse, Rome). These circumstances created very distinct incentives and commitments. As the conditions immediately prior to the negotiation of the Rome and Luena treaties were quite different and yet both were the only two successful treaties, there does not seem to be a correlation between battlefield dynamics immediately prior to negotiations and the outcome of those treaties.

What is much harder to tease out, however, is the distinction between perceived battlefield stalemate versus actual long-term stalemate. While the concept of 'ripeness' is persuasive in Zartman's account,[11] identifying it in real time is difficult. This is especially because what could look like a stalemate could in fact be a short-term status, a strategic operational pause, as sides use the pause of negotiating to rearm and prepare to resume violence. This was clearly the case in some instances. For example, going into and during the Lusaka negotiations, with both sides using discussions as a pause during which to increase their military abilities for future campaigns. In contrast, going into the Bicesse and Rome negotiations, there also seemed to be a perception of battlefield stalemate, but for different reasons. It is possible this stalemate was perceived as more obdurate, perhaps due to the external pressures discussed in the previous section, because it was reliant on factors beyond the control of the warring parties. Still, this is a difficult distinction to make, between real and tactical stalemate. Taken together, these cases demonstrate the challenge in identifying Zartman's moment of 'ripeness' with accuracy,[12] even with hindsight's benefit. Acknowledging the role of battlefield defeat,[13] even if it is impossible to know whether this would have been a lasting condition, it seems much clearer when examining the military dynamics immediately prior to the Luena negotiations (see Chapter 5), but grey areas still remain.

The even more complicated distinction lies between perceptions of any kind of battlefield stalemate and war weariness, on the part of the combatants and even on the population involved in the conflict as well. Although claims have been made that Mozambique's negotiations were undertaken in a climate of war weariness, determining what this actually means, how it can be measured and how it interacts with the myriad other factors already identified seems too complex for this simple statement. Additionally, the argument for war weariness in either case fails to consider the complex psychological processes needed to move from seeing the opposing side as requiring violent death on an existential basis to merely political opponents who can be debated, negotiated and compromised with. Claiming war weariness implies a higher revulsion towards continued fighting than towards acknowledging to some degree the legitimacy of the enemy, but given that all four parties accused the others of horrific atrocities within a few years of negotiations starting, this seems a difficult psychological claim to make, especially in the case of Angola where successively failed treaties only deepened distrust and hatreds.[14] Therefore, this book does not find any correlation or clear links between war weariness and negotiation commencement, much less between war weariness and success or failure of peace treaties. This is interesting and important because it casts some doubt on the centrality of a theme that is heavily emphasized in much of the existing literature.

In examining other potential factors that could have influenced the move to negotiations, the economic and humanitarian conditions in all four cases were quite dire, with no particular differences between the two successful treaties (Rome, Luena) and the two failed ones (Bicesse, Lusaka). Similarly, there was no significant technological difference either on the battlefield or in charge of mass media between any of the cases.

Therefore, in examining these factors, there is one significant difference in the lead up to negotiations between the two treaties that were successfully implemented and the two that were not. This was that in the former, the parties were firmly committed to negotiating instead of fighting, whereas in the latter, negotiations were externally imposed and seen by the parties themselves as providing breathing space in order to prepare for future military action. This book has argued that the main accounting for these different stances is not war weariness, external pressure or imminent defeat, nor classic resource-based greed, but rather the fact that all four parties were motivated by control over the political centre and chose to negotiate when they calculated that acquiring this political power was more likely through talks than on the battlefield.

Process of negotiating: The importance of dignity

When looking at the actual process of negotiating peace treaties, the two main claims of this book are, first, that the specifics of who is at the table matter. Second, that the combination of who is at the table and how the negotiations process is run impacts the terms and provisions agreed upon, as well as the climate of implementation. While these claims may seem straightforward, the literature to date focuses primarily on the characteristics of mediators (see, for example, Zartman & Berman; Kissinger; Beardsley, Quinn, Biwas and Wilkenfield),[15] with only a few scholars (Dudouet, Jett and Stedman)[16] examining the characteristics of the conflict protagonists. Still, even amongst this second category, researchers tend to focus more on institutional incentives (i.e. spoilers or relative strength) than on personal characteristics and relationships of participants and negotiators, as well as the processes through which negotiations are managed.

Who was at the negotiating table

One of the undertakings of this book has been to examine actors' motives going into negotiations in order to assess their willingness not only to negotiate a treaty but to actually implement the agreed-upon provisions. This book argues that agency matters in this realm and that individual characteristics are deeply relevant to understanding the interpersonal dynamics of negotiations. These interpersonal dynamics are in turn important at the implementation stage, and how this evolves is tied directly to the success or failure of peace. This section will first analyse in depth who was at the various negotiations and what personal characteristics may have been influential and then focus on the concept of dignity and perceptions of equality during the process of negotiations. One of the consistent themes across the chapters has been the analysis of the specifics of who was at the table for each party, and the argument that individual characteristics, including educational background, personal relationships, perceptions of dignified or unequal treatment or standing during negotiations and more, have an impact on the negotiations and therefore the provisions in the final treaty.

In both the Angolan and Mozambican civil wars, though most dramatically in the latter, there was a significant difference in educational background between most of the 'rebel' negotiators (UNITA and RENAMO) and the government interlocutors (MPLA and FRELIMO). Although Savimbi, the leader of UNITA, was highly educated, as were some of the other high-level members in the group, UNITA more broadly were explicitly representatives of the Ovimbundu, Angola's largest identity group, which dominated the interior of Angola and therefore had much less exposure to Portuguese colonization (see Chapter 2), including the Portuguese education systems and the Portuguese language. As senior leaders within UNITA defected (see Chapter 4) or died (see Chapter 5), UNITA's negotiating capacity began to erode (see Chapter 5), as they had fewer leaders with similar educational and professional backgrounds to match MPLA negotiators.

The atmosphere of internationally sponsored negotiations gave native Portuguese-speaking MPLA negotiators easier access to informal assistance and perks in Bicesse, Portugal, where the first treaty was negotiated. It also made it easier for MPLA negotiators to converse with international actors, who, even if they did not speak Portuguese, were more likely to have access to Portuguese translators than Ovimbundu negotiators. Furthermore, most of the MPLA's negotiators and senior leaders had been educated in Portugal and spent much of their leisure time there, giving them increased familiarity and ease in these negotiating circumstances,[17] compared to some in the UNITA delegation, for whom the surroundings were much more foreign, and thus potentially more nerve-wracking and uncomfortable.[18] In addition, the MPLA had been governing Angola since independence and from 1993 was recognized by all countries, giving the group direct experience of government administration, bureaucracy and institutional norms that UNITA members did not have. Another potentially relevant note is the marked difference in physical appearance between the lighter-skinned MPLA delegation and the notably darker-skinned UNITA contingent which was raised in interviews. While no claims of racism were made by either group, unconscious bias on the part of Western actors may have occurred,[19] especially as they were likely to have been culturally and linguistically more comfortable with the Portuguese-speaking and more cosmopolitan adjusted than MPLA representatives already. These psychological differences are difficult to measure in this context but important to consider as possible factors.

Admittedly, there were complaints in UN reports during the Lusaka negotiations that the location of the negotiations – though much closer to the Angolan conflict than Bicesse had been – were nevertheless too comfortable to encourage speedy discussions because negotiators would enjoy the physical respite from the front lines too much to feel the need to urgently negotiate. Still, it is worth considering how big a change it was to negotiate in neighbouring Zambia, where UNITA both had many more allies and where UNITA leaders had more first-hand knowledge, compared to negotiating in isolated Bicesse, where the MPLA had such a distinct linguistic and cultural advantage. Coupled with the military incentives discussed in the previous section, which likely inhibited negotiations to resolve the conflict politically in 1994 regardless of location, it is interesting to consider what impact the location of Lusaka had on the length of time the negotiations dragged on for.

The dynamics between the two Mozambican sides were similar in terms of structural inequalities to those between the Angolan sides. FRELIMO actors consistently had more access to standardized Western education in general, as well as exposure to Portuguese language. While this had a somewhat smaller impact on the Mozambicans, due to the Italian-based nature of the location of the negotiations in Rome, translation between Portuguese and Italian was nevertheless simpler than between the two main indigenous languages that most of RENAMO's negotiators preferred to communicate in. Additionally, RENAMO was notorious for having coerced and kidnapped the majority of their recruits, which inhibited individuals from seeking educational opportunities once part of RENAMO's organization, especially as kidnappings often targeted teenagers. Even for those who joined voluntarily, because Mozambique had received almost no educational development of any kind under colonialism, this meant that those who had risen to senior leadership in the group by the early 1990s often had barely completed 5–6 years of formal schooling.[20] While in many environments this was not a significant impediment, during technocratic peace treaty negotiations, this educational gap was starkly obvious to all involved, resulting in delays when some participants had to have foundational concepts explained,[21] including demobilization, party formation and election processes (see Chapter 3).

Beyond education, language and experience, the other factor this book has investigated is what impact the involvement of military officers had on the negotiations and the resulting peace treaties. This was more difficult to untangle than expected, especially because the line between which negotiators were 'fully' military officers and which were not was particularly hard to distinguish. This was especially true amongst RENAMO and, to a lesser degree, UNITA actors. This line was clearest in the Rome and Bicesse negotiations; during both processes, military and non-military issues were dealt with by distinct sections of the treaty and negotiated by different people within the parties. In Bicesse, there were two negotiation rooms: one for 'political' and one for 'military' participants, allowing for a direct comparison between these two types of treaty provisions. Interviews with every American involved in both rooms, as well as comparisons of the treaty terms and secondary literature (see Chapter 3), showed that military negotiations moved much more quickly to agree on both general principles and technocratic specifics, to the extent that those in the 'political' room intervened to slow discussions down to maintain leverage for the political topics. This directly contrasts with Themner's finding that military actors may be less inclined to compromise than political actors.[22] This shows the importance of having military actors involved in negotiations as equal partners, as in this case, military negotiators were more willing and able to come to agreements than political ones; an important finding in the interests of maintaining speed and momentum of negotiations. In addition, the subordination of the military room by the politicians highlights the pitfalls of privileging the traditionally political over the necessary military knowledge as the Bicesse Treaty itself set the stage for a succession of treaties that relied on political compromises, but without sufficiently developed military implementation plans – thus continually leading to failures in enabling these plans for peace to succeed. When compared with the Luena Treaty, which was negotiated entirely by military actors and around military topics and successfully negotiated and implemented much faster than any of the other treaties, the importance of including military actors as empowered negotiators is demonstrated further. This has clear policy implications for peace treaties in a variety of other cases, including when the battlefield imbalance between sides is so stark.

Interviews with three of the international participants, as well as investigations of first-person accounts, showed a similar trend in the Rome process, where military issues were seen as much more straightforward and easier to agree on. This is interesting because there is a near-unanimous agreement in the theoretical literature on peace treaties that consensus on security provisions is the most difficult element to achieve. This book's examination of the negotiations aspect of the peace treaties seems to belie that finding: every treaty examined here shows that the *implementation* of security provisions in every treaty discussed was definitely the trickiest part of these provisions, not reaching agreement on the plans. This suggests that the theoretical literature does not currently have a solid enough distinction between the process of agreeing to security provisions and that of actually implementing them.

In terms of international actors, the most directly involved group in the Angolan negotiations were the Americans and the UN, in that order. The United States had a relatively stable contingent for the negotiations around Namibian independence (which included the MPLA), the Bicesse negotiations and the Lusaka negotiations, composed mainly of US State Department officials specializing in African affairs, with some specialists from the Department of Defence. The UN had a cast of participants that rotated more frequently, led by a few different special representatives and UN peacekeeping commanders. All of these international actors were intent on securing a peace treaty, implementation and focused particularly on elections (see later section in this chapter). None were particular experts on either Angola as a country or its conflict, and only a few spoke Portuguese, much less any indigenous languages or much time in the country. It is therefore hard to compare whether the participation of more informed outsiders would have made a difference across Angolan negotiations, as the only comparison extant is between the two treaties, on the one hand, that were facilitated predominantly by these outsiders (Bicesse and Lusaka) and the one that had an explicit lack of any similar involvement on the other (Luena).

Where the comparison is more constructive, is between the background and attitude of international actors involved in the Angolan treaties and the Mozambican one. Mozambique's is nearly unique amongst peace negotiations, in that the main mediator in this case was neither another government nor a recognized foreign leader, but a small NGO, Sant Egidio. While this was considered unusual both at the time and in hindsight, it has also been considered by Mozambican and international actors to be a key mechanism of success in the negotiations in Mozambique. Another smaller but still significant beneficial involvement from the international community was the informal coalition of foreign ambassadors in Maputo and in Rome who, from the late 1980s onwards, regularly met to discuss and align policies related to Mozambique in order to coordinate pressures (mainly vis-a-vis the recognized government of FRELIMO) in order to signify a united international front. What is significant about this group of ambassadors is that they were permanently in Maputo, Mozambique's capital, and therefore had access to long-standing and real-time information about conditions and realities on the ground. This therefore separates these international diplomats from 'Groups of Friends' arrangements which are focused around the UN, rather than locally.[23] The consistency of this group during both Sant Egidio-led negotiations and UN-led implementation confirms the importance of long-term commitments from international actors highlighted in the theoretical literature, for example, by Stedman, Rothchild and Cousens.[24]

Sant Egidio succeeded as a mediator for a variety of reasons. These are worth examining because they are not unique to Sant Egidio itself and may therefore be applicable to other negotiations. First, Sant Egidio became the official negotiations mediator following over a decade of involvement in Mozambique, both in the cities and countryside. This enabled the group to develop a detailed knowledge of Mozambique and its current conditions, as well as a wealth of relationships and networks with the two main parties and with significant civil society actors like religious leaders. While this did not necessarily lead to hugely different terms and provisions in between the provisions agreed on in the Mozambican Treaty and those seen in more internationally driven treaties, for example, in Angola, it did create a negotiations atmosphere where the two Mozambican parties were considered the drivers of the discussions. This stands in contrast with the Angolan negotiations, during which many of the priorities and provisions came from outside actors like the US and the UN.

Second, Sant Egidio itself had no capacity to force either side to do anything: it did not have the money to mandate the removal of negotiations to a closed location, thus forcing an expedited focus on discussions the way the Portuguese and Americans had with the Bicesse Accords; it did not have the financial means to pressure either side into joining or continuing discussions, as the US and USSR had in Bicesse; it did not have any military power with which to explicitly or implicitly threaten; it did not have relationships with major corporations or international financial institutions through which to create pressures or incentives. This seeming powerlessness, however, was actually a huge feature. As a result, the incentives that brought both sides to the table, kept them from abandoning the process and resulted in a signed treaty were the result of promises that both sides felt willing and able to uphold themselves, without external pressure applied by Sant Egidio.[25] In turn, much less external commitment was required in the implementation stage to force parties to stick to the agreement. This agency-focused approach likely contributed to the extended timeline of the Rome negotiations, which took three years to complete, rather than the much faster Bicesse, Lusaka and Luena agreements. In the long term, however, slower negotiations but more commitment to the terms seems a worthwhile trade-off.

The lessons about international actors in negotiations thus seem relatively clear and are in fact similar to ideas raised in the earlier section regarding external pressure and those discussed later regarding the UN's attitude. International actors can be incredibly beneficial during the negotiations process when they 'act as servants of the peace, rather than masters'.[26] This confirms much of the literature and UN's own writings on peace processes; the comparison of Angola, where the international community was heavily involved, versus Mozambique, which also had significant but qualitatively different involvement, contributes to the literature by adding nuance to the understanding of not just how the quantity of international involvement impacts treaty negotiations, but the qualitative differences as well.

Dignity

One of the key contributions this book seeks to make to the literature is to highlight the importance of dignity and the perceptions of personal equality, during peace treaty negotiations. This is building off of two pieces of literature: Bekoe's 2008 book examining the peace agreements in Angola, Mozambique and Liberia, and Albin and Druckman's 2012 piece 'Equality Matters: Negotiating an End to Civil Wars'. The theoretical argument of Bekoe's work emphasizes the idea of 'mutual vulnerability', that both sides must feel equally at risk in order to feel secure enough to move forward. She argues that external actors must ensure that implementation timelines require equal concessions from both sides, which is consistent with this book's examination of all the Angolan and Mozambican treaties in which neither side was militarily dominant. Although this seems to negate the premise of the argument and the book's contribution, as demonstrated in Chapter 5, the Luena Treaty, although negotiated by a militarily dominant MPLA, was in fact explicitly built off of the previous two treaties negotiated in quite different environments and therefore cannot be considered entirely separate to those negotiations and environments. Furthermore, some of the specific terms included in the Luena Treaty, notably the provision of generalships for UNITA leaders (see Chapter 5 for more details), show that even with military dominance, the MPLA was attuned to particular measures of dignity for key UNITA leaders in order to encourage compliance. This suggests that dignity and perceptions of dignity are important negotiation considerations even in conditions of battlefield victory. This is an important nuance that this book contributes to the existing literature.

This book goes further, arguing that the idea of perceived mutual vulnerability in fact applies to treaty negotiations as well as implementation: delays in negotiations are often a function of one side's perception that the other is less committed to talks, is less vulnerable in talks and therefore the delaying party does not feel sufficiently valued and empowered to continue to negotiate. This is an additional nuance of the security dilemma theory[27] and information asymmetry discussed for example by Wennman and Bekoe.[28] With the Angolan treaties, this was consistently how UNITA and their leader Savimbi positioned themselves during treaty negotiations. During the failed Gbadolite talks, UNITA accused regional actors of enacting pressure; during the Lusaka discussions during which UNITA felt that the international community singled UNITA out as being the sole cause of renewed violence (see Chapter 4), which was something UNITA also accused all four peacekeeping missions deployed in Angola during this time. Similar complaints were made by RENAMO, embodied in instances including the rejection of negotiation attempts until they perceived FRELIMO to be in a sufficiently weakened position; in the demand that US diplomats travel into the bush or to his ally in Kenya to persuade RENAMO's leader to participate, rather than require him to travel somewhere convenient to them, and others.

This is similar to the concept put forward by Albin and Druckman about 'procedural equality' or 'procedural justice', which posits that equality in how negotiations are conducted leads to more equal, and therefore more acceptable, terms and provisions. They suggest that equal treatment during negotiations leads to increased trust, even intangibly, which makes agreements, once reached, more durable in implementation. This again is consistent with the negotiations examined in this book; for example, the emphasis on clarity of general principles around equal participation in elections, political power, ratios in integrated militaries and more, even before actual specifics could be discussed. This idea of perceptions of equality during negotiations is also confirmed by more psychologically focused research, such as Hickerson's examination of the role that mental illness can play during mediation and negotiation,[29] a consideration worth remembering particularly when thinking about individual participants such as Savimbi.

Beyond terms-based perceptions of equality, however, this book argues that perceptions of equality and dignity are hugely impactful for the individuals involved in negotiations (and as will be argued in the later section on assembly areas during implementation as well). For the individual negotiators, feeling linguistically and educationally at a disadvantage has already been discussed in the previous section (as well as in Chapters 3 and 4), and although drawing a clear line from those differences to direct outcomes in terms of treaty provisions is difficult, they cannot be ignored.

Interviews conducted by the author point to other areas of equality that were quite important in both cases, particularly in relation to the Bicesse and Rome negotiations. As has already been discussed, both the MPLA and FRELIMO negotiators, being government ministers, already had bureaucratic experience going into the negotiations. This experience may or may not have included discussions of technocratic issues like how to run a democratic election, but it did include familiarity with Western business attire, Western meeting norms and the drafting and use of white papers and memos. These were not skills held by all of UNITA's negotiators and were almost entirely unknown to those representing RENAMO. Interviews conducted for this book consistently revealed anecdotes about how, for example, the Italian government paid for RENAMO negotiators to purchase nice Italian suits and shoes, in order for the delegation to feel sufficiently presentable to meet with representatives of Sant Egidio, the United States and FRELIMO during the Rome negotiations as discussed in Chapter 3. Other incentives present during both the Rome negotiations and the Lusaka discussions included foreign governments paying for hotels and restaurants for RENAMO and UNITA respectively, which anecdotally was seen to have direct positive impacts on these participants' willingness to continue to participate even when there were unexpected delays in the process.

Perceptions of strength, weakness and therefore political leverage and willingness to participate were constant themes throughout the examination of the various negotiations included in this book. Although concepts like trust and vulnerability may be difficult to measure or prove, there is sufficient evidence in the academic literature and, importantly, in the attestations of those involved on the ground[30] to strongly encourage that mediation and negotiation processes take these fewer tangible measures into account. This is particularly worth emphasizing given the relative ease with which perceptions of individual vulnerability can be addressed: hotels, clothing, transportation, a few dedicated aides or personal assistants, some basic instruction on behavioural norms and expectations and so on. While it is perhaps reductive to reduce a recommendation down to buying negotiation success for the price of a few suits, it is certainly not too generalized a takeaway, either.

This book consistently builds on the work of those who have emphasized the importance of perception (Bekoe), perceptions of equality (Albin and Druckman) and unconscious bias[31] to argue that these fewer tangible elements are nonetheless central to negotiation success. This argument contributes to the existing literature by illustrating particular examples, specifically in the contexts of civil, not inter-state, war, as well as from both situations of UN involvement, NGO involvement and military victory, thus providing a range of situations in which these aspects are still significant.

Terms and provisions

This section deals with the lessons learned by comparing the four treaties and the existing academic literature on what should be written into peace treaties regarding security provisions. This section reflects on some of the secondary research questions raised in Chapter 1. These next subsections look at specific treaty provisions and generally find that specificity in treaty terms is important. However, this book argues that part of the necessary specificity are built-in mechanisms for flexibility during implementation, in order for provisions to be implemented without relying on trust and goodwill between sides to adjust for inevitable real-world delays. While there is interesting literature on the importance of inclusivity, trust-building and more regarding more holistic definitions of peace (see Mac Ginty),[32] this section argues that there are technocratic methods of improving prospects for treaty implementation, extending Rothchild and Kingma's work,[33] especially around the need for flexible specifications for addressing problems that arise during implementation.

Elections vs security

While this book is not hugely concerned with examining post-conflict elections as a specific focus, there is a consistent way in which elections are relevant to the understanding of security provisions and implementation throughout all the treaties examined here. Put simply, this is the maxim that elections must happen after disarmament and demobilization, if not all of the reintegration programmes, have been completed. This is a lesson that was immediately recognized as the key cause of the collapse of the Bicesse process,[34] and yet, provisions to avoid similar problems were only clearly built into one of the three treaties that followed: Mozambique's. The conclusion that elections caused problems in Angola's first treaty has been well established in the academic and practitioner literature. This book examines the specific negotiations that led to this decision as well as the provisions and how they interacted more closely. This book therefore is able to add nuanced analysis in explaining exactly how elections can be effectively included in peace treaties without harming demobilization efforts, by comparing the contrasting cases of Mozambique and Angola. While Angola's second two treaties more accurately recognized that demobilization was that priority, by not setting elections as a clear goal, the Lusaka Treaty created years of delays without any incentive (aka winning an election) with which to leverage progress, and in the Luena Treaty, a lack of scheduled elections hampered the process of transitioning from fighting for grievances via military means into political ones by not replacing the battlefield with another arena to contest influence.

In Mozambique's Rome agreement, on the other hand, the balance was successfully struck between flexibility to ensure demobilization was complete before elections even with delays and enough strictness to ensure elections could not be delayed indefinitely. This was done by instituting a clear deadline for demobilization to be completed by, but then also a pre-specified extension to allow for more time to complete the process before elections that could be triggered if delays set in. Importantly, this trigger was exclusively under the control of the third-party implementer, in this case, the UN mission ONUMOZ, which meant that it could not be used by one side against the other to either delay or speed election preparations, which also increased the trust that neither party was purposefully causing delays solely to be able to use this extension option. This is consistent with the role Collier, Hoeffler and Söderbom see third parties playing in reducing election-related violence[35] as well as Joshi, Melander and Quinn's work on election-related sequencing in post-conflict environments.[36] Joshi and Quinn have also done comparative work on this issue by comparing similar processes in Nepal, Liberia, Macedonia, Indonesia (Aceh) and South Sudan, highlighting the same point of delaying elections until demobilization is complete,[37] suggesting a more generalizable lesson.

The lesson that complete demobilization must precede elections is therefore very much confirmed by the academic literature, and yet specific treaty provisions are often not focused on creating mechanisms to ensure this sequencing is followed. Mac Ginty, for example, notes that liberal democratic peace theory (which heavily influenced the first two Angolan treaties that had strong US influences) tends to follow a specific template that includes elections as the main step towards democratization, but that this template is applied too rigidly to take into account the practical considerations of most contexts and thus prioritizes fast elections over reducing security risks.[38] This is almost exactly the situation of the Bicesse negotiations, in which the Americans presented a format for elections explicitly based on the agreement for Namibian independence a few years before that was a completely different political context, despite being Angola's next-door neighbour.

In the Bicesse process, there was no procedure for extension. In the Lusaka Treaty, there was no set deadline for elections, and so demobilization kept being delayed indefinitely, which decreased incentives on both sides to participate. Both treaties failed to demobilize and complete elections. The provision linking elections to demobilization is therefore important but must be carefully balanced as was successfully done in Mozambique.

Role of opposition leaders

What the case studies of Angola and Mozambique show is that determining an acceptable role for the loser of a winner-takes-all election is one of the key pieces of both reaching an agreement and successfully implementing it. Academic literature (see Call, Jarstad & Nilsson) is generally unanimous that winner-takes-all systems are difficult to implement successfully, as perceptions of political exclusion are one of the biggest reasons for treaty non-compliance in post-conflict settings.[39] What these two cases also highlight, however, is how much still remains to be understood about why some leaders are more willing to compromise than others. Biographies have been written on both Savimbi and Dhlakama; as much as can be known about their thoughts have long since been excavated, and yet why one was willing to compromise and accept not being president while the other was so determinedly not is still an open question.

Some theories to consider include that Savimbi was simply a 'classic spoiler' in Stedman's typography,[40] and consistently believed that he would be more likely to succeed on the battlefield, thus predisposing negotiations to always be secondary in his priorities. Maybe Dhlakama was simply less ambitious, or more tired from fighting, than Savimbi and therefore more willing to compromise.

Perhaps the main factor was not about the particulars of Savimbi or Dhlakama themselves, but rather how external actors coordinated their responses to them. Savimbi was well known for being able to play different factions off of each other, from simultaneously claiming support from China and the United States in UNITA's early days (see Chapter 2), to supporting various regional leaders in opposition to the MPLA (see Chapter 5), to getting along with multiple different US administrations before then failing to successfully recapture their alliance (see Chapters 2 and 4). In Mozambique, on the other hand, with the exception of Zimbabwe and South Africa, nearly every other international actor was consistent with its approach to RENAMO, and importantly from the start of negotiations well after the conclusion of the UN mission was not only consistent but internally coordinated about their messages to Dhlakama. Perhaps this difference therefore convinced Savimbi that he had more leeway and pathways to achieve his goal rather than by complying with treaties, whereas Dhlakama saw compliance as his best option.

Maybe there were structural incentives built into the situation in Mozambique but not in Angola, that enabled spoilers in the latter but not the former, as suggested by Greenhill and Major.[41] Perhaps Dhlakama accepted that RENAMO was a movement only slowly transitioning into a successful political party and did not feel able to mount a challenge; whereas Savimbi consistently positioned himself and UNITA as representing the largest share of Angola's population, with a therefore obvious implied relationship to electoral success. While much of the academic literature on warlordism and the emphasis on resource acquisition for the sake of financial gain is often reductive,[42] particularly when contrasted with UNITA and Savimbi's consistent statements about seeking political power,[43] the structural incentives around war-time economic dynamics, especially around oil and diamonds (see Chapter 5) is an important consideration. Alternatively, perhaps the problem was about lack of sufficient trust to reach a settlement as posited by Stanley and Call;[44] in Mozambique both sides accepted they could not win outright, whereas neither Angolan parties ever came to that conclusion.

The available evidence strongly suggests a combination of factors common in conflicts, but of course cannot be truly definitive in clarifying exactly what accounts for this extremely important difference between the two cases. Still, it nonetheless highlights the ways in which one leader can have huge impacts on both negotiations and implementation.

Role of the UN during negotiations

For treaty terms and provisions, the lessons learned for how to deal with the involvement of UN peacekeeping is relatively clear and quite separate from less tangible aspects like mission attitude, prioritization and coordination (which will be dealt with in a later section under implementation). For what is written in the actual treaty, the role of the UN follows many of the same general principles as the other aspects of treaty provisions, namely that making clear decisions in the treaty about the extent of UN authority over implementation purview reduces risk of uncertainty, arguments and delays in implementation. This outlining of the UN's role includes determining the extent to which the mission has a mandate to merely observe, or whether more active tasks around verifying or implementing provisions are allocated. The provisions also include to what extent the mission is both involved in and in charge of decision-making in implementation-phase committees.

By comparing the four UN peacekeeping missions deployed across the two cases, the example of ONUMOZ clearly shows three key factors that enabled the mission to succeed. First, having a third party take an active role in chairing committees. Second, holding the 'trigger' on preset decision conditions. Finally, being the authority in charge of determining compliance for high-risk provisions like DDR created relative equality between the two sides as neither is elevated above the other while also having an authoritative tiebreaker able to avert deadlock. The example set by ONUMOZ is confirmed by quantitative studies on the role of UN peacekeeping missions in assisting peace processes; see Caplan's work arguing that making peacekeeping missions in charge of DDR rather than having them act merely as observers improves the likelihood of peace durability.[45] Taken together, the qualitative examples from this book and quantitative literature confirm Howard and Dayal's finding that when UN missions are created using templates (unfortunately frequently, as evidenced by the few deviations seen between the four different missions deployed to Angola despite dramatically different conditions on the ground) the results are deeply problematic.[46] This is for a number of reasons, including the lack of inclusion of the specific contexts and political situations that templates are able, or enabled, to take into account, for example, differences in both political contexts and political personalities between the two rebel leaders examined in this book.

Security provisions

When it comes to security-specific treaty provisions, there are a number of aspects to consider. One important factor to note is the near-unanimity in the academic literature regarding the centrality of security provisions to the successful implementation of peace treaties (see Hartzell, Hoddie & Rothchild).[47] This book has taken this as a starting point and then examined specific security provisions in more detail across the four peace treaties and found some key aspects to investigate when evaluating peace treaties more broadly. These include whether DDR is implemented for one or all sides, to what extent post-conflict security institutions are created as new institutions or as continuations of old establishments, the balance of numbers within post-conflict security institutions, and to what extent the individual pieces of DDR are emphasized.

First, depending on the political dynamics of the conflict, the initial point of investigation is whether both/all sides of the conflict are required to undergo disarmament, demobilization and reintegration into either civilian or military modes, or whether only one side is required to go through this process. In the cases of Angola and Mozambique, both the Bicesse and Rome processes required equal DDR compliance, whereas the Lusaka and Luena treaties focused only on UNITA combatants and made no requirements of MPLA forces.

This book argues that comparable DDR requirements for opposing forces are preferable, as they encourage mutual vulnerability, establish more uniform post-conflict economic opportunities for former combatants (thus mitigating potential for new grievances) and enable the creation of distinctly separate government institutions from war-time bodies. However, as the Bicesse process showed, even if DDR is equally required, if winner-takes-all elections are considered the main goal even before demobilization is complete, both sides are likely to assume that the terms of post-conflict institutions and provisions can be changed if one wins the election, making losing an election seem like an existential threat. The Rome agreement of Mozambique avoided this problem by requiring demobilization to be completed prior to elections (see previous section). The Lusaka and Luena processes only required DDR of UNITA; a dramatic change in the political dynamics of conflict resolution in Angola. In the Lusaka process, there was insufficient enforcement of this provision both from the MPLA and the international community, and perceptions of unfairness and inequality led to mounting delays and eventually the breakdown of the process entirely. It therefore seems reasonable that the Luena Treaty was able to implement this mostly unchanged provision not because of sudden shifts in perceptions of fairness but rather because the military dynamic in 2002 was so much more heavily in favour of MPLA dominance than in 1994, such that the MPLA could successfully enforce compliance. This example, however, suggests that one-sided DDR is most likely to be able to be implemented in conditions of battlefield victory, which is rarely the case in negotiated civil war settlements. Therefore, the main takeaway of these four treaties is that the equal approach to DDR with elections safely initiated after the process is complete, as done in Mozambique, is the more likely generalizable approach.

The second aspect of security-related provisions that this book focused on was the post-conflict integrated military. Specifically, whether it was a new organization or a continuation of a war-time establishment and how numbers and balance between the two sides were determined. This book argues that the evidence shows, following on from the previous point about equality in DDR processes, that an effective peace treaty should include provisions for formally ending existing security formations on both sides, and inaugurating a new integrated security establishment with a new name and new uniforms, because this outcome creates positive incentives for both sides. It creates a viable alternative to a winner-takes-all outcome for the security forces and positions those most at risk for restarting conflict within the context of a new, unified security mission. This corresponds with Toft's arguments about how treaties should be designed to offer benefits to both sides and especially offer ways for security institutions to be shared.[48] This book goes further in examining in detail fully integrated military organizations, not merely ones open to members of the opposing side.

It may be symbolic, but symbols are important in signalling to domestic constituents, international actors and former combatants themselves that the country is entering a distinctly separate phase. Additionally, the creation of a new name and new uniforms can ease psychological barriers when working with former opponents. These are all provisions that were signed and implemented in Mozambique and as part of the Bicesse process in Angola. What the failures of the Angolan Bicesse process shows, clearly, however, is that symbolic inaugurations of the top generals are insufficient to create an integrated military, rank-and-file or at least lower levels of officers must also be included for the institution to seem to exist. The creation of a new institution with a new name and visibly new uniforms is clearly only a first step in creating a new institution, but UN documents regarding the urgency of uniform requests from officers as well as from demobilized troops combined with the contemporary coverage of symbolic disbanding ceremonies and swearing in of generals into the integrated institution show clearly that to actors within militaries on all sides, these kinds of symbols are important initial steps.

In terms of numbers, this book goes into detail about how fraught the negotiations around relative numbers in integrated security institutions were in both cases and all four treaties (see Chapters 4 and 5). Comparing the negotiations, the treaty provisions and the implementation reveals that the principle of 50/50 parity of how many soldiers each side would contribute to the integrated military was important during negotiations in order to maintain political leverage and reduce perceptions of vulnerability. During the implementation stage, however, this principle became less important if rank-and-file combatants had more agency to determine their post-demobilization path and a third-party enforcer can keep the peace during the transition, thus removing some of the security dilemma around DDR processes (see Glassmyer & Sambanis for quantitative research on this last point).[49] These factors were all present in Mozambique, and this book argues they were key reasons that enabled RENAMO to accept an even lower proportion of representation in the integrated security forces than had been initially agreed upon. In Angola, on the other hand, there was little dispute in the final Luena Treaty around the portion of UNITA fighters to be integrated into the MPLA forces, though this book argues this was more to do with the MPLA's aforementioned military dominance, rather than perceptions and acceptance of fairness.

The third aspect of security provisions to examine is to what extent the treaty itself emphasizes the different pieces of the DDR process. While the implementation process also impacts this emphasis, how the priorities are built into the treaty becomes the starting point for assumptions that carry over into the implementation process, especially in terms of international funding. In all of the Angolan treaties, the emphasis was squarely on disarmament and demobilization, with increasing amounts of attention paid to reintegration as the treaties progressed, likely signalling lessons learned from prior failures. The literature, for example, Muggah,[50] suggests this lack of attention on reintegration is a broader failing that still requires improvement. This emphasis on disarmament and demobilization can be seen by examining how much of the treaty focuses in detail on the steps and timelines for the three pieces in comparison, as well as how much time is allocated for each stage. In Mozambique's Treaty, these aspects of the accord show a stronger emphasis on demobilization, followed by reintegration. This initial emphasis on demobilization is a likely influence on how decisions during implementation to focus on this step to the explicit relative exclusion of disarmament came about, though this prioritization is also confirmed in some of the literature, that is, Stedman.[51] This book argues that individuals and circumstances that arise during implementation do have an important impact on how treaties are put into practice, but that the provisions of the treaties themselves shape the conditions and conversations around implementation ahead of time.

Finally, one last issue of security provisions is interesting to consider: to what extent the overall size of the integrated military matters and how much training is called for to enhance a new institution. All four treaties and this book's research into the negotiations process show that in none of the circumstances examined was there concern or debate about the overall size of the integrated military. This suggests that it was considered a mutually acceptable assumption that the purpose of an integrated military was to provide satisfactory jobs for former combatants and a symbol of adherence to mutual vulnerability. Fighting ability (measured by either military size or training) was not a primary concern. This is further emphasized by the fact that none of the treaties mentioned training or skills capabilities for the integrated militaries, and this was not seriously changed during implementation. These two factors were consistent both for the successfully implemented and failed treaties in Angola and Mozambique, as well as those with and without external enforcement and those with and without dominant battlefield balance of power. This argument is also consistent with Ball's work on the purpose of integrated militaries following civil wars and Laitin's on the importance of military size in post-conflict environments.[52] This therefore seems strong evidence that the size of the integrated military, nor its fighting abilities or lack thereof, are particularly important in either treaty provisions or longer-term implementation.

What was left out

The terms and provisions examined in detail in this book primarily focus on security issues and those issues that are immediately related, such as election timetables. Worth a brief mention, however, are the security aspects of the conflicts that were entirely left out of any of the treaties, sometimes on purpose and sometimes without any evident discussion of their inclusion. Joshi and Quinn argue that leaving elements out has one of two effects: it either increases the risk of post-treaty violence, as omissions leave room for violent contestation, or it leads to the necessity of follow-up agreements to address missing elements.[53] Understanding what is left out and trying to determine why it was omitted is therefore an important element in understanding why implementation proceeded in the manner that it did in each of these cases.

The roles of agents whose positions would be redefined by a peace process are amongst the most obvious omissions. In terms of the purposeful omissions, the most glaring is determining the exact status of the loser of Angola's winner-take-all elections, which from 1992 onwards was consistently Savimbi. This was debated and discussed for literal years of negotiations (likely one of the reasons the Lusaka negotiations lasted so long) and yet was never actually resolved on paper, much less in practice. This is an example of Zartman and Berman's recommendation to mediators to agree on general principles and notation – sometimes the biggest issues need to be left out to get something done (this concept was also famously applied during the Oslo Accords regarding the status of Jerusalem).[54] In Angola's case, though, this looming question undermined the implementation of other aspects of the agreement, suggesting that if the largest issues cannot be resolved during negotiations, perhaps the situation is not yet ripe for peace.

For some issues, it remains unclear whether they were omitted purposefully or not. This is predominately the case in broadly security-related entities like the police (unmentioned in the earlier treaties examined here) and the intelligence services (excluded from all four treaties). Neither of these are commonly mentioned in treaties across conflicts in the 1990s, and the intelligence services are still rarely included today. The examination of intelligence services in post-conflict civil war environments is a potential area for further research, either into these two cases or more broadly investigating when and with what impact addressing intelligence services in peace treaties can have and also how post-conflict reforms of intelligence services have been implemented in civil war cases.

Another similarly unclear omitted issue was the topic of justice for war-time actions by any actor. In both cases, Angola and Mozambique, the baseline assumption seemed to be that blanket amnesties were the best option. FRELIMO's attitude of 'accepting the enemy', which in practice meant a lack of any post-conflict justice, is highlighted by van den Bergh as a key aspect of enabling Mozambicans to look forward.[55] The MPLA announced a general amnesty in 2002, exactly as recommended by Joshi, Melander and Quinn,[56] but none of the other treaties or negotiations seem to have mentioned the topic of what, if any, consequences there would be for the war-time actions of the parties involved. Although transitional justice as a concept was relatively new in this era, it is still interesting that it was not considered given that South Africa, the archetype of modern understandings of Truth and Reconciliation Commissions, was involved in both conflicts and was the most immediately influential neighbour. Understanding why transitional justice was not considered a priority in either Angola or Mozambique, and examining the impacts of this decision, suggests another potential avenue for further research.

One issue was omitted only in Angola's treaties rather – the issue of natural resources and mainly UNITA's use of diamond revenues. Chapter 4 goes into the specifics in more detail, but in summary, UNITA funded much of their fighting capacity from the mining and smuggling of diamonds. The UNSC and MPLA worked separately to try and curtail this trade from 1997 onwards and yet diamonds were not specifically mentioned in any of the treaties. It is not clear whether this was discussed in negotiations or during implementation meetings, perhaps due to the preponderance of MPLA and government (US, UN, etc.) sources for these discussions compared to first-hand accounts from UNITA participants. The lack of inclusion of the economic mechanisms of war seems to confirm the conclusions of academic studies (see Wennmann)[57] that indicate that ignoring economic incentives for conflict means a significant aspect of the peace puzzle is missing.

As this section shows and previous chapters explore in detail, leaving issues out of peace treaties was not a successful tactic in the treaties examined in this book, particularly those issues related to the status of key leaders and conflict-fuelling resources. This contrasts with practitioner-focused mediation literature; see Zartman and Berman (often discussing in detail the various Israel-Palestine negotiations) who discuss leaving out critical issues as being a way to move forward in negotiations.[58] However, this book argues that while this method may enable short-term progress in discussions, it significantly hinders implementation and long-term peace, particularly if no plan at all, not even a vague one, is included to address these issues at some point in the process.

How much specificity?

A recurring theme in this book's examination of treaty provisions has been the need for specifying details during negotiations, rather than deferring until the implementation phase, leaving room for delays and accusations to mount and further eroding already tenuous trust. This need for specificity is confirmed in existing academic research such as Crocker & Hampson, DeRouen et al, Rothchild, Kingma and Bakiner.[59] This book, however, illustrates an important nuance of this academic understanding: specificity without rigidity in treaty terms is the key to implementation success. The Bicesse Accords were quite specific about the timelines for demobilization and elections; so specific as to be unchangeable even when events on the ground changed unrecognizably. Thus, the specific rigidity was the treaty's undoing. The Rome Accords, on the other hand, were noteworthy for similar steps, assumptions around elections and timelines, but had a built-in delaying provision to enable flexibility. This flexibility was not in spite of the specificity of the terms laid out; in fact, it enabled the process to be carried out despite on-the-ground delays. The specific flexibility of the terms enhanced implementation, whereas rigid specifications would have inhibited it.

Likewise, the Rome Accords specified a ratio of 50/50 RENAMO to FRELIMO fighters in the combined army but did not otherwise specify linguistic, educational, geographic or other qualifications necessary from combatants from either side. As was discussed in Chapter 4, the number of combatants on both sides who wished to join the military was much smaller than expected. This could have been a juncture at which implementation could break down if either side saw the reduced numbers as a purposeful ploy to break treaty provisions. However, the stark realities of the number of combatants from either side who were willing to join the integrated military – so much smaller than predicted – required revisions to both numbers and ratios. Perhaps the acquiescence of RENAMO to agreeing to a 30/70 ratio instead of a 50/50 was because ONUMOZ and donors focused RENAMO's leadership more on elections and party-building at this junction in the implementation process.

Finally, the most important element that enabled flexible specificity was the creation of implementation-phase committees to oversee processes. Within this key priority, the further specification that a third party, in Mozambique's case ONUMOZ, was officially in charge of the committees with a deciding vote, ensured that the committee could actually function without assuming both conflict participants were always trusting each other. In Angola, equivalent committees only ever stalemated, as by allowing both sides equal and therefore deadlocking abilities, the functioning of the committees required trust between both sides, in short supply generally following civil wars. This corresponds with the importance of third parties as implementation-phase guarantors, as discussed by Crocker & Hampson and Mattes & Savun.[60] This book specifies an additional way in which third parties can be effective in keeping implementation on track: by having decision-making authorization built into the process. This diverges from Crocker & Hampson and Mattes & Savun who assume that third parties are effective at keeping implementation on track due to stronger military force than either adversary,[61] a situation that was not the case in either Angola or Mozambique for any UN mission. This confirms Mac Ginty's argument that review processes must be built into implementation phases in order to ensure the larger picture is kept in mind throughout;[62] this book finds that in Angola and Mozambique at least, third-party-led committees can be effective insurance mechanisms.

Therefore, in returning to some of the initial research questions of this book concerning the degree to which verification committees and detailed planning in treaties (including the creation of verification committees) are needed for implementation success, this book argues the evidence shows these details and concomitant committees lead to success when they are both specific and precisely flexible. This finding is directly contrary to work such as Zartman & Berman and Inbal & Lerner,[63] who argue in favour of constructive ambiguity. The findings of this book argue strongly that detailed provisions, including for how to deal with unexpected and unresolved issues, are absolutely crucial to implementation success. This argument against much of the prevailing literature suggests that more detailed comparative work between treaty provisions and specificity across a wider range of cases and treaties is needed to determine which provisions exactly should be specific, and which, if any, can be left more ambiguous. This book focused only on two cases, the four applicable treaties and specifically the security-related provisions of each treaty; other types of provisions have not been examined in the same detail.

Lessons learned from implementation?

None of the treaties examined in this book were perfect. Lyons convincingly argues that implementation requires both 'push' and 'pull' factors, which, essentially, are incentives to cooperate and barriers to deviation from the plan. This book offers a confirmation of this push-pull idea through the two case studies examined. In Angola, barriers were consistently attempted to avoid recurrence of violence, but few compelling incentives were put forward. In contrast, in Mozambique, incentives for combatants to reintegrate into civilian society were so compelling that both political sides were shocked by how few combatants wanted to remain in fighting positions.

Building on the work of Berdal and Lyons, this book agrees that implementing peace treaties is an important step, and perhaps even riskier, than negotiating a treaty in the first place. Adhering to the provisions and operationalizing the terms is essential to successful peace outcomes. Mac Ginty argues that it is hard to ask combatants to give up weapons, as they often are seen not only as personal protection but also status symbols. This corresponds with Berdal's point that fighters are often not well-equipped economically to adjust to peace time jobs; therefore, economic rather than coercive methods of incentivizing compliance with disarmament are more likely to be successful. Berdal also emphasizes the risks that delays can create in implementation as it reduces confidence and participation in the peace process, something seen in both Angola and Mozambique. This book agrees with these findings and goes further to suggest that providing attractive alternative roles, specifically within the security sector, that meaningfully employ, or at least engage, former combatants is essential to preventing recidivism.

Beyond delays inherent in transition, there is the problem of managing expectations for former combatants, given the high-stakes issue raised by Mac Ginty and the importance of dignity discussed earlier in this chapter. One additional key factor that emerges from the comparison of the four implementation processes in Angola and Mozambique is the impact that the perspective of the UN commander can have when adjusting to conditions on the ground. While ONUMOZ has been noted in existing peacekeeping literature for its adaptability,[64] this book contributes further understanding to the extent to which UN peacekeeping failures in Angola were a function of this particular problem in addition to lack of personnel, supplies and political unity. This follows on from the lessons in the previous chapter about the importance of flexible specificity, which, as this section will show, has important intangible behavioural aspects as well.

Delays

One thing that was consistent across all four implementation periods, regardless of the political will and coordination circumstances involved, was delays from the timetables that had been planned. It is impossible to untangle at this historical distance exactly what every single factor for each delay was and to what extent accusations about purposeful delays for political reasons or security posturing was correct. Despite the differences between the peace treaties and negotiations, the fact that there were delays in every single case suggests that delays happen for a huge variety of reasons and discerning the specific reasons for delays is actually not the lesson to take forward. Instead, the important point about delays is that every single timetable listed in any of these peace treaties, particularly for carrying out security provisions, were wildly unrealistic for mainly logistical reasons which then also included political and security posturing.

In the previous section, the balance between specificity and rigidity has been discussed and delays are a key aspect of implementation where flexibility is most able to manifest. However, even flexible and well-written peace treaties, per the provisions discussed in the previous section, will likely still face delays. One cause is having unrealistic timelines around logistical barriers: none of these treaties adequately considered the logistical difficulty of setting up disarmament camps across countries of these sizes. In addition, the prevalence of landmines specifically along roads and access structures caused delays. Furthermore, the capabilities of communications in the 1990s hindered coordination attempts to solve these problems quickly. Still, landmines are not a problem solely of the past, and UN peacekeeping missions are still often staffed to the extent of just a few peacekeepers for hundreds of square kilometres; therefore, even with improved communication, logistical challenges are still likely to occur if similar timetables are used in peace treaties today.

The lesson from the persistence of delays, therefore, is twofold. First, timetables should assume from the outset that implementing a peace treaty, even just in terms of security provisions, will require at least one year, if not two to three or four, for disarmament and demobilization alone. One reason this is likely to continue to not be the case in treaty provisions, however, is because of the financial and attention pressure that this put on the international community to change its willingness to extend its commitment during the implementation phase despite the numerous pieces of academic research (see DeRouen et al)[65] that point to sustained international commitment as a key peace ingredient. Given that Dayal argues that UN peacekeeping mandates are often designed more through existing templates that have previously secured UNSC approval rather than in response to specific conditions on the ground,[66] this seems unlikely to change.

Still, the lesson to take away is delays are to a degree inevitable, but, also, delays do not automatically mean that an implementation process will fail or that the treaty was badly written. Therefore, implementers should prepare themselves for delays and also prepare participating populations as well as the general national population to expect delays will happen, and this does not mean that the peace has broken down.

Assembly area conditions and expectation management

Relatedly, the single biggest lesson from the implementation of assembly areas for disarmament in both Angola and Mozambique is the importance of expectation management. This applies not only to the soldiers undergoing these processes but also to the civilian populations watching, the politicians in charge of encouraging participation, the third parties on the ground in charge of carrying out these provisions and the international community responsible for both political pressure and humanitarian aid. Delays are inevitable and one of the biggest causes for delays is in creating assembly areas in the first place. The first step – ensuring sufficient security and minimizing violence in order to establish camps for combatants in a long-running conflict that has only recently instituted a ceasefire – is already a tall task. Then, setting up camps to have capacity for thousands or tens of thousands of combatants is quite difficult logistically, particularly when supplies come from many different sources in different ways at different times. In addition, the camps need to be spread evenly around the country so that they can be easily accessed by combatants, but this also makes it difficult for any centrally located efforts to supply these locations.

Beyond logistics, however, there is also the requirement of expectation management around both conditions in the camps and how long combatants should expect to be in them. Combatants, especially when asked to give up their weapons, will often expect quite a lot in return; at the very least, they expect basic standards of living – which was a consistent problem in Angola. Delays in the fulfilment of these expectations can be directly tied to unwillingness to continue to participate in demobilization (see Chapter 4), thus risking the entire peace process.

In the aftermath of a civil war, uncertainty reigns for all actors and that is perhaps one of the largest enemies of implementation; the peace treaty will often outline general principles and goals that are communicated to individual constituencies in a way that seems most likely to garner their enthusiastic participation up to and including tactical inclusions and omissions of information. However, this involves compromises that are already difficult to swallow for participants and delays in fulfilling promises to the parties involved; the perception that promises have been broken result in much more significant consequences when both the soldiers themselves and the population at large have been primed for decades to expect perceived inequality to be resolved solely through violence.

This book therefore confirms and builds on the lessons highlighted by Mac Ginty and others.[67] The early stages of implementation are often the moment that those involved feel the most vulnerable: signing a piece of paper requires words, whereas giving up weapons and moving to designated areas out of your own control involve taking actions which have much higher perceived stakes. This explains Jarstad and Nilsson's finding that military power-sharing (or as this book refers to it, military integration), if successful, is more predictive of peace treaties' success and longevity than political power-sharing in isolation.[68] Therefore, expectation management in the implementation process should not be an afterthought or solely relegated to the realm of public affairs, but instead should be considered central to the mission of the body in charge of implementing the peace treaty.

UN attitude made a difference

During implementation, comparison of these four treaties shows that it not only matters what role the UN is designated in the treaty (see previous section), but also the attitude with which the mission commander approaches the task on the ground as well. This is a less tangible, attitudinal impact of the UN mission, but this book argues that these kinds of aspects, such as the argument around dignity during negotiations, are key factors for success. The demonstration of the importance of attitude can clearly be found in a few examples discussed in previous chapters and generally fall into two categories: behaviours focused around coordination and those centred around flexibility, both exemplified by the ONUMOZ Mission Commander Ajello and lacking from all UN peacekeeping missions in Angola.

For coordination, the UN was merely one international actor involved in the peace negotiations in both cases, and there are of course domestic actors to consider as well. In both countries, there were quite a few instances during the conflicts, negotiations and implementation processes when these various actors were working at cross-purposes (see particularly the argument in Chapter 5 around the impact of international humanitarian aid during continued conflict in Angola). In Angola, the UN peacekeeping missions were both officially designated and acted as merely one amongst many intervenors. ONUMOZ, on the other hand, although given slightly more authority in the peace treaty itself, was not officially given a mandate to coordinate the entire implementation process. Nevertheless, this is what happened, as Ajello made a point of formally working with the group of existing foreign ambassadors in Maputo who had been stationed in Mozambique throughout the war and negotiations process. This coordination meant that all international actors were united on the goals and necessary steps for the peace process, ensuring that neither side of the conflict could try and go around the UN to other international backers, as happened consistently in Angola. This behavioural focus on coordination was not in ONUMOZ's original mandate but was key to ensuring consistent operations amongst the various international actors.

In terms of flexibility, ONUMOZ also went beyond its official mandate in two key ways, the first of which has been discussed in detail in Chapter 4, prioritizing demobilization over disarmament. This was a deviation from the strictest interpretation of ONUMOZ's mandate and treaty-specified role but was made by the force commander in order to respond to conditions on the ground and uphold the larger principles of peace and focus on elections. The second way in which this flexibility manifested was the larger role that ONUMOZ took on in terms not just of overseeing elections in a technical sense (setting up polling stations, registering voters, etc), but also in assisting RENAMO in organizing its campaigning efforts, including providing logistical support such as flight access for RENAMO politicians to travel throughout the country. This decision was made by Commander Ajello and received sharp pushback from his second-in-command (per internal memos now available in the UN archives). Ajello explicitly justified this decision as benefiting the wider goals of the treaty, even though he acknowledged this was a stretched interpretation of the ONUMOZ mandate. The disagreement escalated to UN headquarters in New York, but Ajello's position was upheld.

This instance illustrates just how important this particular person in this particular role at this particular time was in influencing the conditions on the ground, in line with Mac Ginty's extortion that external actors should be 'servants, not masters of the peace',[69] which van den Bergh's research confirms was the case in Mozambique.[70] This example also illustrates Roll's concept of 'pockets of effectiveness',[71] in this case in a post-conflict environment rather than within a national government, but the idea of one piece of a larger entity operating effectively and therefore mitigating excesses (mainly corruption) from connected organizations applies here too.

This book does not go so far as to argue that the individual character of the UN peacekeeping mission, the special representative of the UN Secretary-General (SRSG), is the single key to successful implementation. Rather this book highlights less tangible behavioural aspects, especially around willingness to cooperate and coordinate with others, and to be flexible on the details in order to achieve the larger goals, as being important considerations. Certainly Ajello's unusually pragmatic approach (perhaps from his background in UNDP rather than UN headquarters) was noted by contemporaries, not always happily, yet the outcome speaks to a large degree for itself. In contrast, the Angolan UN missions were headed first by two well-known diplomats and then by less famous UN insiders. For none of these diplomats was a background in UN bureaucracy helpful on the ground. Jett, a US diplomat involved in Mozambique during this time who went on to write about his experiences in Mozambique and with mediation more generally, specifically noted that UN bureaucrats had limitations in the field given their training to make everyone happy; something Ajello did not achieve in the short term, but perhaps with better long-term results.[72]

The comparison of Angola and Mozambique suggests that bureaucratic talent, although key in the development of a UN career and useful in enabling selection to a post in charge of a UN peacekeeping mission, is not in fact necessarily an asset in actually carrying out the mandate. The skills needed to successfully lobby in developed Western nations and at UN headquarters are not necessarily the same as those needed to implement a peace treaty in a tense environment which is transitioning, hopefully, from war to peace. However, UN headquarters remains in charge of the financial and political security of the mission, and is the authority the SRSG reports to, creating a delicate balance to maintain. The examples of Mozambique and Angola confirm the work of Oksamytna, Bove and Lundgren around the characteristics that enable the selection of SRSGs[73] and adds further confirmation that the institutional aspects of post selection and headquarters politics can in fact inhibit the best-suited individuals both from being selected and from being fully empowered once deployed. Both Anstee and Blondin-Beye were known and respected international diplomats who had each previously served in UN posts and both planned to continue working in the UN sphere following their work in Angola.[74] Ajello, on the other hand, came from the UNDP, a distantly non-headquarters-based organization and distinctly had no desire to work further within the UN system.[75] This book argues that these personal preferences, and the related institutional pressures, are relevant to how their tenure and approach to their missions unfolded.

Conclusion: What were the overall lessons learned for military integration?

This book's primary research question was which military reintegration practices are the most effective at reconstructing stable national armed forces after civil wars. While this presumes a universal or relatively generalizable framework is possible to ascertain, it is important to acknowledge that this book examines only two cases in detail and that each reveals specific differences that are unique to their particular circumstances. Therefore, per Robinson's extortion that individual contexts must be treated specifically,[76] this book does not argue for a universal framework. Still, this book does identify certain practices that could be more generally applicable within the context of designing post-conflict integrated military institutions through peace treaties.

This book argues that establishing post-conflict integrated militaries involves a combination of efforts during both treaty negotiations that result in specific treaty provisions, as well as certain steps and behaviours during the implementation phase. Some of the specifics investigated in this book include examining the fighting quality of the integrated military, individual-versus-unit integration, amount of training, number of fighters per side and importance of rank and pay.

In both Angola and Mozambique, as well as in a wider array of militaries per Licklider's edited volume,[77] the fighting quality of the integrated military was not considered either by contemporaries or later analysts to be a key determinant of successful military integration. From the 1990s until today, countries are at far greater risk of internal conflict than having conflict with other countries, and therefore strong militaries that can deter foreign invasions are not in fact relevant to most countries, especially in the post–Cold War era. Therefore, determining integration steps or success via fighting capacity would be irrelevant.

The claim that integrated militaries are more successful on the individual level is hard to test within the context of these two conflicts. In Mozambique's case, the military was integrated to the individual level, and while Angola's treaty implied that individual integration was the plan, it is difficult to ascertain to what degree this was complied with in the Luena Treaty. This is because the FAA was so dominant in negotiating the treaty that previous formulaic ratios of MPLA versus UNITA were ignored and only 5,000 UNITA fighters were integrated into the MPLA, with nine designated as generals but no further details about other ranks or individual-versus-unit integration, which was clarified either in the treaty itself or during the implementation period (see Chapter 5). Given previous integrations of UNITA into the FAA at the individual level, however, it can be presumed that this trend continued. Both militaries integrated at the individual level, and therefore no firm conclusions can be drawn about whether integrating militaries on an individual level is more or less successful than integrating as units either large or small.

Aside from the level of military reintegration, this book finds that integrated militaries do not seem to require any training in order to function. Angola's military does not seem to have provided any particular training to UNITA fighters who joined from 1997 onwards and while equal integration has eluded the force, neither has it disintegrated. More compellingly, Mozambique had two integrated training efforts (the French led a demining effort and the British trained infantry) in the immediate implementation years, but then international training seems to have lapsed from 1997 onwards. Despite this, the FADM has not fractured within based on who did or did not receive this training. While perhaps training can serve the purpose of viewing the integrated military as a more attractive option than going from war directly to civilian life, particularly for those in higher ranks with more to lose starting from scratch as a civilian, it does not seem to have any measurable impact on whether a military stays integrated.

What is clear from analysing the treaties is that in all four cases determining the number of fighters that each side would contribute to the integrated army was by far the largest difficulty related to security provisions during the negotiations. This was more contentious than determining steps or timetables for ceasefires, disarmament or demobilization, despite it being technically much simpler. This is because of the impact, real and perceived, that a relative leverage of numbers would have in the integrated force, with neither side wanting to give the other too much control over the prospective singular security institution in the post-conflict country (see Chapter 4 on the FADM specifically). This is similar to Gaub's argument in favour of quotas within militaries to preserve some balance of power,[78] a prospect not pursued in either Mozambique or Angola.

What comparison of the implementation phases shows, however, is that while the specific numbers and ratios of soldiers were often sticking points during negotiations, the numbers during implementation were often quite different (due to delays, mismanaged expectations of demobilization reducing cooperation incentives for fighters, or sufficiently compelling civilian reintegration packages), and, therefore, these hard-fought numbers in the negotiating room were often useless to both sides in practice. Where they were useful, however, was in preserving the general principle of the integration agreement despite numbers on both sides having been drastically reduced, as was evidenced in Mozambique.

What the Mozambique case also highlights is the importance of rank both in gaining buy-in from combatants for the peace treaty itself as well as for the reintegration of combatants into both military and civilian institutions. First, all sides had military leaders involved in negotiations. They saw this participation as key to ensuring their interests were both clearly delineated and their fighting strength properly leveraged for negotiating positions. This was heightened for UNITA and RENAMO who had more military experts than political ones, but even within the MPLA General 'Ndula was a key figure during negotiations. This suggests that military figures have important perspectives to offer during treaty negotiation, and their inclusion is a likely means through which buy-in throughout the wider organization can be managed as they have more direct operational command of more combatants than politicians usually do. Therefore, mediators and international actors should likewise ensure representative military expertise, as shown successfully in the example of Colonel Snyder in the Bicesse negotiations (see Chapter 3); something that was lacking throughout the Rome discussions and thus required non-military experts like Ambassadors Jett and Hume as well as non-state advisors like Dr Thomashausen to function as military experts despite that not being their particular expertise. While the Bicesse negotiations featured the work of Colonel Synder to a degree by accident, the usefulness of his presence in enabling a separate committee to discuss security issues suggests that in future treaty negotiations outside actors and mediators, if present, should include military and security experts as well as the standard diplomats as part of the core team.

Beyond negotiations, however, the importance of rank was also clear in the implementation phases for most of the treaties examined in this book. The negotiation was not just the overall number of combatants each side would contribute to the military that was contentious, but the number of officer spots, and at which levels, would be allocated. This was continually contested, and lost, by UNITA in every successive Angolan Treaty and was a key point for Mozambican RENAMO officers who specifically sought officership in the FADM, not for its military capacities but for the attendant economic perks of uniforms, salaries and cars. This confirms Alden's research in Mozambique that showed that mid-level and senior officers had more difficulty in adjusting to civilian life given the loss of status.[79] This issue was also examined by Weigink, who showed the unique role that former mid-level officers played in post-conflict criminal networks due to perceptions of loss of status and pressures to continue providing patronage.[80] This is perhaps one aspect behind Porto, Alden and Parsons' finding that in spite of some combatants demobilized as civilians, they nevertheless failed to take on this identity when surveyed in the initial post-conflict years.[81] This suggests that more than absolute numbers or even ratios, peace treaties should make sure to include particular provisions for mid- and senior-level officers. This could result in 'top-heavy' institutions in the initial post-war years, but given the earlier contention regarding no necessity for military capability, this seems a small price to pay.

On the other hand, pay seems to be the key determinant for whether rank-and-file combatants choose civilian life over joining the integrated military, as evidenced by the reactions of Mozambican combatants when offered civilian reintegration packages (see Chapter 4) and UNITA combatants offered even smaller amounts of civilian reintegration support (see Chapter 5). In both cases, however, the amount offered via civilian demobilization was higher than the wages offered in the integrated military, which was a key factor cited by former combatants for their decision-making. Even with that known pay differential, the number of low-level combatants willing to become civilians was surprising to the officers, confirming again the different priorities between these two groups, even within the same organization and conflict-setting.

Therefore, the lessons of this book for building an integrated military include: the participation of military leaders from both sides and the presence of external military experts increases buy-in, if not necessarily realistic implementation timetables, (though this is an area for prospective improvement), the importance of understanding rank differences in terms of demobilization priorities and adjusting expectations and offerings accordingly and the metrics of success that are relevant to post-conflict reintegration (lack of disintegration or in-fighting) rather than the level of training or fighting capacity.

NOTES

Chapter 1

1   Monica Duffy Toft, 'Introduction: Civil War Termination in Historical and Theoretical Context', in *Securing the Peace: The Durable Settlement of Civil Wars* (Princeton University Press, 2009), 1–18. http://www.jstor.org/stable/j.ctt7rzc6.5 (accessed 7 December 2019).
2   Caroline Hartzell, 'Chapter 2: Mixed Motives? Explaining the Decision to Integrate Militaries', in *New Armies from Old: Merging Competing Military Forces After Civil Wars*, ed. Roy Licklider (Washington, DC: Georgetown University Press, 2014), 16. Alex J. Bellamy, Stuart Griffin, and Paul Williams, *Understanding Peacekeeping* (Cambridge: Polity, 2011), 7.
3   Anders Reagan, 'Reframing the Ontology of Peace Studies', *Peace and Conflict Studies* 29, no. 2 (23 May 2023). https://nsuworks.nova.edu/pcs/vol29/iss2/1.
4   Susanna P. Campbell, Michael G. Findley, and Kyosuke Kikuta, 'An Ontology of Peace: Landscapes of Conflict and Cooperation with Application to Colombia', *International Studies Review* 19, no. 1 (1 March 2017): 92–113. https://doi.org/10.1093/isr/vix005.
5   Barbara F. Walter, 'Why Bad Governance Leads to Repeat Civil War', *Journal of Conflict Resolution* 59, no. 7 (1 October 2015): 1242–72. https://doi.org/10.1177/0022002714528006.
6   Anastasia Shesterinina, 'Civil War as a Social Process: Actors and Dynamics from Pre- to Post-War', *European Journal of International Relations* 28, no. 3 (1 September 2022): 538–62. https://doi.org/10.1177/13540661221095970.
7   W. Andy Knight, 'Disarmament, Demobilization, and Reintegration and Post-Conflict Peacebuilding in Africa: An Overview', *African Security* (2008). https://doi.org/10.1080/19362200802285757.
8   Ibid.
9   Roger Mac Ginty, *No War, No Peace: The Rejuvenation of Stalled Peace Processes and Peace Accords* (Basingstoke: Palgrave Macmillan, 2008), 186–7. Inge Ruigrok, 'Whose Justice? Contextualising Angola's Reintegration Process', *African Security Review* 16, no. 1 (2007): 84–98 (p. 91). doi:10.1080/10246029.2007.9627636.
10 Susan Willett, 'New Barbarians at the Gate: Losing the Liberal Peace in Africa', *Review of African Political Economy* 32, no. 106 (2005): 569–94 (p. 583). www.jstor.org/stable/20059109; Toft, 'Introduction', 35.
11 Nicholas Marsh and Júlia Palik, 'Negotiating Disarmament: Lessons Learnt from Colombia, Nepal, the Philippines, South Sudan, Sri Lanka', *PRIO Papers* (n.d.). https://doi.org/https://www.prio.org/publications/12869. (accessed 1 June 2023).
12 Anders Themnér, *Warlord Democrats in Africa: Ex-military Leaders and Electoral Politics* (Uppsala: Nordiska Afrikainstitutet, The Nordic Africa Institute, 2017).

13 Roy Licklider, *New Armies from Old: Merging Competing Military Forces After Civil Wars* (Washington, DC: Georgetown University Press, 2014).
14 Louise Andersen, Bjørn Møller, and Finn Stepputat, *Fragile States and Insecure People?: Violence, Security, and Statehood in the Twenty-first Century* (New York: Palgrave Macmillan, 2007), 177.
15 John Gerring, 'What Is a Case Study and What Is It Good For?', *American Political Science Review* 98, no. 2 (2004): 341–54. https://doi.org/10.1017/s0003055404001182. Toft, 'Introduction'.
16 Shesterinina, 'Civil War as a Social Process'.
17 See for examples: Toft, 'Introduction', 19–38.
18 Although acknowledging the challenges in defining peace (Campbell et al., 'An Ontology of Peace'), this book uses as a rough measurement a lack of battle deaths above a 1,000 deaths per year threshold after the exit of external military enforcers (including UN peacekeepers). Although this definition of peace is negative (Johan Galtung, 'Violence, Peace, and Peace Research', *Journal of Peace Research* 6, no. 3 (September 1969): 167–91. https://doi.org/10.1177/002234336900600301) and focuses on only the military aspect of peace (Campbell et al., 'An Ontology of Peace'), due to the book's focus specifically on the security sector, this definition will be used. This definition incorporates and further enhances the traditional political science statistical definition for civil war recurrence (Nicholas Sambanis, 'What Is Civil War? Conceptual and Empirical Complexities of an Operational Definition', *The Journal of Conflict Resolution* 48, no. 6 (2004): 814–58. https://www.jstor.org/stable/4149797.) by taking into account the role that external enforcers – such as neighbouring countries (Syria in Lebanon 1986–2005) or multilateral peacekeeping missions (UN DPKO) – can play in keeping the peace in post-conflict environments.
19 Caroline Hartzell, Matthew Hoddie, and Donald Rothchild, 'Stabilizing the Peace After Civil War: An Investigation of Some Key Variables', *International Organization* 55, no. 1 (2001): 183–208. doi:10.1162/002081801551450; Donald S. Rothchild, 'Settlement Terms and Postagreement Stability', in *Ending Civil Wars: The Implementation of Peace Agreements*, ed. Stephen John Stedman, Donald Rothchild, and Elizabeth M. Cousens (Boulder, CO: Lynne Rienner, 2002).
20 Gerring, 'What Is a Case Study and What Is It Good For?'.
21 Alexander L. George and Andrew Bennett, *Case Studies and Theory Development in the Social Sciences* (Cambridge, MA: MIT Press, 2007).
22 See, for example: Matthew Hoddie and Caroline Hartzell, *Strengthening Peace in Post-Civil War States* (Chicago: University of Chicago Press, 2003); Florence Gaub, *Military Integration after Civil Wars Multiethnic Armies, Identity, and Post-Conflict Reconstruction* (London: Routledge, 2010); Anna K. Jarstad and Desiree Nilsson, 'From Words to Deeds: The Implementation of Power-Sharing Pacts in Peace Accords', *Conflict Management and Peace Science* 25, no. 3 (2008): 206–23. https://doi.org/10.1080/07388940802218945.
23 Edward George, *The Cuban Intervention in Angola, 1965-1991: From Che Guevara to Cuito Cuanavale* (London: Routledge Taylor & Francis Group, 2012), 67.
24 Ibid., 69.
25 Jarstad and Nilsson, 'From Words to Deeds'.
26 Katherine Glassmyer and Nicholas Sambanis, 'Rebel—Military Integration and Civil War Termination', *Journal of Peace Research* 45, no. 3 (2008): 365–84. https://doi.org/10.1177/0022343308088816.

27   Stephen John Stedman, Donald S. Rothchild, and Elizabeth M. Cousens, *Ending Civil Wars: The Implementation of Peace Agreements* (Boulder, CO: Lynne Rienner, 2002).

28   Charles King, *Ending Civil Wars* (Oxford: Oxford University Press for the International Institute for Strategic Studies, 1997).

29   C. Albin and D. Druckman, 'Equality Matters: Negotiating an End to Civil Wars', *The Journal of Conflict Resolution* 56, no. 2 (2012): 155–82.

30   Dorina Bekoe, *Implementing Peace Agreements: Lessons from Mozambique, Angola, and Liberia* (New York: Palgrave Macmillan, 2016).

31   Madhav Joshi and J. Michael Quinn, 'Is the Sum Greater than the Parts? The Terms of Civil War Peace Agreements and the Commitment Problem Revisited', *Negotiation Journal* 31, no. 1 (2015): 7–30. doi:10.1111/nejo.12077; Michaela Mattes and Burcu Savun, 'Information, Agreement Design, and the Durability of Civil War Settlements', *American Journal of Political Science* 54, no. 2 (2010): 511–24. doi:10.1111/j.1540-5907.2010.00444.x.

32   Rothchild, 'Settlement Terms and Postagreement Stability'.

33   Ira William Zartman and Maureen R. Berman, *The Practical Negotiator* (New Haven: Yale University Press, 2010).

34   Kees Kingma, 'Disarmament, Demobilization And Reintegration of Former Combatants in a Peacebuilding Context', *Policy Sciences* 30, no. 3 (1997): 151–65.

35   Hartzell et al., 'Stabilizing the Peace After Civil War'.

36   Barbara F. Walter, 'Designing Transitions from Civil War: Demobilization, Democratization, and Commitments to Peace', *International Security* 24, no. 1 (1999): 127–55; Barbara F. Walter, 'The Critical Barrier to Civil War Settlement', *International Organization* 51, no. 3 (1997): 335–64. https://doi.org/10.1162/002081897550384.

37   Mattes and Savun, 'Information, Agreement Design, and the Durability of Civil War Settlements'.

38   Terrence Lyons, *Demilitarizing politics: Elections on the Uncertain Road to Peace* (Boulder, CO: Lynne Rienner Publishers, 2005).

39   Stedman et al., *Ending Civil Wars*.

40   Rothchild, 'Settlement Terms and Postagreement Stability'.

41   Mattes and Savun, 'Information, Agreement Design, and the Durability of Civil War Settlements'.

42   Chester A. Crocker and Fen Osler Hampson, 'Making Peace Settlements Work', *Foreign Policy*, no. 104 (1996): 54. doi:10.2307/1148990.

43   Lise Morjé Howard and Anjali Kaushlesh Dayal, 'The Use of Force in UN Peacekeeping', *International Organization* 72, no. 1 (2017): 71–103. doi:10.1017/s0020818317000431.

44   Macartan Humphreys and Jeremy M. Weinstein, 'Demobilization and Reintegration', *Journal of Conflict Resolution* 51, no. 4 (2007): 531–67. https://doi.org/10.1177/0022002707302790.

45   Paul Collier, 'Demobilization and Insecurity: A Study in the Economics of the Transition from War to Peace', *Journal of International Development* 6, no. 3 (1994): 343–51. https://doi.org/10.1002/jid.3380060308.

46   Robert Muggah, *Security and Post-conflict Reconstruction: Dealing with Fighters in the Aftermath of War* (London: Routledge, 2009).

47   Nicole Ball, 'Democratic Governance and the Security Sector in Conflict-affected Countries', in *Governance in Post-Conflict Societies: Rebuilding Fragile States*, ed. Derick W. Brinkerhoff (Oxfordshire: Routledge, 2007).

48   David Laitin, 'The Industrial Organisation of Merged Armies', in *New Armies from Old: Merging Competing Military Forces After Civil Wars*, ed. Roy Licklider (Washington, DC: Georgetown University Press, 2014).

49   Gaub, *Military Integration after Civil Wars Multiethnic Armies, Identity, and Post-conflict Reconstruction*.

Chapter 2

1   Leah Fine, 'Colorblind Colonialism? *Lusotropicalismo* and Portugal's 20th Century Empire in Africa' (PhD diss., Barnard University, 2017), 2–4.

2   Martha Mutisi and Andrea Bartoli, 'Chapter 10: Merging Militaries: Mozambique', in *New Armies from Old: Merging Competing Military Forces After Civil Wars*, ed. Roy Licklider (Washington, DC: Georgetown University Press, 2014), 163.

3   Fernando Andresen Guimarães, *The Origins of the Angolan Civil War: Foreign Intervention and Domestic Political Conflict* (Basingstoke, Hampshire: Palgrave, 2002), 3.

4   Douglas L. Wheeler and Pélissier René, *Angola* (Westport, CT: Greenwood Press, 1978), 35, 37–8.

5   Cameron Hume, *Ending Mozambique's War: The Role of Mediation and Good Offices* (Washington, DC: United States Institute of Peace, 1994), 4.

6   Guimarães, *The Origins of the Angolan Civil War*, 3.

7   Wheeler and René, *Angola*, 33.

8   Michael Wolfers and Jane Bergerol, *Angola in the Frontline* (London: Zed Press, 1983), 103. Wheeler and René, *Angola*, 44.

9   Wheeler and René, *Angola*, 40.

10   Malyn Newitt, *A Short History of Mozambique* (Oxford: Oxford University Press, 2017), 520.

11   Robert Aldrich and Andreas Stucki, *The Colonial World: A History of European Empires, 1780s to the Present* (London: Bloomsbury Academic, 2023), 414.

12   Hilary Andersson, *Mozambique: A War against the People* (London: Palgrave Macmillan, 2014), 11. Alex Vines, *Renamo: From Terrorism to Democracy in Mozambique?* (York: Centre for Southern African Studies, University of York, 1996), 7.

13   Hume, *Ending Mozambique's War*, 5.

14   Colin Darch, *The Mozambican Conflict and the Peace Process in Historical Perspective: A Success Story Gone Wrong?* (Maputo, Mozambique: Friedrich-Ebert-Stiftung Mozambique, 2018), 7.

15   Andersson, *Mozambique*, 9–11. Vines, *Renamo*, 7.

16   Hume, *Ending Mozambique's War*, 5. Fine, 'Colorblind Colonialism?', 3.

17   Justin Pearce, 'Control, Politics and Identity in the Angolan Civil War', *African Affairs* 111, no. 444 (July 2012): 442–65 (p. 449). https://doi.org/10.1093/afraf/ads028. Fine, 'Colorblind Colonialism?', 3.

18   Odd Arne Westad, *The Global Cold War: Third World Interventions and the Making of Our Times* (Cambridge: Cambridge University Press, 2016), 436–7.

19   Darch, *The Mozambican Conflict and the Peace Process in Historical Perspective*, 11. Westad, *The Global Cold War*, 436.

20   Andersson, *Mozambique*, 23.

21 Newitt, *A Short History of Mozambique*, 522, 544. Joao M. Cabrita, *Mozambique: The Tortuous Road to Democracy* (London: Palgrave Macmillan, 2014), 5.

22 Andersson, *Mozambique*, 24. Abiodun Alao, *Brothers at War: Dissidence and Rebellion in Southern Africa* (London: British Academic Press, 1994), 44. Darch, *The Mozambican Conflict and the Peace Process in Historical Perspective*, 7.

23 Lawrence W. Henderson, *Angola: Five Centuries of Conflict* (Itacha: Cornell University Press, 1982), 164–5, 178–9.

24 Alao, *Brothers at War*, 3.

25 Colin Legum and Tony Hodges, *After Angola; The War over Southern Africa* (New York: Africana Publ. Co., 1978), 11–12.

26 Pearce, 'Control, Politics and Identity in the Angolan Civil War', 26.

27 Westad, *The Global Cold War*, 436–7.

28 Wolfers and Bergerol, *Angola in the Frontline*, 110.

29 The phrase 'mixed race' is consistently the phraseology used in the secondary literature and UN archival documents.

30 Westad, *The Global Cold War*, 436–7. Dennis C. Jett, *Why Peacekeeping Fails* (New York: Palgrave Macmillan, 2019), 61.

31 Henderson, *Angola*, 164–5.

32 Pearce, 'Control, Politics and Identity in the Angolan Civil War', 451.

33 Ibid., 443.

34 Jett, *Why Peacekeeping Fails*, 61. Linda Marinda Heywood, *Contested Power in Angola: 1840s to the Present* (Rochester, NY: University of Rochester Press, 2009), 192. Westad, *The Global Cold War*, 436–7.

35 Westad, *The Global Cold War*, 436–7.

36 W. Martin James, *A Political History of the Civil War in Angola, 1974-1990* (New Brunswick: Transaction Publishers, 2011), 51.

37 Wolfers and Bergerol, *Angola in the Frontline*, 110.

38 Heywood, *Contested Power in Angola*, 154.

39 Ibid., 151–2. James, *A Political History of the Civil War in Angola*, 53. Jett, *Why Peacekeeping Fails*, 61.

40 Vines, *Renamo*, 76. Reyko Huang, 'Rebel Diplomacy in Civil War', *International Security* 40, no. 4 (2016): 89–126, muse.jhu.edu/article/617462. Westad, *The Global Cold War*, 438.

41 Heywood, *Contested Power in Angola*, 169. Pearce, 'Control, Politics and Identity in the Angolan Civil War', 21.

42 James, *A Political History of the Civil War in Angola*, 51. Pearce, 'Control, Politics and Identity in the Angolan Civil War', 26.

43 Pearce, 'Control, Politics and Identity in the Angolan Civil War', 443. Heywood, *Contested Power in Angola*, 171–2.

44 Legum and Hodges, *After Angola*, 10, 48. Guimarães, *The Origins of the Angolan Civil War*, 33.

45 Pearce, 'Control, Politics and Identity in the Angolan Civil War', 450. Mutisi and Bartoli, 'Chapter 10', 163.

46 John Marcum, *The Angolan Revolution* (Cambridge, MA: MIT Press, 1969), 241–2. Fine, 'Colorblind Colonialism?', 30–1. Cabrita, *Mozambique*, 34–5.

47 Cabrita, *Mozambique*, 5. Fine, 'Colorblind Colonialism?', 37.

48 Cabrita, *Mozambique*, 3.

49 Newitt, *A Short History of Mozambique*, 541, 543–4. Cabrita, *Mozambique*, 4. James, *A Political History of the Civil War in Angola*, 41. Darch, *The Mozambican Conflict and the Peace Process in Historical Perspective*, 11.

50   Cabrita, *Mozambique*, 4–5.

51   Ibid., 74.

52   Hume, *Ending Mozambique's War*, 6.

53   Andersson, *Mozambique*, 14. Alao, *Brothers at War*, 47. Darch, *The Mozambican Conflict and the Peace Process in Historical Perspective*, 7.

54   Legum and Hodges, *After Angola*, 13.

55   Pearce, 'Control, Politics and Identity in the Angolan Civil War', 27.

56   Alao, *Brothers at War*, 3–4.

57   Pearce, 'Control, Politics and Identity in the Angolan Civil War', 21–2. Westad, *The Global Cold War*, 441–2, 449–50.

58   Hume, *Ending Mozambique's War*, 7.

59   Pearce, 'Control, Politics and Identity in the Angolan Civil War', 17. Westad, *The Global Cold War*, 441–2.

60   Guimarães, *The Origins of the Angolan Civil War*, 152.

61   Ibid.,152. Westad, *The Global Cold War*, 441–2.

62   Westad, *The Global Cold War*, 488.

63   Alao, *Brothers at War*, 14.

64   Guimarães, *The Origins of the Angolan Civil War*, 78. Huang, 'Rebel Diplomacy in Civil War'.

65   James, *A Political History of the Civil War in Angola*, 154. Huang, 'Rebel Diplomacy in Civil War'.

66   Legum and Hodges, *After Angola*, 24. Westad, *The Global Cold War*, 460. Heywood, *Contested Power in Angola*, 151–2, 170.

67   Alao, *Brothers at War*, 3, 16–17. Pearce, 'Control, Politics and Identity in the Angolan Civil War', 25. James, *A Political History of the Civil War in Angola*, 154. Legum and Hodges, *After Angola*, 24. Guimarães, *The Origins of the Angolan Civil War*, 177.

68   Pearce, 'Control, Politics and Identity in the Angolan Civil War', 24.

69   Ibid., 25. Legum and Hodges, *After Angola*, 38. Guimarães, *The Origins of the Angolan Civil War*, 121–2. Westad, *The Global Cold War*, 477, 497.

70   Pearce, 'Control, Politics and Identity in the Angolan Civil War', 446.

71   Legum and Hodges, *After Angola*, chapter 2.

72   Jessica Schafer, *Soldiers at Peace: Veterans and Society after the Civil War in Mozambique* (New York: Palgrave Macmillan, 2007), 36.

73   Alao, *Brothers at War*, 45–6. Nikkie Wiegink, 'Former Military Networks a Threat to Peace? The Demobilisation and Remobilization of Renamo in Central Mozambique', *Stability: International Journal of Security & Development* 4, no. 1 (2015): 3, doi:10.5334/sta.gk.

74   Newitt, *A Short History of Mozambique*, 564.

75   Wiegink, 'Former Military Networks a Threat to Peace?', 3.

76   Mutisi and Bartoli, 'Chapter 10', 163. Hume, *Ending Mozambique's War*, 8–10. Daniel H. Levine, 'Organizational Disruption and Change in Mozambique's Peace Process', *International Peacekeeping* 14, no. 3 (2007): 368–83 (p. 373), doi:10.1080/13533310701422935.

77   Alao, *Brothers at War*, 46.

78   Cabrita, *Mozambique*, 179–81. Andersson, *Mozambique*, 15. Wiegink, 'Former Military Networks a Threat to Peace?', 3.

79   Alao, *Brothers at War*, 46–7. Vines, *Renamo*, 18–20.

80 Schafer, *Soldiers at Peace*, 58. Lisa Hultman, 'The Power to Hurt in Civil War: The Strategic Aim of RENAMO Violence', *Journal of Southern African Studies* 35, no. 4 (2009): 828. https://doi.org/10.1080/03057070903313194.
81 Newitt, *A Short History of Mozambique*, 564–5. Alao, *Brothers at War*, 52. Vines, *Renamo*, 18–20, Wiegink, 'Former Military Networks a Threat to Peace?', 3.
82 Andersson, *Mozambique*, 21.
83 Alao, *Brothers at War*, 57–8.
84 Newitt, *A Short History of Mozambique*, 566–7. Andersson, *Mozambique*, 16–17. Vines, *Renamo*, 1, 7, 87–8. Hultman, 'The Power to Hurt in Civil War', 826.
85 Richard Synge, *Mozambique: UN Peacekeeping in Action 1992-94* (Washington, DC: United States Institute of Peace Press, 1997), 16.
86 Newitt, *A Short History of Mozambique*, 566–7.
87 Ricardo Soares De Oliveira, 'Illiberal Peacebuilding in Angola', *The Journal of Modern African Studies* 49, no. 2 (2011): 290. https://doi.org/10.1017/s0022278x1100005x.
88 Ibid.
89 Vines, *Renamo*, 78. Witney W. Schneidman, 'Africa Notes: Conflict Resolution in Mozambique – February 1990', *Africa Notes: Conflict Resolution in Mozambique – February 1990 | Center for Strategic and International Studies*, 2, 4, www.csis.org/analysis/africa-notes-conflict-resolution-mozambique-february-1990 (accessed 7 October 2018).
90 Alao, *Brothers at War*, 59–62. Hume, *Ending Mozambique's War*, 10–12.
91 Cabrita, *Mozambique*, 225.
92 Pearce, 'Control, Politics and Identity in the Angolan Civil War', 459.
93 James, *A Political History of the Civil War in Angola*, 203.
94 Mutisi and Bartoli, 'Chapter 10', 164. Cabrita, *Mozambique*, 225.
95 Newitt, *A Short History of Mozambique*, 572–4.
96 Vines, *Renamo*, 59, 102–14.

Chapter 3

1 Shawn McCormick, 'Africa Notes: Angola: The Road to Peace – June 1991 . . .', *CSIS*, 1. https://www.csis.org/analysis/africa-notes-angola-road-peace-june-1991 (accessed 7 October 2018). Fernando Andresen Guimarães, *The Origins of the Angolan Civil War: Foreign Intervention and Domestic Political Conflict* (New York: Palgrave, 2002), 121–2.
2 Odd A. Westad, *The Global Cold War* (Cambridge: Cambridge University Press, 2006), 797.
3 Ibid., 477.
4 Ibid., 477. Hilton Hamann, *Days of the Generals: The Untold Story of South Africas Apartheid-Era Military Generals* (Cape Town: Zebra, 2001), 15.
5 Westad, *The Global Cold War*, 800.
6 Interviews conducted by author, August 2019.
7 David Cunningham, 'Blocking Resolution: How External States Can Prolong Civil Wars', *Journal of Peace Research* 47, no. 2 (March 2010): 117. www.jstor.org/stable/25654549.
8 Justin Pearce, 'Global Ideologies, Local Politics: The Cold War as Seen from Central Angola', *Journal of Southern African Studies* 43, no. 1 (2017): 13–27 (p. 17). doi:10.1080/03057070.2017.1266809.

9 W. Martin James, *A Political History of the Civil War in Angola, 1974-1990* (Oxfordshire: Routledge, 2020), 231. Cunningham, 'Blocking Resolution', 116.

10 Herman J. Cohen, *Intervening in Africa: Superpower Peacemaking in a Troubled Continent* (Basingstoke: Macmillan, 2001), 122–3, 238.

11 Interview by author of foreign advisor to RENAMO, 1980–94, conducted 2 August 2019.

12 William J. Durch, *The Evolution of UN Peacekeeping: Case Studies and Comparative Analysis* (Chippenham: A. Rowe, 1995), 355. Cunningham, 'Blocking Resolution', 116.

13 Interview by author with a US diplomat in the Office of Southern African Affairs, circa 1990s, conducted 2 August 2019 and 6 August 2019. Cunningham, 'Blocking Resolution', 117.

14 Joao M. Cabrita, *Mozambique: The Tortuous Road to Democracy* (New York: Palgrave, 2000), 224.

15 Vaughan Lowe, *The United Nations Security Council and War: The Evolution of Thought and Practice since 1945* (Oxford: Oxford University Press, 2008), 200.

16 McCormick, 'Africa Notes: Angola', 1.

17 Durch, *The Evolution of UN Peacekeeping*, 385.

18 First interview by author with a US diplomat in the Office of Southern African Affairs, circa 1990s, conducted 2 August 2019.

19 First interview by author with a US diplomat in the Office of Southern African Affairs, circa 1990s, conducted 2 August 2019. Cabrita, *Mozambique*, 224.

20 Second interview by author with a US diplomat in the Office of Southern African Affairs, circa 1990s, conducted 6 August 2019.

21 George Wright, 'The Clinton Administrations Policy toward Angola: An Assessment', *Review of African Political Economy* 28, no. 90 (2001): 563–76 (pp. 570, 574), doi:10.1080/03056240108704566.

22 Interview by author with US ambassador with African expertise, conducted 16 September 2019.

23 First interview by author with a US diplomat in the Office of Southern African Affairs, circa 1990s, conducted 2 August 2019. Interview conducted by author with former UK ambassador to Angola circa 1990s, conducted on 28 August 2019.

24 Reyko Huang, 'Rebel Diplomacy in Civil War', *International Security* 40, no. 4 (2016). https://doi.org/10.1162/ISEC_a_00237.

25 Ricardo Soares De Oliveira, 'Illiberal Peacebuilding in Angola', *The Journal of Modern African Studies* 49, no. 2 (2011): 287–314 (p. 290). doi:10.1017/s0022278x1100005x. Lowe, *The United Nations Security Council and War*, 187. McCormick, 'Africa Notes: Angola', 2. Interview by author with senior US diplomat working on African affairs, conducted 23 July 2019.

26 Roger Mac Ginty, *No War, No Peace: The Rejuvenation of Stalled Peace Processes and Peace Accords* (Basingstoke: Palgrave Macmillan, 2008), 185.

27 Alex J. Bellamy, Stuart Griffin, and Paul Williams, *Understanding Peacekeeping* (Cambridge: Polity, 2011), 7. World Bank, 'Demobilization and Reintegration of Military Personnel in Africa: The Evidence from Seven Country Case Studies', World Bank Working Paper, October 1993, 83, 41. http://documents1.worldbank .org/curated/en/372941468913782580/text/multi-page.txt (accessed 18 November 2019). McCormick, 'Africa Notes: Angola', 1. Porto João Gomes and Imogen Parsons, *Sustaining the Peace in Angola: An Overview of Current Demobilisation, Disarmament and Reintegration* (Pretoria: Institute for Security Studies, 2003), 24–5.

28 Dennis C. Jett, *Why Peacekeeping Fails* (New York: Palgrave Macmillan, 2019), 116. Pierre Englebert and Denis M. Tull, 'Postconflict Reconstruction in Africa: Flawed Ideas about Failed States', *International Security* 32, no. 4 (2008): 106–39 (p. 118). doi:10.1162/isec.2008.32.4.106.

29 Cohen, *Intervening in Africa*, 237.

30 Interview by author with senior US diplomat working on African affairs, conducted 23 July 2019.

31 George Wright, *The Destruction of a Nation: United States Policy towards Angola since 1945* (London: Pluto Press, 1997), 147.

32 McCormick, 'Africa Notes: Angola', 1. Justin Pearce, 'Control, Politics and Identity in the Angolan Civil War', *African Affairs* 111, no. 444 (July 2012): 459.

33 Interview by author with senior US diplomat working on African affairs, conducted 23 July 2019.

34 Confirmed in two interviews by author with a US diplomat in the Office of Southern African Affairs, circa 1990s, conducted 2 August 2019 and 6 August 2019.

35 First interview by author with a US diplomat in the Office of Southern African Affairs, circa 1990s, conducted 2 August 2019. McCormick, 'Africa Notes: Angola', 1. Chester A. Crocker, *High Noon in Southern Africa: Making Peace in a Rough Neighborhood* (Johannesburg: Jonathan Ball, 1994), 385.

36 Interview of US diplomat in Rome for Mozambique negotiations, conducted by author 18 October 2019.

37 Interview of US diplomat in Rome for Mozambique negotiations, conducted by author 18 October 2019. Jeswald W. Salacuse, 'The Effect of Advice on Negotiations: How Advisors Influence What Negotiators Do', *Negotiation Journal*, 18 April 2016. https://doi.org/10.1111/nejo.12150.

38 McCormick, 'Africa Notes: Angola', 8.

39 Richard Roth, Interview with author 27 August 2019. Jett, *Why Peacekeeping Fails*, 68.

40 Second interview by author with a US diplomat in the Office of Southern African Affairs, circa 1990s, conducted 6 August 2019. Crocker, *High Noon in Southern Africa*, 31.

41 Second interview by author with a US diplomat in the Office of Southern African Affairs, circa 1990s, conducted 6 August 2019. Cohen, *Intervening in Africa*, 109.

42 First interview by author with a US diplomat in the Office of Southern African Affairs, circa 1990s, conducted 2 August 2019.

43 First interview by author with a US diplomat in the Office of Southern African Affairs, circa 1990s, conducted 2 August 2019.

44 Interview by author with US ambassador with African expertise, conducted 16 September 2019.

45 Huang, 'Rebel Diplomacy in Civil War'.

46 Wright, 'The Clinton Administrations Policy toward Angola', 153.

47 Wright, *The Destruction of a Nation*, 574.

48 Ibid., 574.

49 Taisier Mohamed Ahmed Ali and Robert O. Matthews, *Durable Peace: Challenges for Peacebuilding in Africa* (Toronto: University of Toronto Press, 2004), 841. Ian S. Spears, 'Angola's Elusive Peace: The Collapse of the Lusaka Accord', *International Journal* 54, no. 4 (Autumn 1999): 572. https://www.jstor.org/stable/40203416.

50 First interview by author with a US diplomat in the Office of Southern African Affairs, circa 1990s, conducted 2 August 2019. Interview by author of US diplomat

involved in Mozambique negotiations, conducted 12 August 2019. Interview by author of US intelligence and later diplomatic officer with African expertise, conducted 20 September 2019.

51 Interview by author of foreign advisor to RENAMO, 1980–94, conducted 2 August 2019. Interview conducted by author of a senior UN diplomat in ONUMOZ, conducted 13 September 2019.

52 Second interview by author with a US diplomat in the Office of Southern African Affairs, circa 1990s, conducted 6 August 2019. Interview conducted by author of a senior UN diplomat in ONUMOZ, conducted 13 September 2019.

53 Interview by author of US diplomat involved in Mozambique negotiations, conducted 12 August 2019.

54 Alex Vines, *Renamo: From Terrorism to Democracy in Mozambique* (Amsterdam: Centre for Southern African Studies, University of York, 1996), 186.

55 Interview by author of foreign advisor to RENAMO, 1980–94, conducted 2 August 2019. Interview by author with US ambassador with African expertise, conducted 16 September 2019, Richard Synge, *Mozambique: UN Peacekeeping in Action 1992-94* (Washington, DC: United States Institute of Peace Press, 1997), pg 10.

56 Stephen Chan and Moises Vanancio, *War and Peace in Mozambique* (New York: Palgrave Macmillan, 2014), 37.

57 Interview by author of foreign advisor to RENAMO, 1980-1994, conducted 2 August 2019. William J. Durch, *UN Peacekeeping, American Politics, and the Uncivil Wars of the 1990s* (New York: Macmillan, 1997), 278–9, 289.

58 Vines, *Renamo*, 4.

59 Interview by author of a senior US State Department official for African affairs in the 1990s, conducted 27 August 2019.

60 Cabrita, *Mozambique*, 270. Witney W. Schneidman, 'Africa Notes: Conflict Resolution in Mozambique – February 1990', *Africa Notes: Conflict Resolution in Mozambique – February 1990 | Center for Strategic and International Studies*, 28 February 1991, 4. https://www.csis.org/analysis/africa-notes-conflict-resolution-mozambique-february-1990 (accessed 7 October 2018).

61 Interview by the author of a senior representative of the Community of Sant'Egidio, conducted 28 August 2019.

62 Vines, *Renamo*, 129.

63 Interview by author of a senior US State Department official for African affairs in the 1990s, conducted 27 August 2019. Interview by the author of a senior representative of the Community of Sant'Egidio, conducted 28 August 2019.

64 Interview by author of foreign advisor to RENAMO, 1980–94, conducted 2 August 2019.

65 First interview by author with a US diplomat in the Office of Southern African Affairs, circa 1990s, conducted 2 August 2019. Schneidman, 'Africa Notes', 7. Cohen, *Intervening in Africa*, 247. Jett, *Why Peacekeeping Fails*, 67.

66 Interview by the author of a senior representative of the Community of Sant'Egidio, conducted 28 August 2019. Interview by author of US diplomat involved in Mozambique negotiations, conducted 12 August 2019. Chester Crocker, et al., *International Negotiation and Mediation in Violent Conflict: The Changing Context of Peacemaking* (Oxfordshire: Routledge, 2018), 341–2. Lucia Van Den Bergh, 'Why Peace Worked: Mozambicans Look Back', *AWEPA*, 1 August 2013, 129. https://issuu.com/awepainternationale/docs/why_peace_worked_-_mozambicans_look (accessed 10 August 2020).

67   Interview by author of foreign advisor to RENAMO, 1980-1994, conducted 2 August
     2019. Lise Morjé Howard, *UN Peacekeeping in Civil Wars* (Cambridge: Cambridge
     University Press, 2014), 192.
68   Interview by author of foreign advisor to RENAMO, 1980–94, conducted 2 August
     2019.
69   Howard, *UN Peacekeeping in Civil Wars*, 192.
70   Interview of US diplomat in Rome for Mozambique negotiations, conducted by
     author 18 October 2019.
71   First interview by author with a US diplomat in the Office of Southern African
     Affairs, circa 1990s, conducted 2 August 2019.
72   Lowe, *The United Nations Security Council and War*, 192. Schneidman, 'Africa Notes',
     6. Crocker, et al., *International Negotiation and Mediation in Violent Conflict*, 437.
73   Interview by author of US official involved in Mozambique in the 1990s, conducted
     24 September 2019.
74   Interview of US diplomat in Rome for Mozambique negotiations, conducted by
     author 18 October 2019. First interview by author with a US diplomat in the Office
     of Southern African Affairs, circa 1990s, conducted 2 August 2019. Alex Vines,
     Angola and Mozambique: The Aftermath of Conflict (London: Research Institute for
     the Study of Conflict and Terrorism, 1995), 137–9.
75   Interview of US diplomat in Rome for Mozambique negotiations, conducted
     by author 18 October 2019. Interview by author of US diplomat involved in
     Mozambique negotiations, conducted 12 August 2019.
76   Schneidman, 'Africa Notes', 7.
77   Chan and Vanancio, *War and Peace in Mozambique*, 33.
78   Vines, *Angola and Mozambique*, 152. Durch, *UN Peacekeeping, American Politics*,
     290. Howard, *UN Peacekeeping in Civil Wars*, 192.
79   Interview of expert Mozambique-focused journalist with author. 25 November 2019.
     Interview of US diplomat in Rome for Mozambique negotiations, conducted by
     author 18 October 2019. First interview by author with a US diplomat in the Office
     of Southern African Affairs, circa 1990s, conducted 2 August 2019. Interview by
     author of US diplomat involved in Mozambique negotiations, conducted 12 August
     2019.
80   Interview by author of US intelligence and later diplomatic officer with African
     expertise, conducted 20 September 2019. Jett, *Why Peacekeeping Fails*, 131. Vines,
     Angola and Mozambique, 129. Chan and Vanancio, *War and Peace in Mozambique*,
     33. Cohen, *Intervening in Africa*, 188.
81   Interview by author of long-time foreign advisor to RENAMO, conducted 2 August
     2019.
82   Schneidman, 'Africa Notes', 8.
83   Interview by author of US official involved in Mozambique in the 1990s, conducted
     24 September 2019. Interview conducted by author of a senior UN diplomat in
     ONUMOZ, conducted 13 September 2019.
84   Crocker, et al., *International Negotiation and Mediation in Violent Conflict*, 457–8.
85   Interview of US diplomat in Rome for Mozambique negotiations, conducted by
     author 18 October 2019.
86   Interview by author of US official involved in Mozambique in the 1990s, conducted
     24 September 2019. Interview by author of foreign advisor to RENAMO, 1980–
     94, conducted 2 August 2019. Synge, *Mozambique*, 40. Interview by author of
     US intelligence and later diplomatic officer with African expertise, conducted

20 September 2019. First interview by author with a US diplomat in the Office of Southern African Affairs, circa 1990s, conducted 2 August 2019.

87 Interview by author of foreign advisor to RENAMO, 1980–94, conducted 2 August 2019.

88 First interview by author with a US diplomat in the Office of Southern African Affairs, circa 1990s, conducted 2 August 2019. Interview by author of US intelligence and later diplomatic officer with African expertise, conducted 20 September 2019.

89 Jett, Interview of US diplomat in Rome for Mozambique negotiations, conducted by author 18 October 2019. Interview by author of US intelligence and later diplomatic officer with African expertise, conducted 20 September 2019.

90 Interview by author of US diplomat involved in Mozambique negotiations, conducted 12 August 2019.

91 Interview by author of foreign advisor to RENAMO, 1980–94, conducted 2 August 2019. Interview of US diplomat in Rome for Mozambique negotiations, conducted by author 18 October 2019. First interview by author with a US diplomat in the Office of Southern African Affairs, circa 1990s, conducted 2 August 2019.

92 Interview of US diplomat in Rome for Mozambique negotiations, conducted by author 18 October 2019. Interview by author of a senior US State Department official for African affairs in the 1990s, conducted 27 August 2019.

93 Interview by author of US official involved in Mozambique in the 1990s, conducted 24 September 2019.

94 Interview of expert Mozambique-focused journalist with author. 25 November 2019.

95 Interview by the author of a senior representative of the Community of Sant'Egidio, conducted 28 August 2019. Vines, *Angola and Mozambique*, 137–9.

96 Interview by author of foreign advisor to RENAMO, 1980–94, conducted 2 August 2019.

97 Huang, 'Rebel Diplomacy in Civil War'.

98 Interview by author of a senior US State Department official for African affairs in the 1990s, conducted 27 August 2019. Interview by author of foreign advisor to RENAMO, 1980–94, conducted 2 August 2019. First interview by author with a US diplomat in the Office of Southern African Affairs, circa 1990s, conducted 2 August 2019. Schneidman, 'Africa Notes', 8.

99 Interview of US diplomat in Rome for Mozambique negotiations, conducted by author 18 October 2019. Interview by the author of a senior representative of the Community of Sant'Egidio, conducted 28 August 2019. Interview by author of US diplomat involved in Mozambique negotiations, conducted 12 August 2019.

100 Second interview by author with a US diplomat in the Office of Southern African Affairs, circa 1990s, conducted 6 August 2019.

101 'UNTAG', United Nations. https://peacekeeping.un.org/sites/default/files/past/untagS.htm (accessed 18 November 2019).

102 Second interview by author with a US diplomat in the Office of Southern African Affairs, circa 1990s, conducted 6 August 2019.

103 Interview conducted by author with former UK ambassador to Angola circa 1990s, conducted on 28 August 2019.

104 Second interview by author with a US diplomat in the Office of Southern African Affairs, circa 1990s, conducted 6 August 2019.

105 Porto and Parsons, *Sustaining the Peace in Angola*, 23.

106 Durch, *The Evolution of UN Peacekeeping*, 400.

107   Interview by author of US intelligence and later diplomatic officer with African expertise, conducted 20 September 2019.

108   Porto and Parsons, *Sustaining the Peace in Angola*, 23.

109   Bicesse Accords, Attachment IV.

110   Second interview by author with a US diplomat in the Office of Southern African Affairs, circa 1990s, conducted 6 August 2019.

111   Interview by author of US intelligence and later diplomatic officer with African expertise, conducted 20 September 2019.

112   Bicesse Accords.

113   Porto and Parsons, *Sustaining the Peace in Angola*, 23.

114   World Bank, 'Demobilization and Reintegration of Military Personnel in Africa', 83.

115   Bicesse Accords.

116   Durch, *UN Peacekeeping, American Politics*, 24. Jeremy Ginifer, *Beyond the Emergency: Development within UN Peace Missions* (London: Frank Cass, 1997), 58.

117   Alan Doss, *Peacekeeping in Africa: Learning from UN Interventions in Other Peoples Wars* (Boulder, CO: Holmes & Meier, 2020), 209.

118   Second interview by author with a US diplomat in the Office of Southern African Affairs, circa 1990s, conducted 6 August 2019. Trevor Findlay, *The Use of Force in UN Peace Operations* (Stockholm: SIPRI, 2007), 150. Englebert and Tull, 'Postconflict Reconstruction in Africa', 128. Cohen, *Intervening in Africa*, 123–4.

119   Cohen, *Intervening in Africa*, 113.

120   J. Bayo Adekanye, 'Arms and Reconstruction in Post-Conflict Societies', *Journal of Peace Research* 34, no. 3 (1997): 359–66 (p. 363). doi:10.1177/00223433970340 03012.

121   First interview by author with a US diplomat in the Office of Southern African Affairs, circa 1990s, conducted 2 August 2019. Interview by author of foreign advisor to RENAMO, 1980–94, conducted 2 August 2019.

122   Interview conducted by author with senior Mozambican political appointee and diplomat, conducted 28 August 2019. Adekanye, 'Arms and Reconstruction in Post-Conflict Societies', 363. Kristen Eichensehr and W. Michael Reisman, *Stopping Wars and Making Peace Studies in International Intervention* (Leiden: Nijhoff, 2009), 205. Nassrine Azimi and Chang Li Lin, *The Nexus between Peacekeeping and Peace-Building: Debriefing and Lessons: Report of the 1999 Singapore Conference* (Netherlands: Kluwer Law International, 2000), 121.

123   Second interview by author with a US diplomat in the Office of Southern African Affairs, circa 1990s, conducted 6 August 2019. Interview conducted by author with senior Mozambican political appointee and diplomat, conducted 28 August 2019.

124   First interview by author with a US diplomat in the Office of Southern African Affairs, circa 1990s, conducted 2 August 2019. Interview by author of US intelligence and later diplomatic officer with African expertise, conducted 20 September 2019.

125   Interview by author of foreign advisor to RENAMO, 1980–94, conducted 2 August 2019.

126   Eric T. Young, 'The Development of the FADM in Mozambique: Internal and External Dynamics', *African Security Review* 5, no. 1 (1996): 19. https://doi.org/10 .1080/10246029.1996.9627663.

127   Interview conducted by author with senior Mozambican political appointee and diplomat, conducted 28 August 2019.

128   Interview conducted by author with former UK ambassador to Angola circa 1990s, conducted on 28 August 2019. Interview by author of US intelligence and later diplomatic officer with African expertise, conducted 20 September 2019.

129   Durch, *The Evolution of UN Peacekeeping*, 397.

130   Interview of expert Mozambique-focused journalist with author. 25 November 2019. First interview by author with a US diplomat in the Office of Southern African Affairs, circa 1990s, conducted 2 August 2019.

131   Interview by author of foreign advisor to RENAMO, 1980–94, conducted 2 August 2019. Mac Ginty, *No War, No Peace*, 127.

132   Interview conducted by author of a senior UN diplomat in ONUMOZ, conducted 13 September 2019. David H. Levine, 'Organizational Disruption and Change in Mozambique's Peace Process', *International Peacekeeping* 14, no. 3 (2007): 374–5. https://www.tandfonline.com/doi/abs/10.1080/13533310701422935.

133   Abiodun Alao, *Brothers at War: Dissidence and Rebellion in Southern Africa* (London: British Academic Press, 1994), 42.

134   Eric Berman, *Managing Arms in Peace Processes: Mozambique* (New York: United Nations, 1996), 30.

135   Interview by author of foreign advisor to RENAMO, 1980–94, conducted 2 August 2019. Second interview by author with a US diplomat in the Office of Southern African Affairs, circa 1990s, conducted 6 August 2019.

136   Interview by author of US intelligence and later diplomatic officer with African expertise, conducted 20 September 2019. Eichensehr and Reisman, *Stopping Wars*, 205.

137   Jett, *Why Peacekeeping Fails*, 89. Durch, *UN Peacekeeping, American Politics*, 24, 109.

138   Interview conducted by author of a senior UN diplomat in ONUMOZ, conducted 13 September 2019. Interview conducted by author with senior Mozambican political appointee and diplomat, conducted 28 August 2019. Cohen, *Intervening in Africa*, 110–11.

139   Vines, *Angola and Mozambique*, 149–50.

140   Interview conducted by author of a senior UN diplomat in ONUMOZ, conducted 13 September 2019.

141   Vines, *Angola and Mozambique*, 149–50.

142   Interview of expert Mozambique-focused journalist with author. 25 November 2019. Interview conducted by author of a senior UN diplomat in ONUMOZ, conducted 13 September 2019. Eichensehr and Reisman, *Stopping Wars*, 207–8. Durch, *UN Peacekeeping, American Politics*, 24.

143   'ONUMOZ', United Nations. https://peacekeeping.un.org/sites/default/files/past/onumozS.htm (accessed 18 November 2019).

144   Rome Agreement Protocol VI.

145   Interview by author of US intelligence and later diplomatic officer with African expertise, conducted 20 September 2019.

146   Durch, *UN Peacekeeping, American Politics*, 112.

147   Ginifer, *Beyond the Emergency*, 60.

148   Interview conducted by author with former UK ambassador to Angola circa 1990s, conducted on 28 August 2019. Interview by author of US intelligence and later diplomatic officer with African expertise, conducted 20 September 2019.

149   Interview conducted by author with former UK ambassador to Angola circa 1990s, conducted on 28 August 2019. Cohen, *Intervening in Africa*, 123.

150   Berman, *Managing Arms in Peace Processes*, 19.

151 Findlay, *The Use of Force in UN Peace Operations*, 148–9. Synge, *Mozambique*, 7, 21, 30. Lowe, *The United Nations Security Council and War*, 188, 191.

152 Steven R. Ratner, *The New UN Peacekeeping: Building Peace in Lands of Conflict after the Cold War* (New York: Macmillan, 1997), 213. Jett, *Why Peacekeeping Fails*, 73. Margaret Joan Anstee, *Orphan of the Cold War: The Inside Story of the Collapse of the Angolan Peace Process, 1992-93* (London: Macmillan Press, 1996), 34. Vincenzo Bove, Chiara Ruffa and Andrea Ruggeri, *Composing Peace: Mission Composition in UN Peacekeeping* (Oxford: Oxford University Press, 2020), 28.

153 Peter Nadin, et al., *Spoiler Groups and UN Peacekeeping* (Abingdon: Routledge, for the International Institute for Strategic Studies, 2015), 97. Durch, *UN Peacekeeping, American Politics*, 112.

154 Second interview by author with a US diplomat in the Office of Southern African Affairs, circa 1990s, conducted 6 August 2019. Porto and Parsons, *Sustaining the Peace in Angola*, 24–5. Cohen, *Intervening in Africa*, 123–4. Anstee, *Orphan of the Cold War*, 18, 26.

155 Durch, *UN Peacekeeping, American Politics*, 103.

156 'UNAVEM II', United Nations. https://peacekeeping.un.org/mission/past/Unavem2/UnavemIIF.html (accessed 18 November 2019).

157 Ginifer, *Beyond the Emergency*, 60. Durch, *The Evolution of UN Peacekeeping*, 397.

158 Nadin, et al., *Spoiler Groups and UN Peacekeeping*, 97. World Bank, 'Demobilization and Reintegration of Military Personnel in Africa', 27. Durch, *UN Peacekeeping, American Politics*, 397. Anstee, *Orphan of the Cold War*, 18.

159 Second interview by author with a US diplomat in the Office of Southern African Affairs, circa 1990s, conducted 6 August 2019. Durch, *UN Peacekeeping, American Politics*, 112, 397.

160 Kees Kingma, *Demobilization in Subsaharan Africa: The Development and Security Impacts* (New York: Palgrave Macmillan, 2014), 161. Vines, *Renamo*, 8. World Bank, 'Demobilization and Reintegration of Military Personnel in Africa', 26. Anstee, *Orphan of the Cold War*, 19.

161 Cohen, *Intervening in Africa*, 114. Anstee, *Orphan of the Cold War*, 19, 55.

162 Second interview by author with a US diplomat in the Office of Southern African Affairs, circa 1990s, conducted 6 August 2019. Vines, *Renamo*, 8. Virginia Page Fortna, 'A Lost Chance for Peace: The Bicesse Accords in Angola', *Georgetown Journal of International Affairs* 4, no. 1 (Spring 2003): 76. https://www.jstor.org/stable/43134444.

163 Anstee, *Orphan of the Cold War*, 48. World Bank, 'Demobilization and Reintegration of Military Personnel in Africa', 26. Ginifer, *Beyond the Emergency*, 60. Durch, *UN Peacekeeping, American Politics*, 400.

164 First interview by author with a US diplomat in the Office of Southern African Affairs, circa 1990s, conducted 2 August 2019. Interview by author of foreign advisor to RENAMO, 1980–94, conducted 2 August 2019.

165 Huang, 'Rebel Diplomacy in Civil War'.

166 Wright, *The Destruction of a Nation*, 574.

167 Interview by author of US intelligence and later diplomatic officer with African expertise, conducted 20 September 2019. Cohen, *Intervening in Africa*, 113. Wright, 'The Clinton Administrations Policy toward Angola', 166–7.

168 Interview by author with senior US diplomat working on African affairs, conducted 23 July 2019.

169 Huang, 'Rebel Diplomacy in Civil War'.

170 Durch, *UN Peacekeeping, American Politics*, 111.

171 Porto and Parsons, *Sustaining the Peace in Angola*, 26. Alao, *Brothers at War*, 46.

172 Interview conducted by author with former UK ambassador to Angola circa 1990s, conducted on 28 August 2019. Anstee, *Orphan of the Cold War*.

173 Fortna, 'A Lost Chance for Peace', 73, 76.

174 World Bank, 'Demobilization and Reintegration of Military Personnel in Africa', 26.

175 Interview by author with senior US diplomat working on African affairs, conducted 23 July 2019.

176 Alao, *Brothers at War*, 46. Ginifer, *Beyond the Emergency*, 61. Anstee, *Orphan of the Cold War*, 63.

177 Findlay, *The Use of Force in UN Peace Operations*, 150. Ratner, *The New UN Peacekeeping*, 211–12.

178 Interview by author of foreign advisor to RENAMO, 1980-1994, conducted 2 August 2019. Vines, *Angola and Mozambique*, 149–50. Durch, *UN Peacekeeping, American Politics*, 289, 293.

179 Adekanye, 'Arms and Reconstruction in Post-Conflict Societies', 363. Synge, *Mozambique*, 5, 21. Howard, *UN Peacekeeping in Civil Wars*, 194–5.

180 Interview by author of US intelligence and later diplomatic officer with African expertise, conducted 20 September 2019.

181 'ONUMOZ', United Nations. https://peacekeeping.un.org/sites/default/files/past/onumozS.htm.

182 Chan and Vanancio, *War and Peace in Mozambique*, 70, 85. Vines, *Angola and Mozambique*, 149–50.

183 Vines, *Angola and Mozambique*, 149–50.

184 Interview of expert Mozambique-focused journalist with author. 25 November 2019. Interview conducted by author of a senior UN diplomat in ONUMOZ, conducted 13 September 2019.

185 Interview by author of foreign advisor to RENAMO, 1980–94, conducted 2 August 2019. Synge, *Mozambique*, 103.

186 Vines, *Angola and Mozambique*, 153–4. Durch, *UN Peacekeeping, American Politics*, 293.

187 Interview conducted by author of a senior UN diplomat in ONUMOZ, conducted September 13, 2019.

188 Ibid., Lowe, *The United Nations Security Council and War*, 192.

189 Levine, 'Organizational Disruption', 374. Colin Darch, *The Mozambican Conflict and the Peace Process in Historical Perspective: A Success Story Gone Wrong?* (Maputo, Mozambique: Friedrich-Ebert-Stiftung Mozambique, 2018), 17. Alex Vines, 'Prospects for a Sustainable Elite Bargain in Mozambique: Third Time Lucky?', *Chatham House*, 5 August 2019. https://reader.chathamhouse.org/prospects -sustainable-elite-bargain-mozambique-third-time-lucky#key-features-of-past -elite-bargains (accessed 7 October 2018). Severine Rugumamu and Osman Gbla, 'Studies in Reconstruction and Capacity-Building in Post-Conflict Countries in Africa', *The African Capacity Building Foundation*, ACBF Executive Board, May 2004, 35. www.afdb.org/fileadmin/uploads/afdb/Documents/Generic-Documents /PCBSS_Working_Documents/MOZAMBIQUE – Main Report (Revised).pdf (accessed 7 October 2018). Lisa Schirch and Deborah Mancini-Griffoli, *Local Ownership in Security: Case Studies of Peacebuilding Approaches* (The Hague: Alliance for Peacebuilding, 2015). Rachel Waterhouse, *Mozambique: Rising from the Ashes* (Oxford: Oxfam UK and Ireland, 1996), 19.

190 Chris Alden, 'Making Old Soldiers Fade Away: Lessons from the Reintegration of Demobilized Soldiers in Mozambique', *Security Dialogue* 33, no. 3 (2002): 341–56 (p. 343). https://doi.org/10.1177/0967010602033003008.

191 Vines, 'Prospects for a Sustainable Elite Bargain in Mozambique'. Rugumamu and Osman Gbla, 'Studies in Reconstruction', 35. James Dobbins, *The UN's Role in Nation-building: From the Congo to Iraq* (Santa Monica (California): RAND Corporation, 2005), Chapter 6.

192 Darch, *The Mozambican Conflict and the Peace Process in Historical Perspective*, 17. Vines, 'Prospects for a Sustainable Elite Bargain in Mozambique'. Durch, *UN Peacekeeping, American Politics*, 294.

193 Howard, *UN Peacekeeping in Civil Wars*, 193–4. Waterhouse, *Mozambique*, 16.

194 Interview by author of US intelligence and later diplomatic officer with African expertise, conducted 20 September 2019. Interview of expert Mozambique-focused journalist with author. 25 November 2019.

195 Waterhouse, *Mozambique*, 17.

196 Interview by author of US official involved in Mozambique in the 1990s, conducted 24 September 2019. Jessica Schafer, *Soldiers at Peace: The Post-War Politics of Demobilized Soldiers in Mozambique* (New York: Palgrave Macmillan, 2007), 130–1. Mats R. Berdal, *Disarmament and Demobilisation after Civil Wars: Arms, Soldiers and the Termination of Armed Conflicts* (Oxford: Oxford University Press, 1996), 82.

197 Levine, 'Organizational Disruption', 368, 374. Alden, 'Making Old Soldiers Fade Away', 349–50. Rugumamu and Osman Gbla, 'Studies in Reconstruction', 36.

198 Interview by author of US official involved in Mozambique in the 1990s, conducted 24 September 2019. Interview conducted by author of a senior UN diplomat in ONUMOZ, conducted 13 September 2019. Vines, *Angola and Mozambique*, 149–50.

199 Bergh, 'Why Peace Worked', 130–1.

200 Jett, *Why Peacekeeping Fails*, 104.

201 Kyle C. Beardsley, David M. Quinn, Bidisha Biswas, and Jonathan Wilkenfeld, 'Mediation Style and Crisis Outcomes', *Journal of Conflict Resolution* 50, no. 1 (2006): 3. https://doi.org/10.1177/0022002705282862.

202 First interview by author with a US diplomat in the Office of Southern African Affairs, circa 1990s, conducted 2 August 2019.

203 Confirmed by two interviews by author with a US diplomat in the Office of Southern African Affairs, circa 1990s, conducted 2 August 2019 and 6 August 2019.

204 One US diplomat interviewed for this book downplayed the importance of language, but he spoke Italian. Another US diplomat interviewed, who spoke neither Italian nor Portuguese, saw a lack of Portuguese as being a barrier to further US participation in Bicesse.

205 Jett, *Why Peacekeeping Fails*, 67.

206 Cohen, *Intervening in Africa*, 247.

207 Interview by author of US official involved in Mozambique in the 1990s, conducted 24 September 2019.

208 Jannie Lilja, 'Ripening Within? Strategies Used by Rebel Negotiators to End Ethnic War', *Negotiation Journal* 27, no. 3 (18 July 2011): 311–42.

209 First interview by author with a US diplomat in the Office of Southern African Affairs, circa 1990s, conducted 2 August 2019. Interview by author of a senior US State Department official for African affairs in the 1990s, conducted 27 August 2019. Synge, *Mozambique*, 40.

210 Pearce, 'Global Ideologies, Local Politics', 25.

211 Interview of expert Mozambique-focused journalist with author. 25 November 2019.
212 Interview by author of US intelligence and later diplomatic officer with African expertise, conducted 20 September 2019. Interview by author with senior US diplomat working on African affairs, conducted 23 July 2019.
213 Interview of US diplomat in Rome for Mozambique negotiations, conducted by author 18 October 2019. Interview by author of foreign advisor to RENAMO, 1980–94, conducted 2 August 2019. Second interview by author with a US diplomat in the Office of Southern African Affairs, circa 1990s, conducted 6 August 2019.
214 Second interview by author with a US diplomat in the Office of Southern African Affairs, circa 1990s, conducted 6 August 2019. Synge, *Mozambique*, 40.
215 Second interview by author with a US diplomat in the Office of Southern African Affairs, circa 1990s, conducted 6 August 2019. Lilja, 'Ripening Within? Strategies Used by Rebel Negotiators to End Ethnic War'.
216 Second interview by author with a US diplomat in the Office of Southern African Affairs, circa 1990s, conducted 6 August 2019.
217 Interview by author of US diplomat involved in Mozambique negotiations, conducted 12 August 2019.
218 Lilja, 'Ripening Within? Strategies Used by Rebel Negotiators to End Ethnic War'.
219 Wright, *The Destruction of a Nation*, 569.
220 Schneidman, 'Africa Notes', 4. Chan and Vanancio, *War and Peace in Mozambique*, 26.
221 Second interview by author with a US diplomat in the Office of Southern African Affairs, circa 1990s, conducted 6 August 2019.
222 Synge, *Mozambique*, 58.
223 Azimi and Lin, *The Nexus between Peacekeeping and Peace-Building*, 108, 121.
224 Kingma, *Demobilization in Subsaharan Africa*, 111.
225 Bergh, 'Why Peace Worked', 130.
226 Cohen, *Intervening in Africa*, 123. Fortna, 'A Lost Chance for Peace', 73, 77.
227 Second interview by author with a US diplomat in the Office of Southern African Affairs, circa 1990s, conducted 6 August 2019.
228 Ginifer, *Beyond the Emergency*, 60. World Bank, 'Demobilization and Reintegration of Military Personnel in Africa', 96. Fortna, 'A Lost Chance for Peace', 73, 75. Porto and Parsons, *Sustaining the Peace in Angola*, 24–5. Cohen, *Intervening in Africa*, 123.
229 Anstee, *Orphan of the Cold War*, 64.
230 Findlay, *The Use of Force in UN Peace Operations*, 148–50.
231 Interview by author of foreign advisor to RENAMO, 1980–94, conducted 2 August 2019. Interview conducted by author with former UK ambassador to Angola circa 1990s, conducted on 28 August 2019. Interview conducted by author of a senior UN diplomat in ONUMOZ, conducted 13 September 2019. Spears, 'Angola's Elusive Peace', 570. Kseniya Oksamytna, Vincenzo Bove, and Magnus Lundgren, 'Leadership Selection in United Nations Peacekeeping', *International Studies Quarterly*, 4 May 2020. https://doi.org/10.1093/isq/sqaa023.
232 Lowe, *The United Nations Security Council and War*, 192.
233 Interview of expert Mozambique-focused journalist with author 25 November 2019.
234 First interview by author with a US diplomat in the Office of Southern African Affairs, circa 1990s, conducted 2 August 2019. Interview by author of foreign advisor to RENAMO, 1980–94, conducted 2 August 2019. Durch, *UN Peacekeeping, American Politics*, 301. Lowe, *The United Nations Security Council and War*, 192. Waterhouse, *Mozambique*, 16.

235 Interview of expert Mozambique-focused journalist with author. 25 November 2019. Jett, *Why Peacekeeping Fails*, 77.

236 Durch, *UN Peacekeeping, American Politics*, 301. Lowe, *The United Nations Security Council and War*, 192. Bergh, 'Why Peace Worked', 130.

237 Interview by author of US official involved in Mozambique in the 1990s, conducted 24 September 2019. Interview conducted by author of a senior UN diplomat in ONUMOZ, conducted 13 September 2019.

238 Interview of expert Mozambique-focused journalist with author. 25 November 2019.

239 Findlay, *The Use of Force in UN Peace Operations*, 320.

Chapter 4

1 It became even more apparent that allowing each side to choose its own assembly areas without concerns for accessibility, which resulted in a focus on strategic locations, further enabled this swift return to violence especially as there were so few UNAVEM II peacekeepers able to monitor each location. See Chapter 3 for more on location of assembly areas.

2 Alao, *Brothers at War*, 42.

3 Oliveira, 'Illiberal Peacebuilding in Angola', 290. Paul Julian Hare, *Angolas Last Best Chance for Peace: An Insider's Account of the Peace Process* (Washington, DC: United States Institute of peace Press, 1998), 18. Inge Tvedten, *Angola: Struggle for Peace and Reconstruction* (S.l.: Routledge, 2019), 59–61.

4 Doss, *Peacekeeping in Africa*, 206.

5 Christopher Cramer, *Civil War Is Not a Stupid Thing: Accounting for Violence in Developing Countries* (London: Hurst & Company, 2006), 145. James Hamill, 'Angola's Road from under the Rubble', *The World Today* 50, no. 1 (January 1994): 6.

6 Oliveira, 'Illiberal Peacebuilding in Angola', 290. Cramer, *Civil War Is Not a Stupid Thing*, 147.

7 Hare, *Angolas Last Best Chance for Peace*, xv. Cramer, *Civil War Is Not a Stupid Thing*, 144. 'From Military Peace to Social Justice? The Angolan Peace Process: Policy Brief', 2. Philippe Le Billon, *Fuelling War – Natural Resources and Armed Conflicts* (Oxfordshire: Taylor & Francis Ltd, 2017). Gail M. Gerhart and Tony Hodges, 'Angola from Afro-Stalinism to Petro-Diamond Capitalism', *Foreign Affairs* 80, no. 6 (2001): 193. https://doi.org/10.2307/20050391. Assis Malaquias, 'Diamonds Are a Guerrillas Best Friend: The Impact of Illicit Wealth on Insurgency Strategy', *Third World Quarterly* 22, no. 3 (2001): 311–25 (p. 322). https://doi.org/10.1080 /01436590120061624.

8 Hare, *Angolas Last Best Chance for Peace*, xvii. Cramer, *Civil War Is Not a Stupid Thing*, 144.

9 Cramer, *Civil War Is Not a Stupid Thing*, 146.

10 Azimi and Lin, *The Nexus between Peacekeeping and Peace-Building*, 90.

11 Boutros Boutros-Ghali, Aldo Ajello and Alouine Blondin Beye, *Notes of the Secretary-General's Meeting with his Special Representative for Mozambique Mr. Aldo Ajello and his Special Representative for Angola Mr. Blondin Beye [in Maputo]* (17 October 1993), 4.

12 Alao, *Brothers at War*, 42.

13 'UNITA', *Letter from UNITA to Boutros Boutros-Ghali*, 15 January 1993.

14 'UNSC', *S/RES/864*, 15 September 1993.

15 Vines, *Renamo*, 22.

16 Boutros-Ghali, Ajello and Beye, *Notes of the Secretary-General's Meeting with his Special Representative for Mozambique Mr. Aldo Ajello*, 4.

17 Jett, *Why Peacekeeping Fails*, 55. Interview by author of foreign advisor to RENAMO, 1980-1994, conducted 2 August 2019. Séverine Autesserre, *Peaceland: Conflict Resolution and the Everyday Politics Of International Intervention* (Cambridge: Cambridge University Press, 2018).

18 'UNAVEM II', *Report of the Assessment Mission to Angola*, 28 September 1994.

19 Ibid.

20 'UNSC', *S/RES/864*.

21 Wright, 'The Clinton Administration's Policy toward Angola', 563–76.

22 Alao, *Brothers at War*, 42. 'UNAVEM II', *Report of the Assessment Mission to Angola*. Boutros Boutros-Ghali and Alioune Blondin-Beye, *Notes of the Secretary-General's Meeting with the Special Representative of the Secretary-General for Angola, Mr. Alioune Blondin Beye*, 8 May 1994.

23 Hare, *Angolas Last Best Chance for Peace*, 16–17. Spears, 'Angola's Elusive Peace', 562–81. Justin Pearce, *Political Identity and Conflict in Central Angola, 1975–2002* (Cambridge: Cambridge University Press, 2015). A. Vines, *Angola Unravels: The Rise and Fall of the Lusaka Peace Process* (United States of America: Human Rights Watch, 1999), 1.

24 Alao, *Brothers at War*, 44.

25 Hare, *Angolas Last Best Chance for Peace*, 18.

26 Vines, *Angola and Mozambique*, 8.

27 Vines, *Renamo*, 6–7, 14.

28 Hare, *Angolas Last Best Chance for Peace*, 21.

29 Oliveira, 'Illiberal Peacebuilding in Angola', 290.

30 Vines, *Renamo*, 8.

31 Jett, *Why Peacekeeping Fails*, 64.

32 Hare, *Angolas Last Best Chance for Peace*, 18, 56.

33 'UNAVEM II', *Report of the Assessment Mission to Angola*.

34 Véronique Dudouet, 'Mediating Peace with Proscribed Armed Groups', *United States Institute of Peace*, 4 September 2013, 1. https://www.usip.org/publications/2010/06/mediating-peace-proscribed-armed-groups (accessed 25 February 2020). Jett, *Why Peacekeeping Fails*, 47.

35 Dudouet, 'Mediating Peace with Proscribed Armed Groups', 1.

36 Hare, *Angolas Last Best Chance for Peace*, xvii.

37 Nelson Mandela and Alioune Blondin-Beye, *Meeting between President Mandela and the UN Secretary-General's Special Representative to Angola, Mr Alioune Blondin Beye*, 23 June 1994. Oliveira, 'Illiberal Peacebuilding in Angola', 291.

38 Hare, *Angolas Last Best Chance for Peace*, 23.

39 Porto and Parsons, *Sustaining the Peace in Angola*, 23.

40 Ibid. Hare, *Angolas Last Best Chance for Peace*, 78. Boutros Boutros-Ghali, *Talking Points for HE Mr. Venancio de Moura FM of Angola*, 28 September 1994.

41 Howard, *UN Peacekeeping in Civil Wars*, 196. L. M. Howard, *The Failures: Somalia, Rwanda, Angola, and Bosnia. UN Peacekeeping in Civil Wars* (Cambridge: Cambridge University Press, 2007), 39. Dobbins, *The UNs Role in Nation-Building*, executive summary.

42 Porto and Parsons, *Sustaining the Peace in Angola*, 23.

43 Hare, *Angolas Last Best Chance for Peace*, 23. Autesserre, *Peaceland*.

44 Hare, *Angolas Last Best Chance for Peace*, 24.

45 Ibid.

46 Cramer, *Civil War Is Not a Stupid Thing*, 146. Oliveira, 'Illiberal Peacebuilding in Angola', 291.

47 Hare, *Angolas Last Best Chance for Peace*, 24.

48 'UNAVEM II', *Report of the Assessment Mission to Angola.*

49 Interview by author of Senior US diplomat for Angolan peace process, circa 1990s, conducted 7 October 2019.

50 Hare, *Angolas Last Best Chance for Peace*, 23.

51 'UNAVEM II', *Report of the Assessment Mission to Angola.* Interview by author of Senior US diplomat for Angolan peace process, circa 1990s, conducted 7 October 2019. 'From Military Peace to Social Justice? The Angolan Peace Process: Policy Brief', 2.

52 'UNAVEM II', *Report of the Assessment Mission to Angola.* Vines, *Renamo*, 7.

53 Hare, *Angolas Last Best Chance for Peace*, 60.

54 *Lusaka Protocol*, MPLA, UNITA, UN, 15 November 1994, 6–7, 47. Norrie Macqueen, 'Peacekeeping by Attrition: The United Nations in Angola', *The Journal of Modern African Studies* 36, no. 3 (1998): 399–422 (p. 406). https://doi.org/10.1017/s0022278x98002845. Interview by author of Senior US diplomat for Angolan peace process, circa 1990s, conducted 7 October 2019.

55 Cohen, *Intervening in Africa*, 124.

56 Interview by author of Senior US diplomat for Angolan peace process, circa 1990s, conducted October 7, 2019.

57 Ibid., 123.

58 'UNSC', *S/RES/864*, 15 September 1993.

59 *Lusaka Protocol*, MPLA, UNITA, UN, 42–3.

60 Boutros-Ghali and Blondin-Beye, *Notes of the Secretary-General's Meeting with the Special Representative of the Secretary-General for Angola, Mr. Alioune Blondin Beye.*

61 Boutros-Ghali, Ajello and Beye, *Notes of the Secretary-General's Meeting with his Special Representative for Mozambique Mr. Aldo Ajello and his Special Representative for Angola Mr. Blondin Beye [in Maputo]*, 4.

62 Boutros-Ghali and Blondin-Beye, *Notes of the Secretary-General's Meeting with the Special Representative of the Secretary-General for Angola, Mr. Alioune Blondin Beye.*

63 Margaret Anstee, 'The Fight Goes On', *The World Today* 54, no. 10 (October 1998): 256. Spears, 'Angola's Elusive Peace', 566. Kelly M. Greenhill and Solomon Major, 'The Perils of Profiling: Civil War Spoilers and the Collapse of Intrastate Peace Accords', *International Security* 31, no. 3 (2007): 7–40 (p. 21). https://doi.org/10.1162/isec.2007.31.3.7.

64 *Lusaka Protocol*, MPLA, UNITA, UN, 29.

65 Ibid., Hare, *Angolas Last Best Chance for Peace*, 108.

66 Interview by author of Senior US diplomat for Angolan peace process, circa 1990s, conducted 7 October 2019. Interview conducted by author with former UK ambassador to Angola circa 1990s, conducted on 28 August 2019.

67 Boutros-Ghali, *Talking Points for HE Mr. Venancio de Moura FM of Angola.* Porto and Parsons, *Sustaining the Peace in Angola*, 27–8.

68 Hare, *Angolas Last Best Chance for Peace*, 102. Porto and Parsons, *Sustaining the Peace in Angola*, 27–8.

69 Boutros Boutros-Ghali, *Talking Points for HE Mr. Venancio de Moura FM of Angola*, 6 February 1995.

70 'UNAVEM II', *Report of the Assessment Mission to Angola.*

71   Hare, *Angolas Last Best Chance for Peace*, 102.

72   *Lusaka Protocol*, MPLA, UNITA, UN, 10.

73   Cohen, *Intervening in Africa*, 121. *Lusaka Protocol*, MPLA, UNITA, UN, 13–14.

74   *Bicesse Accords,* MPLA, UNITA, UN, 15 May 1991, Annex II.

75   *Lusaka Protocol*, MPLA, UNITA, UN, 63.

76   Donald Rothchild, 'On Implementing Africa's Peace Accords: From Defection to Cooperation', *Africa Today* 42, no. 1 (1995). https://www.jstor.org/stable/4187028. Crocker and Hampson, 'Making Peace Settlements Work'. Porto and Parsons, *Sustaining the Peace in Angola*, 27–8.

77   Interview by author of Senior US diplomat for Angolan peace process, circa 1990s, conducted 7 October 2019. Interview by author with senior US diplomat working on African affairs, conducted 23 July 2019.

78   Boutros-Ghali, *Talking Points for HE Mr. Venancio de Moura FM of Angola*. Porto and Parsons, *Sustaining the Peace in Angola*, 27–8.

79   *Lusaka Protocol*, MPLA, UNITA, UN, 17. Interview by author of Senior US diplomat for Angolan peace process, circa 1990s, conducted 7 October 2019.

80   Eduardo dos Santos, *Unofficial Translation of letter to UNSG*, 5 December 1994.

81   Boutros-Ghali, *Talking Points for HE Mr. Venancio de Moura FM of Angola*.

82   Hare, *Angolas Last Best Chance for Peace*, 78.

83   Howard, *UN Peacekeeping in Civil Wars*, 196. Howard, *The Failures*, 39. Dobbins, *The UNs Role in Nation-Building*, executive summary.

84   *Lusaka Protocol*, MPLA, UNITA, UN, 12–14.

85   Boutros-Ghali, *Talking Points for HE Mr. Venancio de Moura FM of Angola*. *Lusaka Protocol*, MPLA, UNITA, UN, 47. Taisier M. Ali, Robert O. Matthews, and Ian Spears, 'Failures in Peacebuilding: Sudan (1972-1983) and Angola (1991-1998)', in *Durable Peace: Challenges for Peacebuilding in Africa* (Toronto: University of Toronto Press, 1998), 297. Macqueen, 'Peacekeeping by Attrition', 407.

86   Hare, *Angolas Last Best Chance for Peace*, 78.

87   Boutros and Blondin-Beye, *Notes of the Secretary-General's Meeting with the Special Representative of the Secretary-General for Angola, Mr. Alioune Blondin Beye. Lusaka Protocol*, MPLA, UNITA, UN, 26.

88   *Lusaka Protocol*, MPLA, UNITA, UN, 36–40.

89   Cohen, *Intervening in Africa*, 124.

90   Hare, *Angolas Last Best Chance for Peace*, 124.

91   Wright, 'The Clinton Administration's Policy toward Angola'.

92   Unknown, *Briefing Notes for the Secretary-General's Forthcoming Visit to Copenhagen [on] Angola*, 17 September 1992–26 September 1996. Hare, *Angolas Last Best Chance for Peace*, 62–3.

93   Unknown, *Briefing Notes for the Secretary-General's Forthcoming Visit to Copenhagen [on] Angola*. Kofi Annan, *Talking Points for HE Mr. Venancio de Moura FM of Angola*, 26 September 1996.

94   Mandela and Blondin-Beye, *Meeting between President Mandela and the UN Secretary-General's Special Representative to Angola, Mr Alioune Blondin Beye*.

95   Friedrich Plank, 'When Peace Leads to Divorce: The Splintering of Rebel Groups in Powersharing Agreements', *Civil Wars* 19, no. 2 (March 2017): 176–97. https://doi .org/10.1080/13698249.2017.1372004. Stephen John Stedman, 'Spoiler Problems in Peace Processes', *International Security* 22, no. 2 (1997): 5–53. https://doi.org/10 .1162/isec.22.2.5.

96   Porto and Parsons, *Sustaining the Peace in Angola*, 27–8.

97   *Lusaka Protocol*, MPLA, UNITA, UN, 14.
98   Hare, *Angolas Last Best Chance for Peace*, 93.
99   See Chapter 3.
100 Hare, *Angolas Last Best Chance for Peace*, 94, 99.
101 Dobbins, *The UNs Role in Nation-Building*, executive summary.
102 Hare, *Angolas Last Best Chance for Peace*, 100.
103 Boutros Boutros-Ghali, *Talking Points for SG's Phone Conversation with Savimbi*, 20 February 1996.
104 Hare, *Angolas Last Best Chance for Peace*, 101–2.
105 Ibid., 99.
106 Dobbins, *The UNs Role in Nation-Building*, executive summary and Chapter 6.
107 Porto and Parsons, *Sustaining the Peace in Angola*, 31.
108 'UNSC', *S/RES/976*, 8 February 1995.
109 'From Military Peace to Social Justice? The Angolan Peace Process: Policy Brief', 2.
110 Porto and Parsons, *Sustaining the Peace in Angola*, 31.
111 Though there were contentions that UNITA leaders in fact coerced combatants into deciding between demobilization and military integration and this was a one-time choice that could not be changed.
112 Porto and Parsons, *Sustaining the Peace in Angola*, 33.
113 Ibid., 27–8, 32.
114 Boutros-Ghali, *Talking Points for SG's Phone Conversation with Savimbi*.
115 Unknown, *Briefing Notes for the Secretary-General's Forthcoming Visit to Copenhagen [on] Angola*. Annan, *Talking Points for HE Mr. Venancio de Moura FM of Angola*. Porto and Parsons, *Sustaining the Peace in Angola*, 30.
116 Hare, *Angolas Last Best Chance for Peace*, 103. Annan, *Talking Points for HE Mr. Venancio de Moura FM of Angola*.
117 Unknown, *Briefing Notes for the Secretary-General's Forthcoming Visit to Copenhagen [on] Angola*.
118 Annan, *Talking Points for HE Mr. Venancio de Moura FM of Angola*.
119 Porto and Parsons, *Sustaining the Peace in Angola*, 31.
120 Annan, *Talking Points for HE Mr. Venancio de Moura FM of Angola*. Porto and Parsons, *Sustaining the Peace in Angola*, 30.
121 Annan, *Talking Points for HE Mr. Venancio de Moura FM of Angola*.
122 Jett, *Why Peacekeeping Fails*, 107.
123 Hare, *Angolas Last Best Chance for Peace*, 91, 103, 112.
124 Unknown, *Briefing Notes for the Secretary-General's Forthcoming Visit to Copenhagen [on] Angola*.
125 Hare, *Angolas Last Best Chance for Peace*, 69, 91–2. Interview conducted by author with former UK ambassador to Angola circa 1990s, conducted on 28 August 2019.
126 Hare, *Angolas Last Best Chance for Peace*, 70.
127 'UNSC', *S/RES/976*.
128 'Unavem II', United Nations. https://peacekeeping.un.org/sites/default/files/past/Unavem2/UnavemIIF.html (accessed 18 March 2020).
129 'UNSC', *S/RES/976*.
130 Azimi and Lin, *The Nexus between Peacekeeping and Peace-Building*, 90.
131 Boutros-Ghali, *Talking Points for SG's Phone Conversation with Savimbi*.
132 Hare, *Angolas Last Best Chance for Peace*, 70–1.
133 Alex J. Bellamy and Charles T. Hunt, 'Twenty-First Century UN Peace Operations: Protection, Force and the Changing Security Environment', *International Affairs* 91,

no. 6 (2015): 1277–98. https://doi.org/10.1111/1468-2346.12456. Azimi and Lin, *The Nexus between Peacekeeping and Peace-Building*, 90. 'From Military Peace to Social Justice? The Angolan Peace Process: Policy Brief', 2.

134 Interview by author of US official involved in Mozambique in the 1990s, conducted 24 September 2019.

135 Jett, *Why Peacekeeping Fails*, 55, 100.

136 Alden, 'Making Old Soldiers Fade Away', 344. Schafer, *Soldiers at Peace*, 130–1.

137 Interview by author of US official involved in Mozambique in the 1990s, conducted 24 September 2019. Vines, *Angola and Mozambique*, 158.

138 Vines, *Angola and Mozambique*, 1. Rugumamu and Gbla, 'Studies in Reconstruction', 45. Boutros-Ghali, Ajello, and Beye, *Notes of the Secretary-General's Meeting with his Special Representative for Mozambique Mr. Aldo Ajello and his Special Representative for Angola Mr. Blondin Beye [in Maputo]*, 4.

139 Vines, *Angola and Mozambique*.

140 'CCFADM', *Decisions Taken at the Eleventh Session of the CCFADM/011*, 11 March 1994, 3.

141 'ONUMOZ', *Demobilisation: Focus of the Rome Conference*, 1 December 1993–9 February 1994. 'CCFADM', *Notes to the File: CSC Discussion of FADM Salary Structure*, 24 March 1994, 5.

142 Michael Brzoska, 'Introduction: Criteria for Evaluating Post-Conflict Reconstruction and Security Sector Reform in Peace Support Operations', *International Peacekeeping* 13, no. 1 (2006): 1–13 (9–10). https://doi.org/10.1080/13533310500424603. Alden, 'Making Old Soldiers Fade Away', 351. 'ONUMOZ', *Demobilisation: Focus of the Rome Conference*.

143 Brzoska, 'Introduction', 4.

144 Adriano Malache, Paulino Macaringue, and Joao-Paulo Borges Coelho, 'Profound Transformations and Regional Conflagrations: The History of Mozambique's Armed Forces from 1975–2005', in *Evolutions and Revolutions: A Contemporary History of Militaries in Southern Africa* (Cape Town: Institute for Security Studies, 2005), 181.

145 Interview by author of foreign advisor to RENAMO, 1980–94, conducted 2 August 2019.

146 Young, 'The Development of the FADM in Mozambique', 18–24. Malache et al., 'Profound Transformations and Regional Conflagrations', 183.

147 First interview by author with a US diplomat in the Office of Southern African Affairs, circa 1990s, conducted 2 August 2019. Synge, *Mozambique*, 40.

148 Young, 'The Development of the FADM in Mozambique', 15. Malache et al., 'Profound Transformations and Regional Conflagrations', 182.

149 Licklider, *New Armies from Old*, 259. Malache et al., 'Profound Transformations and Regional Conflagrations', 180.

150 'ONUMOZ', *Demobilisation: Focus of the Rome Conference*.

151 Rachel Kleinfeld and Nathaniel Allen, 'Why Security Sector Governance Matters in Fragile States', *Carnegie Endowment for International Peace*. https://carnegieendowment.org/2019/06/11/why-security-sector-governance-matters-in-fragile-states/k2xg (accessed 18 March 2020).

152 Vines, *Angola and Mozambique*.

153 Brzoska, 'Introduction', 9–10.

154 Young, 'The Development of the FADM in Mozambique', 19.

155 Malache et al., 'Profound Transformations and Regional Conflagrations', 182. Jett, *Why Peacekeeping Fails*, 105. Vines, *Angola and Mozambique*, 155.

156 Malache et al., 'Profound Transformations and Regional Conflagrations', 180, 183.
157 Jett, *Why Peacekeeping Fails*, 105. Young, 'The Development of the FADM in Mozambique', 19.
158 Malache et al., 'Profound Transformations and Regional Conflagrations', 182. Vines, *Angola and Mozambique*, 155.
159 Malache et al., 'Profound Transformations and Regional Conflagrations', 182. Jett, *Why Peacekeeping Fails*, 105.
160 Darch, *The Mozambican Conflict and the Peace Process in Historical Perspective*, 18.
161 Young, 'The Development of the FADM in Mozambique', 19.
162 Vines, *Angola and Mozambique*, 152–3.
163 Berdal, *Disarmament and Demobilisation after Civil Wars*, 75.
164 Darch, *The Mozambican Conflict and the Peace Process in Historical Perspective*, 18. Berdal, *Disarmament and Demobilisation after Civil Wars*, 87.
165 'ONUMOZ', *Status of Forces Agreement: The Formation of the New Mozambican Defence Force*, 19 April 1993.
166 'ONUMOZ', *Minutes of the Cease-Fire Commission*, 28 January 1994.
167 'ONUMOZ', *Tri-paritite Meeting to Establish an Equivalent Between the Ranks Used by RENAMO and by the Government*, 12 January 1994, 1–2. Interview by author of US official involved in Mozambique in the 1990s, conducted 24 September 2019. Interview by author of foreign advisor to RENAMO, 1980-1994, conducted 2 August 2019. Interview by author of US intelligence and later diplomatic officer with African expertise, conducted 20 September 2019. Charles, interview with author 20 September 2019.
168 Alden, 'Making Old Soldiers Fade Away', 350.
169 Ibid.
170 Ibid. Darch, *The Mozambican Conflict and the Peace Process in Historical Perspective*, 18. Young, 'The Development of the FADM in Mozambique', 20.
171 Darch, *The Mozambican Conflict and the Peace Process in Historical Perspective*, 18. 'ONUMOZ', *Minutes of the 26th Plenary Session of the CSC: Approval of the FADM Salary Structure*, 1994.
172 Schafer, *Soldiers at Peace*. Young, 'The Development of the FADM in Mozambique', 20.
173 'ONUMOZ', *CCFADM Minutes*, 1994. Young, 'The Development of the FADM in Mozambique', 20.
174 'CCFADM', *Decisions Taken at the Eleventh Session of the CCFADM/011*, 4.
175 'ONUMOZ', *CCFADM Informal Meeting*, 6 October 1993, 2.
176 'ONUMOZ', *CCFADM Meeting Meetings: Discussion of Agenda Item (e): Nomination of the Officers for the Second Phase of the Leadership Training Program*, 1994. 'Unknown', *Open Letter to the CCFADM, CSC, ONUMOZ, High Command of the FADM*, 20 September 1994. Young, 'The Development of the FADM in Mozambique', 20.
177 'Unknown', *Open Letter to the CCFADM, CSC, ONUMOZ, High Command of the FADM*.
178 Interview conducted by author of a senior UN diplomat in ONUMOZ, conducted 13 September 2019. Jett, *Why Peacekeeping Fails*, 77.
179 Interview by author of US intelligence and later diplomatic officer with African expertise, conducted 20 September 2019.
180 Interview by author of foreign advisor to RENAMO, 1980–94, conducted 2 August 2019. Interview by author of US intelligence and later diplomatic officer with African expertise, conducted 20 September 2019.

181   Interview of expert Mozambique-focused journalist with author. 25 November
      2019. Interview by author of foreign advisor to RENAMO, 1980-1994,
      conducted 2 August 2019. Darch, *The Mozambican Conflict and the Peace
      Process in Historical Perspective*, 18. 'Unknown', *Open Letter to the CCFADM,
      CSC, ONUMOZ, High Command of the FADM.*. Young, 'The Development of the
      FADM in Mozambique', 20.
182   Malache et al., 'Profound Transformations and Regional Conflagrations', 180–91.
      Vines, *Angola and Mozambique*, 155. 'ONUMOZ', *Status of Forces Agreement: The
      Formation of the New Mozambican Defence Force*.
183   Vines, *Angola and Mozambique*, 155. 'ONUMOZ', *Minutes of the 23rd Plenary
      Session of the CCFADM*, 1994, 6. 'ONUMOZ', *CCFADM Informal Meeting*, 2. Young,
      'The Development of the FADM in Mozambique', 22.
184   Aldo Ajello, *Letter to UNSG: Training of the New Armed Forces*, 15 November 1993.
      Kofi Annan, *Letter to ONUMOZ Ajello: Training centres for FADM*, 15 November
      1993.
185   'ONUMOZ', *Reintegration Support Scheme: Rehabilitation of Training Centers*, 1994.
186   Malache et al., 'Profound Transformations and Regional Conflagrations', 180–91.
187   Young, 'The Development of the FADM in Mozambique', 21.
188   Vines, *Angola and Mozambique*, 152–3, 155. 'ONUMOZ', *Reintegration Support
      Scheme: FADM Troop Strength*, 1994.
189   Vines, *Angola and Mozambique*, 155.
190   'ONUMOZ', *Reintegration Support Scheme: FADM Troop Strength*, 6.
191   'ONUMOZ', *Reintegration Support Scheme: Rehabilitation of Training Centers*.
192   Jett, *Why Peacekeeping Fails*, 105. CCFADM, *Decisions Taken at the Eleventh Session
      of the CCFADM/011*, 3. 'CCFADM', *Situation Report – British Training Team*,
      5 August 1994.
193   'ONUMOZ', *Minutes of the 23rd Plenary Session of the CCFADM*, 10. 'CCFADM',
      Situation Report – British Training Team.
194   Peter Batchelor, Kees Kingma and Guy Lamb, *Demilitarisation and Peace-Building
      in Southern Africa* (Aldershot, Hants: Ashgate, 2004), 48. 'ONUMOZ', *Reintegration
      Support Scheme: FADM Troop Strength*, 4.
195   'ONUMOZ', *Pre-election Training for the FADM – Amendment 1*, May 1994, 1–2,
      A-1, A-8.
196   'ONUMOZ', *Overview of the Operation*, March-August 1994, 2.
197   Emily Knowles and Jahara Matisek, 'Is Human Rights Training Working with
      Foreign Militaries? No One Knows and That's O.K', *War on the Rocks*, 11 May 2020,
      warontherocks.com/2020/05/is-human-rights-training-working-with-foreign-mil
      itaries-no-one-knows-and-thats-o-k/.
198   'How to Build Better Militaries in Africa: Lessons from Niger', *Council on Foreign
      Relations*. https://www.cfr.org/blog/how-build-better-militaries-africa-lessons-niger
      (accessed 2 October 2020).
199   'ONUMOZ', *Overview of the Operation*, 6.
200   'ONUMOZ', *CCFADM Informal Meeting*, 3. 'ONUMOZ', *Minutes of the 26th Plenary
      Session of the CSC: Approval of the FA DM Salary Structure*, 2.
201   'ONUMOZ', *Overview of the Operation*, 5. 'ONUMOZ', *Status of the FADM*,
      5 September 1994.
202   'ONUMOZ', *CCFADM Informal Meeting*, 3.
203   Malache et al., 'Profound Transformations and Regional Conflagrations', 181.
204   Jett, *Why Peacekeeping Fails*, 105.

205 Synge, *Mozambique*, 160.
206 Malache et al., 'Profound Transformations and Regional Conflagrations', 181.
207 Ibid.
208 Schafer, *Soldiers at Peace*, 125, 129. Berdal, *Disarmament and Demobilisation after Civil Wars*, 82. 'CCFADM', *Situation Report – British Training Team*, 6.
209 Jett, *Why Peacekeeping Fails*, 105.
210 Batchelor et al., *Demilitarisation and Peace-Building in Southern Africa*, 49–50. Young, 'The Development of the FADM in Mozambique', 22.
211 Darch, *The Mozambican Conflict and the Peace Process in Historical Perspective*, 18. Interview by author of foreign advisor to RENAMO, 1980-1994, conducted 2 August 2019.
212 Jett, *Why Peacekeeping Fails*, 55.
213 Vines, 'Prospects for a Sustainable Elite Bargain in Mozambique'.
214 In interviews with two American and one British diplomat involved in Angolan negotiations cumulatively from 1986 to 1995, all three recollected that Savimbi had a habit of showing off his historical knowledge and linguistic capabilities by quoting famous leaders from the country of whichever foreign diplomat he was currently meeting with. In the personal experience of these interviewees, specific mention was made of George Washington and Winston Churchill in particular. Interview by author with senior US diplomat working on African affairs, conducted 23 July 2019. Interview by author with a US diplomat in the Office of Southern African Affairs, circa 1990s, conducted 2 August 2019 and 6 August 2019. Interview conducted by author with former UK ambassador to Angola circa 1990s, conducted on 28 August 2019.
215 Azimi and Lin, *The Nexus between Peacekeeping and Peace-Building*, 90.
216 Porto and Parsons, *Sustaining the Peace in Angola*, 29–30.
217 Brzoska, 'Introduction'.

Chapter 5

1 'UNSC', *Notes for Mr. Miyet, Angola: Briefing to the Security Council*, July 1997, 1–3. 'UNAVEM III', *Debriefing of General Chris Garuba*, 17 October 1995. David Simon, 'Angola: The Peace Is Not Yet Fully Won', *Review of African Political Economy* 25, no. 77 (1998): 497–8.
2 Macqueen, 'Peacekeeping by Attrition', 412. Howard, *UN Peacekeeping in Civil Wars*, 40.
3 Bekoe, *Implementing Peace Agreements*, 91.
4 Gwinyayi A. Dzinesa, 'Postconflict Disarmament, Demobilization, and Reintegration of Former Combatants in Southern Africa', *International Studies Perspectives* 8, no. 1 (February 2007): 77. https://doi.org/10.1111/j.1528-3585.2007.00270.x. Barry Munslow, 'Angola: The Politics of Unsustainable Development', *Third World Quarterly* 20, no. 3 (June 1999): 552. https://www.jstor.org/stable/3993321. Willett, 'New Barbarians at the Gate', 574.
5 Achim Wennmann, 'Getting Armed Groups to the Table: Peace Processes, the Political Economy of Conflict and the Mediated State', *Third World Quarterly* 30, no. 6 (2009): 1123–38 (p. 1127). doi:10.1080/01436590903037416, pg 1127. Munslow, 'Angola', 556.

6   Macqueen, 'Peacekeeping by Attrition', 407, 413. Spears, 'Angola's Elusive Peace', 562, 572.

7   Azimi and Lin, *The Nexus between Peacekeeping and Peace-Building*, 90. Macqueen, 'Peacekeeping by Attrition', 407.

8   'UNAVEM III', *Debriefing of General Chris Garuba.*

9   Ali and Matthews, *Durable Peace*, 777, 819. Bekoe, *Implementing Peace Agreements*, 95. Vines, *Renamo,* 24. Macqueen, 'Peacekeeping by Attrition', 412.

10 Todd Howland, 'UN Human Rights Field Presence as Proactive Instrument of Peace and Social Change: Lessons from Angola', *Human Rights Quarterly* 26, no. 1 (February 2004): 12. Paul Robson, 'Angola After Savimbi', *Review of African Political Economy* 29, no. 91 (March 2002): 131. https://www.jstor.org/stable/4006868. Nigel Davidson, *The Lion That Didnt Roar: Can the Kimberley Process Stop the Blood Diamonds Trade?* (Acton, ACT: ANU Press, 2016), 26. Nuema Grobbelaar, 'Angola in Search of Peace: Spoilers, Saints and Strategic Regional Interests', *Clingendael* (2003): 26. https://www.clingendael.org/sites/default/files/pdfs/20031000_cru _working_paper_14.pdf.

11 Simon, 'Angola', 496. Vines, *Angola and Mozambique,* 24.

12 Howard, *UN Peacekeeping in Civil Wars*, 40.

13 Macqueen, 'Peacekeeping by Attrition', 412. S/1997/640 (1997), 5.

14 Ali and Matthews, *Durable Peace*, 836–7. Bekoe, *Implementing Peace Agreements*, 77. Macqueen, 'Peacekeeping by Attrition', 412. Howard, *UN Peacekeeping in Civil Wars*, 40.

15 Bekoe, *Implementing Peace Agreements*, 77.

16 Mats R. Berdal, *Reintegrating Armed Groups after Conflict: Politics, Violence and Transition* (Abingdon: Routledge, 2009), 203.

17 Ali and Matthews, *Durable Peace*, 299. Bekoe, *Implementing Peace Agreements*, 91.

18 J. C. Cilliers and C. Dietrich (eds), 'Angola's War Economy: The Role of Oil and Diamonds', *Johannesburg, South Africa: Institute for Security Studies* (2001): 85. https://issafrica.s3.amazonaws.com/site/uploads/2000-11-01-book-angolas-war -economy.pdf.

19 Marika Landau-Wells, 'High Stakes and Low Bars', *International Security* 43, no. 1 (Summer 2018): 102, 104, 120–5, 135–7. https://static1.squarespace.com/static/56a ac3450ab37725a3850c35/t/5c8ab1e9104c7be301fb6cd0/1552593385662/Landau -Wells_2018_High Stakes.pdf.

20 Howard, *UN Peacekeeping in Civil Wars*, 38.

21 Wright, 'The Clinton Administrations Policy toward Angola', 572.

22 'UNAVEM III', *Note to Mr. Kittani, Visit of the Military Advisor to Angola*, late November 1996, 1.

23 Willett, 'New Barbarians at the Gate', 572–3.

24 Bekoe, *Implementing Peace Agreements*, 89. Marcus Power, 'Patrimonialism & Petro-diamond Capitalism: Peace, Geopolitics & the Economics of War in Angola', *Review of African Political Economy* 28, no. 90 (2001): 493. https://www .tandfonline.com/doi/abs/10.1080/03056240108704561. Levine, 'Organizational Disruption', 375.

25 Porto and Parsons, *Sustaining the Peace in Angola*, 29–30. Munslow, 'Angola', 556.

26 Willett, 'New Barbarians at the Gate', 572–3.

27 Simon, 'Angola', 497.

28 Berdal, *Reintegrating Armed Groups after Conflict*, 203. Macqueen, 'Peacekeeping by Attrition', 405.

29 Macqueen, 'Peacekeeping by Attrition', 421.

30 Ibid., 416.

31 Ibid.

32 Howland, 'UN Human Rights Field Presence as Proactive Instrument of Peace', 2–3.

33 Macqueen, 'Peacekeeping by Attrition', 415–16.

34 UN Peacekeeping website.

35 'UCAH', *Memo to MONUA*, 11 August 1997.

36 'MONUA', *Report on Tasks Still to Complete, Focus on Military Tasks*, 1997, 4.

37 'UNAVEM III', *Demobilisation of Underage UNITA Soldiers*, 21 October 1996, 1, 2. Levine, 'Organizational Disruption', 375.

38 'MONUA', *Recruitment and Regrouping of Troops by UNITA*, 31 July 1997.

39 S/1997/640 (1997), 8.

40 Simon, 'Angola', 497. 'MONUA', *Report on Tasks Still to Complete, Focus on Military Tasks*.

41 'UNAVEM III', *Debriefing of General Chris Garuba*. Power, 'Patrimonialism & Petro-diamond Capitalism', 493.

42 Simon, 'Angola', 497. 'MONUA', *Report on MONUA Completion of Mission, 'Part II: Obstructions to MONUA'*, Spring 1999, 9.

43 'MONUA', *Report on MONUA Completion of Mission, 'Part II: Obstructions to MONUA'*, 12–13.

44 S/1997/640 (1997), 4. Howard, *UN Peacekeeping in Civil Wars*, 41.

45 'MONUA', *Declaration Completion of Demilitarisation of UNITA*, 10 March 1998, 1, 2.

46 'MONUA', *Report on Tasks Still to Complete, Focus on Military Tasks*.

47 Ibid.

48 Ibid., 4. Interview by author with senior US diplomat working on African affairs, conducted 23 July 2019.

49 'MONUA', *Report on Tasks Still to Complete, Focus on Military Tasks*, 4. 'MONUA', *Executive Summary: Lessons Learnt*, Spring 1999, 4.

50 'UNAVEM III', *Status Report February 1995-June 1997*, July 1997, 19.

51 Simon, 'Angola', 497.

52 S/1997/640 (1997), 4.

53 Dzinesa, 'Postconflict Disarmament, Demobilization', 77.

54 'MONUA', *Executive Summary: Lessons Learnt*, 2, 7. See also Kingma, *Demobilization in Subsaharan Africa*, 160 for the importance of planning details in advance.

55 'UNAVEM III', *Status Report February 1995–June 1997*, 27.

56 Cilliers and Dietrich, 'Angola's War Economy', 85.

57 Porto and Parsons, *Sustaining the Peace in Angola*, 30.

58 Howland, 'UN Human Rights Field Presence as Proactive Instrument of Peace', 7, 8.

59 Vines, *Angola and Mozambique*, 24.

60 Oliveira, 'Illiberal Peacebuilding in Angola', 288.

61 Wennmann, 'Getting Armed Groups to the Table', 1123.

62 Cramer, *Civil War Is Not a Stupid Thing*, 139.

63 Munslow, 'Angola', 556.

64 Ibid., 555, 557. Crocker, *International Negotiation and Mediation in Violent Conflict*, 683.

65 Grobbelaar, 'Angola in Search of Peace', 29.

66 Cramer, *Civil War Is Not a Stupid Thing*, 144.

67 Berdal, *Reintegrating Armed Groups after Conflict*, 204–5. Malaquias, 'Diamonds Are a Guerrillas Best Friend', 323–34. Grobbelaar, 'Angola in Search of Peace', 25.

68 Cilliers and Dietrich, 'Angola's War Economy', 87, 263–4. Malaquias, 'Diamonds Are a Guerrillas Best Friend', 313.

69 Cilliers and Dietrich, 'Angola's War Economy', 87.

70 Paula Cristina Roque, *Governing in the Shadows: Angola's Securitized State* (Oxford: Oxford University Press, 2021), Chapter 4.

71 Wennmann, 'Getting Armed Groups to the Table', 1130.

72 Ibid.

73 Simon, 'Angola', 500.

74 Munslow, 'Angola', 554.

75 Macqueen, 'Peacekeeping by Attrition', 417.

76 Malaquias, 'Diamonds Are a Guerrillas Best Friend', 313–14, 323–4. Grobbelaar, 'Angola in Search of Peace', 25. Cilliers and Dietrich, 'Angola's War Economy', 351.

77 Howard, *UN Peacekeeping in Civil Wars*, 41.

78 Power, 'Patrimonialism & Petro-diamond Capitalism', 496. Cilliers and Dietrich, 'Angola's War Economy', 269.

79 Pearce, 'Control, Politics and Identity in the Angolan Civil War', 5, 8.

80 'MONUA', *Demilitarisation of UNITA*, 1997-1999, 2.

81 Ibid.

82 Pearce, 'Control, Politics and Identity in the Angolan Civil War', 5, 8.

83 Berdal, *Reintegrating Armed Groups after Conflict*, 205.

84 Vines, *Renamo*, 25.

85 Power, 'Patrimonialism & Petro-diamond Capitalism', 496.

86 Wennmann, 'Getting Armed Groups to the Table', 1130.

87 Vines, *Renamo*, 25. Cilliers and Dietrich, 'Angola's War Economy', 87.

88 Macqueen, 'Peacekeeping by Attrition', 417.

89 Berdal, *Reintegrating Armed Groups after Conflict*, 205.

90 Wennmann, 'Getting Armed Groups to the Table', 1124. Berdal, *Reintegrating Armed Groups after Conflict*, 206.

91 Berdal, *Reintegrating Armed Groups after Conflict*, 206.

92 Vines, *Angola and Mozambique*, 14. Berdal, *Reintegrating Armed Groups after Conflict*, 206. Malaquias, 'Diamonds Are a Guerrillas Best Friend', 167. Ruigrok, 'Whose Justice?', 85.

93 Berdal, *Reintegrating Armed Groups after Conflict*, 206. Ruigrok, 'Whose Justice?', 85.

94 Vines, *Angola and Mozambique*, 14.

95 Cilliers and Dietrich, 'Angola's War Economy', 36.

96 Munslow, 'Angola', 552.

97 Cilliers and Dietrich, 'Angola's War Economy', 84. Grobbelaar, 'Angola in Search of Peace', 26.

98 J. H. Sherman, 'The Clandestine Diamond Economy of Angola', *Journal of International Affairs* 53, no. 2 (2000): 699. Cilliers and Dietrich, 'Angola's War Economy', 271. Malaquias, 'Diamonds Are a Guerrillas Best Friend', 319. Spears, 'Angola's Elusive Peace', 562, 573. Wennmann, 'Getting Armed Groups to the Table', 1124. Pearce, 'Global Ideologies, Local Politics', 461.

99 Malaquias, 'Diamonds Are a Guerrillas Best Friend', 91, 314. Cilliers and Dietrich, 'Angola's War Economy', 36. Pearce, 'Global Ideologies, Local Politics', 461. Grobbelaar, 'Angola in Search of Peace', 355. Conciliation Resources, 'From Military Peace to Social Justice? The Angolan Peace Process: Policy Brief', 1 October 2004, 82. https://www.c-r.org/resource/military-peace-social-justice-angolan-peace -process-policy-brief (accessed 23 February 2020).

100   Munslow, 'Angola', 551.
101   Sherman, 'The Clandestine Diamond Economy of Angola', 701.
102   Cilliers and Dietrich, 'Angola's War Economy', 278. Davidson, *The Lion That Didnt Roar*, 35.
103   Cilliers and Dietrich, 'Angola's War Economy', 287.
104   Hare, *Angolas Last Best Chance for Peace*, 124.
105   Cilliers and Dietrich, 'Angola's War Economy', 89.
106   Howard, *UN Peacekeeping in Civil Wars*, 312.
107   Malaquias, 'Diamonds Are a Guerrillas Best Friend', 313–14.
108   Hare, *Angolas Last Best Chance for Peace*, 124. Cilliers and Dietrich, 'Angola's War Economy', 89.
109   Cilliers and Dietrich, 'Angola's War Economy', 35.
110   Ibid., 290.
111   Ibid.
112   Wennmann, 'Getting Armed Groups to the Table', 1131. Cilliers and Dietrich, 'Angola's War Economy', 278. Davidson, *The Lion That Didnt Roar*, 30.
113   Munslow, 'Angola', 551, 558. Cilliers and Dietrich, 'Angola's War Economy', 278, 285, 352. Malaquias, 'Diamonds Are a Guerrillas Best Friend', 320.
114   Grobbelaar, 'Angola in Search of Peace', 25.
115   Wennmann, 'Getting Armed Groups to the Table', 1131. Cilliers and Dietrich, 'Angola's War Economy', 30, 278. Philippe Le Billon, 'Angola's Political Economy of War: The Role of Oil and Diamonds, 1975-2000', *African Affairs* 100, no. 398 (January 2001): 67.
116   Sherman, 'The Clandestine Diamond Economy of Angola', 700, 717. Willett, 'New Barbarians at the Gate', 574. Cilliers and Dietrich, 'Angola's War Economy', 84. Power, 'Patrimonialism & Petro-diamond Capitalism', 490. Billon, 'Angola's Political Economy of War', 74.
117   Billon, 'Angola's Political Economy of War', 67. Davidson, *The Lion That Didnt Roar*, 30.
118   Wennmann, 'Getting Armed Groups to the Table', 1131.
119   Sherman, 'The Clandestine Diamond Economy of Angola', 717. Power, 'Patrimonialism & Petro-diamond Capitalism', 490. Billon, 'Angola's Political Economy of War', 74.
120   Cilliers and Dietrich, 'Angola's War Economy', 268. Power, 'Patrimonialism & Petro-diamond Capitalism', 490. Billon, 'Angola's Political Economy of War', 74.
121   Wennmann, 'Getting Armed Groups to the Table', 1131. Sherman, 'The Clandestine Diamond Economy of Angola', 717. Billon, 'Angola's Political Economy of War', 74.
122   Willett, 'New Barbarians at the Gate', 575. Sherman, 'The Clandestine Diamond Economy of Angola', 717. Cilliers and Dietrich, 'Angola's War Economy', 285. Billon, 'Angola's Political Economy of War', 74.
123   Hare, *Angolas Last Best Chance for Peace*, 124.
124   Cilliers and Dietrich, 'Angola's War Economy', 173.
125   Sherman, 'The Clandestine Diamond Economy of Angola', 710.
126   Ibid., 717.
127   Davidson, *The Lion That Didnt Roar*, 30, 26.
128   Malaquias, 'Diamonds Are a Guerrillas Best Friend', 312.
129   Davidson, *The Lion That Didnt Roar*, 26.
130   Ibid., 37.
131   Sherman, 'The Clandestine Diamond Economy of Angola', 711.

132   Cilliers and Dietrich, 'Angola's War Economy', 112.

133   Pearce, 'Global Ideologies, Local Politics', 460.

134   Ibid., 461.

135   Crocker, *International Negotiation and Mediation in Violent Conflict*, 186. Willett, 'New Barbarians at the Gate', 570. Malaquias, 'Diamonds Are a Guerrillas Best Friend', 314. Assis Malaquias, *Rebels and Robbers: Violence in Post-Colonial Angola* (Uppsala: Nordiska Afrikainstitutet, 2007), 91.

136   Oliveira, 'Illiberal Peacebuilding in Angola', 290. Roque, *Governing in the Shadows*, Chapter 4.

137   Wright, 'The Clinton Administrations Policy toward Angola', 572–3. Cilliers and Dietrich, 'Angola's War Economy', 220.

138   Ibid.

139   Wright, 'The Clinton Administrations Policy toward Angola', 572–3.

140   Billon, 'Angola's Political Economy of War', 79.

141   Ibid., 75.

142   Anstee, 'The Fight Goes On', 11. Porto and Parsons, *Sustaining the Peace in Angola*, 23. Malaquias, 'Diamonds Are a Guerrillas Best Friend', 313–14.

143   Billon, 'Angola's Political Economy of War', 79. Cilliers and Dietrich, 'Angola's War Economy', 14–15, 359.

144   Power, 'Patrimonialism & Petro-diamond Capitalism', 492–3. Sam Hickey, Abdullgafaru Abdulai, Angelo Izama, and Giles Mohan, 'The Politics of Governing Oil Effectively: A Comparative Study of Two New Oil-Rich States in Africa', *ESID Working Paper* no. 54 (2015). doi:10.2139/ssrn.2695723.

145   Billon, 'Angola's Political Economy of War', 79. Vines, *Renamo*, 25.

146   Billon, 'Angola's Political Economy of War', 75, 79. Cilliers and Dietrich, 'Angola's War Economy', 14–15.

147   Pearce, 'Global Ideologies, Local Politics', 460. Wennmann, 'Getting Armed Groups to the Table', 1129.

148   Vines, *Renamo*, 25.

149   Wright, 'The Clinton Administrations Policy toward Angola', 570.

150   Ibid., 568.

151   Cilliers and Dietrich, 'Angola's War Economy', 14–15.

152   Ibid., 219. Wright, 'The Clinton Administrations Policy toward Angola', 572–3. Robson, 'Angola After Savimbi', 131.

153   Cilliers and Dietrich, 'Angola's War Economy', 14–15, 219–20.

154   Oliveira, 'Illiberal Peacebuilding in Angola', 290.

155   Vines, *Renamo*, 25.

156   Cilliers and Dietrich, 'Angola's War Economy', 351.

157   Malaquias, 'Diamonds Are a Guerrillas Best Friend', 171, 319. Power, 'Patrimonialism & Petro-diamond Capitalism', 492–3.

158   Billon, 'Angola's Political Economy of War', 75.

159   Cilliers and Dietrich, 'Angola's War Economy', 89. Sherman, 'The Clandestine Diamond Economy of Angola', 710. Addisu Lashitew and Eric Werker, 'Are Natural Resources a Curse, a Blessing, or a Double-edged Sword?', *Brookings*, 29 July 2020. https://www.brookings.edu/blog/future-development/2020/07/16/are-natural-resources-a-curse-a-blessing-or-a-double-edged-sword/ (accessed 1 October 2020).

160   Malaquias, 'Diamonds Are a Guerrillas Best Friend', 171, 319. Cilliers and Dietrich, 'Angola's War Economy', 111–12.

161 Munslow, 'Angola', 554. Wennmann, 'Getting Armed Groups to the Table', 1124.
     Sherman, 'The Clandestine Diamond Economy of Angola', 710.
162 Conciliation Resources, 'From Military Peace to Social Justice?', 82. S. Kibble,
     'Angola: Can the Politics of Disorder Become the Politics of Democratisation &
     Development?', *Review of African Political Economy* 33, no. 109 (2006): 525–42.
163 Billon, 'Angola's Political Economy of War', 75. Munslow, 'Angola', 558.
164 Malaquias, 'Diamonds Are a Guerrillas Best Friend', 319.
165 Power, 'Patrimonialism & Petro-diamond Capitalism', 492–3.
166 Spears, 'Angola's Elusive Peace', 567.
167 Vines, *Renamo*, 24. Sherman, 'The Clandestine Diamond Economy of Angola', 709.
     Simon, 'Angola', 496.
168 Cilliers and Dietrich, 'Angola's War Economy', 30, 264–5. Spears, 'Angola's Elusive
     Peace', 567. Munslow, 'Angola', 566.
169 Idean Salehyan, *Rebels without Borders Transnational Insurgencies in World Politics*
     (Ithaca, NY: Cornell University Press, 2011).
170 The reliance of guerilla warfare on small arms made transport particularly easy, as
     did the lightweight and easily concealed nature of diamonds.
171 Power, 'Patrimonialism & Petro-diamond Capitalism', 493, 498. Vines, *Angola
     and Mozambique*, 24. Sherman, 'The Clandestine Diamond Economy of Angola',
     709. Howard, *UN Peacekeeping in Civil Wars*, 41. Cilliers and Dietrich, 'Angola's
     War Economy', 264–5. Simon, 'Angola', 496. Salehyan, *Rebels without Borders
     Transnational Insurgencies in World Politics*.
172 Grobbelaar, 'Angola in Search of Peace', 25.
173 Ibid., 27, 29. Wennmann, 'Getting Armed Groups to the Table', 1129.
174 Roque, *Governing in the Shadows*, Chapter 4.
175 Simon, 'Angola', 496. Grobbelaar, 'Angola in Search of Peace', 29. Salehyan, *Rebels
     without Borders Transnational Insurgencies in World Politics*.
176 Grobbelaar, 'Angola in Search of Peace', 36.
177 Howard, *UN Peacekeeping in Civil Wars*, 41. Simon, 'Angola', 496.
178 Sherman, 'The Clandestine Diamond Economy of Angola', 709. Simon, 'Angola', 496.
     Cilliers and Dietrich, 'Angola's War Economy', 351.
179 Salehyan, *Rebels without Borders Transnational Insurgencies in World Politics*. Roque,
     Governing in the Shadows, Chapter 4.
180 Spears, 'Angola's Elusive Peace', 567. Munslow, 'Angola', 566.
181 Hare, *Angolas Last Best Chance for Peace*, 127.
182 Sherman, 'The Clandestine Diamond Economy of Angola', 709.
183 Cilliers and Dietrich, 'Angola's War Economy', 264–5, 268. Simon, 'Angola', 496.
184 Spears, 'Angola's Elusive Peace', 567.
185 Munslow, 'Angola', 566.
186 Spears, 'Angola's Elusive Peace', 567. Cilliers and Dietrich, 'Angola's War
     Economy', 266.
187 Munslow, 'Angola', 566.
188 Power, 'Patrimonialism & Petro-diamond Capitalism', 498. Cilliers and Dietrich,
     'Angola's War Economy', 266.
189 Simon, 'Angola', 496. Cilliers and Dietrich, 'Angola's War Economy', 266.
190 Spears, 'Angola's Elusive Peace', 567.
191 Cilliers and Dietrich, 'Angola's War Economy', 266.
192 Ibid., 266.
193 Ibid.

194   *Memorandum of Understanding (Luena)*, MPLA, UNITA, 4 April 2002, section 1.2.
195   Ibid.
196   Ibid. Porto and Parsons, *Sustaining the Peace in Angola*, 37.
197   Berdal, *Reintegrating Armed Groups after Conflict*, 206. Porto and Parsons, *Sustaining the Peace in Angola*, 38.
198   Berdal, *Reintegrating Armed Groups after Conflict*, 206. *Memorandum of Understanding (Luena)*, MPLA, UNITA. Porto and Parsons, *Sustaining the Peace in Angola*, 38.
199   Ruigrok, 'Whose Justice?', 85.
200   Ibid. Oliveira, 'Illiberal Peacebuilding in Angola', 292.
201   *Memorandum of Understanding (Luena)*, MPLA, UNITA, 4.
202   Interview by author with senior US diplomat working on African affairs, conducted 23 July 2019. Interview conducted by author with former UK ambassador to Angola circa 1990s, conducted on 28 August 2019. Interview by author with US ambassador with African expertise, conducted 16 September 2019. Interview by author of senior US diplomat for Angolan peace process, circa 1990s, conducted 7 October 2019.
203   Interview by author with senior US diplomat working on African affairs, conducted 23 July 2019. Interview conducted by author with former UK ambassador to Angola circa 1990s, conducted on 28 August 2019.
204   Pearce, 'Control, Politics and Identity in the Angolan Civil War', 2.
205   *Memorandum of Understanding (Luena)*, MPLA, UNITA, 4, section 3.6.
206   Ruigrok, 'Whose Justice?', 85.
207   *Memorandum of Understanding (Luena)*, MPLA, UNITA, section 3.5, section 3.11.
208   Ibid., 4, section b.2 and section b.3. Porto and Parsons, *Sustaining the Peace in Angola*, 38.
209   Porto and Parsons, *Sustaining the Peace in Angola*, 38.
210   *Memorandum of Understanding (Luena)*, MPLA, UNITA, 4, section b.2.
211   Ibid., 14. Malaquias, 'Diamonds Are a Guerrillas Best Friend', 167.
212   Simon, 'Angola', 498. Grobbelaar, 'Angola in Search of Peace', 27.
213   *Memorandum of Understanding (Luena)*, MPLA, UNITA, 14.
214   Porto and Parsons, *Sustaining the Peace in Angola*, 39.
215   Malaquias, 'Diamonds Are a Guerrillas Best Friend', 167.
216   *Memorandum of Understanding (Luena)*, MPLA, UNITA, 21.
217   Berdal, *Reintegrating Armed Groups after Conflict*, 209.
218   *Memorandum of Understanding (Luena)*, MPLA, UNITA, 24. Malaquias, 'Diamonds Are a Guerrillas Best Friend', 167.
219   Malaquias, 'Diamonds Are a Guerrillas Best Friend', 167. Ruigrok, 'Whose Justice?', 87. Porto and Parsons, *Sustaining the Peace in Angola*, 43–4.
220   Kingma, *Demobilization in Subsaharan Africa*, 152. Bekoe, *Implementing Peace Agreements*, 89.
221   Porto and Parsons, *Sustaining the Peace in Angola*, 49.
222   Ibid., 39.
223   Ibid. A. Ozerdem and S. Podder, *Child Soldiers: From Recruitment to Reintegration* (Palgrave Macmillan, 2014), 252. Berdal, *Reintegrating Armed Groups after Conflict*, 207–8.
224   Porto and Parsons, *Sustaining the Peace in Angola*, 42. Berdal, *Reintegrating Armed Groups after Conflict*, 207–8.
225   Berdal, *Reintegrating Armed Groups after Conflict*, 207–8.

226 Porto and Parsons, *Sustaining the Peace in Angola*, 42. Berdal, *Reintegrating Armed Groups after Conflict*, 207–8.

227 Porto and Parsons, *Sustaining the Peace in Angola*, 39. Ozerdem and Podder, *Child Soldiers*, 252. Berdal, *Reintegrating Armed Groups after Conflict*, 207–8. Dzinesa, 'Postconflict Disarmament, Demobilization', 77.

228 Porto and Parsons, *Sustaining the Peace in Angola*, 41.

229 Ibid., 89–90.

230 Ibid., 48.

231 Ibid., 48, 89–90.

232 Ibid., 42, 89–90. Dzinesa, 'Postconflict Disarmament, Demobilization', 77.

233 Porto and Parsons, *Sustaining the Peace in Angola*, 42. Dzinesa, 'Postconflict Disarmament, Demobilization', 77. Berdal, *Reintegrating Armed Groups after Conflict*, 209.

234 Porto and Parsons, *Sustaining the Peace in Angola*, 72, 90.

235 Ibid., 71, 73.

236 Ozerdem and Podder, *Child Soldiers*, 250.

237 Porto and Parsons, *Sustaining the Peace in Angola*, 43–4. Ozerdem and Podder, *Child Soldiers*, 250.

238 Berdal, *Reintegrating Armed Groups after Conflict*, 207–8.

239 Porto and Parsons, *Sustaining the Peace in Angola*, 7.

240 Ibid., 44. Conciliation Resources, 'From Military Peace to Social Justice?', 5. Berdal, *Reintegrating Armed Groups after Conflict*, 208.

241 Conciliation Resources, 'From Military Peace to Social Justice?', 5.

242 Ruigrok, 'Whose Justice?', 55–6.

243 Berdal, *Reintegrating Armed Groups after Conflict*, 207–8.

244 Ibid. Dzinesa, 'Postconflict Disarmament, Demobilization', 77.

245 Porto and Parsons, *Sustaining the Peace in Angola*, 43–4.

246 Ozerdem and Podder, *Child Soldiers*, 250.

247 Ibid.

248 Ruigrok, 'Whose Justice?', 88.

249 Porto and Parsons, *Sustaining the Peace in Angola*, 54.

250 Oliveira, 'Illiberal Peacebuilding in Angola', 292.

251 Porto and Parsons, *Sustaining the Peace in Angola*, 48.

252 Ibid.

253 Ibid., 7.

254 Ruigrok, 'Whose Justice?', 89. Porto and Parsons, *Sustaining the Peace in Angola*, 51, 56.

255 Ruigrok, 'Whose Justice?', 91 Berdal, *Reintegrating Armed Groups after Conflict*, 207.

256 Ozerdem and Podder, *Child Soldiers*, 207.

257 Ibid., 209–10.

258 Ibid., 251.

259 Porto and Parsons, *Sustaining the Peace in Angola*, 7, 48. Ruigrok, 'Whose Justice?', 89. Ozerdem and Podder, *Child Soldiers*, 251.

260 Ruigrok, 'Whose Justice?', 91.

261 Berdal, *Reintegrating Armed Groups after Conflict*, 209–10.

262 Ruigrok, 'Whose Justice?', 91. Porto and Parsons, *Sustaining the Peace in Angola*, 51.

263 Ruigrok, 'Whose Justice?', 91. Berdal, *Reintegrating Armed Groups after Conflict*, 209–10.

264 Ozerdem and Podder, *Child Soldiers*, 252.

265 Roque, *Governing in the Shadows*, Chapter 4.

266 Berdal, *Reintegrating Armed Groups after Conflict*, 209.

267 Ibid., 211. Ozerdem and Podder, *Child Soldiers*, 255–6.

268 Ibid.

269 Kibble, 'Angola', 525–42. Roque, *Governing in the Shadows*, Chapter 4.

270 Howland, 'UN Human Rights Field Presence as Proactive Instrument of Peace', 11, 12. Oliveira, 'Illiberal Peacebuilding in Angola', 287.

271 Berdal, *Reintegrating Armed Groups after Conflict*, 213. Malaquias, 'Diamonds Are a Guerrillas Best Friend', 112.

272 Kibble, 'Angola', 525–42. Berdal, *Reintegrating Armed Groups after Conflict*, 213.

273 Pearce, 'Control, Politics and Identity in the Angolan Civil War', 7–8, 10.

274 Berdal, *Reintegrating Armed Groups after Conflict*, 213.

275 Pearce, 'Control, Politics and Identity in the Angolan Civil War', 9, 12. Berdal, *Reintegrating Armed Groups after Conflict*, 213.

276 Oliveira, 'Illiberal Peacebuilding in Angola', 292. Roque, *Governing in the Shadows*, Chapter 4.

277 Ozerdem and Podder, *Child Soldiers*, 252.

278 Carrie Manning, *Politics of Peace in Mozambique: Post-conflict Democratization, 1992-2000* (Westport, CT: Praeger, 2002), 170.

279 Shanaka J. Peiris and Jean A. P. Clément, *Post-Stabilization Economics in Sub-Saharan Africa: Lessons from Mozambique* (Washington DC: International Monetary Fund, 2008), 86.

280 Ibid., 106, 156.

281 Willett, 'New Barbarians at the Gate', 576.

282 T. Bruck, 'Mozambique: The Economic Effects of War', in *Wars and Underdevelopment*, vol. 2 (Oxford: Oxford University Press, 2001), 86–7.

283 Ali and Matthews, *Durable Peace*, 445–7. Willett, 'New Barbarians at the Gate', 576–7. Peiris and Clement, 60–1. Bruck, 'Mozambique', 86–7. Cilliers and Dietrich, 'Angola's War Economy', 14. Howard, *The Failures*, 218. Interview of expert Mozambique-focused journalist with author, 25 November 2019.

284 Ali and Matthews, *Durable Peace*, 403, 445–7, 453. Willett, 'New Barbarians at the Gate', 576. Bruck, 'Mozambique', 86–7. Interview of expert Mozambique-focused journalist with author. 25 November 2019.

285 Rugumamu and Gbla, 'Studies in Reconstruction', 48. Willett, 'New Barbarians at the Gate', 576–7. Schafer, *Soldiers at Peace*, 110–11.

286 Ali and Matthews, *Durable Peace*, 485. Interview of expert Mozambique-focused journalist with author. 25 November 2019.

287 Darch, *The Mozambican Conflict and the Peace Process in Historical Perspective*, 8. Ali and Matthews, *Durable Peace*, 456. Wiegink, 'Former Military Networks a Threat to Peace?', 2. Interview conducted by author of a senior UN diplomat in ONUMOZ, conducted 13 September 2019. Interview by author of US official involved in Mozambique in the 1990s, conducted 24 September 2019.

288 Peiris and Clement, 56, 57.

289 Ali and Matthews, *Durable Peace*, 403. Darch, *The Mozambican Conflict and the Peace Process in Historical Perspective*, 8. Willett, 'New Barbarians at the Gate', 576.

290 Wiegink, 'Former Military Networks a Threat to Peace?', 16.

291 Schafer, *Soldiers at Peace*, 110–11.

292 Ali and Matthews, *Durable Peace*, 487.

293 Ibid., 487. Howard, *The Failures*, 218. Office for Humanitarian Assistance Coordination, *Effective Delivery of Reintegration Programmes for Demobilised Soldiers*, 1993–5, 3.

294 Wiegink, 'Former Military Networks a Threat to Peace?', 5.

295 Ali and Matthews, *Durable Peace*, 403.

296 Ibid., 472–3. Wiegink, 'Former Military Networks a Threat to Peace?', 5.

297 Howard, *The Failures*, 218. Wiegink, 'Former Military Networks a Threat to Peace?', 5. Rugumamu and Gbla, 'Studies in Reconstruction', 45–6.

298 Peiris and Clement, 106, 156.

299 Wiegink, 'Former Military Networks a Threat to Peace?', 5.

300 Rugumamu and Gbla, 'Studies in Reconstruction', 45–6, 48. Ali and Matthews, *Durable Peace*, 403, 456. Interview by author of foreign advisor to RENAMO, 1980-1994, conducted 2 August 2019.

301 Ali and Matthews, *Durable Peace*, 404. Wiegink, 'Former Military Networks a Threat to Peace?', 2, 16.

302 Howard, *The Failures*, 218. Wiegink, 'Former Military Networks a Threat to Peace?', 5.

303 Ali and Matthews, *Durable Peace*, 404. Wiegink, 'Former Military Networks a Threat to Peace?', 2. Interview conducted by author of a senior UN diplomat in ONUMOZ, conducted 13 September 2019. Interview by author of US official involved in Mozambique in the 1990s, conducted 24 September 2019.

304 Rugumamu and Gbla, 'Studies in Reconstruction', 48. Ali and Matthews, *Durable Peace*, 403, 445–7. Peiris and Clement, 106, 156.

305 Bruck, 'Mozambique', 86–7. Cilliers and Dietrich, 'Angola's War Economy', 14. Schafer, *Soldiers at Peace*, 125.

306 Schafer, *Soldiers at Peace*, 129.

307 Ibid., 125. Interview by author of foreign advisor to RENAMO, 1980-1994, conducted 2 August 2019.

308 Schafer, *Soldiers at Peace*, 125. Howard, *The Failures*, 218.

309 Interview by author of US official involved in Mozambique in the 1990s, conducted 24 September 2019. Interview by author of foreign advisor to RENAMO, 1980-1994, conducted 2 August 2019.

310 Ali and Matthews, *Durable Peace*, 485. Interview by author of foreign advisor to RENAMO, 1980–94, conducted 2 August 2019.

311 Interview by author of foreign advisor to RENAMO, 1980–94, conducted 2 August 2019.

312 Ali and Matthews, *Durable Peace*, 404. Darch, *The Mozambican Conflict and the Peace Process in Historical Perspective*, 11.

313 Howard, *The Failures*, 218.

314 Ali and Matthews, *Durable Peace*, 486. Willett, 'New Barbarians at the Gate', 576. Darch, *The Mozambican Conflict and the Peace Process in Historical Perspective*, 11.

315 Crocker, *High Noon in Southern Africa*, 815. Kingma, *Demobilization in Subsaharan Africa*, 160. Interview conducted by author of a senior UN diplomat in ONUMOZ, conducted 13 September 2019.

316 Interview conducted by author of a senior UN diplomat in ONUMOZ, conducted 13 September 2019.

317 Crocker, *High Noon in Southern Africa*, 815.

318 Kingma, *Demobilization in Subsaharan Africa*, 160. Interview conducted by author of a senior UN diplomat in ONUMOZ, conducted 13 September 2019.

319 Willett, 'New Barbarians at the Gate', 572–3.

320 Ibid.

321 Ibid., 572.

322 On the importance of security processes, see Walter's work, as well as Rothchild, 'Settlement Terms and Postagreement Stability', and Jarstad and Nilsson, 'From Words to Deeds'. For the economic aspect, see Wennmann, 'Getting Armed Groups to the Table'. Alexander Costy, *From Civil War to Civil Society? Aid, NGOs and Hegemonic Construction in Mozambique* (Ann Arbor, MI: University of Michigan, 2002), and Carrie Manning, 'Party-Building on the Heels of War: El Salvador, Bosnia, Kosovo and Mozambique', *Democratisation* 14 (2007): 253–72.

Chapter 6

1 I. William Zartman, 'Ripeness: The Hurting Stalemate and Beyond', in *International Conflict Resolution After the Cold War* (Washington, DC: National Academies Press, 2000).

2 Kyle Beardsley, *The Mediation Dilemma*, 1st edn (Cornell University Press, 2011). http://www.jstor.org/stable/10.7591/j.ctt7zc1z (accessed 15 March 2019).

3 Walter, 'The Critical Barrier to Civil War Settlement', 335–64. Walter, 'Designing Transitions from Civil War', 127–55.

4 Stedman et al., *Ending Civil Wars*.

5 Karl Derouen, Mark J. Ferguson, Samuel Norton, Young Hwan Park, Jenna Lea, and Ashley Streat-Bartlett, 'Civil War Peace Agreement Implementation and State Capacity', *Journal of Peace Research* 47, no. 3 (2010): 333–46. doi:10.1177/0022343310362169. Michael W. Doyle and Nicholas Sambanis, *Making War and Building Peace: United Nations Peace Operations* (Princeton, NJ: Princeton University Press, 2006).

6 King, *Ending Civil Wars*.

7 Bergh, 'Why Peace Worked', 129.

8 Ibid.

9 Kayta Favretto, 'Should Peacemakers Take Sides? Major Power Mediation, Coercion, and Bias', *American Political Science Review* 103, no. 2 (2009): 248–63. doi:10.1017/S0003055409090236. Stedman et al., *Ending Civil Wars*. Walter, 'The Critical Barrier to Civil War Settlement'.

10 Mac Ginty, *No War, No Peace*, 3.

11 Zartman, 'Ripeness'.

12 Ibid.

13 João Gomes Porto, Chris Alden, and Imogen Parsons, *From Soldiers to Citizens Demilitarisation of Conflict and Society* (London: Routledge, Taylor & Francis Group, 2016), 471–3.

14 Ibid., 451.

15 Zartman and Berman, *The Practical Negotiator*. Henry Kissinger, *Diplomacy* (New York City, NY: Touchstone, 1995). Stedman et al., *Ending Civil Wars*. Beardsley, 'Mediation Style and Crisis Outcomes', 58–86.

16 Dudouet, 'Mediating Peace with Proscribed Armed Groups'. Dennis C. Jett, 'Mediation – Its Potential and Its Limits: Developing an Effective Discourse on the

Research and Practice of Peacemaking', *Journal of Law and International Affairs* 2, no. 1 (2013). https://elibrary.law.psu.edu/jlia/vol2/iss1/12/.

17 Malaquias, 'Diamonds Are a Guerrillas Best Friend', 319.

18 Raymond Cohen, 'Resolving Conflict Across Languages', *Negotiation Journal* 17, no. 1 (2001): 17–34. doi:10.1111/j.1571-9979.2001.tb00224.x.

19 Carol Izumi, 'Implicit Bias and the Illusion of Mediator Neutrality', *New Directions in ADR and Clinical Legal Education* 34 (January 2010). openscholarship.wustl.edu/cgi/viewcontent.cgi?article=1054&context=law_journal_law_policy. Jennifer T. Kubota, et al. 'The Price of Racial Bias', *Psychological Science* 24, no. 12 (2013): 2498–504. doi:10.1177/0956797613496435. J. William Breslin, 'Breaking Away from Subtle Biases', *Negotiation Journal* 5, no. 3 (1989): 219–22. doi:10.1111/j.1571-9979.1989.tb00518.x.

20 Nikkie Wiegink, 'Why Did the Soldiers Not Go Home?: Demobilized Combatants, Family Life, and Witchcraft in Postwar Mozambique', *Anthropological Quarterly* 86, no. 1 (2013): 107–32. doi:10.1353/anq.2013.0014. Carrie Manning, 'Party-Building on the Heels of War: El Salvador, Bosnia, Kosovo and Mozambique', *Twenty Years of Studying Democratization* (2018): 4–23 (p. 260). doi:10.4324/9781315757513-1. Alden, 'Making Old Soldiers Fade Away', 350.

21 Interview by author of foreign advisor to RENAMO, 1980–94, conducted 2 August 2019. Interview by author of US diplomat involved in Mozambique negotiations, conducted 12 August 2019.

22 Anders Themnér, *Warlord Democrats in Africa: Ex-military Leaders and Electoral Politics* (Uppsala, Sweden: Nordiska Afrikainstitutet, The Nordic Africa Institute, 2017).

23 Teresa Whitfield, *Friends Indeed?: The United Nations, Groups of Friends, and the Resolution of Conflict* (United States Institute of Peace Press, 2007).

24 Stedman et al., *Ending Civil Wars*.

25 Favretto, 'Should Peacemakers Take Sides?'.

26 Mac Ginty, *No War, No Peace*.

27 Jeremy M. Weinstein, 'Disentangling the Determinants of Successful Demobilization and Reintegration', *Stanford University - Freeman Spogli Institute for International Studies* (2005): 6, 23. doi:10.2139/ssrn.984246. Mac Ginty, *No War, No Peace*, 111–12.

28 Wennmann, 'Getting Armed Groups to the Table', 1130. Bekoe, *Implementing Peace Agreements*, 95. Onur Bakiner, 'Why Do Peace Negotiations Succeed or Fail? Legal Commitment, Transparency, and Inclusion during Peace Negotiations in Colombia (2012–2016) and Turkey (2012–2015)', *Negotiation Journal* 35, no. 4 (2019): 471–513. doi:10.1111/nejo.12301.

29 Glen Hickerson, 'A Bridge over Troubled Water: Managing Parties' Mental Illness in Mediation', *Negotiation Journal* 33, no. 1 (2017): 53–69. doi:10.1111/nejo.12173.

30 Interview by author of US official involved in Mozambique in the 1990s, conducted 24 September 2019. Interview by author of foreign advisor to RENAMO, 1980-1994, conducted 2 August 2019.

31 Izumi, 'Implicit Bias and the Illusion of Mediator Neutrality'. Kubota, et al. 'The Price of Racial Bias'. Breslin, 'Breaking Away from Subtle Biases'.

32 Mac Ginty, *No War, No Peace*.

33 Rothchild, 'On Implementing Africa's Peace Accords'. Kingma, 'Disarmament, Demobilization'. Rothchild, 'Settlement Terms and Postagreement Stability'.

34 Cohen, *Intervening in Africa*, 123. Macqueen, 'Peacekeeping by Attrition', 421. Spears, 'Angola's Elusive Peace', 570.

35   Paul Collier, Anke Hoeffler, and Mans Soderbom, 'Post-Conflict Risks', *Journal of Peace Research* (2008). https://doi.org/10.1177/0022343308091356.

36   Madhav Josh, Erik Melander, and Jason Michael Quinn, 'Sequencing the Peace: How the Order of Peace Agreement Implementation Can Reduce the Destabilizing Effects of Post-accord Elections', *Journal of Conflict Resolution* 61, no. 1 (2016): 4–28. doi:10.1177/0022002715576573. Joshi and Quinn, 'Is the Sum Greater than the Parts?', 7–30.

37   Joshi and Quinn, 'Is the Sum Greater than the Parts?'.

38   Mac Ginty, *No War, No Peace*.

39   Charles Call, *Why Peace Fails: The Causes and Prevention of Civil War Recurrence* (Washington, DC: Georgetown University Press, 2012). Jarstad and Nilsson, 'From Words to Deeds', 206–23.

40   Stedman et al., *Ending Civil Wars*.

41   Greenhill and Major, 'The Perils of Profiling'.

42   Laura Freeman, 'The African Warlord Revisited', *Small Wars & Insurgencies* 26, no. 5 (4 October 2014). https://www.tandfonline.com/doi/full/10.1080/09592318.2015.1072318.

43   Anstee, 'The Fight Goes On', 256. Spears, 'Angola's Elusive Peace', 572. Alao, *Brothers at War*, 16–17.

44   William Stanley and Charles Call, 'Military and Police Reform after Civil Wars', in *Contemporary Peace Making: Conflict, Peace Processes and Post-war Reconstruction* (Basingstoke: Palgrave Macmillan, 2008).

45   Richard Caplan, *Measuring Peace: Principles, Practices, and Politics* (Oxford: Oxford University Press, 2019).

46   Howard and Dayal, 'The Use of Force in UN Peacekeeping', 71–103.

47   Hartzell et al., 'Stabilizing the Peace After Civil War', 183–208.

48   Toft, 'Introduction', 153.

49   Glassmyer and Sambanis, 'Rebel – Military Integration and Civil War Termination', 365–84.

50   Muggah, *Security and Post-conflict Reconstruction*.

51   Stedman et al., *Ending Civil Wars*.

52   Ball, 'Democratic Governance'. Laitin, 'The Industrial Organisation of Merged Armies'.

53   Joshi and Quinn, 'Is the Sum Greater than the Parts?'.

54   Zartman and Berman, *The Practical Negotiator*.

55   Bergh, 'Why Peace Worked'.

56   Joshi et al., 'Sequencing the Peace', 4–28.

57   Wennmann, 'Getting Armed Groups to the Table'.

58   Zartman and Berman, *The Practical Negotiator*.

59   Crocker and Hampson, 'Making Peace Settlements Work', 54. Derouen et al., 'Civil War Peace Agreement Implementation'. Kingma, 'Disarmament, Demobilization'. Bakiner, 'Why Do Peace Negotiations Succeed or Fail?'.

60   Crocker and Hampson, 'Making Peace Settlements Work'. Mattes, Mattes and Savun, 'Information, Agreement Design, and the Durability of Civil War Settlements', 511–24.

61   Ibid.

62   Mac Ginty, *No War, No Peace*.

63   Zartman and Berman, *The Practical Negotiator*. Aliza Belman Inbal and Hanna Lerner, 'Constitutional Design, Identity, and Legitimacy in Post-conflict Reconstruction', *Governance in Post-conflict Societies: Rebuilding Fragile States*, 2006.

64 Howard, *UN Peacekeeping in Civil Wars*, 194. Synge, *Mozambique*, 45, 57. Berdal, *Disarmament and Demobilisation after Civil Wars*.

65 Derouen et al., 'Civil War Peace Agreement Implementation'.

66 Anjali Dayal, 'Research & Writing', *Anjali Dayal*. https://anjali-dayal.squarespace.com/research (accessed 10 August 2020).

67 Mac Ginty, *No War, No Peace*.

68 Jarstad and Nilsson, 'From Words to Deeds'.

69 Mac Ginty, *No War, No Peace*.

70 Bergh, 'Why Peace Worked'.

71 Michael Roll, *The Politics of Public Sector Performance: Pockets of Effectiveness in Developing Countries* (London: Routledge, 2015).

72 Jett, *Why Peacekeeping Fails*.

73 Oksamytna et al., 'Leadership Selection in United Nations Peacekeeping'.

74 Macqueen, 'Peacekeeping by Attrition', 405. Spears, 'Angola's Elusive Peace', 570.

75 Interview conducted by author of a senior UN diplomat in ONUMOZ, conducted 13 September 2019.

76 Colin Robinson, 'Discussion Note: Is a Post-Conflict Army Reconstruction Framework Possible, or Useful?', *Small Wars Journal* (2012). https://smallwarsjournal.com/jrnl/art/discussion-note-is-a-post-conflict-army-reconstruction-framework-possible-or-useful.

77 Licklider, *New Armies from Old*.

78 Gaub, *Military Integration after Civil Wars Multiethnic Armies, Identity, and Post-conflict Reconstruction*.

79 Alden, 'Making Old Soldiers Fade Away'.

80 Wiegink, 'Why Did the Soldiers Not Go Home?'.

81 Porto et al., *From Soldiers to Citizens Demilitarisation of Conflict and Society*.

BIBLIOGRAPHY

Interviews

All interviews have been pseudonymized per ethical approval granted for interviews for this research.

US official in the Office of Southern African Affairs, circa 1990s, interviewed by Miranda Melcher, Skype, 2 August and 6 August 2019.

Senior US official in the Office of Southern African Affairs, circa 1990s, interviewed by Miranda Melcher, Skype, 27 August 2019.

Senior US official on African Affairs, circa 1990s, interviewed by Miranda Melcher, Skype, 23 July 2019.

Senior US State department official on Africa Affairs, circa 1990s, interviewed by Miranda Melcher, Skype, 16 September 2019.

Long-time foreign advisor to RENAMO, 1980–1994, interviewed by Miranda Melcher, Skype, 2 August 2019.

US official involved in Mozambican negotiations in Rome, interviewed by Miranda Melcher, Skype, 12 August 2019.

Senior US diplomat involved in Mozambican negotiations in Rome, interviewed by Miranda Melcher, Skype, 18 October 2019.

Senior representative of the Community of Sant'Egidio, interviewed by Miranda Melcher, Skype, 28 August 2019.

Former UK ambassador in Southern Africa, circa 1990s, interviewed by Miranda Melcher, London, UK, 28 August 2019.

Senior Mozambican political appointee and diplomatic official, interviewed by Miranda Melcher, Skype, 28 August 2019.

Senior civilian UN member of ONUMOZ mission, interviewed by Miranda Melcher, Whatsapp and online correspondence, 13 September 2019.

US intelligence (early 1990s) and later diplomatic officer (later 1990s) for Africa, interviewed by Miranda Melcher, Skype, 20 September 2019.

Senior US diplomat in Mozambique, circa 1990s, interviewed by Miranda Melcher, Skype, 24 September 2019.

Senior US diplomat for Angolan peace process, circa 1990s, interviewed by Miranda Melcher, Skype, 7 October 2019.

Long-time Mozambique issues journalist, interviewed by Miranda Melcher, London, UK, 25 November 2019.

UN Archival Documents

Department of Peacekeeping Operations (DPKO), Office of the Under-Secretary-General (OUSG) (1992-present) fonds, S-1827-0013-0004. 'United Nations Angola Verification Mission III (UNAVEM III) - Military Adviser's trip, 2 November 1996'. 12 September 1996–1 December 1996. United Nations Archives, New York City, New York, USA.

Department of Peacekeeping Operations (DPKO), Office of the Under-Secretary-General (OUSG) (1992-present) fonds, S-1827-0016-0012. 'United Nations Observer Mission in Angola (MONUA) - security'. 26 March 1998–12 June 1998. United Nations Archives, New York City, New York, USA.

Department of Peacekeeping Operations (DPKO), Office of the Under-Secretary-General (OUSG) (1992-present) fonds, S-1827-0016-0013. 'United Nations Angola Verification Mission III (UNAVEM III) - notes for the file'. 2 October 1995–29 December 1995. United Nations Archives, New York City, New York, USA.

Department of Peacekeeping Operations (DPKO), Office of the Under-Secretary-General (OUSG) (1992-present) fonds, S-1827-0024-0007. 'Military Adviser's trips - United Nations Angola Verification Mission III (UNAVEM III) - Luanda, Angola, 2 November 1996'. 21 October 1996–2 November 1996. United Nations Archives, New York City, New York, USA.

Department of Peacekeeping Operations (DPKO), Office of the Under-Secretary-General (OUSG) (1992-present) fonds, S-1827-0024-0008. 'Military Adviser's trips - United Nations Angola Verification Mission III (UNAVEM III) - briefings'. 10 May 1995–12 May 1995. United Nations Archives, New York City, New York, USA.

Department of Peacekeeping Operations (DPKO), Office of the Under-Secretary-General (OUSG) (1992-present) fonds, S-1827-0027-0004. 'United Nations Angola Verification Mission I (UNAVEM I) - Chief Military Observer'. 20 December 1988–28 October 1991. United Nations Archives, New York City, New York, USA.

Department of Peacekeeping Operations (DPKO), Office of the Under-Secretary-General (OUSG) (1992-present) fonds, S-1828-0002-0003. 'United Nations Angola Verification Mission III (UNAVEM III) - guidelines for the Force Commander'. 19 April 1995–30 September 1995. United Nations Archives, New York City, New York, USA

Department of Peacekeeping Operations (DPKO), Office of the Under-Secretary-General (OUSG) (1992-present) fonds, S-1828-0005-0005. 'United Nations Angola Verification Mission III (UNAVEM III) - guidelines for the Force Commander'. 1 February 1993–31 March 1994. United Nations Archives, New York City, New York, USA

Department of Peacekeeping Operations (DPKO), Office of the Under-Secretary-General (OUSG) (1992-present) fonds, S-1828-0010-0002. 'Chronological file on United Nations Angola Verification Mission III (UNAVEM III)'. 12 June 1995–6 December 1995. United Nations Archives, New York City, New York, USA.

Department of Peacekeeping Operations (DPKO), Office of the Under-Secretary-General (OUSG) (1992-present) fonds, S-1828-0010-0003. 'Chronological file on United Nations Angola Verification Mission III (UNAVEM III)'. 2 June 1995–16 August 1995. United Nations Archives, New York City, New York, USA

Department of Peacekeeping Operations (DPKO), Office of the Under-Secretary-General (OUSG) (1992-present) fonds, S-1828-0010-0011. 'United Nations Observer Mission in Angola (MONUA) - directives for the Force Commander and Chief Military Observer'. 7 August 1998. United Nations Archives, New York City, New York, USA.

Department of Peacekeeping Operations (DPKO), Office of the Under-Secretary-General (OUSG) (1992-present) fonds, S-1828-0011-0012. 'United Nations Angola Verification Mission III (UNAVEM III) - Force Commander's directive for the military and police component'. 19 April 1995. United Nations Archives, New York City, New York, USA.

Department of Peacekeeping Operations (DPKO), Office of the Under-Secretary-General (OUSG) (1992-present) fonds, S-1828-0011-0013. 'United Nations Observer Mission in Angola (MONUA) - guidelines for the Force Commander'. 30 September 1995–8 May 1998. United Nations Archives, New York City, New York, USA.

Department of Peacekeeping Operations (DPKO), Office of the Under-Secretary-General (OUSG) (1992-present) fonds, S-1828-0011-0014. 'United Nations Observer Mission in Angola (MONUA) - directives for the Force Commander'. 20 May 1998–22 July 1998. United Nations Archives, New York City, New York, USA.

Department of Peacekeeping Operations (DPKO), Office of the Under-Secretary-General (OUSG) (1992-present) fonds, S-1828-0012-0009. 'United Nations Angola Verification Mission III (UNAVEM III) - miscellaneous'. 22 May 1995–1 June 1997. United Nations Archives, New York City, New York, USA.

Department of Peacekeeping Operations (DPKO), Office of the Under-Secretary-General (OUSG) (1992-present) fonds, S-1828-0012-0011. 'United Nations Operation in Mozambique (ONUMOZ) - Military Component - Observer Group Mozambique (OGMOZ) - Standard Operating Procedures (SOP)'. 1 December 1994–31 December 1994. United Nations Archives, New York City, New York, USA.

Department of Peacekeeping Operations (DPKO), Office of the Under-Secretary-General (OUSG) (1992-present) fonds, S-1828-0012-0011. 'United Nations Operation in Mozambique (ONUMOZ) - Standard Operating Procedures'. 19 March 1993–29 November 1993. United Nations Archives, New York City, New York, USA.

Department of Peacekeeping Operations (DPKO), Office of the Under-Secretary-General (OUSG) (1992-present) fonds, S-1828-0013-0001. 'United Nations Observer Mission in Angola (MONUA) - miscellaneous'. 21 August 1997–9 March 1999. United Nations Archives, New York City, New York, USA.

Department of Peacekeeping Operations (DPKO), Office of the Under-Secretary-General (OUSG) (1992-present) fonds, S-1828-0013-0002. 'United Nations Observer Mission in Angola (MONUA) - miscellaneous'. 2 July 1997–15 August 1997. United Nations Archives, New York City, New York, USA.

Department of Peacekeeping Operations (DPKO), Office of the Under-Secretary-General (OUSG) (1992-present) fonds. 'Military Adviser – Chronological File UNAVEM III'. 12 June–6 December 1995. United Nations Archives, New York City, New York, USA.

Department of Peacekeeping Operations (DPKO), Office of the Under-Secretary-General (OUSG) (1992-present) fonds. 'Military Adviser – Chronological File UNAVEM III'. 2 June–16 August 1995. United Nations Archives, New York City, New York, USA.

Department of Peacekeeping Operations (DPKO), Office of the Under-Secretary-General (OUSG) (1992-present) fonds. 'MONUA – Guidelines for the FC'. 20 May–22 July 1998. United Nations Archives, New York City, New York, USA.

Department of Peacekeeping Operations (DPKO), Office of the Under-Secretary-General (OUSG) (1992-present) fonds. 'MONUA – Guidelines for the FC'. 30 September 1995–8 May 1998. United Nations Archives, New York City, New York, USA.

Department of Peacekeeping Operations (DPKO), Office of the Under-Secretary-General (OUSG) (1992-present) fonds. 'MONUA Directives for the Force Commander and Chief Military Observer'. 7 August 1998. United Nations Archives, New York City, New York, USA.

Department of Peacekeeping Operations (DPKO), Office of the Under-Secretary-General (OUSG) (1992-present) fonds. 'ONUMOZ - Guidelines for the Force Commander'. 1 February 1993–31 March 1994. United Nations Archives, New York City, New York, USA.

Department of Peacekeeping Operations (DPKO), Office of the Under-Secretary-General (OUSG) (1992-present) fonds. 'UNAVEM I Chief Military Observer'. 20 December 1988–28 October 1991. United Nations Archives, New York City, New York, USA.

Secretary-General Boutros Bourtos-Ghali fonds, S-1086-0001. 'Background Brief for the Secretary-General - Angola [1992]'. 17 September 1992–26 September 1996. United Nations Archives, New York City, New York, USA.

Secretary-General Boutros Bourtos-Ghali fonds, S-1086-0001. 'Background Brief for the Secretary-General - Angola [1992]'. 17 September 1992–26 September 1996. United Nations Archives, New York City, New York, USA.

Secretary-General Boutros Bourtos-Ghali fonds, S-1086-0001. 'Briefing Notes for the Secretary-General's Forthcoming Visit to Copenhagen - Angola'. 17 September 1992–26 September 1996. United Nations Archives, New York City, New York, USA.

Secretary-General Boutros Bourtos-Ghali fonds, S-1086-0001. 'Note to the Secretary-General: Talking Points for your meeting with Mr. Lopo Do Nascimento, Political Advisor to the President of Angola [23 November 1993]'. 17 September 1992–26 September 1996. United Nations Archives, New York City, New York, USA.

Secretary-General Boutros Bourtos-Ghali fonds, S-1086-0001. 'Note to the Secretary-General: Your meeting with the Ambassador of Angola [21 October 1992]'. 17 September 1992–26 September 1996. United Nations Archives, New York City, New York, USA

Secretary-General Boutros Bourtos-Ghali fonds, S-1086-0001. 'Talking Points for HE Mr. Venancio de Moura FM of Angola Monday 6 February 1995 noon'. 17 September 1992–26 September 1996. United Nations Archives, New York City, New York, USA.

Secretary-General Boutros Bourtos-Ghali fonds, S-1086-0001. 'Talking Points for HE Mr. Venancio de Moura FM of Angola Thursday 26 September 1996 11.30am'. 17 September 1992–26 September 1996. United Nations Archives, New York City, New York, USA.

Secretary-General Boutros Bourtos-Ghali fonds, S-1086-0001. 'Talking Points for HE Mr. Venancio de Moura FM of Angola Wednesday 28 September 1994 6.30pm'. 17 September 1992–26 September 1996. United Nations Archives, New York City, New York, USA

Secretary-General Boutros Bourtos-Ghali fonds, S-1086-0001. 'Talking Points for SG's phone conversation with Savimbi (Feb 20)'. 17 September 1992–26 September 1996. United Nations Archives, New York City, New York, USA.

Secretary-General Boutros Bourtos-Ghali fonds, S-1086-0001. 'Talking Points for the Secretary-Generals'. Luncheon with the Foreign Ministers of the Permanent Members of the Security Council - Angola [23 Sept 1992]'. 17 September 1992–26 September 1996. United Nations Archives, New York City, New York, USA.

Secretary-General Boutros Bourtos-Ghali fonds, S-1086-0002-05. 'Trouble spots - United Nations Angola Verification Mission II (UNAVEM II) - United Nations in Angola'. 3 October 1994–28 December 1994. United Nations Archives, New York City, New York, USA

Secretary-General Boutros Bourtos-Ghali fonds, S-1086-0002-06. 'Report of the Assessment Mission to Angola 28 September 1994'. 7 July 1994–29 September 1994. United Nations Archives, New York City, New York, USA.

Secretary-General Boutros Bourtos-Ghali fonds, S-1086-0002-07. 'Meeting between President Mandela and the UN Secretary-General's Special Representative to Angola, Mr Alioune Blondin Beye, in Cape Town on 23 June 1994: South African involvement in the negotiations between the Angolan government and UNITA'. 3 January 1994–30 June 1994. United Nations Archives, New York City, New York, USA.

Secretary-General Boutros Bourtos-Ghali fonds, S-1086-0002-07. 'Notes of the Secretary-General's Meeting with the Special Representative of the Secretary-General for Angola [8 April 1994]'. 3 January 1994–30 June 1994. United Nations Archives, New York City, New York, USA.

Secretary-General Boutros Bourtos-Ghali fonds, S-1086-0002-07. 'Notes of the Secretary-General's Meeting with the Special Representative of the Secretary-General for Angola, Mr. Alioune Blondin Beye [8 May 1994]'. 3 January 1994–30 June 1994. United Nations Archives, New York City, New York, USA.

Secretary-General Boutros Bourtos-Ghali fonds, S-1086-0023-03. 'Notes of the Secretary-General's telephone conversation with the President of UNITA Dr Jonas Savimbi'. 16 October 1992–12 November 1992. United Nations Archives, New York City, New York, USA.

Secretary-General Boutros Bourtos-Ghali fonds, S-1086-0023-03. 'Ongoing Code Cable: Views of the Security Council Ad-Hoc Commission on United Nations involvement in a second round election in Angola 16 October 1992, from Anstee to UNSG'. 16 October 1992–12 November 1992. United Nations Archives, New York City, New York, USA.

Secretary-General Boutros Bourtos-Ghali fonds, S-1086-0040-08. 'Letter from President dos Santos to the UN Security Council on 6 Jan 1994'. 4 January 1994–23 December 1994. United Nations Archives, New York City, New York, USA.

Secretary-General Boutros Bourtos-Ghali fonds, S-1086-0040-08. 'Unofficial Translation 5 December 1994 [of dos Santos' letter to UNSG]'. 4 January 1994–23 December 1994. United Nations Archives, New York City, New York, USA

Secretary-General Boutros Bourtos-Ghali fonds, S-1086-0049-01. 'Delegations-Mozambique'. 6 September 1994–28 December 1994. United Nations Archives, New York City, New York, USA.

Secretary-General Boutros Bourtos-Ghali fonds, S-1086-0049-02. 'Delegations-Mozambique'. 1 May 1993–29 August 1994. United Nations Archives, New York City, New York, USA.

Secretary-General Boutros Bourtos-Ghali fonds, S-1086-0049-03. 'Delegations-Mozambique'. 14 January 1994–26 May 1994. United Nations Archives, New York City, New York, USA.

Secretary-General Boutros Bourtos-Ghali fonds, S-1086-0068-08. 'Delegations-Angola'. 1 February 1995–29 December 1995. United Nations Archives, New York City, New York, USA.

Secretary-General Boutros Bourtos-Ghali fonds, S-1086-0076-07. 'Delegations-Mozambique'. 30 December 1994–17 December 1995. United Nations Archives, New York City, New York, USA.

Secretary-General Boutros Bourtos-Ghali fonds, S-1086-0087-11. 'Movement and Concentration of UNITA military people outside control of JMPC and UNAVEM II'. 7 January 1992–30 December 1992. United Nations Archives, New York City, New York, USA.

Secretary-General Boutros Bourtos-Ghali fonds, S-1086-0087-11. 'Notes of telephone conversation: Minister Pik Botha and Dr Jonas Savimbi: Wednesday 23 December

1992, 1500 South African Time'. 7 January 1992–30 December 1992. United Nations
    Archives, New York City, New York, USA.
Secretary-General Boutros Bourtos-Ghali fonds, S-1086-0087-11. 'Protocol of
    Agreement to be followed in carrying out the terms of the Angolan peace accords'.
    7 January 1992–30 December1992. United Nations Archives, New York City, New
    York, USA.
Secretary-General Boutros Bourtos-Ghali fonds, S-1086-0087-11. 'Transcription of
    the entire speech by Jonas Savimbi made at Jamba 17 July 1992'. 7 January 1992–30
    December 1992. United Nations Archives, New York City, New York, USA.
Secretary-General Boutros Bourtos-Ghali fonds, S-1086-0096-09. 'Delegations-
    Mozambique'. 22 September 1992–31 March 1993. United Nations Archives, New York
    City, New York, USA.
Secretary-General Boutros Bourtos-Ghali fonds, S-1086-0096-11. 'Delegations-
    Mozambique'. 2 January 1992–10 September 1992. United Nations Archives, New York
    City, New York, USA.
Secretary-General Boutros Bourtos-Ghali fonds, S-1086-0114-07. 'Letter from UNITA
    to Boutrous-Boutros-Ghali 15 January 1993'. 15 January 1993–10 March 1994. United
    Nations Archives, New York City, New York, USA.
Secretary-General Boutros Bourtos-Ghali fonds, S-1086-0114-07. 'Notes on the Secretary-
    General's meeting with the President of Angola 27 June 1993'. 15 January 1993–10
    March 1994. United Nations Archives, New York City, New York, USA.
Secretary-General Boutros Bourtos-Ghali fonds, S-1086-0114-07. 'Peace Plan of the
    Angolan Government 22 September 1993'. 15 January 1993–10 March 1994. United
    Nations Archives, New York City, New York, USA.
Secretary-General Boutros Bourtos-Ghali fonds, S-1086-0124-20. 'Delegations-
    Mozambique'. 27 July 1993–31 December 1993. United Nations Archives, New York
    City, New York, USA.
Secretary-General Boutros Bourtos-Ghali fonds, S-1086-0124-21. 'Delegations-
    Mozambique'. 1 March 1993–27 July 1993. United Nations Archives, New York City,
    New York, USA.
Secretary-General Boutros Bourtos-Ghali fonds, S-1086-0124-22. 'Delegations-
    Mozambique'. 1 January 1993–31 March 1993. United Nations Archives, New York
    City, New York, USA.
Secretary-General Boutros Bourtos-Ghali fonds, S-1086-0145-09. 'Letter dated 11 July
    1996 from the permanent representative of Angola to the United Nations addressed
    to the president of the Security Council'. 12 January 1996–12 December 1996. United
    Nations Archives, New York City, New York, USA.
Secretary-General Boutros Bourtos-Ghali fonds. 'Annex VIII.B United Nations Operation
    in Mozambique Summary job descriptions for professional civilian staff'. 27 July–31
    December 1993. United Nations Archives, New York City, New York, USA.
Secretary-General Boutros Bourtos-Ghali fonds. 'Meeting with the president of RENAMO
    25 February 1993'. 4 January–31 March 1993. United Nations Archives, New York City,
    New York, USA.
Secretary-General Boutros Bourtos-Ghali fonds. 'Notes of the Secretary-General's meeting
    with his special representative for Mozambique Mr. Aldo Ajello and his special
    representative for Angola Mr. Blondin Beye [in Maputo] 17 October 1993'. 27 July–31
    July 1993. United Nations Archives, New York City, New York, USA.
Secretary-General Boutros Bourtos-Ghali fonds. 'Notes of the Secretary-General's meeting
    with International Members of the Supverision and Monitoring Commission (CSC)

established under the Rome Agreement (Mozambique) 19 October 1993'. 27 July–31 July 1993. United Nations Archives, New York City, New York, USA.

Secretary-General Boutros Bourtos-Ghali fonds. 'Notes of the Secretary-General's meeting with the President of Mozambique 18 October 1993'. 27 July–31 July 1993. United Nations Archives, New York City, New York, USA.

Secretary-General Boutros Bourtos-Ghali fonds. 'Notes of the Secretary-General's meeting with the President of Mozambique, H.E Mr. Joaquim Chissano, and the President of RENAMO, Mr. Alfonso Dhlakama'. 27 July–31 July 1993. United Nations Archives, New York City, New York, USA.

Secretary-General Boutros Bourtos-Ghali fonds. 'Notes on the Secretary-General's meeting with the Foreign Minister of Portugal 15 June 1993'. 27 July –31 July 1993. United Nations Archives, New York City, New York, USA.

Secretary-General Boutros Bourtos-Ghali fonds. 'Notes on the Secretary-General's meeting with the President of Mozambique 27 June 1993'. 27 July–31 July 1993. United Nations Archives, New York City, New York, USA.

Secretary-General Boutros Bourtos-Ghali fonds. 'Secretary-General announces major breakthrough in Mozambican peace process'. 27 July–31 July 1993. United Nations Archives, New York City, New York, USA.

Secretary-General Javier Perez de Cuellar fonds, S-1024-0004-04. 'Third Round of Quadriparite Talks on Angola/Namibia 11 July 1988'. 13 February 1988–18 November 1988. United Nations Archives, New York City, New York, USA.

Secretary-General Javier Perez de Cuellar fonds, S-1024-0004-07. 'Angola Verification Mission'. 3 March 1988–13 February 1989. United Nations Archives, New York City, New York, USA.

Secretary-General Javier Perez de Cuellar fonds, S-1024-0133-15. 'Angola'. 27 January 1987–15 December 1987. United Nations Archives, New York City, New York, USA.

Secretary-General Javier Perez de Cuellar fonds, S-1024-0133-16. 'Angola'. 3 March 1988–13 February 1989. United Nations Archives, New York City, New York, USA.

Secretary-General Javier Perez de Cuellar fonds, S-1024-0141-0004. 'Angola'. 3 March 1988–13 February 1989. United Nations Archives, New York City, New York, USA.

Secretary-General Javier Perez de Cuellar fonds, S-1024-0153-0003. 'Mozambique'. 31 December 1988–22 August 1989. United Nations Archives, New York City, New York, USA.

Secretary-General Javier Perez de Cuellar fonds, S-1024-0158-0011. 'Angola'. 3 January 1990–21 February 1991. United Nations Archives, New York City, New York, USA.

Secretary-General Javier Perez de Cuellar fonds, S-1024-0158-0012. 'Angola'. 29 January 1988–29 December 1988. United Nations Archives, New York City, New York, USA.

Secretary-General Javier Perez de Cuellar fonds, S-1024-0163-0016. 'Mozambique'. 3 January 1990–11 February 1991. United Nations Archives, New York City, New York, USA.

Secretary-General Javier Perez de Cuellar fonds, S-1024-0172-0004. 'Mozambique'. 2 October 1991–31 October 1991. United Nations Archives, New York City, New York, USA.

United Nations Department of Political and General Assembly Affairs (1972–1991) fonds, S-1808-0124-0001. 'Security Council - Angola' ?-24 March 1982. United Nations Archives, New York City, New York, USA.

Selected documents from: United Nations Observer Mission in Angola (MONUA) (1997–1999) fonds. 316 boxes. United Nations Archives, New York City, New York, USA

United Nations Observer Mission in Angola (MONUA) (1997–1999) fonds. 'Angola Peace Talks 19 November 1993–12 August 1994'. United Nations Archives, New York City, New York, USA.

United Nations Observer Mission in Angola (MONUA) (1997–1999) fonds. 'Angolan Armed Forces 17 July–22 October 1992'. United Nations Archives, New York City, New York, USA.

United Nations Observer Mission in Angola (MONUA) (1997–1999) fonds. 'Demobilisation of UNITA 11 December 1997–20 December 1998'. United Nations Archives, New York City, New York, USA.

United Nations Observer Mission in Angola (MONUA) (1997–1999) fonds. 'Demobilisation/Formation of FAA 17 July–19 August 1997'. United Nations Archives, New York City, New York, USA.

United Nations Observer Mission in Angola (MONUA) (1997–1999) fonds. 'Demobilisation/Formation of FAA 20 November 1996–6 January 1997'. United Nations Archives, New York City, New York, USA.

United Nations Observer Mission in Angola (MONUA) (1997–1999) fonds. 'FAA and UNITA meetings 10 November 1994–10 January 1995'. United Nations Archives, New York City, New York, USA

United Nations Observer Mission in Angola (MONUA) (1997–1999) fonds. 'Joint Political-Military Commission Peace Agreement Implementation 24 April–11 June 1992'. United Nations Archives, New York City, New York, USA.

United Nations Observer Mission in Angola (MONUA) (1997–1999) fonds. 'Joint Political-Military Commission/Joint Verification and Monitoring Commission 19 December 1991–25 November 1992'. United Nations Archives, New York City, New York, USA.

United Nations Observer Mission in Angola (MONUA) (1997–1999) fonds. 'Lessons learnt from UNAVEM III and MONUA 16 July 1997–3 June 1999'. United Nations Archives, New York City, New York, USA.

United Nations Observer Mission in Angola (MONUA) (1997–1999) fonds. 'Meeting of the Military Staffs of the Government, UNITA, and UNAVEM II following the initialling of the Lusaka protocols 4 Oct 1994'. United Nations Archives, New York City, New York, USA.

United Nations Observer Mission in Angola (MONUA) (1997–1999) fonds. 'Peace talks in Abidjan 21 January–21 September 1993'. United Nations Archives, New York City, New York, USA.

United Nations Observer Mission in Angola (MONUA) (1997–1999) fonds. 'Security 26 March – 12 June 1998'. United Nations Archives, New York City, New York, USA.

United Nations Observer Mission in Angola (MONUA) (1997–1999) fonds. 'Status of the UNITA president 2 January 1997–23 July 1998'. United Nations Archives, New York City, New York, USA.

United Nations Observer Mission in Angola (MONUA) (1997–1999) fonds. 'UNITA 15 December 1997–19 February 1999'. United Nations Archives, New York City, New York, USA.

United Nations Observer Mission in Angola (MONUA) (1997–1999) fonds. 'UNITA 17 March 1997–17 January 1998'. United Nations Archives, New York City, New York, USA.

United Nations Observer Mission in Angola (MONUA) (1997–1999) fonds. 'UNITA 2 April–29 May 1998'. United Nations Archives, New York City, New York, USA.

United Nations Observer Mission in Angola (MONUA) (1997–1999) fonds. 'UNITA 24 March – 8 June 1998'. United Nations Archives, New York City, New York, USA.

Selected documents from: United Nations Operation in Mozambique (ONUMOZ) (1992–1994) fonds. 149 boxes. United Nations Archives, New York City, New York, USA.

United Nations Operation in Mozambique (ONUMOZ) (1992–1994) fonds. "'Demobilisation – Certain Observations" [from Ajello to Annan 22 January 1994]'. United Nations Archives, New York City, New York, USA.

United Nations Operation in Mozambique (ONUMOZ) (1992–1994) fonds. 'Afonso Dhlakama 25 October 1993–3 October 1994'. United Nations Archives, New York City, New York, USA.

United Nations Operation in Mozambique (ONUMOZ) (1992–1994) fonds. 'Armed Forces for the Defence of Mozambique 22 November 1993–8 November 1994'. United Nations Archives, New York City, New York, USA.

United Nations Operation in Mozambique (ONUMOZ) (1992–1994) fonds. 'Assembly Areas 1-22 November 1993'. United Nations Archives, New York City, New York, USA.

United Nations Operation in Mozambique (ONUMOZ) (1992–1994) fonds. 'Assembly Areas 16 February–23 August 1994 - "Issues raised by soldiers in the assembly areas"'. United Nations Archives, New York City, New York, USA.

United Nations Operation in Mozambique (ONUMOZ) (1992–1994) fonds. 'Assembly Areas 16 February–23 August 1994'. United Nations Archives, New York City, New York, USA.

United Nations Operation in Mozambique (ONUMOZ) (1992–1994) fonds. 'Assembly Areas 22 December 1993-15 February 1994'. United Nations Archives, New York City, New York, USA.

United Nations Operation in Mozambique (ONUMOZ) (1992–1994) fonds. 'Assembly Areas 23 November 1993–17 December 1993'. United Nations Archives, New York City, New York, USA.

United Nations Operation in Mozambique (ONUMOZ) (1992–1994) fonds. 'Assembly Areas 24 August–28 October 1993'. United Nations Archives, New York City, New York, USA.

United Nations Operation in Mozambique (ONUMOZ) (1992–1994) fonds. 'Assembly Areas Policies and Directives 29 October 1993–27 January 1994'. United Nations Archives, New York City, New York, USA.

United Nations Operation in Mozambique (ONUMOZ) (1992–1994) fonds. 'Cease-fire Commission 3 January–16 February 1994'. United Nations Archives, New York City, New York, USA.

United Nations Operation in Mozambique (ONUMOZ) (1992–1994) fonds. 'Cease-fire Commission 3 October–10 November 1994'. United Nations Archives, New York City, New York, USA.

United Nations Operation in Mozambique (ONUMOZ) (1992–1994) fonds. 'Civilian Police 1 July–22 August 1994'. United Nations Archives, New York City, New York, USA.

United Nations Operation in Mozambique (ONUMOZ) (1992–1994) fonds. 'Demobilisation – Verification Activities 4 August–4 November 1994'. United Nations Archives, New York City, New York, USA.

United Nations Operation in Mozambique (ONUMOZ) (1992–1994) fonds. 'Demobilisation – Verification Activities 6 September–20 October 1994'. United Nations Archives, New York City, New York, USA.

United Nations Operation in Mozambique (ONUMOZ) (1992–1994) fonds. 'Demobilisation 1 December 1993–9 February 1994 - "Demobilisation: focus of the Rome Conference"'. United Nations Archives, New York City, New York, USA.

United Nations Operation in Mozambique (ONUMOZ) (1992–1994) fonds. 'Demobilisation 1 December 1993–9 February 1994'. United Nations Archives, New York City, New York, USA.

United Nations Operation in Mozambique (ONUMOZ) (1992–1994) fonds. 'Demobilisation 10 February–10 May 1994'. United Nations Archives, New York City, New York, USA.

United Nations Operation in Mozambique (ONUMOZ) (1992–1994) fonds. 'Demobilisation 18 September 1992–29 November 1993'. United Nations Archives, New York City, New York, USA.

United Nations Operation in Mozambique (ONUMOZ) (1992–1994) fonds. 'Documentation of Demobilised Soldiers 11 January 1993–17 August 1994'. United Nations Archives, New York City, New York, USA.

United Nations Operation in Mozambique (ONUMOZ) (1992–1994) fonds. 'Documentation of Demobilised Soldiers 15 January 1993–3 November 1994'. United Nations Archives, New York City, New York, USA.

United Nations Operation in Mozambique (ONUMOZ) (1992–1994) fonds. 'Information and Social Reintegration Programme 29 August–8 November 1994'. United Nations Archives, New York City, New York, USA.

United Nations Operation in Mozambique (ONUMOZ) (1992–1994) fonds. 'Information and Social Reintegration Programme 5 August 1993–19 August 1993'. United Nations Archives, New York City, New York, USA.

United Nations Operation in Mozambique (ONUMOZ) (1992–1994) fonds. 'Joint Commission for the Formation of the Mozambican Defence Force (CCFADM) 11–20 August 1994'. United Nations Archives, New York City, New York, USA.

United Nations Operation in Mozambique (ONUMOZ) (1992–1994) fonds. 'Joint Commission for the Formation of the Mozambican Defence Force (CCFADM) 13–19 July 1994'. United Nations Archives, New York City, New York, USA.

United Nations Operation in Mozambique (ONUMOZ) (1992–1994) fonds. 'Joint Commission for the Formation of the Mozambican Defence Force (CCFADM) 15 June–4 July 1994'. United Nations Archives, New York City, New York, USA.

United Nations Operation in Mozambique (ONUMOZ) (1992–1994) fonds. 'Joint Commission for the Formation of the Mozambican Defence Force (CCFADM) 16 November 1993–15 March 1994'. United Nations Archives, New York City, New York, USA.

United Nations Operation in Mozambique (ONUMOZ) (1992–1994) fonds. 'Joint Commission for the Formation of the Mozambican Defence Force (CCFADM) 2 March–9 December 1994'. United Nations Archives, New York City, New York, USA.

United Nations Operation in Mozambique (ONUMOZ) (1992–1994) fonds. 'Joint Commission for the Formation of the Mozambican Defence Force (CCFADM) 2–30 September 1994'. United Nations Archives, New York City, New York, USA.

United Nations Operation in Mozambique (ONUMOZ) (1992–1994) fonds. 'Joint Commission for the Formation of the Mozambican Defence Force (CCFADM) 20 July–4 August 1994'. United Nations Archives, New York City, New York, USA.

United Nations Operation in Mozambique (ONUMOZ) (1992–1994) fonds. 'Joint Commission for the Formation of the Mozambican Defence Force (CCFADM) 22–31 August 1994'. United Nations Archives, New York City, New York, USA.

United Nations Operation in Mozambique (ONUMOZ) (1992–1994) fonds. 'Joint Commission for the Formation of the Mozambican Defence Force (CCFADM)

24 October–25 November 1994'. United Nations Archives, New York City, New York, USA.

United Nations Operation in Mozambique (ONUMOZ) (1992–1994) fonds. 'Joint Commission for the Formation of the Mozambican Defence Force (CCFADM) 25 May–14 June 1994'. United Nations Archives, New York City, New York, USA.

United Nations Operation in Mozambique (ONUMOZ) (1992–1994) fonds. 'Joint Commission for the Formation of the Mozambican Defence Force (CCFADM) 25 November 1994'. United Nations Archives, New York City, New York, USA.

United Nations Operation in Mozambique (ONUMOZ) (1992–1994) fonds. 'Joint Commission for the Formation of the Mozambican Defence Force (CCFADM) 26 July–3 Aug 1994'. United Nations Archives, New York City, New York, USA.

United Nations Operation in Mozambique (ONUMOZ) (1992–1994) fonds. 'Joint Commission for the Formation of the Mozambican Defence Force (CCFADM) 30 November–9 December 1994'. United Nations Archives, New York City, New York, USA.

United Nations Operation in Mozambique (ONUMOZ) (1992–1994) fonds. 'Joint Commission for the Formation of the Mozambican Defence Force (CCFADM) 4–10 August 1994'. United Nations Archives, New York City, New York, USA.

United Nations Operation in Mozambique (ONUMOZ) (1992–1994) fonds. 'Joint Commission for the Formation of the Mozambican Defence Force (CCFADM) 5–24 October 1994'. United Nations Archives, New York City, New York, USA.

United Nations Operation in Mozambique (ONUMOZ) (1992–1994) fonds. 'Joint Commission for the Formation of the Mozambican Defence Force (CCFADM) 6 April–24 May 1994'. United Nations Archives, New York City, New York, USA.

United Nations Operation in Mozambique (ONUMOZ) (1992–1994) fonds. 'Joint Commission for the Formation of the Mozambican Defence Force (CCFADM) 6 September–4 October 1994'. United Nations Archives, New York City, New York, USA.

United Nations Operation in Mozambique (ONUMOZ) (1992–1994) fonds. 'Joint Commission for the Formation of the Mozambican Defence Force (CCFADM) 6–12 July 1994'. United Nations Archives, New York City, New York, USA.

United Nations Operation in Mozambique (ONUMOZ) (1992–1994) fonds. 'Joint Commission for the Formation of the Mozambican Defence Force (CCFADM) 8 August–3 October 1994'. United Nations Archives, New York City, New York, USA.

United Nations Operation in Mozambique (ONUMOZ) (1992–1994) fonds. 'Joint Commission for the Formation of the Mozambican Defence Forces 10 May–29 July 1994'. United Nations Archives, New York City, New York, USA.

United Nations Operation in Mozambique (ONUMOZ) (1992–1994) fonds. 'Joint Commission for the Formation of the Mozambican Defence Forces 13 August–25 November 1993'. United Nations Archives, New York City, New York, USA.

United Nations Operation in Mozambique (ONUMOZ) (1992–1994) fonds. 'Joint Commission for the Formation of the Mozambican Defence Forces 14 April–12 May 1994'. United Nations Archives, New York City, New York, USA.

United Nations Operation in Mozambique (ONUMOZ) (1992–1994) fonds. 'Joint Commission for the Formation of the Mozambican Defence Forces 29 September 1993–17 January 1994'. United Nations Archives, New York City, New York, USA.

United Nations Operation in Mozambique (ONUMOZ) (1992–1994) fonds. 'Joint Commission for the Formation of the Mozambican Defence Forces 30 November 1993–28 January 1994'. United Nations Archives, New York City, New York, USA.

United Nations Operation in Mozambique (ONUMOZ) (1992–1994) fonds. 'Joint Commission for the Formation of the Mozambican Defence Forces 4 February–13 April 1994'. United Nations Archives, New York City, New York, USA.

United Nations Operation in Mozambique (ONUMOZ) (1992–1994) fonds. 'Joint Commission for the Formation of the Mozambican Defence Forces 1 August–25 October 1994'. United Nations Archives, New York City, New York, USA.

United Nations Operation in Mozambique (ONUMOZ) (1992–1994) fonds. 'Military 1 December 1993–25 May 1994'. United Nations Archives, New York City, New York, USA.

United Nations Operation in Mozambique (ONUMOZ) (1992–1994) fonds. 'Military 17 September–30 November 1993'. United Nations Archives, New York City, New York, USA.

United Nations Operation in Mozambique (ONUMOZ) (1992–1994) fonds. 'Military 2 December 1993–20 May 1994'. United Nations Archives, New York City, New York, USA.

United Nations Operation in Mozambique (ONUMOZ) (1992–1994) fonds. 'Military 2 June–11 November 1994'. United Nations Archives, New York City, New York, USA.

United Nations Operation in Mozambique (ONUMOZ) (1992–1994) fonds. 'Military 20 September–30 November 1993'. United Nations Archives, New York City, New York, USA.

United Nations Operation in Mozambique (ONUMOZ) (1992–1994) fonds. 'Military 21 October 1993–2 May 1994'. United Nations Archives, New York City, New York, USA.

United Nations Operation in Mozambique (ONUMOZ) (1992–1994) fonds. 'Military 6 June–7 November 1994'. United Nations Archives, New York City, New York, USA.

United Nations Operation in Mozambique (ONUMOZ) (1992–1994) fonds. 'Military Component Observer Group 1-31 December 1994'. United Nations Archives, New York City, New York, USA.

United Nations Operation in Mozambique (ONUMOZ) (1992–1994) fonds. 'Military Observers 15 November–29 September 1993'. United Nations Archives, New York City, New York, USA.

United Nations Operation in Mozambique (ONUMOZ) (1992–1994) fonds. 'Military Observers 28 September 1993–12 October 1994'. United Nations Archives, New York City, New York, USA.

United Nations Operation in Mozambique (ONUMOZ) (1992–1994) fonds. 'Mozambican National Resistance RENAMO 30 May–20 November 1994'. United Nations Archives, New York City, New York, USA.

United Nations Operation in Mozambique (ONUMOZ) (1992–1994) fonds. 'Mozambican National Resistance RENAMO 7 January 1993–27 April 1994'. United Nations Archives, New York City, New York, USA.

United Nations Operation in Mozambique (ONUMOZ) (1992–1994) fonds. 'Paramilitary Disbandment Team 22 December 1993–3 March 1994'. United Nations Archives, New York City, New York, USA.

United Nations Operation in Mozambique (ONUMOZ) (1992–1994) fonds. 'Paramilitary Forces Disbandment 14 January–2 September 1994'. United Nations Archives, New York City, New York, USA.

United Nations Operation in Mozambique (ONUMOZ) (1992–1994) fonds. 'Peacekeeping 11 October 1993–28 April 1994'. United Nations Archives, New York City, New York, USA.

United Nations Operation in Mozambique (ONUMOZ) (1992–1994) fonds.
'Peacekeeping 2 May –12 October 1994'. United Nations Archives, New York City, New York, USA.

United Nations Operation in Mozambique (ONUMOZ) (1992–1994) fonds.
'Reintegration 1–17 November 1993'. United Nations Archives, New York City, New York, USA.

United Nations Operation in Mozambique (ONUMOZ) (1992–1994) fonds.
'Reintegration 11 July–19 November 1993'. United Nations Archives, New York City, New York, USA.

United Nations Operation in Mozambique (ONUMOZ) (1992–1994) fonds.
'Reintegration 15 December 1993'. United Nations Archives, New York City, New York, USA.

United Nations Operation in Mozambique (ONUMOZ) (1992–1994) fonds.
'Reintegration 22 November 1993–12 January 1994'. United Nations Archives, New York City, New York, USA.

United Nations Operation in Mozambique (ONUMOZ) (1992–1994) fonds.
'Reintegration 24 Janusry–15 August 1994'. United Nations Archives, New York City, New York, USA.

United Nations Operation in Mozambique (ONUMOZ) (1992–1994) fonds.
'Reintegration 29 November 1992–3 January 1994'. United Nations Archives, New York City, New York, USA.

United Nations Operation in Mozambique (ONUMOZ) (1992–1994) fonds.
'Reintegration Commission CORE 31 15 October 1993–18 March 1994'. United Nations Archives, New York City, New York, USA.

United Nations Operation in Mozambique (ONUMOZ) (1992–1994) fonds.
'Reintegration Commission CORE 31 March–20 July 1994'. United Nations Archives, New York City, New York, USA.

United Nations Operation in Mozambique (ONUMOZ) (1992–1994) fonds.
'Reintegration Support Scheme 1 Jan – 24 June 1994'. United Nations Archives, New York City, New York, USA.

United Nations Operation in Mozambique (ONUMOZ) (1992–1994) fonds.
'Reintegration Support Scheme 14 March 1994–30 November 1994'. United Nations Archives, New York City, New York, USA.

United Nations Operation in Mozambique (ONUMOZ) (1992–1994) fonds.
'Reintegration Support Scheme 16 December 1993–11 March 1994'. United Nations Archives, New York City, New York, USA.

United Nations Operation in Mozambique (ONUMOZ) (1992–1994) fonds. 'Report 14–25 October 1994'. United Nations Archives, New York City, New York, USA.

United Nations Operation in Mozambique (ONUMOZ) (1992–1994) fonds. 'Requests for Assistance 19 April–21 November 1994'. United Nations Archives, New York City, New York, USA.

United Nations Operation in Mozambique (ONUMOZ) (1992–1994) fonds. 'Resettlement 2 June 1993–15 April 1994'. United Nations Archives, New York City, New York, USA.

United Nations Operation in Mozambique (ONUMOZ) (1992–1994) fonds. 'Rules of Conduct and Procedures 20 May–22 August 1994'. United Nations Archives, New York City, New York, USA.

United Nations Operation in Mozambique (ONUMOZ) (1992–1994) fonds. 'Status of Forces Agreement 19 April 1993–16 May 1994'. United Nations Archives, New York City, New York, USA.

United Nations Operation in Mozambique (ONUMOZ) (1992–1994) fonds. 'Supervision and Monitoring Commission 1 October 1993–14 January 1994'. United Nations Archives, New York City, New York, USA.

United Nations Operation in Mozambique (ONUMOZ) (1992–1994) fonds. 'Supervision and Monitoring Commission 18 August–20 September 1993'. United Nations Archives, New York City, New York, USA.

United Nations Operation in Mozambique (ONUMOZ) (1992–1994) fonds. 'Supervision and Monitoring Commission 18 January–12 March 1994'. United Nations Archives, New York City, New York, USA.

United Nations Operation in Mozambique (ONUMOZ) (1992–1994) fonds. 'Technical Unit for Demobilisation 2 February–12 December 1994'. United Nations Archives, New York City, New York, USA.

United Nations Operation in Mozambique (ONUMOZ) (1992–1994) fonds. 'Visit of the Secretary-General to Mozambique 1–18 October 1993'. United Nations Archives, New York City, New York, USA.

United Nations Operation in Mozambique (ONUMOZ) (1992–1994) fonds. 'Visit of the Secretary-General to Mozambique 24 September–31 December 1993'. United Nations Archives, New York City, New York, USA.

Peace Treaties

'Alvor Accord'. MPLA, UNITA, FNLA, Portugal. November 1975. Alvor, Portugal.

'The Bicesse Accords'. MPLA and UNITA. May 1991. Bicesse, Portugal.

'Rome Accords'. FRELIMO and RENAMO. October 1992. Rome, Italy.

'Lusaka Protocol'. MPLA and UNITA. November 1994. Lusaka, Zambia.

'Luena Memorandum of Understanding'. MPLA and UNITA. April 2002. Luena, Angola.

Secondary Literature

Aall, Pamela R. and Chester A. Crocker. *The Fabric of Peace in Africa: Looking beyond the State*. Waterloo, Ontario: CIGI Press, 2017.

Adekanye, J. Bayo. 'Arms and Reconstruction in Post-Conflict Societies'. *Journal of Peace Research* 34, no. 3 (1997): 359–66. https://doi.org/10.1177/0022343397034003012.

Aid, Christian. 'Mozambique: Weapons of Reconstruction - Mozambique'. *ReliefWeb*, February 2005. https://reliefweb.int/report/mozambique/mozambique-weapons-reconstruction (accessed 5 July 2020).

Alao, Abiodun. *Brothers at War: Dissidence and Rebellion in Southern Africa*. London: British Academic, 1994.

Albin, C., and D. Druckman. 'Equality Matters: Negotiating an End to Civil Wars'. *The Journal of Conflict Resolution* 56, no. 2 (2012): 155–82.

Alden, Chris. *Mozambique and the Construction of the New African State: From Negotiations to Nation Building*. New York: Palgrave, 2001.

Alden, Chris. 'Making Old Soldiers Fade Away: Lessons from the Reintegration of Demobilized Soldiers in Mozambique'. *Security Dialogue* 33, no. 3 (2002): 341–56. https://doi.org/10.1177/0967010602033003008.

Aldrich, Robert and Andreas Stucki. *The Colonial World: A History of European Empires, 1780s to the Present*. London: Bloomsbury Academic, 2023.

Ali, Taisier Mohamed Ahmed and Robert O. Matthews. *Durable Peace: Challenges for Peacebuilding in Africa*. Toronto: University of Toronto Press, 2004.

Andersen, Louise, Bjørn Møller, and Finn Stepputat. *Fragile States and Insecure People?: Violence, Security, and Statehood in the Twenty-First Century*. New York: Palgrave MacMillan, 2007.

Andersson, Hilary. *Mozambique: A War against the People*. London: Palgrave Macmillan, 2014.

Aning, Kwesi and Joseph Siegle. 'Assessing Attitudes of African Security Professionals – Africa Center'. *Africa Center for Strategic Studies*, 26 February 2020. https://africacenter .org/publication/assessing-attitudes-next-generation-african-security-sector -professionals/ (accessed 20 February 2020).

Anstee, Margaret Joan. *Orphan of the Cold War: The Inside Story of the Collapse of the Angolan Peace Process, 1992–93*. New York: Macmillan Press, 1996.

Anstee, Margaret Joan. 'The Fight Goes On'. *The World Today* 54, no. 10 (October 1998): 256–58.

Arjona, Ana, Nelson Kasfir, and Zachariah Cherian Mampilly. *Rebel Governance in Civil War*. Cambridge University Press, 2017.

Autesserre, Séverine. *Peaceland: Conflict Resolution and the Everyday Politics Of International Intervention*. Cambridge University Press, 2018.

Axelson, Eric Victor. *Portuguese in South-East Africa 1600–1700*. Johannesburg: Witwatersrand University Press, 1969.

Azimi, Nassrine and Chang Li Lin. *The Nexus between Peacekeeping and Peace-Building: Debriefing and Lessons: Report of the 1999 Singapore Conference*. Kluwer Law International, 2000.

Bakiner, Onur. 'Why Do Peace Negotiations Succeed or Fail? Legal Commitment, Transparency, and Inclusion during Peace Negotiations in Colombia (2012–2016) and Turkey (2012–2015)'. *Negotiation Journal* 35, no. 4 (2019): 471–513. https://doi.org/10 .1111/nejo.12301.

Ball, Nicole. 'Democratic Governance and the Security Sector in Conflict-Affected Countries'. In *Governance in Post-Conflict Societies: Rebuilding Fragile States*, edited by Derick W. Brinkerhoff. Oxfordshire: Routledge, 2007.

Bank, World. *Demobilization and Reintegration of Military Personnel in Africa: The Evidence from Seven Country Case Studies*. World Bank Working Paper, 1993.

Barnett, Don. *The Making of a Middle Cadre: The Story of Rui De Pinto*. Richmond: LSM Press, 1973.

Barnett, D. B. and Roy Harvey. *The Revolution in Angola: MPLA, Life Histories and Documents*. Indianapolis: Bobbs-Merrill, 1972.

Batchelor, Peter, Kees Kingma, and Guy Lamb. *Demilitarisation and Peace-Building in Southern Africa*. Aldershot, Hants: Ashgate, 2004.

Beardsley, Kyle C., David M. Quinn, Bidisha Biswas, and Jonathan Wilkenfeld. 'Mediation Style and Crisis Outcomes'. *Journal of Conflict Resolution* 50, no. 1 (2006): 58–86. https://doi.org/10.1177/0022002705282862.

Beaumont, Peter. 'From Iraq to Yemen: The Grubby Business of Counting the War Dead'. *The Guardian*, 6 February 2019. https://www.theguardian.com/global-development /2019/feb/06/from-iraq-to-yemen-counting-the-cost-of-war-is-an-inexact-science.

Bekoe, Dorina. *Implementing Peace Agreements: Lessons from Mozambique, Angola, and Liberia*. Palgrave Macmillan, 2016.

Bellamy, Alex J., Stuart Griffin, and Paul Williams. *Understanding Peacekeeping*. Cambridge: Polity, 2011.

Bellamy, Alex J., and Charles T. Hunt. 'Twenty-First Century UN Peace Operations: Protection, Force and the Changing Security Environment'. *International Affairs* 91, no. 6 (2015): 1277–98. https://doi.org/10.1111/1468-2346.12456.

Bennett, Andrew and Jeffrey T. Checkel. *Process Tracing: From Metaphor to Analytic Tool*. Cambridge University Press, 2017.

Berdal, Mats R. *Disarmament and Demobilisation after Civil Wars: Arms, Soldiers and the Termination of Armed Conflicts*. Oxford: Oxford University Press, 1996.

Berdal, Mats R. 'The Security Council and Peacekeeping'. In *The United Nations Security Council and War : The Evolution of Thought and Practice since 1945*, edited by Vaughan Lowe, Adam Roberts, Jennifer Welsh, and Dominik Zaum. Oxford: Oxford University Press, 2006.

Berdal, Mats R. *United Nations Interventionism: 1991–2004*. Cambridge: Cambridge University Press, 2007.

Berdal, Mats R. *Reintegrating Armed Groups after Conflict: Politics, Violence and Transition*. Abingdon: Routledge, 2009.

Berdal, Mats R. and Astri Suhrke. *The Peace in between: Post-War Violence and Peacebuilding*. Routledge, 2012.

Bergh, Lucia Van Den. 'Why Peace Worked: Mozambicans Look Back'. *AWEPA*, 1 August 2013. https://issuu.com/awepainternationale/docs/why_peace_worked_-_mozambicans_look (accessed 5 July 2020).

Berman, Eric. *Managing Arms in Peace Processes: Mozambique: Disarmament and Conflict Resolution Project*. New York: United Nations, 1996.

Billon, Philippe Le. *Fuelling War - Natural Resources and Armed Conflicts*. Taylor & Francis Ltd, 2017.

Bleck, Jaimie and Nicolas Walle. *Electoral Politics in Africa since 1990 Continuity in Change*. Cambridge: Cambridge University Press, 2019.

Bove, Vincenzo. *Composing Peace: Mission Composition in UN Peacekeeping*. Oxford University Press, 2020.

Branch, Adam. 'Against Humanitarian Impunity: Rethinking Responsibility for Displacement and Disaster in Northern Uganda'. *Journal of Intervention and Statebuilding* 13, no. 1 (2006): 151–73.

Breslin, J. William. 'Breaking Away from Subtle Biases'. *Negotiation Journal* 5, no. 3 (1989): 219–22. https://doi.org/10.1111/j.1571-9979.1989.tb00518.x.

Bridgland, Fred. *Jonas Savimbi: A Key to Africa*. Sevenoaks: Coronet, 1988.

Brittain, Victoria. *The Death of Dignity: Angolas Civil War*. Pluto Press, 1998.

Bruck, T. 'Mozambique: The Economic Effects of War'. In *War and Underdevelopment: Volume 2: Country Experiences*, edited by Frances Stewart and Valpy Fitzgerald. Oxford: Oxford University Press, 2001.

Brzoska, Michael. 'Introduction: Criteria for Evaluating Post-Conflict Reconstruction and Security Sector Reform in Peace Support Operations'. *International Peacekeeping* 13, no. 1 (2006): 1–13. https://doi.org/10.1080/13533310500424603.

Byman, Daniel, D. A. Brannan, William Rosenau, Bruce Hoffman, and Peter Chalk. *Trends in Outside Support for Insurgent Movements*. Santa Monica, CA: Rand, 2001.

Cabrita, Joao M. *Mozambique: The Tortuous Road to Democracy*. Palgrave, 2000.

Campbell, Susanna P., Michael G. Findley, and Kyosuke Kikuta. 'An Ontology of Peace: Landscapes of Conflict and Cooperation with Application to Colombia'. *International Studies Review* 19, no. 1 (1 March 2017): 92–113. https://doi.org/10.1093/isr/vix005.

Caplan, Richard. *Measuring Peace: Principles, Practices, and Politics*. Oxford: Oxford University Press, 2019.

Cederman, Lars-Erik. 'Why Do Ethnic Groups Rebel? New Data And Analysis'. *World Politics*, n.d., 87–119.

Chabal, Patrick and Nuno Vidal. *Angola: The Weight of History*. New York: Columbia University Press, 2008.

Chan, Stephen and Moises Vanancio. *War and Peace in Mozambique*. Palgrave Macmillan, 2014.

Cherry, Janet. *Spear of the Nation: South Africas Liberation Army, 1960s - 1980s*. Ohio University, Press, 2011.

Cilliers, J. C. and C. Dietrich. *Angola's War Economy: The Role of Oil and Diamonds*. Institute for Security Studies, 2001. https://issafrica.s3.amazonaws.com/site/uploads /2000-11-01-book-angolas-war-economy.pdf (accessed 20 July 2020).

Cohen, Herman J. *Intervening in Africa: Superpower Peacemaking in a Troubled Continent*. Basingstoke: Macmillan, 2001.

Cohen, Raymond. 'Resolving Conflict Across Languages'. *Negotiation Journal* 17, no. 1 (2001): 17–34. https://doi.org/10.1111/j.1571-9979.2001.tb00224.x.

Collier, Paul. 'Greed and Grievance In Civil War'. *Oxford Economic Papers*, n.d., 563–95.

Collier, Paul. 'Demobilization and Insecurity: A Study in the Economics of the Transition from War to Peace'. *Journal of International Development* 6, no. 3 (1994): 343–51. https://doi.org/10.1002/jid.3380060308.

Collier, Paul. *Breaking the Conflict Trap*. World Bank, 2003. https://doi.org/10.1596/0-8213 -5481-7.

Collier, Paul. 'On the Duration of Civil War'. *Journal of Peace Research j Peace Res* 41, no. 3 (2004): 253–73. https://doi.org/10.1177/0022343304043769.

Collier, Paul, Anke Hoeffler, and Mans Soderbom. 'Post-Conflict Risks'. *Journal of Peace Research*, 2008. https://doi.org/10.1177/0022343308091356.

Collier, Paul and Nicholas Sambanis. *Understanding Civil War: Evidence and Analysis*. World Bank, 2005.

Conciliation Resources. 'From Military Peace to Social Justice? The Angolan Peace Process: Policy Brief'. *Conciliation Resources*, 1 October 2004. https://www.c-r.org/resource/ military-peace-social-justice-angolan-peace-process-policy-brief (accessed 20 July 2020).

Conciliation Resources. 'The Angolan Peace Process: Policy Brief. From Military Peace to Social Justice?', 1 October 2004. https://www.c-r.org/resource/military-peace-social -justice-angolan-peace-process-policy-brief (accessed 20 July 2020).

Corinne, Bara, Annekatrin Deglow, and Sebastian van Baalen. 'Civil War Recurrence and Postwar Violence: Toward an Integrated Research Agenda', 2021. https://journals .sagepub.com/doi/10.1177/13540661211006443.

Costy, Alexander. 'From Civil War to Civil Society?: Aid, NGOs and Hegemonic Construction in Mozambique by Alexander Costy in 2002 by University of Michigan, in Ann Arbor, Michigan, USA', 2000.

Cramer, Christopher. *Civil War Is Not a Stupid Thing: Accounting for Violence in Developing Countries*. London: Hurst & Company, 2006.

Crocker, Chester A. *High Noon in Southern Africa: Making Peace in a Rough Neighborhood*. Jonathan Ball, 1994.

Crocker, Chester A. *International Negotiation and Mediation in Violent Conflict: The Changing Context of Peacemaking*. Routledge, 2018.

Crocker, Chester A. and Fen Osler Hampson. 'Making Peace Settlements Work'. *Foreign Policy*, no. 104 (1996): 54–71.

Cunningham, David. 'Blocking Resolution: How External States Can Prolong Civil Wars'. *Journal of Peace Research* 47, no. 2 (March 2010): 115–27.

Daniels, Lesley-Ann. 'How and When Amnesty during Conflict Affects Conflict Termination'. *Journal of Conflict Resolution*, 25 March 2020, 002200272090988. https://doi.org/10.1177/0022002720909884.

Darby, John. *The Effects of Violence on Peace Processes*. Washington, DC: United States Institute of Peace Press, 2001.

Darby, John and Roger Mac Ginty. *Contemporary Peace Making: Conflict, Violence and Peace Processes*. Palgrave Macmillan, 2002.

Darch, Colin. *The Mozambican Conflict and the Peace Process in Historical Perspective: A Success Story Gone Wrong?* Maputo, Mozambique: Friedrich-Ebert-Stiftung Mozambique, 2018.

Davidson, Nigel. *The Lion That Didnt Roar: Can the Kimberley Process Stop the Blood Diamonds Trade?* Acton, ACT: ANU Press, 2016.

Daxecker, Ursula E. 'The Cost of Exposing Cheating: International Election Monitoring, Fraud, and Post-Election Violence in Africa'. *Journal of Peace Research* 49, no. 4 (July 2012): 503–16.

Dayal, Anjali. 'Research & Writing'. *Anjali Dayal*, 10 August 2020. https://anjali-dayal .squarespace.com/research (accessed 10 August 2020).

'DDR 2009: Analysis of the World's Disarmament, Demobilization, and Reintegration Programs in 2008'. *School for a Culture of Peace*, July 2009, 60–1.

Decalo, Samuel. 'Modalities of Civil-Military Stability in Africa'. *The Journal of Modern African Studies* 27, no. 4 (1989): 547–78.

'Demobilization, and Reintegration of Ex-Combatants'. *Beyond Intractability*, n.d. www .beyondintractability.org/essay/demobilization/.

Denoon, Donald and Balam Nyeko. *Southern Africa Since 1800*. London: Longman, 1992.

Derouen, Karl, Mark J. Ferguson, Samuel Norton, Young Hwan Park, Jenna Lea, and Ashley Streat-Bartlett. 'Civil War Peace Agreement Implementation and State Capacity'. *Journal of Peace Research* 47, no. 3 (2010): 333–46. https://doi.org/10.1177/0022343310362169.

Diehl, Paul F. and Daniel Druckman. 'Not the Same Old Way: Trends in Peace Operations'. *The Brown Journal of World Affairs* 24, no. 1 (2018): 249–60.

Dobbins, James. *The UN's Role in Nation-Building: From the Congo to Iraq*. RAND Corporation, 2005.

Doss, Alan. *A Peacekeeper in Africa: Learning from UN Interventions in Other Peoples Wars*. Boulder, CO: Lynne Rienner Publishers, 2020.

Doyle, Michael W. and Nicholas Sambanis. *Making War and Building Peace: United Nations Peace Operations*. Princeton University Press, 2006.

Dudouet, Véronique. *Mediating Peace with Proscribed Armed Groups*. USIP, 2010.

Dudouet, Véronique. *Mediating Peace with Proscribed Armed Groups*. United States Institute of Peace, 2013. https://www.usip.org/publications/2010/06/mediating-peace -proscribed-armed-groups (accessed 22 January 2018).

Duncan, Walter Raymond. *Soviet Policy in the Third World*. Pergamon Press, 1980.

Durch, William J. *The Evolution of UN Peacekeeping: Case Studies and Comparative Analysis*. Chippenham: A. Rowe, 1995.

Durch, William J. *U.N. Peacekeeping. American Politics, and the Uncivil Wars of the 1990s*. New York: St. Martins Press, 1997.

Duursma, Allard. 'African Solutions to African Challenges: The Role of Legitimacy in Mediating Civil Wars in Africa'. *International Organization* 74, no. 2 (April 2020): 295–330.

Dzinesa, Gwinyayi A. 'Postconflict Disarmament, Demobilization, and Reintegration of Former Combatants in Southern Africa'. *International Studies Perspectives* 8, no. 1 (February 2007). https://doi.org/10.1111/j.1528-3585.2007.00270.x.

Eichensehr, Kristen and W.Michael Reisman. *Stopping Wars and Making Peace Studies in International Intervention*. Nijhoff, 2009.

Emerson, Stephen A. *The Battle for Mozambique the Frelimo-Renamo Struggle, 1977–1992*. Solihull: Helion & Company, 2014.

Englebert, Pierre and Denis M. Tull. 'Postconflict Reconstruction in Africa: Flawed Ideas about Failed States'. *International Security* 32, no. 4 (2008): 106–39. https://doi.org/10 .1162/isec.2008.32.4.106.

Enloe, Cynthia H. *Police, Military, and Ethnicity: Foundations of State Power*. Transaction Books, 1980.

Faria, Paulo C. J. *Post-War Angola: Public Sphere, Political Regime and Democracy*. Cambridge Scholars Publishing, 2013.

Fazal, Tanisha M. *Wars of Law: Unintended Consequences in the Regulation of Armed Conflict*. Cornell University Press, 2020.

Fazal, Tanisha M. and Ryan D. Griffiths. 'Membership Has Its Privileges: The Changing Benefits of Statehood'. *International Studies Review* 16, no. 1 (March 2014): 79–106.

Fearon, James D. 'Why Do Some Civil Wars Last So Much Longer than Others?'. *Journal of Peace Research j Peace Res* 41, no. 3 (2004): 275–301.

Fearon, James D. and David D. Laitin. 'Ethnicity, Insurgency, And Civil War'. *American Political Science Review*, n.d., 75–90.

Filson, Darren and Suzanne Werner. 'A Bargaining Model of War and Peace: Anticipating the Onset, Duration, and Outcome of War'. *American Journal of Political Science* 46, no. 4 (2002): 819–37.

Findlay, Trevor. *The Use of Force in UN Peace Operations*. SIPRI, 2007.

Fine, Leah M. 'Colorblind Colonialism? Lusotropicalismo and Portugal's 20th Century Empire in Africa'. PhD diss., Barnard University, 2017.

Finnegan, William. *A Complicated War: The Harrowing of Mozambique*. Berkeley, CA: University of California Press, 1996.

Foltz, William J. and Henry Bienen. *Arms and the African: Military Influences on Africa's International Relations*. New Haven, CT: Yale University Press, 1985.

Fortna, Virginia Page. 'A Lost Chance for Peace: The Bicesse Accords in Angola'. *Georgetown Journal of International Affairs* 4, no. 1 (2003): 73–9.

Fortna, Virginia Page. 'Does Peacekeeping Keep Peace? International Intervention and the Duration of Peace after Civil War'. *International Studies Quarterly* 48, no. 2 (2004): 269–92. https://doi.org/10.1111/j.0020-8833.2004.00301.x.

Fortna, Virginia Page and Lise Morjé Howard. 'Pitfalls and Prospects in the Peacekeeping Literature'. In *Elgar Handbook of Civil War and Fragile States*, edited by Graham K. Brown and Arnim Langer, 310–26. Elgar Publishing, n.d. https://doi.org/10.4337 /9781781006313.00027.

Freeman, Laura. 'The African Warlord Revisited'. *Small Wars & Insurgencies* 26, no. 5 (4 October 2014): 790–810.

Frelimo, Renamo. 'General Peace Agreement for Mozambique'. *Council on Foreign Relations. Council on Foreign Relations*, 4 October 1992.

Furley, Oliver and Roy May. *Ending Africa's Wars: Progressing to Peace*. Aldershot: Ashgate, 2006.

Galtung, Johan. 'Violence, Peace, and Peace Research'. *Journal of Peace Research* 6, no. 3 (September 1969): 167–91. https://doi.org/10.1177/002234336900600301.

Gaub, Florence. *Military Integration after Civil Wars Multiethnic Armies, Identity, and Post-Conflict Reconstruction*. London: Routledge, 2010.

Gaub, Florence. 'Merging Militaries: The Lebanese Case'. In *New Armies from Old: Merging Competing Military Forces after Civil Wars*, 69–84. Georgetown University Press, 2014. http://www.jstor.org/stable/j.ctt6wpktb.11 (accessed 1 October 2017).

Gawande, Atul. *The Checklist Manifesto: How to Get Things Right*. Gurgaon, India: Penguin Random House, 2014.

George, Alexander L. and Andrew Bennett. *Case Studies and Theory Development in the Social Sciences*. MIT Press, 2007.

George, Edward. *The Cuban Intervention in Angola, 1965–1991: From Che Guevara to Cuito Cuanavale*. London: Routledge Taylor & Francis Group, 2012.

Gerhart, Gail M. and Tony Hodges. 'Angola from Afro-Stalinism to Petro-Diamond Capitalism'. *Foreign Affairs* 80, no. 6 (2001): 193. https://doi.org/10.2307/20050391.

Gerring, John. 'What Is a Case Study and What Is It Good For?'. *American Political Science Review* 98, no. 2 (2004): 341–54. https://doi.org/10.1017/s0003055404001182.

Ginifer, Jeremy. *Beyond the Emergency: Development within UN Peace Missions*. Frank Cass, 1997.

Ginty, Mac. *No Peace: The Rejuvenation of Stalled Peace Processes and Peace Accords*. Palgrave Macmillan, 2008.

Giustozzi, Antonio. *Post-Conflict Disarmament, Demobilization and Reintegration: Bringing State-Building Back In*. New York: Routledge, 2017.

Glassmyer, Katherine and Nicholas Sambanis. 'Rebel—Military Integration and Civil War Termination'. *Journal of Peace Research* 45, no. 3 (2008): 365–84. https://doi.org/10.1177/0022343308088816.

Gleditsch, Skrede Kristian. 'Transnational Dimensions of Civil Wars'. *Journal of Peace Research* 44, no. 3 (May 2007): 293–309.

Greenhill, Kelly M. and Solomon Major. 'The Perils of Profiling: Civil War Spoilers and the Collapse of Intrastate Peace Accords'. *International Security* 31, no. 3 (2007): 7–40. https://doi.org/10.1162/isec.2007.31.3.7.

Grisham, Kevin E. *Transforming Violent Political Movements Rebels Today, What Tomorrow?* Routledge, Taylor & Francis Group, 2014.

Grobbelaar, Neuma. 'Angola in Search of Peace: Spoilers, Saints and Strategic Regional Interests'. *Clingendael Institute*, 1 October 2003.

Guéhenno, Jean-Marie. *The Fog of Peace: A Memoir of International Peacekeeping in the 21st Century*. Brookings Institution Press, 2015.

Guimarães, Fernando Andresen. *The Origins of the Angolan Civil War: Foreign Intervention and Domestic Political Conflict*. Palgrave, 2002.

Gutteridge, William. *Armed Forces in New States*. London: Oxford University Press, 1962.

Hamann, Hilton. *Days of the Generals: The Untold Story of South Africas Apartheid-Era Military Generals*. Cape Town: Zebra Press, 2001.

Hamill, James. 'Angola's Road from under the Rubble'. *The World Today* 50, no. 1 (January 1994): 6–11.

Hanlon, Joseph. *Mozambique: The Revolution under Fire*. London: Zed Books, 1990.

Hanlon, Joseph. *Report of AWEPAs Observation of the Mozambique Electoral Process 1992–1994*. Amsterdam: AWEPA, 1995.

Hanlon, Joseph. *Peace without Profit: How the IMF Blocks Rebuilding in Mozambique*. Irish Mozambique Solidarity & The International African Institute, 1997.

Harding, Jeremy. *Small Wars, Small Mercies*. London: Viking, 1993.

Hare, Paul. *Angolas Last Best Chance for Peace: An Insiders Account of the Peace Process.* Washington, DC: United States Institute of Peace Press, 1998.

Hartzell, Caroline A. 'Mixed Motives? Explaining the Decision to Integrate Militaries at Civil War's End'. In *New Armies from Old,* edited by Roy Licklider, 13–28. Merging Competing Military Forces after Civil Wars. Georgetown University Press, 2014. http://www.jstor.org/stable/j.ctt6wpktb.8 (accessed 1 October 2017).

Hartzell, Caroline A., Matthew Hoddie, and Donald Rothchild. 'Stabilizing the Peace After Civil War: An Investigation of Some Key Variables'. *International Organization* 55, no. 1 (2001): 183–208. https://doi.org/10.1162/002081801551450.

Hazen, Jennifer M. *What Rebels Want: Resources and Supply Networks in Wartime.* Ithaca: Cornell University Press, 2013.

Hegre, Håvard, Lisa Hultman, and Nygård Håvard. 'Evaluating the Conflict-Reducing Effect of UN Peacekeeping Operations'. *The Journal of Politics* 81, no. 1 (January 2019): 215–32.

Heimer, Franz-Wilhelm. *The Decolonization Conflict in Angola, 1974–76: An Essay in Political Sociology.* Genève: Institut Universitaire De Hautes Études Internationales, 1979.

Heitman, Helmoed-Römer. *War in Angola: The Final South African Phase.* Gibraltar: Ashanti Publ, 1990.

Henderson, Lawrence W. *Angola: Five Centuries of Conflict.* Itacha: Cornell University Press, 1982.

Henriksen, Thomas H. 'People's War in Angola, Mozambique, and Guinea-Bissau'. *The Journal of Modern African Studies* 14, no. 3 (September 1976): 377–99.

Henriksen, Thomas H. *Mozambique: A History.* London: Collings, 1978.

Henriksen, Thomas H. *Revolution and Counterrevolution: Mozambiques War of Independence, 1964–1974.* Westport, CT: Greenwood Press, 1983.

Hentges, Harriet and Jean-Marc Coicaud. 'Dividends of Peace: The Economics of Peacekeeping'. *Journal of International Affairs* 55, no. 2 (2002): 351–67.

Heywood, Linda Marinda. *Contested Power in Angola: 1840s to the Present.* Rochester, NY: University of Rochester Press, 2009.

Hickerson, Glen. 'A Bridge over Troubled Water: Managing Parties'. Mental Illness in Mediation'. *Negotiation Journal* 33, no. 1 (2017): 53–69. https://doi.org/10.1111/nejo.12173.

Hickey, Sam, Abdullgafaru Abdulai, Angelo Izama, and Giles Mohan. 'The Politics of Governing Oil Effectively: A Comparative Study of Two New Oil-Rich States in Africa'. *ESID Working Paper,* no. 54 (2015). https://doi.org/10.2139/ssrn.2695723.

Hicks, Donna. *Leading with Dignity.* New Haven, CT: Yale University Press, 2019.

Hicks, Donna and Desmond Tutu. *Dignity: The Essential Role It Plays in Resolving Conflict.* New Haven, CT: Yale University Press, 2011.

Hoddie, Matthew and Caroline A. Hartzell. 'Strengthening Peace in Post-Civil War States'. 2010. https://doi.org/10.7208/chicago/9780226351261.001.0001.

Horowitz, Donald L. *Ethnic Groups in Conflict.* University of California Press, 1985.

Houser, George M. and Herb Shore. *Mozambique: Dream the Size of Freedom.* New York: Africa Fund, 1975.

Howard, Lise Morjé. *UN Peacekeeping in Civil Wars.* Cambridge University Press, 2014.

Howard, Lise Morjé and Anjali Kaushlesh Dayal. 'The Use of Force in UN Peacekeeping'. *International Organization* 72, no. 1 (2017): 71–103. https://doi.org/10.1017/s0020818317000431.

Howland, Todd. 'UN Human Rights Field Presence as Proactive Instrument of Peace and Social Change: Lessons from Angola'. *Human Rights Quarterly* 26, no. 1 (February 2004): 1–28.

Huang, Reyko. 'Rebel Diplomacy in Civil War'. *International Security* 40, no. 4 (2016). https://doi.org/10.1162/ISEC_a_00237.

Huehenno, Jean-Marie. 'On the Challenges and Achievements of Reforming UN Peace Operations, International Peacekeeping'. *International Peacekeeping* 9, no. 2 (2002): 69–80.

Hultman, Lisa. 'The Power to Hurt in Civil War: The Strategic Aim of RENAMO Violence'. *Journal of Southern African Studies* 35, no. 4 (2009): 821–34. https://doi.org/10.1080/03057070903313194.

Hume, Cameron. *Ending Mozambique's War: The Role of Mediation and Good Offices*. Washington, DC: United States Institute of Peace, 1994.

Humphreys, Macartan and Jeremy M. Weinstein. 'Demobilization and Reintegration'. *Journal of Conflict Resolution* 51, no. 4 (2007): 531–67. https://doi.org/10.1177/0022002707302790.

Inbal, Aliza Belman and Hanna Lerner. 'Constitutional Design, Identity, and Legitimacy in Post-Conflict Reconstruction'. In *Governance in Post-Conflict Societies: Rebuilding Fragile States*, edited by Derick W. Brinkerhoff. Oxfordshire: Routledge, 2006.

Isaacman, Allen Frederick and Barbara Isaacman. *Mozambique: From Colonialism to Revolution*. Harare: Zimbabwe Pub. House, 1985.

Isaacman, Allen Frederick and Barbara Isaacman. 'The Tradition of Resistance in Mozambique'. *Africa Today* 22, no. 3 (1976): 37–50.

Ishiyama, John and Anna Batta. 'Swords into Plowshares: The Organizational Transformation of Rebel Groups into Political Parties'. *Communist and Post-Communist Studies* 44, no. 4 (2011): 369–79. https://doi.org/10.1016/j.postcomstud.2011.10.004.

Izumi, Carol. 'Implicit Bias and the Illusion of Mediator Neutrality'. *New Directions in ADR and Clinical Legal Education* 34 (January 2010). https://openscholarship.wustl.edu/cgi/viewcontent.cgi?article=1054&context=law_journal_law_policy.

James, W. Martin. *A Political History of the Civil War in Angola, 1974–1990*. Routledge, 2020.

Jarstad, Anna K. and Desiree Nilsson. 'From Words to Deeds: The Implementation of Power-Sharing Pacts in Peace Accords'. *Conflict Management and Peace Science* 25, no. 3 (2008): 206–23. https://doi.org/10.1080/07388940802218945.

Jarstad, Anna K. and Timothy D. Sisk. *From War to Democracy: Dilemmas of Peacebuilding*. Cambridge University Press, 2009.

Jett, Dennis C. 'Mediation – Its Potential and Its Limits: Developing an Effective Discourse on the Research and Practice of Peacemaking'. *Journal of Law and International Affairs* 2, no. 1 (2013): 103–17.

Jett, Dennis C. *Why Peacekeeping Fails*. Palgrave Macmillan, 2019.

Joshi, Madhav, Erik Melander, and Jason Michael Quinn. 'Sequencing the Peace: How the Order of Peace Agreement Implementation Can Reduce the Destabilizing Effects of Post-Accord Elections'. *Journal of Conflict Resolution* 61, no. 1 (2016): 4–28. https://doi.org/10.1177/0022002715576573.

Joshi, Madhav and J. Michael Quinn. 'Is the Sum Greater than the Parts? The Terms of Civil War Peace Agreements and the Commitment Problem Revisited'. *Negotiation Journal* 31, no. 1 (2015): 7–30. https://doi.org/10.1111/nejo.12077.

Kalley, Jacqueline Audrey, Elna Schoeman, and Lydia Eve Andor. *Southern African Political History: A Chronology of Key Political Events from Independence to Mid-1997*. Westport, CT, 1999.

Kalyvas, Stathis. 'Civil Wars'. In *The Oxford Handbook of Comparative Politics*, edited by Carles Boix and Susan Stokes. Oxford: Oxford University Press, 2009.

Kalyvas, Stathis N. *The Logic of Violence in Civil War*. Cambridge University Press, 2006.

Kalyvas, Stathis N. and Laia Balcells. 'International System and Technologies of Rebellion: How the End of the Cold War Shaped Internal Conflict'. *The American Political Science Review* 104, no. 3 (August 2010): 415–29.

Karazsia, Zachary. 'Evaluating the 'Success'. of Disarmament, Demobilization, and Reintegration Programs: The Case of Congo-Brazzaville'. *Journal of Interdisciplinary Conflict Science* 1, no. 2 (2015). https://nsuworks.nova.edu/jics/vol1/iss2/1/.

Karlin, Mara E. *Building Militaries in Fragile States: Challenges for the United States.* Philadelphia: University of Pennsylvania Press, 2018.

Kibble, S. 'Angola: Can the Politics of Disorder Become the Politics of Democratisation & Development?'. *Review of African Political Economy* 33, no. 109 (2006): 525–42.

King, Charles. *Ending Civil Wars.* Oxford: Oxford University Press for the International Institute for Strategic Studies, 1997.

Kingma, Kees. 'Disarmament, Demobilization And Reintegration of Former Combatants in a Peacebuilding Context'. *Policy Sciences* 30, no. 3 (1997). https://doi.org/10.5040/9780755620302.ch-001.

Kingma, Kees. *Demobilization in Subsaharan Africa: The Development and Security Impacts.* Palgrave Macmillan, 2014.

Kissinger, Henry. *Diplomacy.* Simon & Schuster, 1994.

Kitchen, Helen. *Angola, Mozambique, and the West.* New York: Praeger, 1987.

Kleinfeld, Rachel and Nathaniel Allen. *Why Security Sector Governance Matters in Fragile States.* Carnegie Endowment for International Peace, 2020. https://carnegieendowment.org/2019/06/11/why-security-sector-governance-matters-in-fragile-states/k2xg (accessed 4 July 2020).

Knight, W. Andy. 'Disarmament, Demobilization, and Reintegration and Post-Conflict Peacebuilding in Africa: An Overview'. *African Security* 1, no. 1 (2008): 24–52. https://doi.org/10.1080/19362200802285757.

Knowles, Emily and Jahara Matisek. 'Is Human Rights Training Working with Foreign Militaries? No One Knows and That's O.K'. *War on the Rocks,* 11 May 2020. https://warontherocks.com/2020/05/is-human-rights-training-working-with-foreign-militaries-no-one-knows-and-thats-o-k/ (accessed 11 May 2020).

Koekenbier, Pieter. 'Multi-Ethnic Armies: Lebanese Lessons & Iraqi Implications'. *Conflict Studies Research Center,* June 2005, 0506.

Kovacs, Mimmi Söderberg. 'Bringing the Good, The Bad, and the Ugly into the Peace Fold: The Republic of Sierra Leone's Armed Forces after the Lomé Peace Agreement'. In *New Armies from Old: Merging Competing Military Forces after Civil Wars,* 195–212. Georgetown University Press, 2014. http://www.jstor.org/stable/j.ctt6wpktb.18 (accessed 4 October 2017).

Kubota, Jennifer T., Jian Li, Eyal Bar-David, Mahzarin R. Banaji, and Elizabeth A. Phelps. 'The Price of Racial Bias'. *Psychological Science* 24, no. 12 (2013): 2498–504. https://doi.org/10.1177/0956797613496435.

Kydd, Andrew and Barbara F. Walter. 'Sabotaging the Peace: The Politics of Extremist Violence'. *International Organization* 56, no. 2 (2002): 263–96.

Laitin, David. 'The Industrial Organisation of Merged Armies'. In *New Armies from Old: Merging Competing Military Forces After Civil Wars,* edited by Roy Licklider. Washington, DC: Georgetown University Press, 2014.

Lake, Milli. 'Building the Rule of War: Postconflict Institutions and the Micro-Dynamics of Conflict in Eastern DR Congo'. *International Organization* 71, no. 2 (2017): 281–315. https://doi.org/10.1017/s002081831700008x.

Landau-Wells, Marika. 'High Stakes and Low Bars'. *International Security* 43, no. 1 (2018): 103–37.

Lashitew, Addisu and Eric Werker. 'Are Natural Resources a Curse, a Blessing, or a Double-Edged Sword?', *Brookings*, 29 July 2020. https://www.brookings.edu/blog/future-development/2020/07/16/are-natural-resources-a-curse-a-blessing-or-a-double-edged-sword/ (accessed 30 July 2020).

Leenders, Reinoud. *Spoils of Truce: Corruption and State-Building in Postwar Lebanon.* Cornell University Press, 2012.

Legum, Colin and Tony Hodges. *After Angola: The War over Southern Africa.* New York: Africana, 1978.

Lemke, Douglas, and Charles Crabtree. 'Territorial Contenders in World Politics'. *Journal of Conflict Resolution*, 14 May 2019. https://journals.sagepub.com/doi/10.1177/0022002719847742.

Levine, David H. 'Organizational Disruption and Change in Mozambique's Peace Process'. *International Peacekeeping* 14, no. 3 (2007): 368–83.

Lichtenheld, Adam G. 'Guilt by Location'. *Foreign Policy*, 10 July 2020. https://foreignpolicy.com/2020/07/10/idps-forced-displacement-sorting-populations-guilt-by-location/ (accessed 20 July 2020).

Licklider, Roy. *Stopping the Killing: How Civil Wars End.* New York: New York University Press, 2010.

Licklider, Roy. *New Armies from Old: Merging Competing Military Forces After Civil Wars.* Washington, DC: Georgetown University Press, 2014.

Lilja, Jannie. 'Ripening Within? Strategies Used by Rebel Negotiators to End Ethnic War'. *Negotiation Journal* 27, no. 3 (18 July 2011): 311–42.

Littlejohn, Gary. 'Secret Stockpiles: Arms Caches and Disarmament Efforts in Mozambique'. *Small Arms Survey*, 2015.

Lovell, Julia. *Maoism: A Global History.* London: Vintage, 2020.

Lowe, Vaughan. *The United Nations Security Council and War: The Evolution of Thought and Practice since 1945.* Oxford University Press, 2008.

Lyall, Jason. *Divided Armies Inequality and Battlefield Performance in Modern War.* Princeton University Press, 2020.

Lyons, Terrence. *Demilitarizing Politics: Elections on the Uncertain Road to Peace.* Lynne Rienner Publishers, 2005.

Macqueen, Norrie. 'Peacekeeping by Attrition: The United Nations in Angola'. *The Journal of Modern African Studies* 36, no. 3 (1998): 399–422. https://doi.org/10.1017/s0022278x98002845.

Maier, Karl. *Angola Promises and Lies.* London: Serif Books, 2013.

Malache, Adriano, Paulino Macaringue, and Joao-Paulo Borges Coelho. 'Profound Transformations and Regional Conflagrations: The History of Mozambique's Armed Forces from 1975–2005'. In *Essay. In Evolutions and Revolutions: A Contemporary History of Militaries in Southern Africa.* Institute for Security Studies, 2005.

Malaquias, Assis. 'Diamonds Are a Guerrillas Best Friend: The Impact of Illicit Wealth on Insurgency Strategy'. *Third World Quarterly* 22, no. 3 (2001): 311–25. https://doi.org/10.1080/01436590120061624.

Malaquias, Assis. *Rebels and Robbers: Violence in Post-Colonial Angola.* Nordiska Afrikainstitutet, 2007.

Maley, William and Charles Sampford. *From Civil Strife to Civil Society: Civil and Military Responsibilities in Disrupted States.* Tokyo: United Nations University Press, 2003.

Malone, David M. and Ramesh Thakur. 'UN Peacekeeping: Lessons Learned?'. *Global Governance* 7, no. 1 (2001). http://www.jstor.org/stable/27800283.

Manning, Carrie L. *Politics of Peace in Mozambique: Post-Conflict Democratization, 1992–2000.* Praeger, 2002.

Manning, Carrie L. 'Party-Building on the Heels of War: El Salvador, Bosnia, Kosovo and Mozambique'. *Twenty Years of Studying Democratization* (2018): 4–23. https://doi.org /10.4324/9781315757513-1.

Manning, Carrie L. and Ian Smith. 'Political Party Formation by Former Armed Opposition Groups after Civil War'. *Democratization* 23, no. 6 (2016): 972–89. https:// doi.org/10.1080/13510347.2016.1159556.

Marcum, John. *The Angolan Revolution*. Cambridge, MA: M.I.T. Press, 1969.

Marsh, Nicholas and Júlia Palik. 'Negotiating Disarmament: Lessons Learnt from Colombia, Nepal, the Philippines, South Sudan, Sri Lanka'. *PRIO Papers*, 2021. https:// www.prio.org/publications/12869 (accessed 1 June 2023).

Marshall, Michael Christopher and John Ishiyama. 'Does Political Inclusion of Rebel Parties Promote Peace after Civil Conflict?'. *Democratization* 23, no. 6 (2016): 1009–25.

Matanock, Alia M. 'External Engagement: Explaining the Spread of Electoral Participation Provisions in Civil Conflict Settlements'. *International Studies Quarterly* 62, no. 3 (September 2018): 656–70.

Mattes, Michaela and Burcu Savun. 'Information, Agreement Design, and the Durability of Civil War Settlements'. *American Journal of Political Science* 54, no. 2 (2010): 511–24. https://doi.org/10.1111/j.1540-5907.2010.00444.x.

McCormick, Shawn. *Africa Notes: Angola: The Road to Peace - June 1991*. CSIS, 2021. www .csis.org/analysis/africa-notes-angola-road-peace-june-1991.

McGovern, Mike. *Making War in Côte d'Ivoire*. Chicago: The University of Chicago Press, 2011.

Møller, Bjørn. 'Integration of Former Enemies into National Armies in Fragile African States'. In *Essay. In Fragile States and Insecure People? Violence, Security, and Statehood in the Twenty-First Century*, edited by Louise Andersen, Bjørn Møller, and Finn Stepputat, 1st ed., 177–200. New York: Palgrave Macmillan, 2007.

Mondlane, Eduardo Chivambo. *The Struggle for Mozambique*. Baltimore: Penguin Books, 1969.

Morier-Genoud, Éric. *Sure Road?: Nationalisms in Angola, Guinea-Bissau and Mozambique*. Leiden: Brill, 2012.

'Mozambican Ex-Rebels Renamo in Police Clash'. *BBC News*, April 2013.

'Mozambique Faces Uncertainty as Renamo Ends 1992 Peace Pact'. *Reuters*. Thomson Reuters, 21 October 2013.

'Mozambique: Political Violence Rises'. *The New York Times*, 5 April 2013.

'Mozambique: Weapons of Reconstruction - Mozambique'. *ReliefWeb*, February 2005. https://reliefweb.int/report/mozambique/mozambique-weapons-reconstruction (accessed 5 July 2020).

Muggah, Robert. *Security and Post-Conflict Reconstruction: Dealing with Fighters in the Aftermath of War*. Routledge, 2009.

Munslow, Barry. 'Angola: The Politics of Unsustainable Development'. *Third World Quarterly* 20, no. 3 (June 1999): 551–68.

Mutisi, Martha and Andrea Bartoli. 'Merging Militaries: Mozambique'. In *New Armies from Old: Merging Competing Military Forces after Civil Wars*, edited by Roy Licklider. Washington, DC: Georgetown University Press, 2014.

Nadin, Peter, Patrick Cammaert, and Vesselin Popovski. *Spoiler Groups and UN Peacekeeping*. Abingdon: Routledge, 2015.

Newitt, Malyn. *Portuguese Settlement on the Zambesi*. London: Longman, 1973.

Newitt, Malyn D. D. *A Short History of Mozambique*. Cape Town: Jonathan Ball Publishers, 2018.

Nohlen, Dieter. *Elections in Africa: A Data Handbook*. Oxford: Oxford University Press, 2004.

Noyes, Alexander. 'How to Build Better Militaries in Africa: Lessons from Niger'. *Council on Foreign Relations*, 1 October 2020. https://www.cfr.org/blog/how-build-better -militaries-africa-lessons-niger (accessed 10 October 2020).

Odeh, B. J. Lebanon. *Dynamics of Conflict: A Modern Political History*. Zed Books, 1985.

Ohlson, Thomas. *Power Politics and Peace Policies: Intra-State Conflict Resolution in Southern Africa*. Institutionen För Freds- Och Konfliktforskning, Univ, 1998.

Oksamytna, Kseniya, Vincenzo Bove, and Magnus Lundgren. 'Leadership Selection in United Nations Peacekeeping'. *International Studies Quarterly*, 4 May 2020. https://doi .org/10.1093/isq/sqaa023.

Oliveira, Ricardo Soares De. 'Illiberal Peacebuilding in Angola'. *The Journal of Modern African Studies* 49, no. 2 (2011): 287–314. https://doi.org/10.1017/s0022278x1100005x.

Omer-Cooper, John D. *History of Southern Africa*. Cape Town: Philip, 2003.

Oppenheim, Ben, Abbey Steele, Juan F. Vargas, and Michael Weintraub. 'True Believers, Deserters, and Traitors: Who Leaves Insurgent Groups and Why?'. *Journal of Conflict Resolution* 59, no. 5 (2015): 794–823.

Ovadia, Jesse Salah. *The Petro-Developmental State in Africa: Making Oil Work in Angola, Nigeria and the Gulf of Guinea*. Hurst & Company, 2016.

Ozerdem, A., and S. Podder. *Child Soldiers: From Recruitment to Reintegration*. Palgrave Macmillan, 2014.

Parkinson, Sarah E., and Sherry Zaks. 'Militant and Rebel Organization(s)'. *Comparative Politics* 50, no. 2 (1 January 2018): 271–93. https://doi.org/10.5129/001041518822263610.

Peace Accords Matrix. 'Dispute Resolution Committee'. *Peace Accords Matrix*, 10 August 2020. https://peaceaccords.nd.edu/search-pam?fwp_provision_types=dispute -resolution-committee (accessed 10 August 2020).

Pearce, Justin. 'Control, Politics and Identity in the Angolan Civil War'. *African Affairs* 111, no. 444 (July 2012): 442–65.

Pearce, Justin. 'Global Ideologies, Local Politics: The Cold War as Seen from Central Angola'. *Journal of Southern African Studies* 43, no. 1 (2017): 13–27. https://doi.org/10 .1080/03057070.2017.1266809.

Pearce, Justin. 'From Rebellion to Opposition: UNITA's Social Engagement in Post-War Angola'. *Government and Opposition* 55, no. 3 (2018): 474–89. https://doi.org/10.1017/ gov.2018.36.

Pereira, Anthony. 'The Neglected Tragedy: The Return to War in Angola, 1992 -3'. *The Journal of Modern African Studies* 32, no. 1 (1994): 1–28. https://doi.org/10.1017/ S0022278X00012520.

Plank, Friedrich. 'When Peace Leads to Divorce: The Splintering of Rebel Groups in Powersharing Agreements'. *Civil Wars* 19, no. 2 (2017): 176–97. https://doi.org/10.1080 /13698249.2017.1372004.

Porto, João Gomes, Chris Alden, and Imogen Parsons. *From Soldiers to Citizens Demilitarisation of Conflict and Society*. London: Routledge, Taylor & Francis Group, 2016.

Porto, João Gomes and Imogen Parsons. *Sustaining the Peace in Angola: An Overview of Current Demobilisation, Disarmament and Reintegration*. Pretoria: Institute for Security Studies, 2003.

Power, Marcus. 'Patrimonialism & Petro-diamond Capitalism: Peace, Geopolitics & the Economics of War in Angola'. *Review of African Political Economy* 28, no. 90 (2001): 489–502.

Radtke, Mitchell and Hyeran Jo. 'Fighting the Hydra: United Nations Sanctions and Rebel Groups'. *Journal of Peace Research* 55, no. 6 (August 2018). https://doi.org/10.1177 /0022343318788127.

Ratner, Steven R. *The New UN Peacekeeping: Building Peace in Lands of Conflict after the Cold War*. Macmillan, 1997.

Reagan, Anders. 'Reframing the Ontology of Peace Studies'. *Peace and Conflict Studies* 29, no. 2 (23 May 2023). https://nsuworks.nova.edu/pcs/vol29/iss2/1.

Regan, P. M. 'Greed, Grievance, And Mobilization In Civil Wars'. *Journal of Conflict Resolution*, n.d., 319–336.

Reuters. 'Mozambique: 1992 Peace Pact Collapses'. *The New York Times*, 21 October 2013.

Robinson, Colin. 'Army Reconstruction in the Democratic Republic of the Congo 2003–2009'. *Small Wars & Insurgencies* 23, no. 3 (2012): 474–99.

Robinson, Colin. 'Discussion Note: Is a Post-Conflict Army Reconstruction Framework Possible, or Useful?', *Small Wars Journal* (2012). https://smallwarsjournal.com/jrnl/art/discussion-note-is-a-post-conflict-army-reconstruction-framework-possible-or-useful.

Robson, Paul. 'Angola After Savimbi'. *Review of African Political Economy* 29, no. 91 (March 2002): 130–32.

Robson, Paul. 'Communities and Reconstruction in Angola: The Prospects for Reconstruction in Angola from the Community Perspective'. *Development Workshop*, 2001.

Roll, Michael. *The Politics of Public Sector Performance: Pockets of Effectiveness in Developing Countries*. London: Routledge, 2015.

Roque, Paula Cristina. *Governing in the Shadows: Angola's Securitized State*. Oxford University Press, 2021.

Rothchild, Donald S. 'On Implementing Africa's Peace Accords: From Defection to Cooperation'. *Africa Today* 42, no. 1 (1995). https://www.jstor.org/stable/4187028.

Rothchild, Donald S. 'Settlement Terms and Postagreement Stability'. In *Ending Civil Wars: The Implementation of Peace Agreements*, edited by Stephen John Stedman, Donald Rothchild, and Elizabeth M. Cousens. Boulder, CO: Lynne Rienner, 2002.

Rugumamu, Severine and Osman Gbla. 'Studies in Reconstruction and Capacity-Building in Post-Conflict Countries in Africa'. *The African Capacity Building Foundation*, May 2004. https://www.afdb.org/fileadmin/uploads/afdb/Documents/Generic-Documents/PCBSS_Working_Documents/MOZAMBIQUE%20-%20Main%20Report%20(Revised).pdf (accessed 25 April 2018).

Ruigrok, Inge. 'Whose Justice? Contextualising Angolas Reintegration Process'. *African Security Review* 16, no. 1 (2007): 84–98. https://doi.org/10.1080/10246029.2007.9627636.

Rupiya, Martin. *Evolutions and Revolutions: A Contemporary History of Militaries in Southern Africa*. Institute for Security Studies, 2005.

Rustad, Siri Aas and Helga Malmin Binningsbø. 'A Price Worth Fighting For? Natural Resources and Conflict Recurrence'. *Journal of Peace Research* 49, no. 4 (2012): 531–46. https://doi.org/10.1177/0022343312444942.

Sabaratnam, Meera. *Decolonising Intervention: International Statebuilding in Mozambique*. Lanham: Rowman & Littlefield Publishers, 2018.

Salacuse, Jeswald W. 'The Effect of Advice on Negotiations: How Advisors Influence What Negotiators Do'. *Negotiation Journal*, 18 April 2016. https://doi.org/10.1111/nejo.12150.

Salehyan, Idean. *Rebels without Borders Transnational Insurgencies in World Politics*. Ithaca, NY: Cornell University Press, 2011.

Sambanis, Nicholas. 'Short-Term And Long-Term Effects Of United Nations Peace Operations'. *Policy Research Working Papers*, 2007. https://doi.org/10.1596/1813-9450-4207.

Sambanis, Nicholas. 'What Is Civil War? Conceptual and Empirical Complexities of an Operational Definition'. *The Journal of Conflict Resolution* 48, no. 6 (2004): 814–58. https://www.jstor.org/stable/4149797.

Sambanis, Nicholas and Jonah Schulhofer-Wohl. 'What's in a Line? Is Partition a Solution to Civil War?'. *International Security* 34, no. 2 (2009): 82–118.

Sambanis, Nicholas and Moses Shayo. 'Social Identification and Ethnic Conflict'. *American Political Science Review* (n.d.): 294–325. https://doi.org/10.2139/ssrn.1955111.

Sarkees, Meredith Reid. *The COW Typology of War: Defining and Categorizing Wars.* Correlates of War Project, n.d. https://correlatesofwar.org/wp-content/uploads/COW -Website-Typology-of-war.pdf (accessed 16 October 2017).

Schafer, Jessica. *Soldiers at Peace: The Post-War Politics of Demobilized Soldiers in Mozambique.* New York: Palgrave Macmillan, 2007.

Schafer, Jessica. *Soldiers at Peace Veterans and Society after the Civil War in Mozambique.* New York: Palgrave Macmillan, 2007.

Schiff, Amira. 'Pre-Negotiation and Its Limits in Ethno-National Conflicts: A Systematic Analysis of Process and Outcomes in the Cyprus Negotiations'. *International Negotiation* 13, no. 3 (January 2008): 387–412.

Schirch, Lisa and Deborah Mancini-Griffoli. *Local Ownership in Security: Case Studies of Peacebuilding Approaches.* Alliance for Peacebuilding, 2015.

Schneckener, U. 'Making Power-Sharing Work: Lessons from Successes and Failures in Ethnic Conflict Regulation'. *Journal of Peace Research* 39, no. 2 (2002): 203–28. https:// doi.org/10.1177/0022343302039002004.

Schneidman, Witney W. 'Africa Notes: Conflict Resolution in Mozambique - February 1990'. In *Africa Notes: Conflict Resolution in Mozambique*, 1990. www.csis.org/analysis/ africa-notes-conflict-resolution-mozambique-february-1990.

Schoon, Eric W. 'Why Does Armed Conflict Begin Again? A New Analytic Approach'. *International Journal of Comparative Sociology* 59, no. 5–6 (10 December 2018): 480–515.

Seiler, John. *Southern Africa Since the Portuguese Coup.* Routledge, 2019.

Sherman, J. H. 'The Clandestine Diamond Economy of Angola'. *Journal of International Affairs* 53, no. 2 (2000): 699–719.

Shesterinina, Anastasia. 'Civil War as a Social Process: Actors and Dynamics from Pre- to Post-War'. *European Journal of International Relations* 28, no. 3 (1 September 2022): 538–62. https://doi.org/10.1177/13540661221095970.

Simon, David. 'Angola: The Peace Is Not Yet Fully Won'. *Review of African Political Economy* 25, no. 77 (1998): 495–503.

Slantchev, Branislav L. 'The Principle of Convergence in Wartime Negotiations'. *American Political Science Review* 97, no. 4 (2003): 621–32.

Söderberg, Mimmi. *From Rebellion to Politics: The Transformation of Rebel Groups to Political Parties in Civil War Peace Processes.* Uppsala Universitet, 2007.

Söderström, Johanna. *Peacebuilding and Ex-Combatants: Political Reintegration in Liberia.* Abingdon, Oxon: Routledge, Taylor & Francis Group, 2015.

Spears, Ian S. 'Angolas Elusive Peace: The Collapse of the Lusaka Accord'. *International Journal* 54, no. 4 (1999): 562. https://doi.org/10.2307/40203416.

Staniland, Paul. *Networks of Rebellion: Explaining Insurgent Cohesion and Collapse.* Cornell University Press, 2014.

Stanley, William and Charles Call. 'Military and Police Reform after Civil Wars'. In *Contemporary Peace Making: Conflict, Peace Processes and Post-War Reconstruction*, edited by John Darby and Roger Mac Ginty. Basingstoke: Palgrave Macmillan, 2008.

Stedman, Stephen John. *Peacemaking in Civil War: International Mediation in Zimbabwe, 1974–1980.* Boulder, CO: Rienner, 1991.

Stedman, Stephen John. 'Spoiler Problems in Peace Processes'. *International Security* 22, no. 2 (1997): 5–53. https://doi.org/10.1162/isec.22.2.5.

Stedman, Stephen John, Donald S. Rothchild, and Elizabeth M. Cousens. *Ending Civil Wars: The Implementation of Peace Agreements.* Boulder, CO: Lynne Rienner, 2002.

Stockwell, John. *In Search of Enemies: A CIA Story.* New York: Norton, 1984.

Synge, Richard. *Mozambique: UN Peacekeeping in Action, 1992–94.* Washington, DC: United States Institute of Peace Press, 1997.

Taylor, Adam. 'Venezuela's Maduro Still Has a Diplomatic Lifeline - And It's in the Heart of New York City'. *The Washington Post*, 16 February 2019. https://www .washingtonpost.com/world/2019/02/16/venezuelas-maduro-still-has-diplomatic -lifeline-its-heart-new-york-city/.

Themnér, Anders. *Warlord Democrats in Africa: Ex-Military Leaders and Electoral Politics.* Uppsala, Sweden: Nordiska Afrikainstitutet, The Nordic Africa Institute, 2017.

Thomashausen, Andre. *The Concept and Implementation of 'Gradual Decentralisation' in Mozambique.* Oxford: Oxford University Press, n.d.

Toft, Monica Duffy. *Securing the Peace: The Durable Settlement of Civil Wars.* Princeton University Press, 2010.

Tveden, Inge. *Angola: Struggle for Peace and Reconstruction.* Boulder, CO: Westview Press, 1997.

UNDPKO. 'ONUMOZ'. *United Nations.* Peacekeeping.Un.Org/Sites/Default/Files/Past/ OnumozS.Htm, n.d.

UNDPKO. 'UNAVEM II'. United Nations, n.d.

UNDPKO. 'UNTAG'. *United Nations,* Peacekeeping.Un.Org/Sites/Default/Files/Past/ UntagS.Htm, n.d.

Union, European. *European Union Election Observer Mission.* Angola: Final Report Parliamentary Elections, 2008.

Vines, Alex. *No Democracy without Money: The Road to Peace in Mozambique, 1982–1992.* London: Catholic Institute for International Relations, 1994.

Vines, Alex. *Angola and Mozambique: The Aftermath of Conflict.* London: Research Institute for the Study of Conflict and Terrorism, 1995.

Vines, Alex. *Renamo: From Terrorism to Democracy in Mozambique?* York: Centre for Southern African Studies, University of York in Association with J. Currey, 1996.

Vines, Alex. 'War Number Four'. *The World Today* 55, no. 6 (June 1999): 24–5.

Vines, Alex. 'Beyond Savimbi'. *The World Today* 58, no. 4 (2002): 14–15.

Vines, Alex. *Prospects for a Sustainable Elite Bargain in Mozambique: Third Time Lucky?* Chatham House, 2019. https://reader.chathamhouse.org/prospects-sustainable-elite -bargain-mozambique-third-time-lucky#key-features-of-past-elite-bargains (accessed 20 August 2019).

Walker, Eric A. *A History of Southern Africa.* London: Longmans, 1957.

Walter, Barbara F. 'The Critical Barrier to Civil War Settlement'. *International Organization* 51, no. 3 (1997): 335–64. https://doi.org/10.1162/002081897550384.

Walter, Barbara F. 'Designing Transitions from Civil War: Demobilization, Democratization, and Commitments to Peace'. *International Security* 24, no. 1 (1999): 127–55.

Walter, Barbara F. 'Does Conflict Beget Conflict? Explaining Recurring Civil War'. *Journal of Peace Research j Peace Res* 41, no. 3 (2004): 371–88. https://doi.org/10.1177 /0022343304043775.

Walter, Barbara F. 'Why Bad Governance Leads to Repeat Civil War'. *Journal of Conflict Resolution* 59, no. 7 (1 October 2015): 1242–72. https://doi.org/10.1177 /0022002714528006.

Waterhouse, Rachel. *Mozambique: Rising from the Ashes*. Oxfam UK and Ireland, 1996.

Weinstein, Jeremy M. *Disentangling the Determinants of Successful Demobilization and Reintegration*. Stanford University - Freeman Spogli Institute for International Studies, 2005. https://doi.org/10.2139/ssrn.984246.

Wennmann, Achim. 'Getting Armed Groups to the Table: Peace Processes, the Political Economy of Conflict and the Mediated State'. *Third World Quarterly* 30, no. 6 (2009): 1123–38. https://doi.org/10.1080/01436590903037416.

Westad, Odd Arne. *The Global Cold War: Third World Interventions and the Making of Our Times*. Cambridge: Cambridge University Press, 2016.

Wheeler, Douglas L. and René Pélissier. *Angola*. New York: Praeger, 1971.

Whitfield, Teresa. *Friends Indeed?: The United Nations, Groups of Friends, and the Resolution of Conflict*. United States Institute of Peace Press, 2007.

Wiegink, Nikkie. 'Why Did the Soldiers Not Go Home?: Demobilized Combatants, Family Life, and Witchcraft in Postwar Mozambique'. *Anthropological Quarterly* 86, no. 1 (2013): 107–32. https://doi.org/10.1353/anq.2013.0014.

Wiegink, Nikkie. 'Former Military Networks a Threat to Peace? The Demobilisation and Remobilization of Renamo in Central Mozambique'. *International Journal of Security and Development* 4, no. 1 (2015): 1–16.

Wiegink, Nikkie. '"It Will Be Our Time To Eat": Former Renamo Combatants and Big-Man Dynamics in Central Mozambique'. *Journal of Southern African Studies* 41, no. 4 (2015): 869–85. https://doi.org/10.1080/03057070.2015.1060090.

Willett, Susan. 'New Barbarians at the Gate: Losing the Liberal Peace in Africa'. *Review of African Political Economy* 32, no. 106 (2005): 569–94. https://doi.org/10.1080 /03056240500467062.

Wolfers, Michael and J. Bergerol. *Angola in the Frontline*. London: Zed Books, 1985.

Wren, Christopher S. 'Finally, Mozambique Sees a Way to Halt Its Own Devastation'. *The New York Times*. *The New York Times*, 5 August 1989.

Wright, George. *The Destruction of a Nation: United States Policy towards Angola since 1945*. Pluto Press, 1997.

Wright, George. 'The Clinton Administrations Policy toward Angola: An Assessment'. *Review of African Political Economy* 28, no. 90 (2001): 563–76. https://doi.org/10.1080 /03056240108704566.

Young, Eric T. 'The Development of the Fadm in Mozambique: Internal and External Dynamics'. *African Security Review* 5, no. 1 (1996): 18–24. https://doi.org/10.1080 /10246029.1996.9627663.

Young, Thomas-Durrell. 'Experimentation Can Help Build Better Security Partners'. *War on the Rocks*, 30 August 2019. https://warontherocks.com/2019/08/experimentation -can-help-build-better-security-partners/ (accessed 31 August 2019).

Zaks, Sheryl. 'Resilience Beyond Rebellion: How Wartime Organizational Structures Affect Rebel-to-Party Transformation'. PhD diss., UC Berkeley, 2017.

Zartman, Ira William. *Collapsed States: The Disintegration and Restoration of Legitimate Authority*. L. Rienner Publishers, 1995.

Zartman, Ira William. 'Ripeness: The Hurting Stalemate and Beyond'. In *International Conflict Resolution After the Cold War*, edited by National Research Council. Washington, DC: National Academies Press, 2000. https://doi.org/10.17226/9897.

Zartman, Ira William and Maureen R. Berman. *The Practical Negotiator*. New Haven, CT: Yale University Press, 2010.

Zeeuw, Jeroen De. *From Soldiers to Politicians: Transforming Rebel Movements after Civil War*. Boulder, CO: Lynne Rienner Publishers, 2008.

INDEX

www.ingramcontent.com/pod-product-compliance
Lightning Source LLC
Chambersburg PA
CBHW071852270326
41929CB00013B/2205